D1745330

History & Women, Culture & Faith

Volume 1

History and Women, Culture and Faith:
Selected Writings of Elizabeth Fox-Genovese
David Moltke-Hansen, General Editor

History & Women

Culture & Faith

Selected Writings of
Elizabeth Fox-Genovese

David Moltke-Hansen, General Editor

Volume 1
Women Past and Present

Edited by Deborah A. Symonds
Foreword by Peter N. Stearns

The University of South Carolina Press

© 2011 University of South Carolina

Published by the University of South Carolina Press
Columbia, South Carolina 29208

www.sc.edu/uscpress

Manufactured in the United States of America

20 19 18 17 16 15 14 13 12 11   10 9 8 7 6 5 4 3 2 1

Library of Congress Cataloging-in-Publication Data

Fox-Genovese, Elizabeth, 1941–2007.

History and women, culture and faith : selected writings of Elizabeth
Fox-Genovese / David Moltke-Hansen, general editor.
    p. cm.
Includes bibliographical references and index.
ISBN 978-1-57003-990-4 (cloth : alk. paper)—ISBN 978-1-57003-991-1
(cloth : alk. paper)—ISBN 978-1-57003-992-8 (cloth : alk. paper)—
ISBN 978-1-57003-993-5 (cloth : alk. paper)—ISBN 978-1-57003-994-2
(cloth : alk. paper) 1. Women—History. 2. Culture. 3. Feminism.
4. Fox-Genovese, Elizabeth, 1941–2007. I. Moltke-Hansen, David. II. Title.

HQ1121.F64 2011
305.409—dc22   2010048764

Publication of *History & Women, Culture & Faith* is made possible in part by
the generous support of the Watson-Brown Foundation.

This book was printed on Glatfelter Natures, a recycled paper with 30 percent
postconsumer waste content.

Contents

General Editorial Note

This is one of five volumes of the selected essays and reflections of Elizabeth Fox-Genovese. First conceived a week after Fox-Genovese's funeral service, the project received generous support from the Watson-Brown Foundation, on whose Hickory Hill Forum advisory board Fox-Genovese served. Also making this edition possible was the collaboration of a dozen of her former colleagues and students, as well as her sister. Helping this diverse group keep on schedule, the Institute for Southern Studies of the University of South Carolina provided administrative support and the superb assistance of history graduate student Ehren K. Foley, compiler of the selected bibliographies for the first four of the five volumes of the edition.

Because the essays and chapters included were published in some seventy-five different venues, spelling and punctuation vary. No effort was made to standardize either these things or the forms of citation. English spellings are not as common as American but do occur. The editors did correct an occasional, obvious error silently or did insert in brackets missing words or elements of citations. In addition they put all original notes at the ends of pieces. The few editors' notes are placed as footnotes.

Each volume stands on its own, covering an area of Fox-Genovese's long-term scholarly and intellectual involvements. The fifth volume, the reader, is drawn largely from the others to give a broad sampling of the range of her work. It does, nevertheless, also include a couple of items by Fox-Genovese not found in the first four volumes, together with a number of remembrances of her.

The decisions about the contents of individual volumes were the responsibility of the editor or editors of each volume. The editors of the first four volumes nominated items for inclusion in the reader. They were guided in the selections for their own volumes by principles to which they all subscribed at the outset or, in a couple of cases, when joining the project a bit later on. Selections from the books Fox-Genovese wrote, co-wrote, and saw through publication are excluded. These titles are widely known and available. The editors also generally tried to choose more substantial over more popular pieces and limited each volume to a little over one hundred thousand words of her writings and some thirty thousand words of apparatus, including notes and bibliography. These decisions necessitated exclusion of at least a third of her fugitive writings. As a result the present edition includes no more than roughly 20 percent of her total published work.

For background to these materials and for related correspondence, readers are directed to the Southern Historical Collection of the University of North Carolina at Chapel Hill, repository of Elizabeth Fox-Genovese's papers. An aid to finding the papers is currently available at http://www.lib.unc.edu/mss/inv/f/Fox-Genovese,Elizabeth.html.

Foreword

Contributions in Women's History

Peter N. Stearns

This collection is, above all, an invitation to understand the complexities of women's issues and common feminist political assumptions in modern society and, particularly, the United States. The volume captures deep and fairly consistent concerns about excessive individualism and a commitment to work for real improvements in women's lives, along with a desire to use both history and a sense of contemporary social issues to suggest alternatives to conventional priorities. The essays reveal deep and wide reading, particularly in theory and intellectual history but also in social history, and an eager quest for clarity and common sense in the obviously contested arena of gender.

Superficially, of course, the theme that jumps out from the essays is the evolution from an ardent and apparently conventional feminist position on key issues to a defiance of majority feminist thinking on a host of crucial contemporary problems as well as theoretical underpinnings. It is no news that Elizabeth Fox-Genovese became a target for a great deal of bitter feminist criticism of the sort reserved for presumed abandoners of the cause, and while the articles in this volume do not convey her reactions directly, there is evidence of some understandable sniping in turn in some of the generalizations about feminism.

Perceptive commentators have long pointed out that Betsey's evolution was far from complete. Early on in her scholarship the concern for the social basis of individual rights, and the belief that more conventional Western rights formulations began to move too far away from this basis from the late seventeenth century onward, revealed a basic vision that was never shared by the majority of feminist theorists. Another consistency, though a simpler one, must also be noted. Despite clashes with feminism in the later stages of her career, Betsey never abandoned a deep commitment to trying to figure out the best possible systems for women and the best ways to rectify older as well as newer types of subordination and abuse. That her solutions ultimately swam against the feminist mainstream must not conceal the attachment to the cause. At no point was Betsey an apologist for older systems of gender relations in the style of many nonfeminists.

As the initial article in this volume suggests, Betsey early was concerned with the dependence of liberal thought on the individual as sole source of, and referent for, rights, noting how Hobbes and Locke were logically compelled to see the family as a voluntary union of individuals rather than as a social derivative.[1] While the focus on the collective was initially Marxist, it was reinforced at the outset by wide reading in Christian theology. The concern was at first theoretical, as Betsey noted that Hobbes, particularly, managed to salvage the family through the subordination of women. But her focus would deepen over time, as she witnessed the obvious dependence of modern feminism on the individual rights argument and, increasingly, believed that she saw its corrosive effects on institutions vital to women and to society alike. Many of her feminist commentators, in turn, even the few who were somewhat sympathetic, simply could not fathom an alternative to the individual rights approach, an indirect confirmation of Betsey's findings.[2]

But Betsey's increasing disagreements with mainstream feminism depended on more than her distinctive take on the primacy of society over the individual. It depended as well on an increasingly articulated belief in the inherent differences between men and women, another take that put Betsey at odds with most feminist spokeswomen. She correctly delineated the historical oscillation of feminists over the question of special feminine qualities and functions versus essential gender equivalence. Betsey's position in some ways harked back to the late-nineteenth-century emphasis on the rights women deserve as distinctive nurturers, but this has not of course been the dominant feminist view more recently.[3]

The final elements of the mounting attack on conventional feminism stemmed from Betsey's deep belief that feminism was not representing most women's needs or interests, or even their articulated goals, and that positions on abortion and other questions led not only to an alienation of the majority from the feminist cause, but also to a privileging of the individual rights strategy over any interest in family preservation or the protection of children.

The gap that grew between Betsey and dominant feminism led, it is fair to say, to oversimplifications on both sides, and nastiness on at least one. The articles in this collection do not directly capture the bitterness of feminist indignation against a scholar who initially seemed firmly aligned with a leftist take on women's issues (even though this had not been entirely the case) but who now seemed to have abandoned the cause.[4] Contemporary feminism has often been deeply unkind to dissent, especially around key symbols such as abortion, and when dissent combined with seeming betrayal, the attacks became scathing and, often, quite unfair.

For her part, and here several of the later articles in this volume do offer illustration, Betsey could misleadingly paint feminists as far more uniform than they actually were or are and could use labels such as antifamily and antichild in dubious ways. Here the collection that follows illustrates not just the fascinating interplay between consistency and change in Betsey's own approaches to feminism, but some of the less constructive aspects of ideological warfare as well.

But the larger point is the complexity of Betsey's thinking about women and the really difficult balance she tried to develop in her work. For this was no rubber-stamp, conservative antifeminist, even though comments on conservative limitations tended to recede in favor of the more obvious conflicts with feminism. Along with her critiques of feminism, Betsey consistently welcomed gains women had made in politics and in intellectual life and even in the workforce, where, however, she had more reservations.[5] She routinely championed the need to protect women from many traditional forms of subordination, even though she had her own approach as to how best to do so. She vigorously sought opportunities to use some specific feminist platforms along with a more social-institutional approach to improve women's lives, against contemporary dangers and past injustices alike.

All of this makes for a truly nuanced intellectual mix. It was not absolutely unique. Betsey herself noted other critics who shared many of her assessments at least on a number of points,[6] and reviewers (both friendly and hostile) have done the same. But the search for a distinctive combination of newer and older gender elements and the attack on mainstream feminism (combined with the enthusiastic defense of many women's gains) generate challenging reading. And that reading, overall, is what the articles in this collection provide. They urge an examination of basic assumptions and a candid appraisal of current gender problems alike, and they easily repay a thoughtful consideration.

The assessment of feminism and the development of the distinctive effort to combine enhancement of women's lives with a less individualistic rendering of the quest for rights shine through the majority of articles in this collection, especially the materials from the early 1990s onward. Several essays are particularly probing.[7] In addition to these basic issues, several articles lay out challenging assertions about some of the problems most important to conventional feminist hearts—not only abortion, but date rape and marital rape as well. One cannot dismiss out of hand Betsey's argument that defense of individual rights in such areas encourages women to sidestep responsibility for sexual behavior (in the date or acquaintance rape scenario) and, even more, undercuts the primacy of the family unit (in the case of spousal rape). Contentions of this sort, by no means intended to justify male violence or ignore problems of women's subordination (Betsey was fiercely opposed to spousal rape), force either a rethinking of some current liberal conventions or, at the least, a more thoughtful statement of basic assumptions. Either way the force of Betsey's arguments is real and salutary—even if one ultimately disagrees on some points.

Small wonder that other commentators, not content merely to dismiss the currently less fashionable as hopelessly antifeminist, have really struggled with this fundamental aspect of Betsey's work, conveyed here in the majority of articles that follow and of course presented as well in her three books on feminism and on the family.[8] The question posed by one scholar—can there be a conservative feminism?—though naive and by implication too facilely negative in one sense, reveals the dilemma of combining a critique of dominant feminism with obvious compassion for the issues women faced and face. Betsey's views are not easy to pin down on a contemporary roadmap.[9]

Another tension, less obvious than the effort to challenge conventional feminism while defending women's achievements and needs, informs many essays in this collection. This, too, begins with early evaluations herein of the relationship between elite and ordinary women and also derives from the types of evidence most often invoked.

Betsey was trained as an intellectual historian, and her interests here infuse the vast majority of the essays that follow. But she worked at a time when social history (and even some of the newer forms of cultural history) were gaining prominence, and the essays also reveal her wide reading in this area with regard to European women's history. Her own work, as is well known, migrated from early modern intellectual history to southern women's history (not directly represented in this volume), where she contributed significantly to what any historian will recognize as the social history field, though with emphasis on reading texts rather than, say, quantitative evidence. In this volume, however, the relationship between intellectual history and social claims is less explicitly articulated than might be desired.

Interest in women with intellectual or spiritual accomplishments was a natural for a woman scholar entering the ranks in the 1970s. The achievements helped such scholars soften any sense of treating women merely as historical victims (another consistent position through the evolution of Betsey's work). This interest obviously continued to mark that work and the work of other writers and intellectuals in more recent times.[10] A probing early article in this collection also highlights the tension between the history

of women, as being mainly focused on private life, and mainstream historical topics dealing with political systems. This tension bothered Betsey, who
looked to women's larger contribution, beyond the private experience, in
her own work.[11] The embrace of social history here was somewhat qualified.

More familiar—and here we approach feminist issues again—was Betsey's
deep and abiding belief that the theoretical (individualistic) foundations of
liberalism and feminism create fundamental flaws that, translated through
specifics such as the individual rights approach to abortion, could tear apart
social institutions such as the family. The intellectual substructure of abortion somehow teaches men as well as women that family responsibilities are
purely a matter of personal choice. This may well be so, but the mechanism
of transmission, from intellectual system to social reality, needs attention.
The intellectual angle shines through much more clearly than what is surely
a more complicated, and potentially varied, social reality.

This is all the more the case in dealing with one of Betsey's central contentions from the 1990s onward: that feminists are out of touch with real
women and real women's issues. Her ultimate tendency to dismiss feminists
as elitists is a bit distracting here, as feminism obviously cuts a wider swath
than an elite of upper-class and intellectual women alone. But the larger question is how Betsey knew what ordinary women think and want—particularly
working-class women who were her principal frame of reference. Here is
another confrontation with the need for social evidence. There is no elabo-
rate sociological inquiry in these articles (which doubtless makes them more
readable). A reference to polling data would surely have revealed more complexities than Betsey chose to acknowledge about support for abortion rights,
for example. Betsey asserted a social reality on the basis, apparently, of some
interviews (not specified), discussions with her students (who did not feel as
oppressed as feminists might want them to, which understandably intrigued
Betsey), and selective reference to undeniable social issues—with the plight
of single mothers resonating most vividly. The assertions may all be true
(except about professed majority views on abortion), but the connective evidence, between the intellectual bases of rights arguments and social results,
is at least debatable.

Nothing infuriates the leaders of an ideological movement—whether
socialist or feminist—more than being told that they do not know the real
issues or real interests of their proclaimed constituency. So these aspects of
Betsey's work inevitably drew fire, as she knew they would. And while some
of the critiques can be dismissed as rhetorical bombast—in trying for example to write Betsey out of feminism altogether—the fact is that the methods of social analysis ultimately required to undergird Betsey's claims are not
foregrounded in these essays.

For, despite their author's affinity for intellectual evidence, Betsey's claims are sociological. She argued recurrently (and to my mind persuasively, in principle at least) that women are more divided by class than united by gender (both in the past and now). This approach informed her early historical statements and, of course, her work on southern women with its sharp divides between slave women and free white women, and it undergirds her assertions that feminists and lower-class women are two separate groups, with distinct and sometimes hostile interests. Some elite women, either childless or possessed of abundant daycare, thus contrast obviously with the female majority who deal with children directly and, Betsey asserted, have a far more child-centered view of life than their privileged sisters.[12] Both in past and in present, different groups of women have had quite different definitions of freedom. Again the argument is strong, its plausibility considerable—but some further evidentiary steps are essential. Betsey was hardly the first intellectual historian to range into social analysis, and it is vital to note her wide and intelligent reading in social history—even aside from her specialist work on southern women's history. But her contemporary analysis does reveal some problems characteristic of the intellectual history orbit.

Betsey was a distinguished historical scholar, and while the essays in this volume deal only glancingly with her central historical work, the historical perspective is obvious. Most specifically there are several fine articles either summing up the state of work on women's history at several points in the recent past or using this scholarship to generalize about topics such as pre-industrial women's work. An assessment of historical causation, however, is largely missing in these accounts save for the deep belief in the power of intellectual systems.

More to the point of the collection as a whole is an important, indeed inescapable, historical topic to which Betsey turned often. Inevitably, if not always systematically, Betsey grappled with the question of declension—of how women's conditions today compare to those of the past. It is a tough issue for her—or for any scholar not simplistically Whiggish. It is also fundamental to her claims that contemporary feminism, with its individualistic approach and its focus on the wrong, because elitist, issues, has done more harm than good. The argument comes through in several forms, and it is invariably worth serious consideration. Typically, however, the argument is also debatable—partly because it is a very complex case to make on its face and partly because, here too, the kind of social data needed to drive the points home conclusively are not always present.

Two articles offer particularly ready ammunition. The little piece on violence,[13] contending that physical abuse against women has gone up because family cohesion and protection have been stripped away, is at the least too slight and assertive to bear the historical weight it carries. It is worth noting, to be sure, that John Demos and others have ventured similar arguments about child abuse—that there was less in the past than now—but, even with Demos's widened scope and more detailed analysis, the argument is impossible to demonstrate conclusively.[14] Concern about violence to women (and children) has gone up in the political realm. We know that some acts that were once assumed to be private matters are now punishable as criminal. We also know, however, that local community norms and enforcement have lost some sting—and possibly a lot of sting (this is Demos's argument)—as families have become more private. This, of course, is Betsey's contention as well. But whether overall violence, as currently defined, has increased is truly difficult to affirm.

A more substantial later effort had Betsey dealing with the complexities of actual family history to contend that, despite past varieties and undeniable problems, the family is worse off today than ever.[15] She briefly acknowledged historical work that shows limitations on actual family life, especially among the poor, in many prior eras of Western history, though she does not quite get to the systematic efforts to debunk idealization of families past.[16] But she insisted that things are worse today because only today has any group—read contemporary feminism—turned against the family itself. This is, frankly, contestable, for it depends on a more detailed reading of history but also on a more careful assessment of the family today in actuality and not in some rhetorical renderings. Historical judgments of progress or deterioration are notoriously hard to make because of the range of variations and perceptions involved, and short articles almost inevitably preclude a full rendering.

Historical perspective also suggests some desirable additions to Betsey's sense of family causation, including the causation involved in dealing with children—always assuming that a model of deterioration is appropriate in the first place. More active use of the so-called European-style family as a crucial social backdrop to her comments on Western women's history, particularly in the premodern period, would have deepened her analysis at several points.[17] Betsey saw modern history in terms of male irresponsibility (which she did not belabor) encouraged in turn by feminist dismissal of family concerns and insistence on individual evaluation and consent. But some of the central trends of the modern family are determined by far more than this.

Thus Betsey's concern about care for children is surely legitimate, but children have been affected by changes far greater than feminism over the last century. It is really the impact of an industrial, urban economy that should sit at the base of assessments of modern childhood, with the reduction of the economic utility of children and the strains associated with moving most work outside the family context. This is of course why the issue crops up in other industrial societies without feminist movements comparable to the American one, and it produces new questions about what children are for, as well as about adult responsibilities. American feminism certainly has a role in the ongoing discussions, but it is not a primary moving force in them.[18]

The fact is that, with industrialization, the whole economic position of the family shifted—diminished, in fact—whether a strong feminist movement was present or not. Since it was no longer the context for most economic production (since jobs were almost entirely outside the home), a reevaluation of family motivation was essential. Thus in contemporary Japan, lacking much individualistic feminism or an individual rights tradition more generally, more and more women simply do not find the formation of families worth the bother. But there is no set formula here, as other motivations and attachments can also be discovered—whether feminism is a strong factor or not. Thus while many of Betsey's family concerns continue to ring true—even though the causation involved is broader than she suggests—unexpected signs of new commitment have emerged among many Americans since the early 1990s, including an increase (quite at odds with a declension model) in parental time devoted to children and even, at an extreme, the new phenomenon of helicopter parenting.[19] Family issues, in sum, are wider than a feminist agenda can encompass and less predictable than assumptions of some overarching individualism would allow.

A final vantage point on the essays in this collection involves a comparative approach. Few of the essays venture much by way of comparison, and the resolutely Western concentration is intriguing in an age of increasingly global history.[20] One article did move into comparative territory, when Betsey blasted American shortcomings in light of greater European, and especially Scandinavian, social commitments. Here she took American conservatives to task for espousing family values but opposing relevant social programs, such as government-sponsored daycare, that would really help families and women alike—another sign of Betsey's hard-to-label political approach and the links between her early Marxism and later Catholicism. Exactly why the United States went astray, since its sharing of European-derived individualistic values is such a key intellectual point in Betsey's work, is not entirely clear, but the weakness of American social institutions is undeniable and undeniably significant whatever one's views on feminism. It might even be noted that Betsey's own passionate emphasis on the family may reflect a larger American dependence on this particular institution, given the historical weakness of community and (until relatively recently) state in a nation of divided ethnicities and unusual geographic mobility.

An accompanying comparative point, however, raises some warning flags. Betsey noted the unusually high American illegitimacy and teenage pregnancy rates, and she wanted to pin them on the decline of moral responsibility as well. But American rates of adolescent sex are not in fact unusually high by the standards of contemporary industrial societies. What is more obviously distinctive is the national unwillingness to extend easily available birth control and the preference for "just say no" abstinence efforts that do not work—and this reflects the conservative rather than the individual rights agenda.

I confess some hesitation as well over Betsey's ultimate rejection of efforts to deal with global population pressure as a "sorely misguided" sign of "hysteria."[21] She was right that birth control rates have begun a global decline.[22] But the record of opposition to women's efforts to limit births in many contemporary settings and the problems that excessive numbers of children can still create for women and societies suggest that a more balanced view would be preferable—a view more in keeping with Betsey's usual effort at sympathetic realism where women's problems are concerned. More attention to issues in developing countries, rather than an implicitly United States–focused hostility to birth control arguments, would yield a more nuanced comparative approach.

A final comparative element, however, though one that Betsey quite understandably did not take up, returns us to the central strengths of the essays that follow. Recent evaluations by several African and Asian social scientists offer intriguing support for Betsey's critiques of Western feminism and of the harmful isolation it helps impose on women. In the past several years a number of intellectuals have detailed how Western impositions and imitations have limited community and family life outside the West and have reduced both the levels of women's well-being and important, if informal, sources of women's power.[23] Without exploring the details of Western intellectual history—as Betsey did—they pick up many of the same elements that she detailed in the American and Western context. Like Betsey, they hope for an approach to women's issues that will correct the limitations of individualism and offer new but more collective approaches to advance the cause.

Elizabeth Fox-Genovese had an extraordinary scholarly and political journey, and the essays in this collection include some key portions of her project. She became probably the most distinguished spokeswoman for conservative feminism, recasting what those terms meant and anchoring the movement within academia as well as its polemical discourse. She also contributed to several branches of historical scholarship, and though this aspect of her achievement is more fully illustrated in other volumes, there is solid historical work in the essays that follow as well.

Obviously the work represented here spurs various arguments and discussions. I have tried to suggest some issues of historical perspective and (somewhat less fairly, because here the comments go beyond Betsey's intent) some possible comparative insights as well. The issues can be raised only because the work itself is so thought provoking; they are intended as a tribute, as an extension of inquiry.

For in the end I am grateful for the opportunity to participate in this collection, even in a small way. By disposition a vaguely liberal feminist myself, though not a systematically passionate one, I was impressed by the challenge Betsey's essays raise to rethink or at least more fully justify some key positions. The invitation to assess what is really happening to women in real life and to scrutinize some of feminism's standard symbolism remains as valid as when Betsey began her own evaluation. At a time—late 2009—when many voices apparently preferred to reject health-care reform in favor of abortion orthodoxy, specific contemporary debates arguably bring home some of the questions about priorities that Betsey's work already raised. Betsey's evolution led some to strident dismissals without further thought. These essays join several other sober reassessments in calling for more serious reading, beyond knee-jerk partisan rancor.

And one final point: as noted this collection readily highlights Betsey's thoughts about individualism and, in the later offering, her repeated concerns about family and children.[24] In watching Betsey pass to the offensive against mainstream feminism, it might be too easy to pass over her effort to provide constructive alternatives. Here, ultimately, her essay "The Legal Status of Families as Institutions" may particularly reward attention. Betsey posited in this article the need for new options, as against feminism and conservatism alike, in calling for a new concept of family as a corporate entity, not an individual contract but also not an institution dependent on the subordination of women. Whatever one thinks of the specifics attached, like limitations on divorce rights, the ambition and even the optimism of the larger vision cannot fail to impress. The essay, like the collection as a whole, deserves more than labeling as feminist or conservative, calling for attention to underlying consistencies and basic goals and also to some perspectives missed that encourage ongoing debates about the vital issues raised.

Notes

1. Elizabeth Fox-Genovese, "Property and Patriarchy in Classical Bourgeois Political Theory," *Radical History Review* 4, nos. 2–3 (1977): 36–59; reprinted in this volume, pp. 1–20.

2. Chris Beasely, *What Is Feminism? An Introduction to Feminist Theory* (London: Sage, 1999); Angela Dillard, "Adventures in Conservative Feminism," *Society* 42, no. 3 (2005): 25–27.

3. Amy R. Baehr, "Conservatism, Feminism, and Elizabeth Fox-Genovese," *Hypatia* 24, no. 2 (2009): 101–24.

4. Elizabeth Minnich, "Feminist Attacks on Feminism: Patriarchy's Prodigal Daughters," *Feminist Studies* 24, no. 1 (1998): 159–75; Tricia Rose, "Feminism and Its Discontents," *Women's Review of Books* 13 (September 1996): 18.

5. Elizabeth Fox-Genovese, "The New Female Literary Culture," *Antioch Review* 38 (Spring 1980): 193–217; Elizabeth Fox-Genovese, "Severing the Ties That Bind: Women, the Family, and Social Institutions," *Intercollegiate Review* 34 (Fall 1998): 26–30; reprinted in this volume, pp. 229–34.

6. Timothy Heppell, "Conservative Feminism?" Research Centre for Democracy and Governance, 2004, http://www2.hud.ac.uk/hhs/cdg/research/conferences/0411/papers/femcon.htm (accessed July 27, 2006).

7. Elizabeth Fox-Genovese, "Feminism and the Rhetoric of Individual Rights, Part One," *Common Knowledge* 1, no. 1 (1992): 43–53, and "Feminism and the Rhetoric of Individual Rights, Part Two," *Common Knowledge* 1, no. 2 (1992): 63–73; reprinted in this volume, pp. 120–31 and pp. 132–43, respectively.

8. Elizabeth Fox-Genovese, *Marriage: The Dream That Refuses to Die* (Wilmington, Del.: Intercollegiate Studies Institute, 2008); *"Feminism Is Not the Story of My Life": How Today's Feminist Elite Has Lost Touch with the Real Concerns of Women* (New York: Nan A. Talese, 1996); *Feminism without Illusions: A Critique of Individualism* (Chapel Hill: University of North Carolina Press, 1991).

9. Baehr, "Conservatism, Feminism, and Elizabeth Fox-Genovese."

10. Elizabeth Fox-Genovese, "Culture and Consciousness in the Intellectual History of European Women," *Signs* 12 (Spring 1987): 529–47; reprinted in this volume, pp. 92–111.

11. Elizabeth Fox-Genovese, "Placing Women's History in History," *New Left Review* 133 (May/June 1982): 5–29; reprinted in this volume, pp. 45–74.

12. Elizabeth Fox-Genovese, "Contested Meanings: Women and the Problem of Freedom in the Mid-Nineteenth-Century United States," in *Historical Change and Human Rights: The Oxford Amnesty Lectures 1994*, ed. Olwen Hufton (New York: Basic, 1995), 179–215; reprinted in this volume, pp. 167–96.

13. Elizabeth Fox-Genovese, "Beyond Autonomy: Sex, Repression, and Violence against Women," *Common Knowledge* 4, no. 3 (1995): 64–71; reprinted in this volume, pp. 203–10.

14. John Putnam Demos, *Past, Present and Personal: The Family and the Life Course in American History* (New York: Oxford University Press, 1988).

15. Elizabeth Fox-Genovese, "Thoughts on the History of the Family," in *The Family, Civil Society, and the State*, ed. Christopher Wolfe (Lanham, Md.: Rowman & Littlefield, 1998), 3–15; reprinted in this volume, pp. 253–66.

16. John R. Gillis, *A World of Their Own Making: Myth, Ritual and the Quest for Family Values* (New York: Basic, 1996).

17. Mary S. Hartman, *The Household and the Making of History: A Subversive View of the Western Past* (Cambridge: Cambridge University Press, 2004).

18. Peter N. Stearns, *Childhood in World History* (New York: Routledge, 2006).

19. Peter N. Stearns, *Anxious Parents: A History of Modern Childrearing in America* (New York: New York University Press, 2003).

20. Fox-Genovese, "Thoughts on the History."

21. Elizabeth Fox-Genovese, "Feminism and the Unraveling of the Social Bond," *Voices: Women for Faith and Family* 19 (Michaelmas 2004): 9–14; reprinted in this volume, pp. 282–93.

22. Perdita Huston, *Third World Women Speak Out* (New York: Praeger, 1979).

23. Ifi Amadiume, *Male Daughters, Female Husbands: Gender and Sex in an African Society* (London: Zed, 1997).

24. Elizabeth Fox-Genovese, "The Legal Status of Families as Institutions," *Cornell Law Review* 77 (1992): 992–96; reprinted in this volume, pp. 144–48.

Introduction

"For as long as I can remember"—
Elizabeth Fox-Genovese as Historian

Deborah A. Symonds

Thirty years ago, sitting in on an undergraduate lecture by a new faculty member, Elizabeth Fox-Genovese, I heard one of my fellow graduate students—an older woman whose husband was an economist—remark quietly but firmly, "Betsey is a class act."[1] At that moment I thought it was an offhand comment, but I never forgot it, and by the time I finished my dissertation, I knew that it was true. Erudite by force of her own will, she was well educated by institutions now severely eroded, and her marriage to Eugene D. Genovese provided yet another education. Elegant and formidable in public, she was intense, compelling, driven, and yet respectful of students, colleagues, staff, and service workers in everyday life. She could cook. She was funny. She and her husband performed—and performed is the right word—lengthy, hilarious dialogues on baseball, the true nature of girls, why cats kill, and a number of other topics on which they disagreed. I miss them. Betsey, as all of her students (at Binghamton, at least) came to call her, could "dish it out and take it"; she was the smartest person I had ever met, and I privately called her "the Fox."[2] I knew her for the last 40 percent of her life, by which time she was a distinguished intellectual of the political Left and, then, of the Right. This apparent shift belies what is ultimately so profound about her life and what should confound those on the left and the right who have or have not grasped the range of her work: Elizabeth Fox-Genovese did not change very much at all; she was a distinguished intellectual, never the property of the Left or the Right.

Her sustained critique of individualism was complex and arose out of her initial, and carefully respectful, interest in a very long eighteenth century from Hobbes through, as she put it in 1978, the moment when "weighty political events cut short Marie Antoinette's romping and eventually her head as well."[3] Her mastery in both detail and major architecture of the work of the great men of the period from Hobbes through more than the French Revolution, including Marx, Freud, Gramsci, and the major commentaries on their work, served her well. And it was, as she noted in "The New Female Literary Culture," always supplemented by her familiarity and respect for the great as well as the unknown women of the period, from the early novelists through the later "books by women,"[4] including anonymous, and to some degree collective, peasant and genteel transmitters of folk tales and ballads. Yet her critique of individualism was, like her other work, always dialectical. As Mark Bauerlein so perfectly put it, "as soon as one began to settle into a firm understanding and expected her to concur, Betsey would insert a thoughtful qualification or gentle warning."[5] The sustained critique could, in other words, turn on a dime into a defense, for no one has ever articulated more clearly that individualism in all of its material and cultural manifestations did not come to men and women of various ranks at the same time, in the same form, or with the same social implications. Betsey, one might add, loved a good car.

After publishing her dissertation as *The Origins of Physiocracy: Economic Revolution and Social Order in Eighteenth-Century France* in 1976, she rapidly moved on to Hobbes and Locke, and their participation "in the as yet unresolved assault upon divine authority."[6] Locke took the assault much further, attacking patriarchy and absolutism as embodied in the family and the wife's subordination to the husband. In the first article in this collection, "Property and Patriarchy in Classical Bourgeois Political Theory," women emerge in Locke as contenders for the same right to "absolute property in oneself" that bourgeois political theory offered men, without being able to realize what would remain a theoretical right. And so, as Fox-Genovese put it, implicitly male "individualism triumphed on the ruins of the dreams of equality."[7]

With subtlety and irony, Fox-Genovese brought her mastery of Western thought to bear not only on the critique of the absolutists' defense of patriarchy that Locke made, and to which Hobbes ever so slightly opened the door, but on the three components of their work that would haunt her until her death: women, the family, and individualism. Her own first endnote captures the scholarly literature of the 1970s, but the notes reflect the times, and among the references to Gordon Schochet and Leo Strauss is another, to Ginevra Conti Odorsio writing about Hobbes in DWF: *Donna, Woman, Femme* in 1976. Women's history was an emerging, not a recognized field, and the questions on the table in the late 1970s among both grassroots members of the women's movement and scholars interested in women were often shaped, and then reshaped, by the much-abused word *patriarchy*.[8] So it was no accident that Fox-Genovese, a self-identified Marxist since the

1960s, plunged into the debates on women by dissecting Hobbes, Locke, and Filmer in an article the title of which began with the words *property* and *patriarchy*. To paraphrase Virginia Woolf, if patriarchy was not to be found in, or rather understood through, classical bourgeois political theory, it was not to be understood at all.[9]

By 1978 Betsey had finished a very different essay for *Marxist Perspectives*, "Yves Saint Laurent's Peasant Revolution." No longer moored to the eighteenth century, but not entirely adrift from it, she established another lifelong interest, fashion in its most profound relations to culture, to the female self, to the mediation of that self by designers, and to the economy. In this piece one can see Fox-Genovese reading the *New York Times* on July 29, 1976, and follow her immediate train of thought: Saint Laurent's new peasant collection; the price of the clothes; the market; the cultural position of haute couture; and ultimately to her point of historical departure: "Saint Laurent's genius lay in costuming the rich as peasants."[10] At this moment the eighteenth century takes center stage, and we see Marie Antoinette as milkmaid, followed by the comparison between Saint Laurent and Rousseau, then Beau Brummel, Adam Smith, clothing as commodity, and ultimately, we find ourselves in a discussion of the female self—the individual—enmeshed in a powerful culture. Even kleptomania and anorexia nervosa appear briefly as "fashion clearly holds its sway in the relationship between consciousness and social being."[11]

Fox-Genovese always understood power, from "economic exigency" to subtle psychological and theoretical implications, and in this article she creates a complex historical context around one item of front-page news, combining references to peasant revolution and the search for community with Dior, the 1950s, and—more striking to her recent audience than to readers in the late 1970s—the use of a feminist vocabulary, including "domestic self-abnegation" and "right-wing reaction."[12] But her defense of abortion was specific and qualified: "the opposition to abortion flies for the jugular of workingclass women."[13] And her catalog of enemies on the right leaves the door open to consideration of their arguments: "Life would be much simpler if all or even most adherents of the traditional family, the domestic role of women, the right to life, and the sanctity of the free market and the American way of life could be dismissed as hypocrites, fools, or dupes. They cannot."[14] In short this defense of abortion was grounded in her knowledge of the harshness and exigencies of working-class life in the present, just as much as that of peasant life in the past; it was not grounded in a defense of sexual freedom or individual pleasure. And her recognition of the seriousness of opposing arguments, equally a hallmark of her thought, marks her feminist vocabulary as dialectical rather than ideological.

Two years after the encyclopedic essay on fashion, work, feminism, and the female self, Fox-Genovese published "The New Female Literary Culture," reflecting her own broad and careful reading of early and contemporary women's fiction. The essay begins, "For as long as I can remember, books by women have mattered to me, and in the most compelling ways." Within a few sentences, she delineated the double consciousness familiar to women readers aware of the canon in 1980 and, no doubt, earlier: "I just never thought much about my ready acceptance of standards that had no place for so many of the works of literature that nourished my soul." While not the same as the double consciousness described by W. E. B. DuBois, to which Fox-Genovese later frequently referred, it is akin to it, and it captures an important aspect of second-wave feminist thought, mystified at the time as consciousness-raising but in reality no more than a cascade of rips, rents, and great holes in the fabric of Western ideology, provoked by a critical mass of data regarding women's positions in society, coupled with disciplined dialectical thought.[15] In that first paragraph the king's new clothes, already rather old, were found wanting, and many women, as Fox-Genovese recognized in the essay, were reading voraciously in that "new female literary culture." If a few women may have pored over the work of Hobbes or Locke three hundred years ago, searching for signs of their political viability, an army had descended on the work of Virginia Woolf, Tillie Olsen, Elizabeth Gaskell, and many others by 1980, and on the new journals, magazines, and especially the new novels, searching for something else.[16]

"We must have," Fox-Genovese wrote, "a solid historical and contemporary sociology of women's literary culture."[17] Sketching the possible dimensions of such a culture and addressing some of the novels, Fox-Genovese adopted the pose of someone waiting; she dwelt on Erica Jong's Isadora, who "returns to her husband to wait to see if she will leave him."[18] Like Virginia Woolf in *A Room of One's Own,* posing as the reader of a novel by a fictional young woman, waiting to see if the author can create a situation and resolve it, Fox-Genovese examined the new storytelling about women's lives coming from Doris Lessing, Erica Jong, Marilyn French, Alix Kates Shulman, Gail Godwin, Alison Lurie, Margaret Drabble, and many others to see if the authors will, as Woolf puts it, "jump."[19] Fox-Genovese concluded these authors failed to take the jump, pointing out that Jong "retreats from the insight that personal solutions are socially rooted." If marriage was still the great topic—as it had been for Shakespeare, in "the marriage of true minds," and for Jane Austen and scores of eighteenth- and nineteenth-century novelists—the social structure that was so clear to Austen had now shriveled to a "personalist sensibility," and novelists of the new female literary culture failed to address "why women so deeply needed and wanted the marital structure—as social and economic armor—against which they rebelled." If the discontent was palpable while the solutions were narrow, confessional, and unrealized, the critics, notably Joan Didion, were "staggeringly unfair." True to her opening paragraph, Fox-Genovese consistently acknowledged the dual literary cultures, asking readers "to respect the serious—even when not successful—attempt of women to forge a literary culture faithful to female experience, even if that culture does not conform to the sensibilities and stylistic standards of the dominant male literary culture."[20]

An avid reader who would not separate the new women's literature from the culture that spawned it, Fox-Genovese at thirty-nine, in 1980, left Rochester for Binghamton, then known as the State University of New York at Binghamton. Three years later *Fruits of Merchant Capital: Slavery and Bourgeois Property in the Rise and Expansion of Capitalism* appeared. But in 1982 two very different articles were published, one a brief tour de force on gender, class, and the social construction of both gender and sexuality, the other a review of the state of women's history within the discipline. In the former article, reprinted in the third and fifth volumes of this present edition, Fox-Genovese indirectly addressed the novelists' "personalist sensibility" and supplied the discussion of just where the power to shape women, men, and sexuality, including illusory sexual liberation, to suit the needs of various dominant classes lay. This was the power—the class structure—that the novelists of the 1970s, perhaps with the exception of Marge Piercy, had been unable or unwilling to evoke.[21]

In the latter article, "Placing Women's History in History," Fox-Genovese provided a detailed review of women's history in the United States, Europe, and other places. Noting dryly that "women were invariably doing something," she celebrated the recovery of "annals of women's exploits" but carefully drew a line: "adding women to history is not the same as adding women's history."[22] Always dialectical, she refused to underestimate the importance of "adding women," even as she made clear that this slightly antiquarian pursuit was not to be confused with the field of women's history. In 1982 this precise delineation was something I had come to expect from Betsey, with whom every seminar ended with the sound of the second shoe dropping. In this essay the shoe that dropped was a manifesto setting out the "theoretical implications of placing women's history in history." One, "we must adopt gender system as a fundamental category of historical analysis, understanding that such systems are historically, not biologically, determined." The full meaning of that first point lay in another article, "Gender, Class and Power: Some Theoretical Considerations," published in the same year in *History Teacher.* Two, "the general rubric of patriarchy" obscures more than it illuminates; patriarchy obscures the importance of Hobbes and

Locke, of bourgeois ideology, of property. Three, divorcing women's history from "mainstream history" merely re-creates women as other, echoing Simone de Beauvoir, and thereby continuing the work of mainstream history. Four, "capitalism and the great bourgeois revolutions have tended to generalize gender difference as the custodian of displaced notions of hierarchy and dependence, and thus" to break their promise of "equality for all." Five, "the expansion of capitalism and modern representative government have attempted to bind men of different classes, races, and ethnic groups together through the double promise of individualism in the public sphere and male dominance in the home." Six, "all modern languages of social theory" have accepted this purposefully created gender system without question. Seven, "modern institutions, including the purportedly neutral market, have systematically extended gender difference." Eight, "the family and the sexual division of labour cannot be explained in functional terms"; and nine, "our dominant social theories have provided us with no adequate way to assess the indispensable contributions of women to collective life in society," either among those above or those below.[23]

It was an extraordinary manifesto, written almost a generation ago, calling for nothing less than the reorganization of historical knowledge as the institutions of modern life were exposed as instruments of power, and historians described not only what women habitually did, but why they did it and *cui bono*—to whose advantage. Refocusing the transition from absolutist to bourgeois society through the lens of gender systems allowed her to reveal scores of ideas and their implications, from recent to ancient, from Locke to functionalism, to "the dead end of attempting to establish sexual difference as an agent of historical causation," and to Carl Degler.[24] Like the poles of a magnet pulling iron filings into a distinct pattern, Betsey brought order to recent work and to the classics, bringing them all to the table for a great reckoning. Yet she began with the conflicted self, citing W. E. B. DuBois: "a world which yields him no true self-consciousness, but only lets him see himself through the revelation of the other world." And that was clearly her model for women's history. As she put it, referring to DuBois's consideration of the double consciousness of the African American: "It is the tension itself, the dialectic of his sundered identity that he wishes to live."[25] And she ended with a related plea: "Women's history challenges mainstream history not to substitute the chronicle of the female subject for that of the male, but rather to restore conflict, ambiguity and tragedy to the centre of historical process." But to bring the dialectic full circle, she equated the tension, conflict, ambiguity, and tragedy of the historical process, in an ultimate clause, with "a common destiny."[26]

In 1987, one year after moving from Binghamton to Emory University, Elizabeth Fox-Genovese was building the Emory Institute for Women's Studies, was finishing *Within the Plantation Household: Black and White Women of the Old South,* and had just published "Culture and Consciousness in the Intellectual History of European Women."[27] I mention these three in the same sentence to emphasize the range of her reading, work, and expertise but also to make a different point, for something in her writing had changed by 1987. Betsey had often remarked in the early 1980s that no historian wrote anything very important until he or she was at least fifty. She would explain that the substance of historical work was cumulative but also overwhelming until one had enough experience to both master and simplify the material at hand. Whether she was speaking from experience as she entered her forties I will never know, but the brilliant and also fierce style of the passage I referred to above as a manifesto appears in neither the book being finished nor the article published in 1987. In the preface to *Within the Plantation Household,* Fox-Genovese described a crucial aspect of the antebellum plantation household, working from Sarah Gayle's journal to create a prologue of great simplicity and careful narrative.[28] And in the article "Culture and Consciousness in the Intellectual History of European Women," reprinted here, she began by quietly announcing that in the five years preceding 1987, European women's history had come of age. So, I think, had she.

Reviewing recent work spanning five or six hundred years—including nuns, saints, Christine de Pizan, Joan of Arc, early modern feminist thought, Mary Astell, Mary Wollstonecraft, the Chartists, women's protests in the twentieth century, and more, in chronological order—Betsey made explicit the connections between thought and culture, thought and class, thought and community. She also laid bare the workings of consciousness, for both Christine de Pizan and for one of her biographers, as an aspect of bourgeois individualism that has made the autobiographical stream in de Pizan's work increasingly accessible to us. Consciousness for women is not simply personal and unique, Betsey claimed; it "also derives from their communities' and the larger society's models of womanhood, from structural opportunities for women as women and for working people as members of a class." If consciousness needs social context, "the social determination of women's experience" alone was incomplete without the psychological dimension that consciousness brings. In other words her review of work on women became a study not only of what had been done, but also of how it had been done and how that was also an element of history and subject to historical analysis. One of Elizabeth Fox-Genovese's great strengths was her ability to incorporate, in the richest possible sense of that word, every aspect of material, intellectual, and theoretical life. In the last sentence of an essay that is itself a miniature history of women, she laid out the breadth of her method: "Consciousness is, finally, a matter of language, as are political and social goals. And all three are also matters of political and social relations—of power and its abuses."[29]

If her early work on the French Physiocrats was clearly intellectual history, I cannot imagine even the young Betsey Fox as simply an intellectual historian. I prefer to think of her, early and late, as an omnivore, using every plausible source to give herself and others access to a three-dimensional past that encompassed the intellectual, the psychological, the tactile, and the bluntly political structures of lives that varied by region, dialect, class, dining habits, and a plethora of other aspects. Put in other words, she moved easily between intellectual and social history, her definitions of each were broad, and she never lost sight of the reality of power. Three years before "Culture and Consciousness" was published, "Women and Work" appeared in *French Women and the Age of Enlightenment*,[30] demonstrating a grasp of how women's work fit into French society and the "economic life of the state" in which it was embedded.[31] Unlike many other representations of women's work, there are few numbers and no statistics.[32] Without knowing that Betsey had made her mark at the Newberry Institute for Quantitative History in 1978 and developed a serious interest in powerful computers, one might mistake this for disinterest or, worse, inability. It was a conscious choice to use written language and to avoid the generalizations that statistical representation can convey. Instead she wrote that "it is possible to construct a taxonomy of women's work" but qualified that in the next paragraph, adding, "in all likelihood, the rich diversity of women's working experience would not lend itself readily to standardization."[33] To grasp fully the connections within her thought, one might read "Culture and Consciousness," the brief essay on "Women and Work," and finally "The Domestic Bases of Political Economy" from *Fruits of Merchant Capital*. Through the combined impact of these essays from the early and mid-1980s, the reader finds a compelling demonstration of the ways in which intellectual, social, and economic history do more than overlap: each propels the other, creating a three-dimensional, complex, and human past, complemented by the publication of her translation, with a lengthy introduction, of *The Autobiography of Du Pont de Nemours* in 1984.[34]

The 1988 publication of *Within the Plantation Household* marked Fox-Genovese's transformation into a historian of women in the United States, albeit one with an extraordinary background in European history and Western thought. Settled in Atlanta and at Emory University, Fox-Genovese's attention turned to the United States, although she wrote "Women and the Enlightenment" for the 1987 edition of a noted text in European women's history.[35] But it was a complex transformation. Fox-Genovese published history and literary criticism and emerged as a public intellectual addressing the roots of contemporary women's problems, the failures of feminism that emerged from the defeat of the ERA, and the disintegration of a socialist-feminist agenda after the collapse of socialism and the Soviet Union.

After the appearance in 1988 of *Within the Plantation Household,* which contains such precise, complex readings of individuals, especially in the prologue and epilogue and in "My Statue, My Self," Fox-Genovese produced a brief but exacting commentary for *Fanny Kemble: Journal of a Young Actress* in 1990. With surgical precision she dissected what Kemble does and does not tell us and Kemble's "uneasy compromise between the self that experienced those travels and the self that published their account."[36] The foreword is a concise lesson in how to read what women write about themselves for an audience, and it reflects one understanding of the complexity of individual existence. But by 1991, in *Feminism without Illusions,* and then in articles in 1992 on feminism, individual rights, and families, Fox-Genovese began to hammer out a formal, legal, and moral critique, not of individual consciousness but of women's paths to individual rights—not equality—in modern society, and of the rhetoric that paved and still paves the way.

Because I have never been a liberal feminist, an American feminist, or deeply addicted to radical individualism, the pithy indictments of capitalist society that run through her work in the early 1990s—for example, "the atomized individualism grounded in the capitalist market into which our social institutions are collapsing"—have always struck me as perfectly sensible. Between my failure to aspire to atomized individualism and my extended, hard-lived commitment throughout the 1970s to a radical feminism grounded in the belief that women had something different to offer society, different from men and suggested but as yet unrealized by any mainstream socialist or feminist design, I enjoyed the critique of individualism that runs through her two-part essay in *Common Knowledge* in 1992.[37] In the second part, Betsey argued that the defense of women's right to abortion and the defense of the child's right to be born both rely on the tradition of individual rights. And then, leaving me with not much radical feminist ground on which to stand, she added that the belief "that women have a radically different view of the world than men—that women are, for example, especially nurturing—also derives from the tradition of male individualism that has cast women as the other." Yet on a page just before this, she also remarked that "one of the strengths of feminist thinking, in fact, consists in precisely the emphasis on human interconnectedness."[38] I had thought that that might have been one of the alternatives to individualism.

Thought is different from nature, of course, and connections are not the same as nurture. As Fox-Genovese continued to discuss birth, abortion, and society, she insisted that "we remain understandably loathe to admit that innumerable factors resulting from social interdependency impinge upon any definition of life." And then, in a voice I remember from the 1980s as well as the 1990s, she indicted individualism and the society it had spawned: "the right to life means nothing without the means to sustain it," and "we stand effectively alone among industrialized nations in failing to enforce a social context that can truly value and support reproduction."[39] But her target in the two essays for *Common Knowledge* is not society; it is the rhetoric of feminism, in which, she wrote, "women remain hostage to the most robust aspect of Western male thought—the emphasis upon individualism."[40] Rejecting both "radical individualism" and "traditional domesticity," Fox-Genovese noted that "we have, collectively, failed to develop a new narrative of female heroism that preserves the older sense of a special female calling to bind up the wounds of the world and attend to the next generation." And she was determined to press the claims of the collective, and of "an equitable society," not one of atomized individuals.[41] I suspect modern readers will want to read "female heroism" as female heroine and oppose it to the collective; if so one needs only remember Käthe Kollwitz's figure of Black Anna from her series of prints *The Peasants' War* or her *Tower of the Mothers* sculpture from 1938.

Readers of *Feminism without Illusions* in 1991 would not be surprised by Betsey's search for a new feminism and a new feminist rhetoric in these essays, nor by her emphasis on social interconnectedness, interdependence, and family. These latter echoed older notions of social feminism, socialism, and even the traditional, domestic, corporate family for her but were not adequately realized by any of them. Readers of her obituary in the *New York Times* could also quickly do the math and find that she faced a diagnosis of multiple sclerosis in 1992, with the prospect of declining mobility. But those who had known her for many years would also know that she lived the dream of which she wrote to the best of her ability, with an exhausting passion: her family, friends, colleagues, and students formed a complex extended family, and all were welcome guests at the kitchen table. Early in her marriage, she had confessed to wanting twenty-three children, and even without them, she and her husband built an extraordinary family. As Robert P. George put it, "Although unable to have children of their own, they lavished parental care and concern on their students and younger colleagues, who in turn worshipped them."[42] Many of us sat at their kitchen table and in their various dining rooms over the last thirty-some years: equal, interdependent, rowdy, loved, and unchastised—most of the time. We learned, from a constant frisson of unexpected turns of phrase and thought, much, as I continue to learn from Betsey's later work, for much of which I was unprepared.

The third article from 1992 reprinted in this volume, "The Legal Status of Families as Institutions," brings us back to Locke, property, and patriarchy, but also to southern plantation households, creating a far richer pattern of subordination and, by the nineteenth century, restiveness. With the abolition of slavery and the discussion of married women's property rights, family members became individuals bound only by dissoluble contract. Leaving children vulnerable was unacceptable to Fox-Genovese, and she argued something that would shock those of us in the modern world for whom freedom, comfort, and natural rights are personally rather than socially defined: "Perhaps," she wrote, "parents should be denied the right to divorce until their children have attained their majority or are economically self-sufficient." She might, in a longer essay, have explained that this proposal, which is almost outrageous now, would have seemed an unnecessary precaution before the advent of complete divorce and that hallmark of its cultural acceptance, no-fault divorce, in the West between 1900 and 1970.[43] Her point, which was crucial, was that "the dismantling of that [paternal] power [over slaves and wives] has not led to new conceptions of the family as a corporate unit."[44] In short she was asking at what point did one's obligations to one's family, particularly one's children, override one's rights as an individual; she argued that the obligations of parents to children, even if the old formulation of separation of bed and board became necessary for the parents, should prohibit the formation of a new marriage and the creation of new obligations to support new children.[45] She also believed that all adults necessarily dance with authority—much as she described, in 1976, the Physiocrats Quesnay and Mirabeau. The best learn to do it gracefully.[46]

In 1994, on the verge of conversion to Catholicism, with all that entails of the acceptance of authority, obligation, and relief, Fox-Genovese published "Difference, Diversity, and Divisions in an Agenda for the Women's Movement," arguing that "the pursuit of autonomous individualism for women is increasingly exposing the limitations of the model for society as a whole." Arguing from *Feminism without Illusions,* she suggested as remedy "a conception of equity which rests on the notion of individual right as grounded in society rather than prior to it." If natural rights were once a necessary and powerful solvent to the bonds of the old order, Fox-Genovese was done with them in the 1990s, insisting instead that "society, not nature, has endowed us with rights and is entitled to hold us accountable for meeting the attendant responsibilities."[47] She was deeply engaged in meeting those attendant responsibilities by 1994, determined to turn her years of study to good account as a public intellectual. This was at considerable cost to herself.

Part of that cost accrued as a result of her rejection of abortion, not only on moral grounds, which she expressed much later, but simply as useless: "At best, access to abortion will permit a poor woman to re-engage the dreary struggle for a more promising future without the encumbrance of a child, but it will not necessarily improve her education or her job prospects, provide her with medical insurance, or increase the likelihood that she will marry. And access to abortion does nothing for the poor woman who chooses to keep her child."[48] Written in 1994, this was a materialist argument, attentive to the needs of those who had real needs. Betsey discussed the importance of rejecting abortion and embracing life in the course of her conversion to Catholicism in "A Conversion Story," among other essays, but it is important to remember that she found abortion a misleading, ineffective solution for women before her conversion in late 1995.[49]

Betsey also raised the specter of infanticide, citing Toni Morrison's novel *Beloved* in her 1994 Oxford Amnesty Lecture, published as "Contested Meanings: Women and the Problem of Freedom in the Mid-Nineteenth-Century United States." Deftly juxtaposing Orlando Patterson's definition of slavery as "social death" with personal, civic, and sovereignal freedom, she then muddied the water by discussing the degree to which Lockean, if not modern, individualism rests on personal and sometimes civic freedom. If "early Lockean" individual freedom was, she argued, consistent with "the previous and still pervasive religious vision of governance and political obligation," then the later "antithesis between freedom and slavery is a distinctly modern phenomenon, born of the era of the American, French, and Haitian revolutions." And that antithesis was precisely what she then contested, using the positions of abolitionist women, Lowell factory women, plantation mistresses, and slave and freedwomen to demonstrate that there was no such simple opposition of slavery and freedom in the United States in the middle of the nineteenth century.[50] She wrote with stark elegance that "the experience of women in general and of slave women in particular challenges any simple understanding of the meaning of freedom in the history of the American republic."[51] Of course after such a statement, the devil is in the details, but the detail here is rich, drawing from her early work on Locke and her familiarity with nineteenth-century women in the North and even more so in the South, where personal papers and novels yield evidence that "freedom has always been contested" and that neither freedom nor slavery, Patterson notwithstanding, was absolute in life.[52] With respect to the topics of this volume—women and history—this is the last substantial historical essay reprinted here. Those that follow are the work of a public intellectual, after 1999 an "out" Catholic, who remained as thoroughly informed by history, literature, Marx, and Freud as she had been in the 1970s.[53]

In these last nine essays, written between 1995 and 2004, Fox-Genovese was determined to find a third way, neither the majority feminist nor the conservative, for women, children, and men to acknowledge their interdependence and their responsibility to and for each other. Because American reform movements, including first- and second-wave feminism, have been so thoroughly shaped by a liberal, individualist vision, Betsey's insistence on ties between individuals, and binding ties at that, has been heard as a call for reactionary, hierarchical, perhaps virtually enslaving obligations that would reiterate women's subjection in the traditional family. But a reader would be hard pressed to find that in what she wrote: "We will not begin to define the appropriate relations among women, children, and family until we transcend both the feminist insistence upon equality and the conservative celebration of domesticity as usual. Only when we recognize that both an unattainable equality and a punitive inequality deepen the antagonism between the needs of women and children will we begin to imagine a model of equity that may serve the needs of both."[54] The equity Betsey had in mind would be deeply embedded in society, not simply in personal relations, for "to encourage mothers to put children first, we must encourage fathers and especially employers and public policies to do the same."[55]

For the next decade she would prod and examine the points at which she saw society breaking down: rape, the discourse about it, and "Freud's underlying insight about the importance of individual restraint to a tolerable common life";[56] divorce, poverty for women, and the waning responsibility of men to and for their children; and abortion as an aspect of the female individual striving to compete in a rigidly defined equality with men. Betsey was chronicling the collapse of social institutions as individualism reached an apogee, partially driven by feminist urgency and sometimes underpinned, as she admitted, by "a massive movement of married women and mothers of small children into the labor force."[57] She was also arguing that Americans' (and she often wrote *feminists* when she might have written *Americans*) emphasis on the lone individual has allowed the United States to offer little or nothing in support of families and children. In "Severing the Ties That Bind: Women, the Family, and Social Institutions," written in 1998, Betsey listed the failures of the state to provide even a minimal level of support for children and parents.[58] By 2004 she was advocating a new feminism, grounded in Catholic theology, welcoming women's difference, and quietly calling for "a measure of self-denial and self-abnegation."[59] I can only imagine what a relief it must have been to her, living in the late twentieth century's festival of self-absorption, to discover the shelter of a principled religious community, and what it meant to a serious critic of individualism to advocate finally "a measure of self-denial."

Betsey wrote fewer essays in the last years of her life, but she and Gene finished *The Mind of the Master Class* in 2005, and much of *Slavery in White and Black* by the time of her death, so sympathetic clucking about her diminished output is out of place. She worked until she died, rather like Elizabeth I, who refused to sit until she could no longer stand. And in the midst of her later work, she sometimes used a more personal voice, writing in 2004 that "as a child, I dreamed of becoming the first woman president of the United States and of having twenty-three children. I have accomplished neither."[60] But, as she added, "the spirit that informed those dreams" persisted, and the result was both a profoundly serious career, devoted to taking women—of all sorts—seriously, and a consistent concern with preserving, rather than discarding, the ties that bind individuals to each other, and especially to children.[61] She said even more in "Advocacy and the Writing of American Women's History" in 1997, discussing the ideas that shaped her early career: the importance of history, Marx, Freud, and, earlier still, the "Calvinist traditions" of her family, which confirmed for her that "intellectual honesty and personal accountability were not only possible but necessary."[62] Thus in 2004, in the last article reprinted here, Betsey wrote another of her short histories of the making of the modern world. Written for a specifically Catholic and, perhaps, broadly Christian audience, "Feminism and the Unraveling of the Social Bond" describes the rise of the West, and if she chides feminists for ignoring the big picture, she chastises global capitalism and quotes Eric Hobsbawm on our collective and personal inability to come to terms with globalization.[63] This short essay should be read as contiguous with Niall Ferguson's *The War of the World*, because it is the same story, told from a different but complementary perspective.

Many years ago, when I was struggling with turning my dissertation into the book I wanted it to be, I told Betsey a long and, I suspect, rather gothic tale of all the roadblocks, fears, and childhood crises in my way. She listened patiently, said little, and promised to lend me a book that would help. The book turned out to be a murder mystery, and one of its larger lessons was delivered in the form of a motto that Vasco da Gama had had carved into his flagship. I have not forgotten it. I am sure that it was Betsey's message to me, and perhaps to all of us: It is necessary to sail; it is not necessary to live. Betsey chose to sail, although she sailed with fresh salad, good wine, and all the ingredients for Gene's dinner on board.

Notes

The phrase "For as long as I can remember" is from Elizabeth Fox-Genovese, "The New Female Literary Culture," in the *Antioch Review* 38 (Spring 1980): 193. This volume excludes more than it includes, as do all of the volumes in this series, and other volumes address Fox-Genovese as a historian. Fox-Genovese's work on southern women, for example, is the focus of volume 2 of this series, *Ghosts and Memories: White and Black Southern Women's Lives and Writings,* edited by Kibibi Mack-Shelton and Christina Bieber Lake. I am indebted to the general editor, David Moltke-Hansen, and Eugene D. Genovese for their support, wisdom, and patience.

1. Ellen Leiman, a graduate student at Binghamton in 1980, called Fox-Genovese a class act.

2. Jeff Vanke, HNN blog, January 10, 2007, at http://hnn.us/readcomment.php?id =104346&bheaders=1.

3. Elizabeth Fox-Genovese, "Yves Saint Laurent's Peasant Revolution," *Marxist Perspectives* 1 (Summer 1978): 61; article reprinted in this volume, pp. 21–44.

4. Fox-Genovese, "New Female Literary Culture," 193. This essay could not be reprinted here but reflects Betsey's wide reading and early commitment to women's literature.

5. Mark Bauerlein, "Foreword: A Literary Theorist of the Positive Kind," in volume 2 of this selected edition, *Ghosts and Memories: White and Black Southern Women's Lives and Writings,* ed. Kibibi Mack-Shelton and Christina Bieber Lake (Columbia: University of South Carolina Press, forthcoming).

6. Elizabeth Fox-Genovese, "Property and Patriarchy in Classical Bourgeois Political Theory," *Radical History Review* 4, nos. 2–3 (1977): 36; article reprinted in this volume, pp. 1–20.

7. Fox-Genovese, "Property and Patriarchy," 40.

8. On Odorsio, see ibid., 56n3; a subsequent article worth noting is Mary Lyndon Shanley, "Marriage Contract and Social Contract in Seventeenth Century English Political Thought," *Western Political Quarterly* 32 (March 1979): 79–91, which Fox-Genovese mentions in "Placing Women's History in History," *New Left Review* 133 (May/June 1982): 20n21; article reprinted in this volume, pp. 45–74.

9. Virginia Woolf, *A Room of One's Own* (New York: Harcourt, Brace, 1929), 25; her sentence is "If truth is not to be found on the shelves of the British Museum, where, I asked myself, picking up a notebook and a pencil, is truth?"

10. Fox-Genovese, "Yves Saint Laurent's Peasant Revolution," 59.

11. Ibid., 70.

12. Ibid., 81, 83.

13. Ibid., 84.

14. Ibid.

15. For DuBois, see Fox-Genovese, "Placing Women's History in History," 5.

16. Elizabeth Fox-Genovese, "New Female Literary Culture," 193; for consciousness-raising, see 204.

17. Ibid., 196.

18. Ibid., 207. The reference is to Erica Jong's *Fear of Flying.*

19. Woolf, *Room of One's Own,* 85.

20. Fox-Genovese, "New Female Literary Culture," 208–11.

21. Elizabeth Fox-Genovese, "Gender, Class, and Power: Some Theoretical Considerations," *History Teacher* 15 (February 1982): 255–76. Elizabeth Fox-Genovese and Eugene D. Genovese, *Fruits of Merchant Capital: Slavery and Bourgeois Property in the Rise and Expansion of Capitalism* (New York: Oxford University Press, 1983).

22. Fox-Genovese, "Placing Women's History," 6.

23. Ibid., 6–7.

24. Ibid., 15, and for Degler, 13.

25. Ibid., 5, 6.

26. Ibid., 29.

27. Elizabeth Fox-Genovese, "Culture and Consciousness in the Intellectual History of European Women," *Signs: Journal of Women in Culture and Society* 12 (Spring 1987): 529–47; reprinted in this volume, pp. 92–111. She published two articles in 1987, one textbook chapter, and two encyclopedia entries; three were on Europe, one was on the United States, and the one on fashion was transatlantic.

28. See the prologue to Elizabeth Fox-Genovese, *Within the Plantation Household: Black and White Women of the Old South* (Chapel Hill: University of North Carolina Press, 1988), 1–36.

29. Fox-Genovese, "Culture and Consciousness," 547. On Christine de Pizan, see 538; on consciousness, see 546.

30. Elizabeth Fox-Genovese, "Women and Work," in *French Women and the Age of Enlightenment,* ed. Samia I. Spencer (Bloomington: Indiana University Press, 1984), 111–27; reprinted in this volume, pp. 75–91.

31. For the phrase "economic life of the state," see Alice Clark, *The Working Life of Women in Seventeenth Century England* (1919; repr., London: Routledge & Kegan Paul, 1982).

32. For an example of quantitative presentation, see Joan Scott and Louise Tilly, *Women, Work, and Family* (New York: Holt, Rinehart & Winston, 1978).

33. Fox-Genovese, "Women and Work," 112.

34. Elizabeth Fox-Genovese and Eugene D. Genovese, "The Ideological Bases of Domestic Economy: The Representation of Women and the Family in the Age of Expansion," in Fox-Genovese and Genovese, *Fruits of Merchant Capital,* 299–336; Pierre Samuel Du Pont de Nemours, *The Autobiography of Du Pont de Nemours,* trans. Elizabeth Fox-Genovese (Wilmington, Del.: Scholarly Resources, 1984), two sections of the introduction are to be included in volume 5 of this edition.

35. Elizabeth Fox-Genovese, "Women and the Enlightenment," in *Becoming Visible: Women in European History,* 2nd ed., ed. Renate Bridenthal, Claudia Koonz, and Susan Stuard (New York: Houghton Mifflin, 1987), 251–77.

36. Elizabeth Fox-Genovese, foreword to *Fanny Kemble: Journal of a Young Actress,* ed. Monica Gough (New York: Columbia University Press, 1990), xix; article reprinted in this volume, pp. 112–19.

37. Elizabeth Fox-Genovese, "Feminism and the Rhetoric of Individual Rights, Part One," *Common Knowledge* 1, no. 1 (1992): 43–53; "Feminism and the Rhetoric of Individual Rights, Part Two," *Common Knowledge* 1, no. 2 (1992): 63–73; reprinted in this volume, pp. 120–31 and pp. 132–43, respectively.

38. Fox-Genovese, "Feminism and the Rhetoric of Individual Rights, Part Two," 68–69.

39. Ibid., 71.

40. Ibid., 69.

41. Ibid., 71–72.

42. Robert P. George, "The Story of a Life Well-Lived," *National Review Online,* January 3, 2007, http://article.nationalreview.com/302160/the-story-of-a-well-lived-life/robert-p-george (accessed September 8, 2010); to be collected in volume 5 of this selected edition, *Unbought Grace: An Elizabeth Fox-Genovese Reader,* ed. Rebecca Fox and Robert L. Paquette (Columbia: University of South Carolina Press, forthcoming).

43. See Elizabeth Fox-Genovese, "The Legal Status of Families as Institutions," *Cornell Law Review* 77 (July 1992): 995; article reprinted in this volume, pp. 144–48. To comprehend the historical background from which this brief legal point was drawn, see not only "Property and Patriarchy," but also Fox-Genovese, *Within the Plantation Household,* chap. 7, "And Women Who Did Not," 334–71; Elizabeth Fox-Genovese and Eugene D. Genovese, *Slavery in White and Black: Class and Race in the Southern Slaveholders' New World Order* (Cambridge: Cambridge University Press, 2008), chap. 6, "Perceptions and Realities," 234–88.

44. Fox-Genovese, "Legal Status of Families," 994.

45. Ibid., 995.

46. Elizabeth Fox-Genovese, *The Origins of Physiocracy: Economic Revolution and Social Order in Eighteenth-Century France* (Ithaca, N.Y.: Cornell University Press, 1976), 18–19.

47. Elizabeth Fox-Genovese, "Difference, Diversity, and Divisions in the Women's Movement," in *Color, Class and Country: Experiences of Gender,* ed. Gay Young and Bette J. Dickerson (London: Zed, 1994), 238; article reprinted in this volume, pp. 149–66.

48. Ibid., 239.

49. Elizabeth Fox-Genovese, "A Conversion Story," *First Things* 102 (April 2000): 39–43.

50. See Elizabeth Fox-Genovese, "Contested Meanings: Women and the Problem of Freedom in the Mid-Nineteenth-Century United States," in *Historical Change and Human Rights: The Oxford Amnesty Lectures 1994,* ed. Olwen Hufton (New York: Basic, 1995), 183, 181; article reprinted in this volume, pp. 167–96.

51. Ibid., 185.

52. Ibid., 214.

53. I use 1999 based on material considered for this volume.

54. Elizabeth Fox-Genovese, "Feminism, Children, and the Family," *Harvard Journal of Law and Public Policy,* 18 (Spring 1995): 508; article reprinted in this volume, pp. 197–202.

55. Ibid., 507.

56. Elizabeth Fox-Genovese, "Beyond Autonomy: Sex, Repression, and Violence against Women," *Common Knowledge* 4, no. 3 (1995): 64; article reprinted in this volume, pp. 203–10.

57. Elizabeth Fox-Genovese, "Severing the Ties That Bind: Women, the Family, and Social Institutions," *Intercollegiate Journal* 34 (Fall 1998): 27; article reprinted in this volume, pp. 229–34. Also available online at http://www.firstprinciplesjournal.com/articles.aspx?article=485&theme=home&page=2&loc=b&type=ctbf (accessed October 25, 2010).

58. Ibid. By 2004 she was warning against "an ominous strengthening of the state" with regard to "attempts to legislate away" the consequences of women's difference; see

"Equality, Difference, and the Practical Problems of a New Feminism," in *Women in Christ: Toward a New Feminism,* ed. Michele M. Schumacher (Grand Rapids, Mich.: Eerdmans, 2004), 303; article reprinted in this volume, pp. 267–81.

59. Fox-Genovese, "Equality, Difference," 304.

60. Elizabeth Fox-Genovese, "Feminism and the Unraveling of the Social Bond," *Voices: Women for Faith and Family* 19 (Michaelmas 2004): 9; article reprinted in this volume, pp. 282–93.

61. Ibid. The words that follow the quotation are mine; Betsey claimed on that page only that she was led to continuing "aspirations for a just and humane society."

62. Elizabeth Fox-Genovese, "Advocacy and the Writing of Women's History," in *Religious Advocacy and American History,* ed. Bruce Kuklick and D. G. Hart (Grand Rapids, Mich.: Eerdmans, 1997), 105; to be collected in volume 4 of this selected edition, *Explorations and Commitments: Religion, Faith, and Culture,* ed. Ann Hartle and Sheila O'Connor-Ambrose (Columbia: University of South Carolina Press, forthcoming).

63. Fox-Genovese, "Feminism and the Unraveling," 11.

History & Women, Culture & Faith
Volume 1

Elizabeth Fox-Genovese.
Courtesy of Eugene D. Genovese

One

Property and Patriarchy in Classical Bourgeois Political Theory

> Locke fell into a swoon,
>   The garden died.
> God took the spinning jenny
>   Out of his side.
>
> *W. B. Yeats*

Classical bourgeois political theory articulated the political revolution that established possessive individualism as the basis of legitimate government and the foundation of civil society. In this respect, it inaugurated the systematic investigation of the objective rules governing subjective human existence. The work of Thomas Hobbes and of John Locke, like classical political economy and modern social science, rest squarely upon the notion of theoretical individualism—at least in the public domain. Both men, diverse prescriptive solutions notwithstanding, thus participated in the as yet unresolved assault upon divine authority. By rejecting divine sanction in favor of rationality as the first principle of civil society, they helped to establish the individual as the justification for and fundamental unit of political society. The theoretical clarity of bourgeois individualism, however, as Hegel and Marx respectively insisted, masked deep psychological and social—i.e., historical—contradictions, not the least of which concerned the appropriate social role of women.

"Property and Patriarchy in Classical Bourgeois Political Theory." *Radical History Review* 4, nos. 2–3 (1977): 36–59. Copyright 1977, MARHO: The Radical Historians Organization, Inc. All rights reserved. Used by permission of the present publisher, Duke University Press.

The revolution in the idea of legitimate political authority that occurred in England in the seventeenth century brought into question the entire theoretical structure of society. From this perspective, it can perhaps most usefully be understood as a rereading of collective experience. As a rereading—and a reformulation of norms—it simultaneously embodied a radical rupture with previous symbolic formulations and a very real continuity, not to say conservative comfort, with previous social relations. Hence the difficulty in assessing the actual content of its rhetoric, which tended, in the temporary heat of struggle, to advance social claims beyond the narrower political goals of its progenitors. Underlying the various revolutionary pronouncements lay a central determination to displace divine authority in the public sphere and to replace it with a rational, individually anchored authority. To effect their goal, however, both Hobbes and Locke, in one small but pivotal detail, relied upon a notion of women's domestic role to express their challenge to the system they purported to supplant. Their performance should not be scanned for any particular interest in women as women, much less for the least hint of feminist intent. Nothing could have been further from the minds of those formulating the new ideology of rational political society.

Hobbes and Locke turned to the domestic role of women to drive home their point for the simple reason that those advancing the claims of divine authority had come increasingly to rely upon the family as the model for a legitimate society, the human vessel of divine intent. Divine authority had assumed the guise of the *pater familias;* the patriarchal model claimed divine sanction. The emergence of the patriarchal ideology on the ruins of a far less self-conscious lineage system constitutes another subject. The expressed ideology incorporated a long historical legacy as well as previous ideological positions, which it transformed in such a way that the divinely sanctioned and omnipotent father appeared as the necessary custodian of political order. At the very moment of its political demise, the family emerged as the highest symbol of political coherence, and the father figured as the unquestioned and unrivaled head of the family. Patriarchal ideology thus sought to unite the public and the private—the juridical and the domestic—realms conceptually and symbolically just at the point when they were decisively apart. The defenders of a more traditional view of social and political organization isolated the father, as head of the family, and invested him with complete domestic and political authority. Their ideological wedding of the two realms established the immediate symbolization against which the theorists of rational political life would have to argue.[1]

The formulation of familial authority as the paradigm for political authority barely survived its first theoretical expression. By treating domestic relations as the model for the juridical realm, the patriarchalists exposed their cherished institution to systematic attack. Both Hobbes and Locke initially found the familial model sufficiently compelling to demand refutation in its own terms. They started, in other words, not by dismissing family relations as irrelevant to, or different in kind from, political relations, but by insisting that their opponents erred in the characterization of domestic relations. For individualism to triumph politically, it had to be shown to operate domestically. In this sense, Hobbes and Locke did accept the theoretical identity of the public and private realms: the principles that dominated the social relations of the one would have to dominate the social relations of the other.

The individualists' theoretical and political victory relieved them of the necessity to implement their insights. Their concern to free propertied individuals from externally imposed authority had led them to a more thorough questioning of authority than their practical victory would require or their psychological necessities tolerate. With their theoretical rereading secure in the political sphere, history and social experience could be allowed to reassert their claims in the domestic sphere—increasingly portrayed as "naturally" separate. An emerging political economy and historical sociology confirmed this disjuncture by emphasizing the triumph of individual (propertied, male) rationality while rationally accepting the world (women and social classes) as given. Henceforth, the family would be viewed theoretically and experienced psychologically as a unit of, or even a counter-weight to, a juridical system—a political realm—that was increasingly responsive to a market or individualist logic. The family, having temporarily figured as the locus of individualism was resurrected, in traditional—if mystifying—splendor as its antidote.

Because of their preoccupation with the sources of legitimate authority, the early bourgeois political theorists abstracted from prevailing social relations in order to provide a natural or universal basis for individualism. The theorists found that basis in innate human rationality, considered as an attribute, if not a realization, throughout the species. Authority must derive from contract or consent. This line of thought posited slavery as the absolute antithesis of legitimate authority. The explorations of the nature of slavery as a psychological condition—so brilliantly formulated by Hegel—require separate consideration.[2] But, by common consensus, the position of women and slaves remained the touchstones, theoretically speaking, of the relative political and economic freedom prevailing in different societies. The freedom and equality of women never attained the ideological centrality accorded to the absolute condition of slavery, which increasingly figured not merely as the actual state of blacks in the colonies, but as the antithesis of all human liberty: men, normally living with women from whose devotion and relative subordination they benefited, tended to espouse limited notions of the freedom befitting a female being. But the conditions of women and slaves were regularly linked as the limiting cases of the nature of any given society—as the most sensitive barometers of its freedom and decency.

In Hegelian terms, slavery and the subjection of women forced the question of dependency upon the individualist consciousness. The strength—if potential inconvenience—of the contract or consensual approach to social relations lay in its requirement of two or more equal participants. The equality, to be sure, needed to extend no further than the ability to consent, but for the consent to be valid it had to be freely given. The importance of this attitude for capitalist social relations of production have been dissected beginning with Marx. The model, however, also carried important psychological overtones. For the bourgeois theorists discerned in slavery a distorting rather than a flattering mirror of the individual human condition. Slavery bespoke dependence, tyranny, despotism; precisely all those attributes of the form of authority they sought to overthrow. If the political realm was to be freed from the chains of arbitrary domination, so must all relations between men—however much the inequalities persisted in unpleasant social fact. Inequality would become the individual responsibility of the unfortunate, not the God-given responsibility of the master. It required centuries to dismantle the social household with its slaves, domestics, retainers, but the principles of that dismantling had been sketched out in the original individualist assault on patriarchalism. Absolute property in one's self, extended to all at the small price of simultaneously accepting the accumulated properties of the "labor" of others, provided the working basis for social relations.

The mirror of equality, however, proved to generate as much anxiety as fraternity. In this respect, Hegel's discussion of lordship and bondage captures the psychological character of bourgeois social relations as neatly as it does those of the master-slave relation which individualism sought to repudiate. As the commercialization of social relations "liberated" more and more of the old domestic sphere, opening it to the wonders of the market, the remaining domestic kernel seems to have acquired a progressively greater psychological importance. The Victorians would produce the apotheosis of the female as so unequal as to be naturally of another human order. The theoretical retreat from domestic equality, however, began almost as soon as that equality had been enunciated. Individualism triumphed on the ruins of the dreams of equality, and founded its historical career on the twin pillars of absolute property and absolute dominion over a domestic mirror.

Women, avowedly, get short shrift in political theory. The early ideological struggle purported to establish the "rights of man"—which in effect meant "of men." Nevertheless, texts reveal that those rights depended theoretically, if not practically, upon the rights of women. Thomas Hobbes, hardly a feminist, could not avoid postulating a theoretical equality, although he immediately retreated from any practical implications.[3] In Hobbes' view, dominion was acquired, not by divine right, but either by generation or by conquest. "The right of Dominion by Generation," he explained, "is that, which the parent hath over his Children; and is called PATERNALL. And is not so derived from the Generation, as if therefore the Parent had Dominion over his Child because he begat him; but from the Childs Consent, either expresse, or by other sufficient arguments declared."[4] Hobbes argues thus to prove that any participation in civil society derives from consent or contract. That Hobbes' authoritarianism appalled his liberal successors in no way mitigates his individualist postulates. No more than Locke, Hutcheson, Hume, or Smith did Hobbes expect political organization to derive from a transcendent authority. Like his more optimistic successors, he found it necessary to undermine the theoretical basis for that authority in the irreducible social unit—the family.

To assert the consensual relationship between father and children did not suffice. Hobbes continues: "For as to the Generation, God hath ordained to man a helper; and there be alwayes two that are equally Parents: the Dominion therefore over the Child should belong equally to both; and he be equally subject to both. . . ."[5] Hobbes' notions of order do not mesh with such dual sovereignty, and he completes his sentence by repudiating the equal power of parents on the grounds that the equal subjection of the child "is impossible; for no Man can obey two Masters."[6] Unwilling to permit this retreat to trap him into affirming the natural political supremacy of the father—that gambit having been forestalled by his rejection of patriarchal authority as politically rational—he subjects the family to a rational analysis. "And whereas some," he continues, lavishly mingling historical and theoretical precedents, "have attributed the Dominion to the Man only, as being of the more excellent Sex; they misreckon it. For there is not always that difference of strength or prudence between the man and the woman, as that the right can be determined without War. In Common-wealths, this controversie is decided by the Civill Law. . . ." Most commonwealths, he allows, have decided in favor of the father, "not by the Mothers of families." But in the state of nature which includes no laws of matrimony, nor of education other than the law of nature itself and the natural inclination of the sexes, "in this condition of meer Nature, either the Parents between themselves dispose of the dominion over the Child by Contract: or do not dispose thereof at all." And, in the absence of contract, "the Dominion is in the Mother. For in the condition of meer Nature, where there are no matrimoniall lawes, it cannot be known who is the Father, unlesse it be declared by the Mother;

and therefore the right of Dominion over the Child dependeth on her will and is consequently hers."[7]

Hobbes' discussion contains a number of assumptions about women. First, as he states more explicitly elsewhere, "men, are naturally fitter than women, for actions of labour and danger."[8] Second, in the absence of matrimonial laws, women have natural dominion over their off-spring. Third, within the matrimonial state, women normally relinquish their dominion over children to the fathers of their children, but do so by consent. Fourth, the theoretical equality of women as parents—not as physical or intellectual beings—confirms the individualist basis of civil society. Hobbes, in other words, repudiates women's rights to the independent exercise of their sovereignty once they have yielded the right by contract, just as he repudiates the right of any member of a commonwealth to exercise his sovereignty once he has yielded it, by contract, to the sovereign. For Hobbes, therefore, paternal authority need not be sex-specific: "If the Mother be the Fathers subject, the Child, is in the Fathers power: and if the Father be the Mothers subject . . . the Child is subject to the Mother; because the Father also is her subject."[9] Yet Hobbes' logic does, unwittingly, parallel the patriarchal argument by insisting that identical principles govern the political and the familial realms.[10]

Hobbes perceived and shuddered at the logic of possessive individualist or market society. This recognition of individualism merely prompted him to guard against its political expression. His analysis and his political prescription take full account of both the subjective and the objective aspects of bourgeois man as prey to competition for Honour and Dignity and to a "restless striving after powere that ceaseth only in death." Among such men arises "Envy and Hatred, and finally Warre."[11] That simple, driven individual, however, constitutes the basis of all political organization. Dominion arises from the consent of individuals, not from some necessary divine order imposed upon them. Hobbes' contemporaries understood the radical character of his thought. As Bramhall put it, Hobbes "taketh a pride in removing all ancient land-marks, between prince and subject, father and child, husband and wife, master and servant, man and man."[12] Historical process, especially the rise of capitalist society since the time of Hobbes, tends to obscure the full force of his logic. His liberal heirs, in both theory and practice, strove to veil the domination inherent in capitalist social relations and, accordingly, focussed on Hobbes' authoritarian resolution of the political, social, and psychological tensions of an individualist society; they thus sacrificed his underlying premises, the starkness of which they simply repudiated. Liberal theory, however, has not kept pace with history, and conditions in the post-Freudian world require that serious attention be given to Hobbes' analysis even if his conclusions are not accepted. Above all, Hobbes left no natural basis for domination standing, not even the domination of men over women. Prefiguring Hegel's attack on slavery in *Philosophy of Right*, Hobbes denies that one human being can become the creature of another's will, for, paradoxically, he or she must consent to do so.

Thus, Hobbes stipulates the historical conditions of servitude explicitly: conquest or victory can give rise to that dominion which "some Writers call DESPOTICALL . . . which signifieth a *Lord* or *Master*, and is the Dominion of the Master over his Servant." But, Hobbes insists, the victor acquires this dominion only "when the vanquished, to avoyd the present stroke of death, covenanteth either in expresse words, or by other sufficient signes of the will, that so long as his life, and the liberty of his body is allowed him, the Victor shall have use thereof, at his pleasure. And after such Covenant made, the Vanquished is a SERVANT, and not before. . . ."[13] Such dominion hardly appeals to modern sensibilities, and succeeding theorists exercised enormous ingenuity in trying to mitigate its brutality. Did not bourgeois hegemony depend heavily on convincing working people that wage servitude constituted a plausible foundation for individual self-respect and human dignity? For Hobbes, the contract, however violently extracted, signified the willing acceptance of the relationship and differentiated it from non-viable forms of servitude, notably slavery. For, he explains, "by the word *Servant* . . . is not meant a Captive, which is kept in prison, or bonds, till the owner of him that took him, or brought him of one that did, shall consider what to do with him. . . ."[14] Men so coerced can never be trusted. For "such men, (commonly called Slaves,) have no obligation at all; but may break their bonds, or the prison; and kill or carry away captive their Master justly."[15]

Even to its interstices, civil society must rest upon consent. The decisive and related roles of women and slaves would reappear regularly in subsequent political theory and political economy. Increasingly, liberal theorists would argue from fact, nature, and history to justify the subjection of women who were seen to benefit economically from their loss of selfhood. Even committed feminists would argue from the perspective of women's special sphere. The conversion of bourgeois individualism, from a radical position that required an arbitrary solution to a law of nature embedded in natural historical development, would entail sacrificing Hobbes' greatest insights, namely that civil society derives from human choice; that it is, therefore, arbitrary not natural; and that with respect to civil society all human beings are equal and must willingly consent to the sacrifice of any freedom they relinquish in the interests of an ordered polity.

Leviathan (1651) did not win Hobbes popularity in most circles. Sir Robert Filmer (d. 1653) drafted a series of treatises to demonstrate the organic and religious foundation of divine right monarchy; John Locke (1632–1704) responded directly to Filmer, but seems throughout to have been aware of Hobbes.[16] The nature of and basis for authority constitute the central point of contention between Filmer and Locke, and, in different ways, between both of them and Hobbes. For Hobbes, authority could only be understood as a political question: Filmer retreats from that arena to the realms of scripture, nature, and history; Locke moves the discussion toward the terrain of political economy. Neither Filmer nor Locke devotes many pages to women; both, however, rest a major part of their arguments on the relationship between men and women.

Filmer's reliance upon dubious historical precedent derived from scripture makes his account easy to dismiss. No more than Locke are modern readers likely to be swayed by such arguments as: "Adam was the father, king, and lord over his family: a son, a subject, and a servant, or slave, were one and the same thing at first. The father had power to dispose or sell his children or servants. . . ." Nor would we be convinced by the assertion that "Law is nothing else but the will of him that hath the power of the supreme father. . . . It was God's ordinance that the supremacy should be unlimited in Adam, and as large as all the acts of his will; and as in him, so in all others that have supreme power."[17]

The power ascribed to Adam derived in Filmer's view directly from God and was first instituted, not surprisingly, in relation to Eve. "If God," Filmer questions rhetorically, "created only Adam, and of a piece of him made the woman, and if by generation from them two, as parts of them, all mankind be propagated; if also God gave to Adam not only the dominion over the woman and the children that issue from them, but also over all the earth to subdue it . . . I wonder. . ."[18] Filmer wonders how an honest man could conceive of any other basis for domination, or more important, how an honest man could rebel against authority founded on such solid grounds. Woman having been created from man and he having been granted explicit governance over her, the rest follows logically, and—more to Filmer's point—historically.

Locke completely rejects Filmer's reasoning. The *First Treatise on Government* (1690) announces, in its subtitle, its intent to detect and to overthrow "the false principles and foundation of Sir Robert Filmer and his followers."[19] The first chapter, "On Slavery," raises the central issue directly. Filmer, according to Locke, purports to demonstrate "*That all government is absolute monarchy.*" And, continues Locke, "the ground he builds on is this: *That no man is born free.*"[20] Locke is not, in this instance, addressing the historical institution of slavery that has preoccupied modern historians, but the absolute condition of slavery as it affects the foundations of political society. Locke understands Filmer's link between the condition of slavery and political authority and explains, in terms reminiscent of Hobbes, that Filmer's case rests upon the notion that "men are not born free and therefore could never have the liberty to choose either governors or forms of government. Princes," he continues, "have their power absolute and by divine right; for slaves could never have a right to compact or consent."[21] Locke then proceeds to demolish Filmer's case point by point. In Chapter V, he gets around to "Adam's title to Sovereignty by the Subjection of Eve."

Locke begins the chapter by repeating the quote from *Genesis* used by Filmer, that in which God instructs Eve "And thy desire shall be to thy husband and he shall rule over thee." In this instruction, according to Filmer, could be found the original grant of government, which proves "that the supreme power is settled in the fatherhood, and limited to one kind of government, that is, to monarchy."[22] Locke fails to see the glorious triumph in God's pronouncement. "The words," he reminds his readers "are the curse of God upon the woman for having been the first and forwardest in disobedience." But, he cautions, ponder the circumstances: "If we will consider the occasion of what God says here to our first parents that He was denouncing judgment and declaring His wrath against them both for their disobedience, we cannot suppose that this was the time wherein God was granting Adam prerogatives and privileges, investing him with dignity and authority, elevating him to dominion and monarchy."[23] Need we be reminded that Adam too had a share in the fall. "It would be hard to imagine that God, in the same breath, should make him universal monarch over all mankind and a day-labourer for his life," simultaneously "turn him out of paradise to till the ground" and "advance him to a throne and all the privileges and case of absolute power."[24]

Having thus questioned the compatibility between the ultimate punishment and the ultimate power, Locke continues to examine the specifics of Eve's case. God's strictures about rule, Locke points out, were intended to chastise Eve and were directed to her alone. "Neither indeed was there any grant in them made to Adam . . . and if we will take them as they were directed in particular to her, or in her, as their representative, to all other women, they will at most concern the female sex only, and import no more but that subjection they should ordinarily be in to their husbands."[25] Even that minimal domestic subjection cannot, however, fully satisfy Locke. After all, he muses, "There is here no more law to oblige a woman to such subjection, if the circumstances either of her condition or contract with her husband should exempt her from it, than there is that she should bring forth her children in sorrow and pain, if there could be found a remedy for it, which is also part of the same curse upon her. . . ."[26]

So much for monarchical government by way of the subjection of Eve. Nor should anyone, on account of these words, "think the weaker sex, as by law so subjected to the curse contained in them that it is their duty not to endeavour to avoid it."[27] Locke implicitly argues that just as women have the right to triumph over their physical constitution (the pains of childbirth) through the assistance of medical science, so have they the right to triumph over their subjection to their husbands. Human beings may progress from their original sinful state. Locke will not concede that God, in the text of the curse, actually grants any authority whatsoever. Assuredly, he cannot see that God "gives . . . any authority to Adam over Eve, or to men over their wives, but only foretells what should be woman's lot, how by his providence he would order it so that she should be subject to her husband, as we see that generally the laws of mankind and customs of nations have ordered it so, and there is, I grant, a foundation in nature for it."[28]

Locke's ambiguity here should not pass unremarked. While denying the patriarchalists the Biblical subjection of women as authority for their preferred vision of political order, he proves quite willing to readmit the historical, customary, and natural bases for female inferiority. His slight concession to the sociological perspective and his willingness to incorporate it, however tentatively, into his political theory foreshadow the arguments of his eighteenth-century heirs, even as they prefigure that new history which will transpose this feminine teleology from the sphere of divine intent to that of "natural" development.[29]

In the first treatise, Locke attacks Filmer on Filmer's chosen terrain. And Filmer's scriptural and historical arguments do not withstand Locke's scathing criticism, at least so far as the specifics of the genesis of political authority are concerned. Filmer's arguments, however, mask a potentially far more serious statement about the nature of political authority. For Filmer maintains that all authority originated in paternal authority, and he relies on a historical method to prove his point. No matter that Filmer's historical sources served him poorly: the paradigmatic role of the family in all relations of superordination and subordination has returned to the modern debates via historical materialism, psychoanalytic theory, and anthropology. In the first treatise, Locke himself accepts historical precedent to explain the role of women. On the basis of historical experience, Locke is even prepared to concede a natural basis for the subordination of women to men. Filmer, however, perceives history as the working out of immutable principles. The original patriarchal authority subsists unaltered through the succession of generations and the increasing complexity of social and economic existence. In this respect, Filmer relies upon as abstract and rigid a formulation as Hobbes does. Apparently, in the eyes of these seventeenth-century theorists, the principles of law do not change. The original basis for authority must persist unaltered: the Garden of Eden and the State of Nature may appear to prescribe different laws of polity, but as models they function identically. Neither side of the debate could rely on the fickle progress of history; both the organic and the contractual positions depended upon an extra-temporal paradigm continually anchoring the more chaotic surface of events.[30]

Filmer was less concerned with subjecting women to men than with subjecting the progeny of women to their fathers. Locke, while not disputing the common historical subjection of women to men, is determined to free women's off-spring from dominion. To this end, he distinguishes between husband—which Adam was—and king—which he was not. In Locke's reading, *Genesis* merely provides for "the subjection of the inferior ranks of creatures to mankind, and the . . . subjection that is due from a wife to her husband, both far enough from that which subjects owe the governors of political societies."[31]

Locke's statements about women in the *First Treatise* foreshadow the theoretical and practical tendencies of bourgeois society. The arguments based on historical precedent and common experience tolerate the existence of two spheres which operate according to different principles. Familial society must be held separate from political society and the two must obey different laws. By this logic, the man who enters civil society as a consenting individual remains an unhampered despot at home. Locke did not, however, rest his case for civil society upon this dualism.

The *Second Treatise,* however polemical the circumstances of its composition, embodies Locke's considered view of the proper basis and character of political society. Significantly, he repeatedly describes political society as a community.[32] Gone is the preoccupation with authoritarian sovereignty that haunted the discussions of Hobbes and Filmer. Sovereignty has been displaced to the propertied individuals who comprise the political community, and they affirm the rights of the magistrates by a consent that they can revoke. The basis of individual sovereignty resides in the quality of men who are born "free and rational."[33] Such men owe their creator their self-preservation. Their condition in civil society cannot be that of slavery for, as he argues in terms reminiscent of those of Hobbes, "the perfect condition of slavery . . . is nothing else but the state of war continued between a lawful conqueror and a captive"; once "compact enter between them and make an agreement for a limited power on the one side and obedience on the other, the state of war and slavery ceases as long as the compact endures. . . ."[34] This repudiation of slavery accompanies Locke's definition of the liberty of man in society which "is to be under no other legislative power but that established by consent in the commonwealth, nor under the dominion of any will or restraint of any law but what that legislative shall enact according to the trust put in it."[35]

Locke grounds the freedom and rationality of individuals not merely in divine purpose, but in economic and social attributes, specifically in people's aptitude for acquiring property. The argument for property requires only brief review. A man, by mixing his labor with the land, acquires a right in it; the miraculous powers of money permit the indefinite extension of that right without doing violence to the moral imperative that would prohibit one man from selfishly hoarding food that might be essential to others. With a little ingenuity, the right to the material basis of freedom for all has been transformed into the "estates" of some without sacrificing the fundamental moral principle.

The simultaneous grounding of individualism in religion and economic discourse constitutes the most difficult and yet historically most faithful aspect of Locke's thought. By identifying the two, he contributed to an ideology, not to say political and social myth, that portrayed property as the necessary extension of the individual's psychological identity. Via the mediating individual, property becomes divine, or more accurately, sacred. Thus are the internal sources of individual freedom, developed in the Protestant tradition, externalized to provide the fundamental limit on the exercise of political authority. The superimposition of the economic and the religious, so characteristic of Locke's thought, did not survive indefinitely.[36] But, long after its demise, it continued to haunt the conception of women's proper social role. For after Locke, government could be seen as guaranteeing the religion and property of the individual in negative terms—by non-interference. Religion and economics could, therefore, be relegated to the private sphere. Locke accomplishes the theoretical divorce that Hobbes failed to effect between family and polity. According to Locke, they simply obey different moral principles. Thus, in the political sphere, despotical power over the lives, liberties, and estates of individuals constitutes the antithesis of that "Reason, which God hath given to be the Rule betwixt Man and Man, and the common bond whereby human kind is united into one fellowship and society. . . ."[37] In the domestic sphere, however, the logic is not so clear.

Locke's introduction of property as the cornerstone of individualism moved even his most rationalistic and abstract arguments towards a reconciliation with the prevailing relations of production and social authority. Nonetheless, in facing the spectre of patriarchal authority as the prototype for political authority, he resorts to the same stratagem as Hobbes. Men have been led to mistake the import of paternal power, he warns. Those who have seen this power as a model for political arrangements, however, have taken it "to place the power of parents over their children wholly in the father, as if the mother had to share in it; whereas, if we consult reason or revelation, we shall find she has an equal title." This observation prompts Locke to propose substituting "parental" for paternal power, "for whatever obligation nature and the right of generation lays on children, it must certainly bind them equally to both concurrent causes of it."[38]

The relationship between man and wife figures at the core of Locke's discussion of "Political or Civil Society." The first society, he argues, "was between man and wife, which gave beginning to that between parents and children; to which, in time, that between master and servant came to be added. . . ." But although one might argue that the master and mistress had some form of rule, this family, this little commonwealth, "came short of political society, as we shall see if we consider the different ends, ties, and bounds of each of these." The family has as its chief end procreation, or, as we might say, reproduction. This conjugal society derives from "a voluntary compact between man and woman." And "though it consist chiefly in such a communion and right in one another's bodies as is necessary to . . . procreation, yet it draws with it mutual support and assistance, and a communion of interests" necessary not only to their common care and affection, but to the nurture and rearing of their young.[39] Locke argues further that this conjugal society must necessarily endure through time, since the female produces successive off-spring each of which requires an extended period of maturation. Nevertheless, he observes that one may ask why this compact, like all other voluntary compacts, may not be terminated by consent once its essential functions have been fulfilled, "there being no necessity in the nature of the thing nor to the ends of it that it should always be for life; I mean, to such as are under no restraint of any positive law which ordains all such contracts to be perpetual."[40]

Theoretically, Locke requires the equality of husband and wife to counter the claims of paternal authority; practically, he doubts that such equality could provide for domestic tranquility. For "the husband and wife, though they have but one common concern, yet having different understandings, will unavoidably sometimes have different wills too. . . ." The contingency of opposing selfhoods can, however, be forestalled by placing the last determination with one or the other: the rule "naturally falls to the man's share as the abler and the stronger."[41]

Locke does not wish to leave the impression that he has reduced the wife to a state of slavery or even of unnatural subordination. After all, his dominion reaches only "to the things of their common interest and property" and leaves the wife in full possession "of what by contract is her peculiar right, and gives the husband no more power over her life than she has over his."

The power of the husband, Locke solemnly avers, "being so far from that of an absolute monarch that the wife has in many cases a liberty to separate from him where natural right or their contract allows it, whether that contract be made by themselves in the state of nature, or by the customs or the laws of the country they live in. . . ."[42]

Which laws and which customs? we may be permitted to ask. For Locke, by positing both a pre-social spiritual individualism and a pre-social property, has established that much of human life transpires beyond the permissible meddling of political authority. Furthermore, by casting those arrangements as natural, he has allowed a large variety of customs of the country to persist in harmony with the reigning propertied and rational individualism. His blithe mingling of rationalistic and natural-historical arguments enjoyed a much longer life than the more consistent formulations of Hobbes and Filmer, precisely because of its superimposition of two different visions. The more generous of his arguments succumbed to the realities of historical process and class struggle, even as their ideological core continued to justify the aspirations of those to whom political and economic exigencies denied their full access. Property in one's own labor-power has proved a double-edged sword, as have the liberties of women within the marriage contract. The theoretical equality of women necessary to the liberty and to the hegemony of bourgeois male individuals rapidly foundered on the economic and psychological arrangements necessary to the survival and class dominance of those same bourgeois male individuals.[43]

In time and place, Locke's political theory carried a markedly progressive character that, under different circumstances, could have permitted—and in America did permit—a democratic as well as a Whig reading. To the extent that Locke, even in time and place, espoused a cautious social conservatism, he relegated it to the familial sphere. It seems likely, although the subject requires extended treatment, that his successors—in both theory and practice— also did so.[44] Thus, with the secularization of the public sphere, women, as custodians of the domestic sphere, were assigned special responsibility for religious life, for non-competitive values. In this respect, the domestic and political spheres moved further and further apart ideologically, with, initially at least, each liberalization in the public arena entailing further curtailment in the private.[45]

Locke actually bequeathed to women a far more radical legacy than his promptly qualified assertion of their equality within the family. His psychology, with its emphasis on the rational attributes of the human mind and the decisive role of sense impressions in the development of thought, potentially offered women the same possibilities for personal development as men. And with Reason, by Locke's own admission, as the bond of the public sphere, no innate characteristics should have denied women's equal access to it. As Sophia, a person of quality, wrote in 1739: "It is the known truth, that the difference of sexes regards only the body, and that merely as it relates to the propagation of human nature. But the soul concurring to it only by consent, actuates all after the same manner, so that in *that* there is *no sex* at All. . . . And since there is not at most any greater difference between the souls of *Women* and *Men*, there can be no real diversity contracted from the body: all the diversity then must come from *education, exercise,* and the *impressions* of those external objects which surround us in different Circumstances."[46] Thus, inadvertently, Locke furnished future feminists with a language of rights and rationality such as would characterize the writings of Maria Edgeworth and Mary Wollstonecraft.[47]

The triumph of the language of property, rights, and rationality, born as it was in the growing commercialization of social relations, carried other consequences as well. In the realm of theory and ideology, Hume's repudiation of any original contract may have legitimately demolished a myth and done much to advance the rational investigation of human social relations, but it also harbored some sinister implications.[48] The assault on the patriarchal case for transcendent authority had moved from Hobbes' assertion of the artificial nature of political society, based on a contract as binding as Filmer's version of the original grant to Adam would be, to Locke's more naturalistic view of the contract, ever-renewed by the consent of successive generations. Hume, by denying the contract altogether, opened the way for the reappearance of organic social bonds, now seen as deriving from historical process.

The great political debates of the seventeenth century, and the revolutions they attended, established the contours of Anglo-Saxon political norms. Disagreements would persist about the appropriate size of the political community—the qualifications for participating individualism, as it were; but the vast majority accepted the new basis of political life, and opposition focused on denouncing corruption or demanding expanded participation. The structural and ideological revolution itself remained surprisingly unquestioned. And with the structural and ideological ground rules secure, attention turned increasingly to supplying the historical, social, and economic content of the model. Myths of the state of nature gave way to the systematic investigation of historical development and contemporary conditions. The greatest advances came in political economy, which, progressively disengaged from the notion of the social household, sought to describe and explain the open-ended production of wealth, and the beneficent commerce of social relations that made such wonders possible.

As political economy thus intruded upon the political, emphasis shifted from natural law, understood as an abstract norm, to natural process, understood as how things are and have come to be. The relationship between the condition of women, slavery, and legitimate political authority signaled by the seventeenth-century theorists continues to haunt the theoretical discourse; but those cases that had proved so essential to the original shift in paradigms fell rapidly to the periphery as attention turned to real—in contradistinction to theoretical—problems. Indeed, to the extent that women's actual subordination evinced itself essential to supporting the gains effected by propertied male individuals, real women and slaves could find themselves (individual souls and autonomous reasons notwithstanding) redefined according to realistic or natural criteria. The full treatment of women in eighteenth-century sociology and political economy must await another occasion, but the outstandingly acute and unusually frank observations of Adam Smith in his Glasgow lectures indicate the underlying logic of the transformation.

Smith's *Lectures* make a significant transformation of the public discourse from the moral and political to the economic. Smith remained deeply preoccupied with moral questions, but he rests his case against slavery, which he genuinely abhors, on the grounds that free workers would be more profitable. In discussing marriage, Smith adopts a combination of the historical, sociological, and economic methods. He observes practice and analyzes the social logic of the institution. In the course of his observations, he notes that love has become more respectable; that only despotism favors and supports polygamy; and that divorce undermines society, for "when both parties have the power of divorce, they can have no mutual trust nor dependence upon each other, but their interests are quite separate." Having leisurely considered the different species of marriage, however, Smith arrives at his main point: "The effect of marriage is to legitimate the children." Utility turns on the succession of property. Yet Smith points beyond the economics to the psychology of bourgeois individualism. The first duty of marriage, he affirms, "is fidelity of the wife to the husband; breach of chastity is the greatest of offences. Spurious children may be introduced into the family, and come to the succession instead of lawful ones." The interest of property will not, however, suffice to account for the outrage such infidelity arouses. Public indignation against such women derives from "sympathy with the jealousy of the husband. . . ." The sentiment of jealousy, moreover, is not chiefly founded, or rather not at all, upon the idea of a spurious off-spring. It is not from the particular act that the jealousy arises, but he considers her infidelity as an entire alienation of that preference to all other persons which she owed him.[49] This understanding of psychological dependence foreshadows Hegel, and beyond him Freud.

The relationships between theory and practice on the one hand and theory and ideology on the other remain problematic. Theorists draw upon previous intellectual traditions and even think in inherited vocabularies. To the extent that their own experience differs from that of their predecessors, they may inform the words with new content, but rarely even in their most radical departures do they effect a complete rupture with previous problematics and previous discourses. In this sense, theory simultaneously abstracts from the current experience (cultural, religious, and psychological, as well as social, political, and economic), which it attempts to describe according to plausible constructs, and engages previous theories, which it purports to answer in logical (or normative) as well as experiential terms. Any given theory thus adheres to at least two discrete systems: the intellectual tradition to which it is heir, and the contemporaneous society some or more facets of which it attempts to articulate. Theory differs from life or historical process as epistemology differs from actual experience. However acute the theoretical reading of an experience, the theory can never be identical to the experience; rather, all theory mediates between past or present and future experience. This mediation affords the connecting link, or overlap between theory and ideology. In a complex dialectical process, ideology both feeds and draws upon theory, extrudes strands that theoretical work organizes systematically and assimilates theoretical findings into ideological foundations from the most bastardized propaganda to the most complex and thorough of world views.

Much work is needed before we begin fully to grasp these processes. Nonetheless, the ways in which human minds transform past ideologies and explain present conditions to themselves correspond to and even impinge upon the history of social relations. The work of the great bourgeois political theorists offers some insight into the ways in which the early capitalist social and political relations were perceived, and the visions of human dignity and equality that could be drawn from them. Neither Hobbes nor Locke broke completely with the assumptions of their contemporaneous and inherited political culture, yet on that decisive margin where revolutions do occur they reread their heritage in ways that would transform the prism through which subsequent generations would view the polity. Their treatment of women and the family permits a glimpse into the continuity and the change. Had they not, on some level, accepted the patriarchalist notion of family as mirror of the polity, they would never have been drawn (on, say, feminist grounds) into asserting the equality of women within the family. That accepting so much, they still asserted that equality reveals the breadth of their assault on the patriarchal vision. Their successors, struggling with the practical implications of the broad theoretical claims, jettisoned the vestiges of the family/polity identity and raised the family to the antidote of the public sphere. The mythology of the family as refuge, like that of rural organicism, served to veil the intrusion of capitalism into the innermost crannies of human existence. The reassertion of patriarchalism at home recalls, once again, Hegel's dialectic of lordship and bondage, complete with the ironies of the lord's dependency. And the mythology of the sexual division of labor masked the original insight that a slave, however well-treated, may provide the reflection of his master's own dependency but never of his freedom as an individual.

Notes

1. See Gordon Schochet, *Patriarchalism in Political Thought: The Authoritarian Family and Political Speculation and Attitudes Especially in Seventeenth-Century England* (New York: Basic Books, 1975). See also, Mervyn James, *Family, Lineage, and Civil Society: A Study of Society, Politics, and Mentality in the Durham Region, 1500–1640* (Oxford: The Clarendon Press, 1974); Jean Bodin, *Les Six Livres de la République* (1576); Meyer Fortes, *Kinship and the Social Order: The Legacy of Lewis Henry Morgan* (London: Routledge and Kegan Paul, 1969). Cf. Alain Marie, "Rapports de Parenté et Rapports de Production dans les Sociétés Lignagères," in *L'Anthropologie Economique: Courants et Problèmes,* ed. by François Pouillon (Paris: F. Maspero, 1976), 86–116; and Claude Meillassoux, *Femmes, greniers, et capitaux* (Paris: F. Maspero, 1975).

2. G. W. F. Hegel, *The Philosophy of Right,* trans. by T. M. Knox (London, Oxford, New York: Oxford University Press, 1952; pb. 1967), esp. 40–57.

3. On Hobbes, see Leo Strauss, *The Political Philosophy of Hobbes: Its Basis and Genesis,* trans. by Elsa M. Sinclair (Oxford: The Clarendon Press, 1936; pb. 1973); Michael Oakeshott, *Hobbes on Civil Association* (Berkeley: University of California Press, 1975); Howard Warrender, *The Political Philosophy of Hobbes: His Theory of Obligation* (Oxford: The Clarendon Press, 1957); Maurice Cranston and Richard Peters (eds.), *Hobbes and Rousseau* (Garden City: Anchor Books, 1972); Ginevra Conti Odorsio, "La funzione del matriarcato in Hobbes," *DWF: donna, woman, femme,* I (1976), 21–33.

4. Thomas Hobbes, *Leviathan,* ed. by C. B. MacPherson (Baltimore: Penguin, 1968), 253. All references will be to this edition. Hobbes' general treatment of women, cf. also B. Tovey and G. Tovey, "Women's Philosophical Friends and Enemies," *Social Science Quarterly,* 55 (1974).

5. *Leviathan,* 253.

6. Ibid.

7. Ibid.

8. Ibid., 250.

9. Ibid., 254.

10. Ibid., 256. "In summe the Rights and Consequences of both *Paternall* and *Despoticall* Domination are the very same with those of a Soveraign by Institution; and for the same reasons. . . ."

11. Ibid., 226.

12. Quoted by Quentin Skinner in Cranston and Peters, *op. cit.,* 139. Cf. Sheldon S. Wolin, *Hobbes and the Epic Tradition of Political Theory* (Los Angeles: William Andrews

Clark Memorial Library, 1970), 50. See also Samuel I. Mintz, *The Hunting of Leviathan: Seventeenth Century Reactions to the Materialism and Moral Philosophy of Thomas Hobbes* (Cambridge: Cambridge University Press, 1962).

13. *Leviathan,* 255.

14. Ibid.

15. Ibid.

16. See Peter Laslett's Introduction to John Locke, *Two Treatises of Government,* ed. by Peter Laslett (Cambridge: Cambridge University Press, 1970). All references will be to this edition, but will be indicated by paragraph number, rather than page.

17. Sir Robert Filmer, *Patriarchia and Other Political Works,* ed. by Peter Laslett (Oxford: Oxford University Press, 1949), "Observations Upon Aristotle's Politiques . . . ," 88.

18. Filmer, "Observations on Mr. Hobbes's *Leviathan*: or his Artificial man—a Commonwealth," *loc. cit.,* 24.

19. The title page reads: *Two Treatises of Government: In the Former, the False Principles and Foundations of Sir Robert Filmer, and His Followers, are Detected and Overthrown. The Latter is an Essay Concerning The True Original, Extent, and End of Civil-Government.*

20. John Locke, *Two Treatises of Government,* Book I, par. 2.

21. Ibid., par. 5.

22. Ibid., par. 44.

23. Ibid.

24. Ibid.

25. Ibid., par. 47.

26. Ibid.

27. Ibid.

28. Ibid.

29. See Duncan Forbes, *Hume's Philosophical Politics* (Cambridge: Cambridge University Press, 1975), and Ronald Meek, *Social Science and the Noble Savage* (Cambridge: Cambridge University Press, 1976).

30. Cf. Schochet, *Patriarchalism,* 262.

31. Locke, *loc. cit.,* Book I, par. 49.

32. Locke, *loc. cit.,* Laslett's introduction. See Book II, *passim,* for frequent reference to "community," e.g., par. 87, "And thus all private judgment of every particular member being excluded, the Community comes to be Umpires, by settled standing Rules, indifferent and the same to all Parties. . . ."

33. Locke, *loc. cit.,* Book II, par. 61.

34. Ibid., par. 24.

35. Ibid., par. 22.

36. On the religious basis and content of Locke's politics, see John Dunn, *The Political Thought of John Locke: An Historical Account of the Argument of the 'Two Treatises of Government'* (Cambridge: Cambridge University Press, 1969), esp. 245–61. I do not think that Dunn's very intelligent and sensitive reading of Locke is as incompatible with MacPherson's argument as Dunn suggests. My conception of the superimposition of economic and religious individualism and the over-determination of their mutual reinforcement, however, is not identical to the argument advanced by Max Weber in *The Protestant Ethic and the Spirit of Capitalism.*

37. John Locke, *loc. cit.,* Book II, par. 172.

38. Ibid., par. 52.

39. Ibid., par. 78.

40. Ibid., par. 81.

41. Ibid., par. 82.

42. Ibid.

43. The problems attendant upon understanding this shift, its causes, the time at which it occurred, and even the extent to which the practice of diverse social groups (including the bourgeoisie) conformed to the "bourgeois" ideology of womanhood remain tremendous. My own best guess is that the French Revolution constituted a real watershed, in England as well as in France, perhaps because its visible, external violence crystallized—even mythologized—more deep-rooted trends of both class and sexual relations. The evidence for understanding and acceptance of female sexuality, at least within marriage, among various literate groups of the seventeenth and eighteenth centuries is extensive. See, for example, Defoe's novels, esp. *Moll Flanders* and *Roxana*. See also, Paula Backsheider, "Defoe's Women: Snares and Prey," *Studies in Eighteenth-Century Culture* 5 (1976): 103–20; Peter Earle, *The World of Defoe* (London: Weidenfeld and Nicolson, 1976), esp. 243–71. With respect to France, for the post-Revolutionary repudiating of the loose morality of the ancien régime, see, among many, Clarie de Rémusat, *Essai sur l'éducation des femmes,* ed. by [Octave] Gréard (Paris: Hachette, 1903).

44. For Locke's early conservatism, see John Locke, *Two Tracts on Government,* ed. by Philip Abrams (Cambridge: Cambridge University Press, 1967).

45. See, for example, Leonore Davidoff, *The Best Circles* (London: Croom Helm, 1973), and also Leonore Davidoff, Jean L'Esperance and Howard Newby, "Landscape with Figures: Home and Community in English Society," in Mitchell and Oakely (eds.), *Rights and Wrongs* (Harmondsworth: Penguin, 1976), 139–75. Eli Zaretsky, *Capitalism, the Family, and Personal Life* (New York: Harper and Row, 1976), develops a similar argument.

46. Sophia, a person of quality (Lady Mary Wortley Montagu?), *Woman not Inferior to Man* (London: Brentham Press, 1939; reprinted 1975), 23.

47. Mary Wollstonecraft, *Vindication of the Rights of Women,* ed. by Miriam Kramnick (Harmondsworth: Penguin, 1975). See Kramnick's introduction, and also, Margaret George, *One Woman's 'Situation': A Study of Mary Wollstonecraft* (Urbana: University of Illinois Press, 1970). Cf. Marilyn Butler, *Maria Edgeworth: A Literary Biography* (Oxford: The Clarendon Press, 1972) and her *Jane Austen and the War of Ideas* (Oxford: The Clarendon Press, 1975); Regina James, "Mary, Mary, Quite Contrary, Or, Mary Astell and Mary Wollstonecraft Compared," *Studies in Eighteenth-Century Culture,* vol. 5, ed. by Ronald C. Rosbottom (Madison: University of Wisconsin Press, 1976), 121–36.

48. David Hume, "Of the Original Contract," in Sir Ernest Barker (ed.), *Social Contract: Essays by Locke, Hume, and Rousseau* (London, Oxford, New York: Oxford University Press, 1970 (1947)), and *A Treatise of Human Nature,* ed. by L. A. Selby-Bigge (Oxford: The Clarendon Press, 1968 (1888)), especially Book III, "Of Morals."

49. Adam Smith, *Lectures on Justice, Police, Revenue, and Arms,* ed. by Edwin Cannan (Oxford: The Clarendon Press, 1896). Hutcheson had also mentioned that affection due from the wife to her husband, but only briefly and without Smith's psychological development.

Two

Yves Saint Laurent's Peasant Revolution

Thursday, July 29, 1976. A scant month after the bicentennial celebration, the front page of the New York *Times* announced the outbreak of another revolution: the new peasant collection of Yves Saint Laurent. Front page status, unusual for fashion events, continued to herald the new look through the summer and fall. *Time* and *New York Magazine* rivaled the fashion magazines of Western Europe and the United States in lengthy speculations. European fashion magazines, led by the French, had a field day. Opinions diverged wildly: Women will not buy such garb; women will dabble with occasional pieces of the line but reject the totality; the garments, at $400 for openers, will not be kept in the stores. The reasons advanced for the collection's potential and influence ran as wide a gamut: the peasant look itself; the element of costume; the artistry; the return to femininity; and, for *L'Officiel* (would you believe?), the warmth.

Everyone, to be sure, agreed that success would turn on the market—the women who did or did not buy. The significance of their buying or not—the elusive psychology of fashion—remained subject to vague speculation. And the structural and cultural, if much impoverished, legacy of the look seems, as of spring 1978, to have escaped attention. Saint Laurent's recent collection figures, once again, as one among many.

One thing seems clear: The firmament set ablaze in Paris on July 28 confirmed Yves Saint Laurent's position as "the king," undisputed heir of those other monarchs of *haute couture*, Charles Frederick Worth and Paul Poiret.

"Yves Saint Laurent's Peasant Revolution." *Marxist Perspectives* 1, no. 1 (Summer 1978): 58–92. Copyright 1978. All rights reserved.

His current status as *primus inter pares* rather than that of absolute monarch, which he enjoyed last year, testifies merely to momentary disorder in the world of fashion and should not distract from his considerable triumph in shoring up the fortunes of *haute couture* as a whole. Like his illustrious predecessors, Saint Laurent has proved himself both genial artist and consummate business man. The unerring aesthetic virtuosity, the sense of color, of drama, of spatial configuration single him out as *maestro extraordinario*. Quite simply, Saint Laurent's harshest critics could not fairly deny that his peasant creations, taken on their own terms, were startlingly beautiful. And the entrepreneurial acumen, so indispensable to modern royalty, has extended his domain from the cutting rooms of Paris, to the boutiques bearing his name that dot the globe, and even to the counters of the "democratic" department stores where his perfumes, soaps, scarves, ties, sheets, shower-curtains, and belts titillate mass purchasing power.

Saint Laurent's "Peasant Revolution" combined the two predominant, if superficially opposed, trends of recent fashion in a masterful and breath-taking synthesis. In one superb outflanking maneuver, he skirted the world of work-a-day fashion to marry the pop-culture themes of the street to high fashion itself. Thus—hardly by accident coming from one of Saint Laurent's talent—he appears to have provided the hard-pressed domain of high fashion with a new lease on life, just as, along the way, he crystallized a new image of femininity and coopted the growing ethnic consciousness and pastoral nostalgia for the guardians of multinational finance and class stability.

I.

However mediated or ambiguous the ultimate outcome, the reception of Saint Laurent's *coup de main* commands attention. His designs have not triumphed in precisely their original form, but the interest they aroused testifies to their creator's uncanny feel for cultural and social trends. Much talk has circulated in recent years about the street influences on designing in the fashion industry: Popular models in expensive fabrics and expensive cuts in popular fabrics have been with us for a while. Lately, the more alert could have discerned a return to more complex, delicate, and stylized models in the pages of *Vogue* and elsewhere. These expensive-to-buy, costly-to-maintain, and difficult-to-copy creations have suggested that a radical break between elite and common apparel might lie just around the bend—a cultural equivalent of the rich getting richer, the poor poorer, and the middle classes floundering in between. Fifth Avenue (increasingly supported by wealthy Europeans in flight from communist and socialist threats at home) and 125th Street. With no one left to pay the taxes. Although one can fantasize the army of laundresses required to keep the new models fresh. And the French

Communist Party has spoken out in favor of luxury—shades of Cantillon and Graslin—on the grounds of employment for seamstresses.

Saint Laurent's genius lay in costuming the rich as peasants, and thus in restoring to wealth the prerogatives of cultural hegemony that the young, the ethnic, and the reform-minded had threatened to usurp. His fabrics, colors, and cut defied cheap emulation; yet, his models suggested a lost social harmony, a simpler past, and even echoed the rising tide of regionalism from Scotland, to the Basque country, to the Italian-American League. The year 1975 had, after all, seen Emanuel Leroy Ladurie's scholarly *Montaillou, village occitan* scale the heights of bestsellerdom; and a popular occitanian theatre still draws enthusiasts from all over France while the local meridional population cultivates its archaic regional language and produces poetry in the mode and tongue of Mistral. Capitalizing in innumerable subtle and sensitive ways on the aspirations of so many during the past decade, Saint Laurent's pageantry could have been taken as boding ill—for those who take cultural barometers seriously—for the future of the woman's movement and of the related social gains of the 1960s.

The peasant gambit is not new. One thinks of William Morris and the ascendancy of Liberty's. The original peasant look, however, inaugurated precisely the birth of modern fashion itself and coincided with the American Revolution and the publication of *The Wealth of Nations*—those twin pillars of individual freedom and individual enterprise, the celebration of whose birthdays mirrored Saint Laurent's extravaganza. The initiative for the elite's pursuit of peasant simplicity has been attributed to Jean-Jacques Rousseau, prophet par excellence of domestic sentimentality, confessional self-exploration, and the problematical nature of political democracy. And not coincidentally, Rousseau's more esoteric concerns with the origins of language and society have returned to vogue under the pen of the structuralist anthropologist Claude Lévi-Strauss, who has done so much to popularize primitive cultures and the use of anthropology in all the social sciences. No more than Saint Laurent invented ethnicity, folk-culture-nostalgia, or the peasantry did Rousseau "invent" nature, the self, or self-mirroring women. English gardens, pastorals, conjugal domesticity, and the obligation to nurse one's own children had been percolating towards broad cultural consciousness. But like Saint Laurent, Rousseau codified, articulated, and popularized; his uncanny sensitivity made him something of a conduit for cultural tensions and aspirations, and his unusual talent formulated the disparate strands in a recognition-commanding image.

Rousseau's legacy hangs heavy indeed, but Rousseau did not himself model women's fashions. That role fell to the lot of the fragile, childlike, self-indulgent queen of France, Marie Antoinette, who tiring of the formal demands of Versailles, retired to the rustic simplicity of the palace grounds, where she and her court pursued unpretentious, Rousseauesque tranquility, appropriately dressed as milkmaids.

Marie Antoinette's quest for the simple life did not noticeably reduce the royal budget, avert impending political upheaval, nor yet reflect a commitment to social leveling. It did, however, incidentally help to solidify the rising career of one Rose Bertin, who, in that fateful year 1776, had established the milliners' guild in Paris, thus launching modern couture. It also provided subject matter for the infant business of women's magazines and models for the celebrated dolls that carried the image of Parisian fashion to the backward courts of Eastern Europe.

Weighty political events cut short Marie Antoinette's romping and eventually her head as well. Revolution forced, temporarily, a drastic simplification of fashion for all. But the fledgling fashion industry survived the Terror so many of its customers did not, and emerged fortified both by rudimentary political individualism and the beginnings of industrialization. For, the great Revolution that destroyed divine-right monarchy paved the way for the emergence of Society. Such kings and emperors as returned to grace the nineteenth century did so as individual Frenchmen among many. Like their English "cousins" of the same period, they, no more than American presidents, could afford to confuse their wishes with the will of God. Commerce in general, and industrial production in particular, began to contribute major fortunes and new faces to the social lives of the various countries. Parliamentary governments, however restricted their constituencies, conducted their business away from the royal courts.

Social gatherings centered more and more on theatres, assemblies, and private homes. Matrons of substance (frequently corporal as well as financial and social) established the network of rules, of "knowing" and "not knowing," of inviting and not inviting, of dressing and redressing for each hour of the day. And, after the brief outbreak of bared female flesh and general exuberance that characterized the Directory and Empire—the Emperor, altogether Rousseauesque in his notions of female modesty and submission, did not approve, but continued to have extra logs piled on the fires at the Luxembourg to protect his scantily clad guests from chill—their ideas of dressing tended more and more towards the ample, the covered, and the laced.

The now-derided and prudish behavior of our early Victorian ancestors might seem irrelevant to the present scene, were it not that underlying their outmoded notions of fashion lurked powerful forces. The industrial revolution and the beginnings of mass consumption contributed much to setting fashion on its course. Based upon the production of textiles, early industrialization fed upon each extension of that textile market: new fabrics for different seasons, occasions, hours of the day, and mere chic; new consumers for the new fabrics. Prior to the invention of the sewing machine in the 1840s, and ever less easily thereafter, merchant and industrial capital managed a mutually tolerant and beneficial division of the market in such a way that artisanal, neodomestic, and mass production coexisted in relative peace. Indeed, the great extension of French luxury production, from lace, to Lyon silks, to artificial flowers paralleled the emergence of factory-produced textiles. The appearance of department stores, one thinks of Stewart's and *Bon Marché,* in the 1830s similarly intertwined with the development of *haute couture,* the career of Worth for example. The popular, middle-class, and luxury markets unfolded within an intersecting cultural network but without serious internecine struggles.

In the new world of the bourgeoisie, bathing, laundry, change of clothes became *de rigueur.* The proliferation of a universal cultural norm of sobriety, cleanliness, industry, and thrift, including the more highly articulated sexual division of labor, sought to contain disorder within a normative framework as well as to mobilize everyone for their appropriate market roles. The wide marketing of fabrics, and later of ready-to-wear clothes, carried certain risks of overzealous emulation on the part of the lower classes. No woman relished seeing her servant in her dress, or even a mediocre copy. But increasing wealth continued to provide means and opportunity for its own display quite beyond the means of ordinary folk. It has been claimed that when servants too enthusiastically took to wearing bonnets their mistresses switched to hats.

Society sparkled in a veritable crystal palace of conspicuous consumption. For fashion, as Thorstein Veblen long ago pointed out, took much of its glory and prestige from its embodiment of leisure—the manifest inability of its exponents to do anything. The exigencies of class society, as well as the vanities of individuals, fostered the notion that the lower classes should aspire to imitate their betters. No sooner did they approach success (in the words of Georg Simmel, thereby both "crossing the line of demarcation [that] the upper classes have drawn and destroying the uniformity of their coherence"), than "the upper classes turn away from this style and adopt a new one, which in its turn differentiates them from the masses; and thus the game goes merrily on." And, as Simmel also noted, with implicit reference to the specific developments of the nineteenth century, the same process can obtain between different sets within the upper classes so that "the more nearly one set has approached another, the more frantic becomes the desire for imitation from below and the seeking for the new from above." The increase of wealth, Simmel insists, can only accelerate the process and render it more visible. The acceleration and the visibility of fashion since the beginning of the nineteenth century reflected, however, not merely increasing wealth, but revolutionary changes in the production of wealth. If quantitative increase at first masked qualitative change, by the end of the century the shift could no longer be called in doubt. Nor can its significance.

Nineteenth-century fashion meant, overwhelmingly, female fashion. The industrial age was not built by those whose corsets promised them vapors at best and ribs piercing their livers at worst (for such was the cause of death of one twenty-three year old, zealously corseted beauty). Indeed, the same age that brought us political and economic liberalism brought us a renewed emphasis upon the special role and nature of women—another legacy of Rousseau. A recent debate in the pages of *Signs* over tight-lacing—who submitted to or indulged in it, how frequently, and why—risks obscuring the inescapable truth of tight-lacing as model, as standard of femininity. Many women undoubtedly shirked the extreme rigors of tight-lacing, even as they observed the general dictates of which it constituted the image of excellence. That their clothes never fit quite the way they looked as if they should, probably passed lightly over the strongest egos, and probably left the psychologically frailer with nothing more than a pervasive feeling of guilt, inferiority, or inadequacy. The motives of those who accepted the discipline and met the standard probably ranged from robust narcissism to displaced eroticism to outright masochism. The tight-laced vision of femininity long withstood the breaches, excesses, illness, and pain in its observance. And it proved a powerful conduit in disseminating the model of the woman-belle ideal, as well as the centrality of a particular female self-construction to the forward march of civilization and the assimilation of working people to the ranks of respectability. Nowhere more clearly than in fashion was the essence of the sexual division of labor displayed. And the fashionable display underscored the sexual division of labor as the *sine qua non* of social harmony.

As the price for the worlds of business and politics in the new age, men forsook their time-honored sartorial parity with women and settled comfortably into the sober garb that has characterized real power ever since. What sartorial aspirations they retained were channeled, following the prescriptions of that quintessential dandy George Brummel, into perfection of cut, cleanliness of linen, and subtlety of tone. Their loss in splendor went a long way towards freeing them from treating themselves as objects of beauty—from one potentially consuming facet of narcissism—thus releasing their energies for what Sigmund Freud dubbed sublimation. Whatever its eventual fate, the original dandy impulse, however self-centered, arose from an impulse to wield power from a position of autonomy, self-possession, and individual superiority: Brummel's two-pronged condemnation of aristocratic, including regal, *laissez-aller* and bourgeois philistinism had little in common with the role of retiring dependence offered women. Brummel may have made a career—even something of a crusade if crusades had not demanded too much visible earnestness—out of antiutilitarianism, but the self-containment, the cleanliness, the fanatical sobriety betray a purposeful individualism less far removed than one might think from the purposefulness of Manchester magnates.

In *The Theory of Moral Sentiments* Adam Smith had roundly castigated the frivolity and moral dependency of the "foolish thing called a man of fashion," contrasting them with "the solid and masculine virtues of a warrior, a statesman, a philosopher, or a legislator." In Smith's view, all "the great and awful virtues, all the virtues which can fit, either for the council, the senate, or the field, are, by the insolent and insignificant flatterers, who commonly figure the most in such corrupted societies (the courts of princes, the drawing-rooms of the great), held in the utmost contempt and derision." Brummel informed male fashion with an appropriately masculine seriousness. Dependency and flattery were allocated to women.

Women gained on the narcissism front. The point did not escape Mary Wollstonecraft who reported in her *Vindication* that in "Dr. Smith's Theory of Moral Sentiments, I have found a general character of people of rank and fortune, that, in my opinion, might with the greatest propriety be applied to the female sex." And Wollstonecraft's resounding condemnation of the fostering of debilitating female narcissism includes the pernicious role of clothing. "Men order their clothes to be made, and have done with the subject; women make their own clothes, necessary or ornamental, and are continually talking about them; and their thoughts follow their hands. It is not indeed the making of necessaries that weakens the mind; but the frippery of dress." And again: "The thoughts of women ever hover round their persons, and is it surprising that their persons are reckoned most valuable? Yet some degree of liberty of mind is necessary even to form the person. . . ." Women remain in "slavery" to their first, most dependent and immature, emotions—to that childhood to which their lives ever draw them back.

Provided that they were wealthy enough, women could devote most of their lives to the adornment of their own persons. And since the new mystique of womanhood denied their sexuality, and the new social codes hedged them round with a barrier of gentility, they could settle down to a lifetime of objecthood. Custodians of religion, the home, sartorial brilliance, consumption in all its forms, and chastity, they took upon themselves those social responsibilities which hindered the forward march of rational progress. That dressing the part cost increasing amounts of money and thus actually contributed to the oiling of the expanding market can be seen as one more miraculous proof of the existence of the Invisible Hand. The connection is not fortuitous. For the same Adam Smith who lauded the virtues of the market also explained that the psychological ease of any male engaged in the wonders of a market economy required a female who would prefer him to all others and, by her preference, fortify his spirit against the competitive pressures of entrepreneurship. Rousseau, less enamored of modernity and economic progress, while even more attuned to the regressive pulls towards dependency that threatened men [who are] prey to the psychological market of competition, concurred wholeheartedly.

To be sure, many women never became fashionable women. Preoccupied with homes that even with the assistance of a servant required constant attention and effort, confined by frequent pregnancies, and engaged in a range of charitable and religious activities, they fell short of the perfection propagated by the increasing number of women's magazines. During the course of the century, however, the expanding function of consumption rather than domestic production in women's lives drew them more and more into the market. That women's appointed market role confirmed their passivity and dependency did not figure prominently in their assigned role. The dominant cultural messages cultivated their needs and desires in a language that emphasized every plausible note from social and familial responsibility to merited self-reward.

Dress reformers protested, in the tradition of Wollstonecraft. But their case for health and functionalism too frequently smacked of eccentricity and overseriousness. Life had not changed sufficiently, nor had social crisis appeared so ominous that the language of moral reform could compete, at least with respect to female dress, with sophistication, brilliance, and wealth. But the price must have been high for many. Emile Zola, in *Au Paradis des Dames,* evokes the magical new world of the department store. The glittering array of goods sparkles and shimmers, reflected in the eyes of women whose desires and compulsions constitute their value. The hands itch, the pulse quickens, the fever of possession takes hold. A nameless anxiety forces ever more purchases to ease its cutting edge, to fill the terrifying emptiness within. Zola, prefiguring modern psychiatric wisdom, links kleptomania to the endless possibilities of buying—and portrays it as a female disease.

II.

Fashion ranks as the most fickle and elusive of deities—a demon to some—and all embroiled in her tentacles instinctively look for the genius or villain establishing her sway. For fashion does dictate. Women have been known to blame the great taste-setters, the Mephistophelean couturiers—in recent mythology, those sadistic homosexuals. The couturiers claim to be as putty in the hands of their clients or the spirit of the age. And, in fact, the great

Worth could not decree the end of the crinoline when he chose, nor could his star client, the Empress Eugenie, abandon it prematurely. More sophisticated women will readily charge the fashion industry with forcing the pace of their consumption. But retailers and manufacturers retort with equal certainty that they have no such power. The failure of the maxi must still burn in many minds.

Fashion defies the neat and tidy, necessary and sufficient, kind of definition tailored to the needs of dictionary precision: Fashion is . . . The extensive literature circles and weaves, rarely committing itself to hard-and-fastness. The discussions themselves follow the paths of intellectual fashion, emphasizing in turn the universal and the particular, the behavioral and the symbolic, the expressive and the hierarchical, the artistic and the economic, *ad infinitum*. Notions of individual and collective identity figure in most discussions. In one of the few attempts at straightforward definition, Kurt and Gladys Lang assert that fashion "is a process by which the taste of a mass of people is collectively redefined." This sensible discussion further takes account of the importance of novelty and of the continuing tension between self and collectivity. The authors situate fashion in the realm of "all those market decisions in which individual preferences are reflected and those of others affirmed or rejected." Choices of fashion "express a need for individuation without the risk of group disapproval." So far, so good. Fashion mediates, in some way, between self and society, or between some aspects of self and some aspects of society. All the good recent treatments of fashion lean towards one or another variant of the socio-cultural approach.

And as a catchall, society and culture do nicely for a first approximation. Unrefined, however, the concepts beg the most difficult and tantalizing questions, not least of which must be the relationship between society and culture. Fashion raises every intractable question about the nature of collective human social existence. It can be interpreted from the economic, the psychological, the sociological, the historical, the aesthetic, or the religious perspective. Within each perspective it can be addressed under a range of theoretical rubrics. A comprehensive study of fashion, moreover, would touch upon almost every facet of human experience. For fashion is cultural, social, economic, psychological, and historical. In this respect, thinking fashion requires thinking complexity, indeterminancy, subjectivity, and hard theory. In the first instance, fashion might be conceived of as a social cement, a form of communication, a social representation. Ritual and metaphor, no matter how *au courant* as modes of designation, remove fashion too far from its solid foundations in commodities. Overly spiritualizing the day-to-day of dressing, for example, risks committing the psychoanalytic fallacy of intellectualization, which drains the experience of its lived content. And fashion has become a mundane and recurring fact of most people's lives, spanning the continuum from minor purchase to self-representation. Yet, fashion cannot be identified with the commodity purchased. The commodity remains dress, or chain, or blue jean, or car, or waterbed, no matter what aura fashionability may lend. Nor, one hopes, is the self, him-herself, fashion. Although here pessimists may be inclined to doubt.

Fashion is, or better qualifies, social interconnectedness, social relationship, the mode of connecting and relating. It is, in fact, adjective and, above all, adverb rather than noun, much less verb. The strength of fashion, however, can best be captured in its ability to figure as noun or verb. From its origins, fashion has sought to fashion isomorphism between its objects, its manifestations, and itself. It invariably aspires to totality and identity. Even fashion as mode of social differentiation, as encoded in sumptuary laws, affirmed the importance of its custodians in a manner that comprehended the negation of those excluded. The exclusion itself offered an identity, a social being, based on a nonbeing. Such language merely points towards fashion as a qualification, accentuation, articulation of prevailing social relations of production. It is neither coterminous with those social relations of production nor extraneous to them. Nor can it be reduced to direct emanation of them. Its undeniable links with artistic expression and production, its elements of symbolization and of play, of craft and of artifact, invite a more nuanced appreciation. It remains, nonetheless, art with a particular social function. And in contemporary society it is tending more and more towards a barely mediated ideology of commodities.

Thomas Carlyle spoke readily of the philosophy of clothes. His phrase evokes the realms of metaphysics, ethics, and epistemology. Philosophy, in his sense, referred to elements of motivation and meaning, intentionality and causation, origins and ends. Communications theory and semiology— society as language, society as text—attempt to dis-embed the teleological legacy of philosophy in Carlyle's sense and to reconstitute social discourse as a system of signs or messages. Roland Barthes' *Système de la Mode* provocatively applies semiotics to the language of fashion and lays bare the internal, circular, and psychologically dictatorial logic of women's fashion magazines. He brilliantly demonstrates the consistency with which such magazines batter their readers with the message that they will become what they wear, that fashion dictates what they wear, that they must be fashionable to be. In this respect, although he does not put it this way, he underscores the notion of fashion as mediation between commodity and self—a mediation that, in denying female consciousness and choice, tends towards identifying commodity and self. His virtuosity nonetheless ends with his own admission that a full discussion of fashion, in contradistinction to its verbal signs, would require moving beyond the words to their referents. And the referents, in their multiplicity, defy tidy cataloguing.

As Edward Sapir, in what remains one of the finest treatments of fashion, argues, it "is emphatically a historical concept. A specific fashion is utterly unintelligible if lifted out of its place in a sequence of forms." Sapir further insists on the special danger of rationalizing or psychologizing "a particular fashion on the basis of general principles which might be considered applicable to the class of forms of which it seems to be an example." The point, well taken, would be better taken yet if Sapir were calling attention not merely to the sequential development of form but to the historical development of social relations of production and reproduction as well. Mary Douglas' general caveat to broad interpretations of culture, *qua* culture, obtains: Culture can only be understood in relation to discrete societies. Moreover, Sapir's own extremely useful negative delineation of fashion as neither custom, taste, nor fad should have led him to dwell more specifically on its historical context and substance.

Sapir does, nonetheless, recognize the substitution of an "aristocracy of wealth" for one of rank as a critical element in the emergence of modern fashion, and he underscores the importance of "a psychological if not an economic leveling of classes because of the feeling that wealth is an accidental or accreted quality of an individual as contrasted with blood. In an aristocracy of wealth everyone, even the poorest, is potentially wealthy both in legal theory and in private fancy." Indeed, one critical strategy of bourgeois culture has been its encouragement of private fancy—not to say fantasy— as a substitute for public—not to say political—consciousness. Thus, Sapir's hasty dismissal of psychology as a valid tool for interpreting fashion may be related to his resounding silence on the hard economic questions. The very notion of an aristocracy of wealth blurs the specific characteristics of class society.

Reigning psychoanalytic interpretations of fashion also tend to blur such distinctions. Even such sensitive analysts as J. G. Flugel fall into something like banality in expounding on the sexual symbolism of any fashion. However valid the general insights, their universalism leads them perilously close to archetypal formulations. And they singularly fail to explain the predominance of one particular form of sexual symbolism in a given period, much less the change from one to another. In this respect, psychoanalytic interpretations tend to apply the basic stages of individual psycho-sexual development to a society as a whole, thereby ignoring the compelling terrain of social psychology as interaction. The important territory that should indubitably fall to a psychological reading of fashion lies in the realm of the mobilization, containment, and distortion of fundamental intrapsychic conflicts rather than in the simple unfolding of sexual symbolization. For, fashion clearly holds its sway in the relationship between consciousness and social being. Kleptomania or anorexia nervosa constitute socially rooted intrapsychic disorders.

Nor can any consideration of fashion afford to neglect the objective conditions of social being. The mode of production, the prevailing social relations of production and reproduction, the extent of the market, even the relative levels of accumulation and profit impinge upon that social life and social consciousness which fashion seeks to order and encompass. If fashion as convention in part obeys an internal sequential logic—if waists having risen so high must drop, if skirts having become so wide must narrow—it does so within the contours of its social and economic possibilities. If social history and social psychology cannot alone account for the development of an art form, much less the variable of individual creation, art for art's sake and the myth of creativity cannot alone account for the vagaries of so socially corrupted an art as fashion.

III.

Historians and theorists of fashion frequently discuss their subject as if it pertained equally to all times and places. And all historical peoples seem to have had preferred modes of dress, adornment, artifacts. Such modes do not, in themselves, constitute fashion. Traditional peasant dress may reflect custom rather than fashion: Fashion itself can neither be understood independent of notions of change and novelty nor identified with passing fads perceived as such. One of the peculiar elements of fashion lies in its quality of presenting change or novelty as necessary, hence endowing the temporary with a psychological illusion of permanence. Indications of what the modern world understands as fashion can be found throughout European history, particularly at courts and in cities. These imitative, restrictive, and conventional modes of dress, adornment, and furnishing cannot be dismissed. Nor should they be allowed to shape our understanding of modern fashion completely. They qualified and gave expression to traditional social arrangements, much as fashionable goods resulted from precapitalist forms of production. Such goods circulated on the markets constructed by merchant capital, which sought more to organize existing social relations of production than to transform them. In this perspective, the fashion that characterizes modern capitalist society, although not without historical origin and antecedent, constitutes as new a phenomenon as does capitalist society itself.

The pervasiveness and elusiveness of fashion have acquired particular intensity since the American, French, and industrial revolutions. And that market society of which we are all members notoriously lacks a single center of gravity. If our world is anything, it is a web, a texture, a system of interlocking and mutually interdependent relationships. It is a fair or a meeting place—a society in which we all look to each other for the reflection and measure of who and what we are. A department store, as Zola suggested. And, quintessentially, Bloomingdale's on Saturday afternoons when anxious glances at mirrors, at the faces, forms, and appearance of others shade off into the compensatory fixation on the glitter of objects and garb, each promising to relieve the anxiety by creating a self through possession of commodities. In such a world, fashion becomes the external manifestation of our belonging and our individualism, our persona, our identity, although the "our" of display, as against that of attainment, has been primarily assumed by women in this democratic market.

Too fickle to be fully controlled or manipulated, fashion did play an important role in the development of capitalist society. In particular it lubricated the transformation of luxuries into necessities, thus facilitating eager, individual commitment to the unceasing expansion of commodity production. It helped to draw ever wider segments of the population into full market existence. It mirrored the emergence of labor-power as a commodity and eased the pain of alienation by recasting loss of autonomy as the realization of fantasy. Fashion mediated production and consumption, economic exigency and individual self-perception. The growth of advertising as the commanding form of social discourse publicized and codified aspirations to comfort, dignity, and respect. That along the way it substituted consumption for politics, passivity for action, simply testifies to its strength in recasting individual aspiration and in extending alienation to the realm of fantasy itself.

Originally, the bourgeoisie had sought to enforce social discipline through harsher means. Emphasizing thrift, hard work, repression, it promoted fashion in the sense of cleanliness, modesty, decorum. In the same vein bourgeois culture exaggerated the social import of the sexual division of labor, which it stringently defended in the name of lost harmony and social order. But by the beginning of the twentieth century, if not sooner, the unprecedented economic success of capitalism permitted a certain relaxation of traditional values in the interests of increased consumption. Increasingly, the commodities themselves—named, valued, and bedecked by the advertising discourse—could be counted on to identify selfhood with consumption. Ultimately, as Stuart Ewen has argued, the corporation proposed itself, rather than the family, paternal wisdom, or female domesticity, as the source of reassurance and nurture. This recent development suggests a decisive erosion of bourgeois culture and may portend a real shift in the nature and function of fashion. For, the fashion of bourgeois hegemony must be understood as a counterpart of bourgeois etiquette—an attempt at ordering and regulating. The bourgeoisie recognized the personal as political and sought to repress it. In so doing, it carved up human psyches, allocating achievement to men and narcissism to women.

IV.

Bourgeois fashion has shaped women—and with their complicity. Slavery did not long survive the advent of wage-labor. Voluntary servitude better flatters the image of the upstanding, independent, democratic citizen, even if his need to submit casts doubts on his pretensions to autonomy. A thoroughly convincing psychology, much less a social psychology of women, has yet to be elaborated. For, if Freud gave us the indispensable building blocks, he failed to assemble them in a manner that articulated the interaction between the subjective and objective elements of female selfhood. The woman's movement may already be recasting the terms of the debate to such an extent that when the psychology of the contemporary woman is formulated it may differ in important particulars from that of her Victorian forerunner. But, the modern woman is a relatively recent and fragile creation: the newborn product of the efforts of a multitude of women who refuse to be excluded from the world of selfhood (socially validated subjective existence), production, activity, and power, and yet refuse to sacrifice what they deem the essence of their femininity. It has already become clear that femininity can no longer be defined as the opposite of male norms or as the mere satisfaction of male needs. Nor can it be reduced to narrow waists flanked by welcoming curves. Nor to domesticity. Nor to the restoration of traditional family life. Nor even to the voluptuous display of ethnic yearnings, artistic relief from the depressing aspect of contemporary civilization—a blaze of warmth and comfort from an earlier time. Nor to fantasies of personal liberation independent of social fabric.

Saint Laurent's peasant garb, in its happy unification of the streets and the salons, promised small place for the working woman who has emerged during the past decade. His visual imagery highlights contradictory messages of predatory female sadism and masochistic female submission. The steelsharp clack of the gold boot taps across the psyches of men like a Cossack dancing on a marble floor. The nurture and warmth promised by the inviting décolletage of the bodice and the seductive volume of the petticoats evoke sirens and Laurelei as much as nurturing acceptance. And the costliness of the fabrics denies the very ethnic simplicity the models seem to embody. The element of costume may entrance, but costume invariably refers to artificial or constructed persona. To the extent that such dress suggests female power, it suggests the power of female ruler—of the tsarist princess. It thus brings the image of explicit hierarchy to embellish the mere fact of conspicu-ous consumption. It caricatures, in a word, feminist notions of legitimate female power and independence. And it implicitly challenges, even as it mocks, feminist notions of femininity. From that perspective, Saint Laurent makes Diane von Furstenberg, however inflated her publicity and openly capitalist her allegiance, look very, very good.

Nothing forced women to buy the peasant look. Few could afford the real thing in any case. And many did not buy it, although lack of alternatives may soon force them into buying its heirs. Be that as it may, surface cultural phenomena, particularly fashion, have had a way of taking their toll on even the best integrated female psyches. And Saint Laurent has ominously earned his standing by an uncanny sensibility that picks up the vibrant elements in the culture and recasts them in original creations which influence the way the members of the culture think about themselves. Women's contribution to the social good lies all too frequently in their role as consumers, and fash-ion remains one of the prime commodities that they can be persuaded to consume as much out of psychological as economic need.

Fashion plays its role in the many forces that encourage women to see themselves less as productive beings and more as the objects of others' desires, or as the saintly custodians of values necessary to decent human life but incompatible with market competition—not uncommonly represented intrapsychically as sexual competition. Not coincidentally, recent changes in fashion have paralleled the massive entry of women into and their depar-ture from the labor force. Particularly the entries and departures of women socially represented as middle class or normative.

During the twentieth century traditional female dress in its various stylis-tic embodiments has gradually given way to more utilitarian, if less inspiring, garb. The complex progress, most evident in the improvement of under-wear, the shortening of skirts, and the acceptability of pants, has included a marked and superficially confusing trend away from mature (voluptuous and maternal) femininity and toward varying degrees of boyishness. The revolu-tionary increase in the exposure of bared female flesh should not in itself be taken as an acceptance of female sexuality. For, if women favored less restric-tive underwear, or none at all, the fashionable and pornographic—and at the upper reaches of fashion the two merge more closely than one might expect—depiction of the liberation of the female body looks more like a dis-torted male fantasy of female sexuality as threat than a natural acceptance of the female body and being. How else are we to read the pictorial allusions to female masturbation or the photograph in a recent *Vogue* that portrayed a white, blond-haired woman in a skimpy red bathing suit between two extraordinarily large, tribally-garbed, black men?

These confusing trends hopelessly complicate any appraisal of Saint Laurent's peasant collection. Few, even among feminists, will begrudge a return to an appreciation of a properly female identity and the acceptance, for women, of maturation. (Be it not naively romantic to think such ever existed.) A female adulthood would come as a blessing. It would provide a welcome relief from the dilemma of manifest female masochism versus female-denying masculinity (a higher form of masochism). But Saint Laurent's collection, in its innuendos and implications, did not resolve that dilemma: It boldly sketched a return to full nineteenth-century femininity of a kind none have dared for decades. Its evocation of organic restoration could not, however, fully mask its inescapable engagement with contemporary problems. The fantasy of bliss it proposed has rapidly decomposed, revealing more sinister cultural and social dispositions.

V.

Dior's celebrated "new look" of 1947 attempted nothing so sweeping, although it too favored the small waist and the floating skirt over petticoats. In 1947, of course, sensible women, still mindful of their independence and war work, insisted that they were not about to throw out entire wardrobes for such a trivial matter as fashion. Throw them out they did. But then, the factories were throwing out the women in order to make room for men. Dior's new look, in other words, coincided with the beginning of the years dominated by what Betty Friedan termed "the feminine mystique." Those poor frustrated housewives (our mothers, the voluntary homemakers) trapped in the suburbs, married to the men in the grey flannel suits, raising unnecessarily large families under intense psycho-cultural pressures, buying the image of themselves dished out by the *Ladies Home Journal,* Doctor Spock, et. al., wore the new look.

Remember Audrey Hepburn, Debbie Reynolds, Doris Day, and, quintessentially, Kim Novak in *Strangers When We Meet?* They all had tiny waists and undulating skirts: None of them had jobs, at least not jobs they kept after Mr. Right came along. The new look should not be held responsible for their plight. They may only have bought it out of boredom and self-doubt. The world of work was hardly offering them substantive alternatives. The advertising phalanx was doing its best to persuade them to free themselves for the serious business of consumption. Yet, they probably found the new look charming and gracious. And more likely than not it helped seduce them into finding a "meaning" in domestic self-abnegation that transcended the crass material values of the world outside. The essence of mystification lies in the sad truth that in their wistful pursuit of a meaning that would transcend the materialism of the cash nexus they performed the most essential economic function.

The postwar economy benefited from the increased domestic consumption characteristic of the new suburban life, and even then had its eyes on the child market. The advertising industry did its bit in bolstering the image of this sweet custodian of traditional values, but, having long since proved its ability to pitch its message at almost any cultural stereotype, it is now happily peddling "liberation" and "black is beautiful." Had the half-conscious yearnings for a new stability and a new prosperity-at-any-cost not permeated the culture, Dior's venture might well have died stillborn.

Yet, no Machiavellian manipulator perpetrated the new look and its attendant cultural syndrome on women. The worst of it is that the values the new look subtly enshrined are not all bad. No more are those captured in Saint Laurent's phantasmagoric peasants. The reaction against scandal, corruption, impersonality, bureaucratization, the erosion of personal bonds, the loss of community, and on and on, runs rife through the Western world.

The various quests for a simpler, more organic past abound: Crafts flourish from the American suburbs to the Scottish highlands; American historians, so long the apostles of our individualistic and inherently entrepreneurial origins, are hot on the trail of the peasant character of colonial society; young people, facing the glutted job market, set up in communes, or bake bread, or sport long flowered skirts; the celebration of ethnic origins and identity prevails where only recently assimilation predominated; religious cults of all varieties are on the rise; and Claude Lévi-Strauss' structural anthropology, with its avowed preference for cold (unchanging or "primitive") societies over their hot (growth-oriented) counterparts, sets the tone for the most sophisticated intellectual work. The peasants are in.

But the peasant community so many seek constitutes a myth. The essential dynamic in this cultural explosion remains the reaction against the excesses, the depersonalization, the alienation of advanced industrial society. The reaction testifies to the extent of disillusionment with the values of our liberal, individualistic tradition and its political, social, and economic institutions. But our technology and our awesome interdependence are here to stay. A vast, collective fantasy, however compelling, will solve nothing. The exigencies of running the world reduce this cultural revolution to a blind delusion that may actually perpetuate the evils it thought to protest.

However brutal those realities of peasant existence which the fanciful re-creations staunchly deny, peasant societies did form communities and did embody genuine social and economic relationships. The social relations of production, upon which the current peasant mystique rests, remain intractably those of advanced capitalist society—of alienation and extreme individualistic fragmentation. And corporate capitalism, particularly in its multinational variant, seems prepared to live with an extraordinary variety of cultural forms and individual predilections. As the ethic of consumption steadily usurps the once privileged ethic of work, business adapts to selling anything to anyone. It even seems flexible enough to substitute personal and sexual liberation for religion as the opiate of the people. The order of multinational capitalism has moved so far from its original class and national roots as to tolerate seemingly endless quantities of disorder in daily life. The merciless logic of the computer can coexist with dizzying light shows of cultural pluralism. All business requires is a mounting tide of personal anxiety and dependency that can only be assuaged by ever-renewed purchase. Of fashion, it requires novelty, not meaningful or ordering cultural symbolism. Hence, the seven-billion-dollar-a-year cosmetics industry that feeds off the time-honored quest for beauty, but even more off the panicky fear of aging: a fear constantly exacerbated by stern reminders that retaining a job depends upon the appearance of youth. Women, long habituated to such self-eroding demons, may well wonder whether to gloat or to moan at their current assault upon men.

The peasant look turned explicitly to women to embody—to display—those values which cannot be assimilated into the nitty-gritty of modern life and must therefore be left to culture. Like children playing house, women may yet be persuaded to return to their dolls. And if the ERA goes down or the right to abortion is further compromised, or if the equilibrium of capitalist economies necessitates the abstinence of women from salaried and wage labor, perhaps those engaged in creating the new traditionalism will not notice.

The peasant look itself schizophrenically straddled the disparate tensions of multinational cultural anarchy and bourgeois class reaction. Unlike corporate permissiveness, the right-wing reaction has serious ideological commitments. Its vision of social order includes a full-scale assault on the substantive gains made by human liberation movements during the past decade, in particular the woman's movement. But its assault on so-called cultural disorder rests upon firm class commitments and an attempt to retain the social space appropriated by the bourgeoisie during the nineteenth century. In this respect, it has more sharply attacked the political and social dimensions of the women's movement than the cultural. The personal careers of the female leaders of the anti-ERA battalions constitute no secret. Only an implicit class position can reconcile the career performance with the ideological pronouncements. The sexuality of the "total woman" figures as the object of celebration, provided it remains contained within a traditional domestic role. The opposition to abortion flies for the jugular of working-class women on the assumption that their middle-class sisters can afford a few mistakes. Given individuals within the right-wing camp indisputably take the ideological questions with deep seriousness. Life would be much simpler if all or even most adherents of the traditional family, the domestic role of women, the right to life, and the sanctity of the free market and the American way of life could be dismissed as hypocrites, fools, or dupes. They cannot. Elements of sincerity and commitment notwithstanding, the reaction of traditionalism constitutes an objective class position, albeit at odds with that of other elements of the ruling class. And present cultural trends, those of fashion especially, suggest that class distinctions may be about to stage a real comeback.

VI.

The new look is said, to wit Bernadine Morris in the New York *Times* (July 29, 1976), to have succumbed only at the presentation of Saint Laurent's peasant collection. And by the logic of fashion itself, the analysis makes sense. The conventional or formal life of any fashion allows a given style to develop to a certain point, exhaust its paradigmatic possibilities, and ultimately give way to something new. The aesthetic dynamic cannot be unilaterally reduced to psychological, economic, or social determinants. In part, the survival of fashion with a capital F turns on surmounting context, on preserving the hegemony of high style against the mounting tide of utilitarianism.

By this logic, the most serious blow to the new look, *qua* Fashion, came not from Saint Laurent but from the early 1960s, from Jackie Kennedy's reign in the White House, and from the early glimmerings of the women's and other protest movements. Jackie's impact could easily be dismissed by those more preoccupied with deep social and cultural forces—all the more since she herself has moved on to pursue the extravagances of high fashion with all the avidity of an addict. But the A-line skirt, Chanel suit and bag, and relatively easy hairdo, in their deceptive simplicity, permitted successful copies in easy-to-wear, easy-to-care-for fabrics. A woman could wear them to the office with no cost to femininity or professionalism. They at least opened a bridge to the middle and lower-middle classes. As they gave way to pants suits, blunt-edged haircuts, and turtleneck sweaters, they opened the causeway across which the blue jeans, long hair, and beads of the street culture could pass. The meeting of the two created an easy, wearable fashion for women that owed little to the cutting rooms of Paris, which in turn went *prêt-à-porter*, adopting accepted practice along the way.

Those brief halcyon years, in which the heretofore extravagant *Times Magazine* fashion supplement, to say nothing of *Vogue* and *Harpers*, featured "the life and clothes of a woman like you," may now have run their course. But they, not Saint Laurent's brilliant counterattack, constituted the revolution. And these days, *Vogue*'s idea of the life and clothes of the working woman focuses on Mary Wells Lawrence with her "millions-of-dollars clout in a 'man's world,'" jetting home to Dallas from New York to spend the weekend with her husband, chairman of the board of Braniff International, or jetting off to recuperate at their hideaway, La Fiorentina, "the most beautiful house in the south of France." The MWL story is offered to reassure us all that a woman can make it to the top "without damage to husband, children, job, or self; without coming, finally, to resemble the career-driven neurotic of old Joan Crawford movies." Thus interpreted, the woman's movement should not require the ERA or abortion. You've come a long way baby, and all it took was a little cash. Such a woman can work in appropriately feminine designer creations and easily sport the latest extravaganzas in her leisure hours. How absurd to argue that reasonably simple and utilitarian clothes made any difference to a woman's position. And maybe they did not, to a woman. But what of women collectively?

Many could be found to argue that the dress of the 1960s and early 1970s sacrificed much of the style, glamour, and panache characteristic of true fashion—that the loss impoverished our culture as a whole. They may even have a point. But, they fail to explain why women should be held responsible for providing society as a whole with the illusion of grace and charm.

The so-called fashions of the late 1960s and early 1970s may actually have heralded the death of fashion as the bourgeois world had known it. The aesthetic cost of such an event would be high, but there should be ways other than a blind restoration of the past to meet the bill. Art, film, urban architecture, graffiti, parks: the possibilities for aesthetic expression are endless. Presumably, the point of such delights is to enhance human experience, not to constrict it—to experience self as perceiving self and object as object of perception—not to be trapped into the paralyzing experience of self as object. Women as the custodians of fashion differ less than they would like to think from women as the victims of rape. From Meg in *Little Women*, caught in the tentacles of *Vanity Fair*, to Gertrude Stein being fitted for her Chanel suit, to the memorable chapter on Jane's despairing shopping (her mother remembered years according to the clothes she had worn) in Gail Godwin's *Odd Woman*, women's literature abounds with women's delighting, anxious, desperate, compulsive relationships to their clothes. The visible self. But what if that facade becomes the only self? Well might *Ms.* and

Spare Rib both ask why women hate their bodies. As apparently all, or at least most, women do.

VII.

"Never a failure of taste, no rift in the deployment of nuances, but a communicative joy in living, an enchanting dynamism for a winter of radiating happiness." So spoke Paris *Vogue*. And *L'Officiel* promised its shiver-prone readers that they would spend "an exquisite winter." The subsequent issue of that prestigious organ of the *Syndicat de Couture* elaborated on the promise while reassuring its readers that the revolutionary upheaval would not be violent. New looks apparently not being enough, it proudly announced the new woman. "The new woman" appropriately lacks a verb—she does nothing, is subject of nothing. She exists as the reference point of fashion in a closed system that transforms her as potential subject into object. *L'Officiel,* undaunted, proceeded to inform its readers that "the enthusiasts—by far the most numerous"—were trumpeting far and wide: "Long live novelty!" (the *vive* of the French clearly echoing the traditional acclamation of monarchs). "Here is something that throws last year's models totally out of fashion." But should any have qualms, they may rest easy: The revolution "is not that of October, but rather that of July, very pacific, the most important since the 'New Look.'"

Bless those literate and savvy French journalists for having made it all so explicit. The ghost of the Bolshevik October Revolution hung heavy over Europe in the fall of 1976. The Italian elections, marked by notable Communist gains, sobered everyone with something to protect. The French bourgeoisie was regrouping to forestall, yet again, any income tax for the propertied. Class lines of a kind not visible in the United States seemed to get sharper every day. In the midst of the general malaise, to predict a radiant winter of joy was to display a willingness to ignore reality worthy of the magic of fairy tales. Joy was to come hard to those hit by the drought, to budgets crippled by inflation, to politicians facing falling currencies and mounting strikes. It was to come harder yet to the increasing unemployed, particularly the women being pressed out of the job market or denied advancement to make room for men. The 25% rise in fuel prices did not help, although it does help to explain the desperate insistence with which the new fashions promised warmth. The coy artificiality of fashion reporting has been with us for a long time, but rarely have those trivial phrases carried so much cynicism. And in preparation for dealing with it all, Valéry Giscard d'Estaing had his chair raised higher than those of his ministers and set about polishing up the emblems of royalty.

The Revolution of July, after all, was a bourgeois revolution. Altogether pacific: Bankers and entrepreneurs encouraged the Parisian working population to take to the streets for a couple of days of almost bloodless barricade-tending in order to permit a more tractable monarch, the mild businesslike Louis-Philippe, to replace his reactionary cousin. The change permitted a smoother functioning of French government and economic development with no threat to the social order. It inaugurated a period of solid bourgeois dominance in which the rich were encouraged to enrich themselves further, while their wives attended to dress and polite society, and the poor stayed in their place.

But the Revolution of July did not adequately do the job. Full industrial development and serious social choices exceeded the capabilities of the French bourgeoisie, which turned to Napoleon III. And Marx, in a book admired even by his harshest critics, explained Napoleon's relationship to the peasantry and the peasantry's relationship to plebiscitary dictatorship. Marx taunted "Napoleon The Little" with presiding over a farce, whereas his uncle had presided over a tragedy. Alas, not even Marx's genius could predict that a third go-round would threaten us with tragedy once again.

At present, with last year's victories in the municipal elections to encourage them, the French Communist and Socialist Parties stand poised on the threshold of national victory. That challenge goes far towards explaining the persisting validity of class consciousness in French society. It also helps elucidate the elements of cynical class consciousness in Saint Laurent's usurpation of popular sensibility. Domestically, French fashion mirrors the centralization of the French State. A strategy of restoring hierarchy haunts the French imagination. In this context, Saint Laurent's display of high fashion rejoins a political sensibility. But to the extent that *haute couture* increasingly serves less to dress individuals and more to sell the name of the designer as trademark for innumerable and disparate commodities, the peasant look also has a multinational dimension.

The United States is not France, nor yet England. For all its injustices, our democracy functions better, our people live better, and our women know a freedom and opportunity still denied to their European sisters. At the very moment of Saint Laurent's revolutionary collection, American fashion seemed to be asserting its own claims against the dominance of Paris. "The Year of the American Woman" fluttered across the pages of fashion magazines and the displays of the big New York stores. A discussion in *New York Magazine* referred to the increased participation of socialites in the organization and aspirations of Seventh Avenue and pointed to a trend towards quiet elegance and exclusive labels. If, as they claimed, everyone was to dress alike, then the name and quality of the model would become the distinguishing features. The trend echoed, although the article did not mention it, the trend in men's clothing inaugurated by Brummel.

Assuredly, the elegance of line and fabric, the subdued and functional apparel did not hinder the class divisions of nineteenth-century society. In such garb the white male bourgeoisie came close to conquering the world and spawned the technology and industrial production that did conquer it. The dress, in a sense, reflected the strength and weakness of the liberal ideology and democratic institutions of its wearers: It offered a model of human dignity (male) and the promise of individual freedom and advancement. Not everyone profited equally from the opportunity—a bitter recognition much with us today. But, the formal equality, whatever its limitations in practice, was better than anything else history had afforded. And a fashion that would embody women's possibility of joining that functional, work- and power-oriented mainstream has more to offer than the reactionary peasant alternative.

More, but perhaps no longer enough. The current fashion scene is so disordered as to defy simple prediction or interpretation. The important political questions, particularly the ERA, still hang in the balance. Spring fashion proposes two major themes: wanton and provocative rumpledness (a caricature of a workingman's fantasy of the female activists of the New Left) or prim and proper femininity. *Vogue* features wrinkled, ill-fitting jackets, with nothing underneath—and everyone knows nakedness teases more effectively under a coat than a nightgown; the most recent Bergdorf Goodman catalogue offers contemporary facsimiles of the pastel shirtdresses of the 1950s and short-sleeved, high-necked blouses with full skirts reminiscent of the late 1940s. The wary, however, would do well to think twice about the promises of individualistic diversity. The common theme of the disparate styles can be found in the return of spike heels for all occasions. The structural legacy of Saint Laurent, once the peasants are gone, lies in the return to waists, curves, longer skirts, and even padded and underwired bras. Without the brilliance of the peasant costume, the structure can easily support an insipid, neodomestic femininity.

Such clothes do not necessarily exclude women from the labor market. Indeed, *Glamour* recently ran an article elaborating the results of its poll of major businesses concerning their preferences in female attire. Preference may be too mild a word. For *Glamour* published the results along with five pictures of diversely dressed young women. The heading ran: Who got the Job? The winner who, should you have missed the point, owed her job to the way she was dressed, wore a soft, contemporary suit with a skirt. The runner-up wore a Diane von Furstenberg dress, identified as simply unexceptionable. The losers were dismissed as too severe (read: masculine)—in a pants suit, what else?—too trendy, and too informal. So much for the acceptance of diversity.

Corporate capitalism can assuredly adapt to female employees, even well-paid female employees, and all the more if they owe their jobs to their appearance rather than their ability. It may not be able to adapt so smoothly to full female employment. Buying off a sufficient number of middle-class women and attributing their success to special individual qualities might work as an antidote to the broad demands of the women's movement. And, in one of those strange historical coincidences in which ruling classes seem to specialize, it might also shore up the American class structure against the international epidemic of socialism. For, with the erosion through taxation and inflation of the professional bourgeoisie—doctors may constitute an exception, and a new magazine is projected to help doctors' wives spend their money—the new rich will be the two-salaried couples, salaried, of course, at a level high enough to justify the wife's working at all. With the rising cost of education and the decline of social services, especially day-care, such an arrangement will hardly benefit workingclass, much less minority, women. And bereft of a united movement backed up by constitutional guarantees, even successful women will remain more vulnerable, than they will want to acknowledge, to the dependency death-traps of female social identity.

VIII.

The peasant fantasy is not new. In 1938 a world, as yet barely recovering from the Depression, faced the acceleration of Hitler's aggression. Women were called upon to do their part: The fashion proposed them included a bunched, or "peasant" skirt and the first hint of a corset. In the words of James Laver, the historian of fashion, the new look pointed "at a new conception of woman, at the end of the woman-as-comrade ideal which had reigned ever since the emancipation of the First World War. Perhaps it is hardly necessary to add that the peasant skirt in question was an Austrian peasant skirt. It was the faint but unmistakeable echo of Hitler's '*Kirche, Kinder, Küche.*'"

Saint Laurent's vision has older and more noble origins: Like that enchanting but frivolous queen, his gilded cooption of harsh peasant experience might be read as telling increasingly unemployed professional and working women, worried about equality for themselves and bread for their families, that they, too, may eat cake.

Three

Placing Women's History in History

'Between me and the other world there is ever an unasked question . . . How does it feel to be a problem?'[1] Thus writes not Simone de Beauvoir, but W. E. B. DuBois. He is speaking, not of women, but of black people—a black male intellectual—within a white world. And he answers his own question: '. . . the Negro is . . . born with a veil, and gifted with second-sight in this American world—a world which yields him no true self-consciousness, but only lets him see himself through the revelation of the other world. It is a peculiar sensation, this double-consciousness, this sense of always looking at one's self through the eyes of others, of measuring one's soul by the tape of a world that looks on in amused contempt and pity. One ever feels his twoness—an American, a Negro; two souls, two thoughts, two unreconciled strivings; two warring ideals in one dark body, whose dogged strength alone keeps it from being torn asunder.'[2] DuBois poignantly insists upon his unwillingness to forgo either side of his twoness: he claims for himself and his people the freedom to be a black American. But fidelity to that twoness requires holding fiercely to both its elements. It is the tension itself, the dialectic of his sundered identity, that he wishes to live: distinct, but equal; of, but not wholly assimilated to. And the free living of that tension necessitates full recognition of the Black past, of a discrete Afro-American history.

It is far from my mind to trivialize the particular meaning of DuBois's words by simply identifying female and Afro-American experience. But however different the problems and histories of women and oppressed racial groups, the living of twoness applies to both. Joan Kelly has suggested as much in writing of the 'doubled vision' of feminist theory. And her remarks have addressed the double perspective of social and sexual oppression that must inform all feminist theory.[3] Increasingly, feminist scholars and theorists are recognizing the intersection of class and gender systems in all systems of male dominance, and, increasingly, they are agreeing, as Michelle Rosaldo has so strongly put it, that male dominance characterizes so much of known human social organization as to function as a general rule—for which, as with all rules, there may be an occasional exception, but no systematic disproof.[4]

I. One History or Two?

To the extent that male dominance, like class dominance, has obtained throughout human history, there is no women's history, nor forms of female power, apart from it. The wealth of studies of women produced in recent years might tempt us into thinking differently. There has been, and remains, so much to be uncovered. The annals of women's exploits, endurances, and contributions are growing steadily. It is now at least acknowledged that while men were performing the feats, building the institutions, producing the goods and cultures, ruling the peoples, and generally busying themselves with those activities we are wont to call history, women were invariably doing something—if only bearing more men to make more history and more women to permit them to do so. And we are now equipped to ask—sources permitting—just what were they doing? But adding women to the received account—especially in the form of a few more neglected worthies or a lot more descriptive social history—does not necessarily change anything substantive in our manner of writing history. Make no mistake, the inclusion of women within conventional historical narratives cannot be dismissed lightly. Their exclusion has been so total that every rectification must be welcome. The sheer quantitative accumulation of information alone will force choices—force us to drop standard material on men and hence sharpen the visibility of women within history. But adding women to history is not the same as adding women's history.

What, then, are the theoretical implications of placing women's history in history? Here, I shall suggest (1) that we must adopt gender system as a fundamental category of historical analysis, understanding that such systems are historically, not biologically, determined; (2) that the forms of male dominance vary historically and cannot be assimilated under the general rubric of patriarchy; (3) that simply to substitute women's history for mainstream history leaves us prisoners of precisely that pernicious status as 'other' to which mainstream history has assigned us; (4) that capitalism and the great bourgeois revolutions have tended to generalize gender difference as the custodian of displaced notions of hierarchy and dependence, and thus practically to repudiate their theoretical promises of equality for all; (5) that the expansion of capitalism and modern representative government has attempted to bind men of different classes, races, and ethnic groups together through the double promise of individualism in the public sphere and male dominance in the home; (6) that all the modern languages of social theory are impregnated with the ideological premises of this gender system; (7) that most modern institutions, including the purportedly neutral market, have systematically extended gender difference as a fundamental part of social order; (8) that official theories of the family and the sexual division of labour cannot be explained in functional terms, but must be understood as the product of class and gender struggle; and (9) that our dominant social theories have provided us with no adequate way to assess the indispensable contributions of women to collective life in society, including class and racial dominance on the one side and the resistance of the oppressed on the other.

The Recovery of Women's Roles

Adding women to history has led scholars to uncover and to chart the regular participation of women in almost all domains of social production and reproduction. But the majority of the evidence they have amassed pertains to arenas and activities that do not normally figure at the centre of conventional history—or do so only under the intentionally depersonalized processes of industrialization, modernization or institution-building. We can now demonstrate, what anyone with a modicum of sense already knew, that women as a group have performed socially necessary labour at least in proportion to their numbers in the population as a whole. We know that women have eased illness, attended childbirth, inspired and sustained religious groups, presided over arcane bodies of knowledge, including magic and religious cults. We know that they have forged bonds among themselves, struggled valiantly for political and social ideals in their own organizations and together with their male comrades, inaugurated and sustained institutions and networks that provided the very substance of the lives of communities.

Anthropologists, ethnographers, and imaginative social historians have recovered many of the previously neglected signs of women's large roles in all pre-capitalist social groups. Many of their insights have proved practically or metaphorically transferable. For those conversant with the literature, it is inviting to seek female powers, female spaces, even discrete female cultures or world-views within the life of any community.[5] Sensitive scholars like Natalie Davis have taught us to trace implicit gender relations, their affirmations and reversals, through cultural forms such as the charivari. We know much of the special and socially validated role of women in bread riots in particular and in defending the norms of the moral economy in general.[6] Pioneers of the first wave of the new women's history, including Nancy Cott,

Kathryn Sklar, Carroll Smith-Rosenberg and many more, have familiarized us with the special worlds of women within American society. More recent studies, including those by Ruth Bordin, Mari Jo Buhle, Carl Degler, William Leach, Winifred Wandersee and others, have placed greater emphasis on women's place in and contributions to the general development of American society and culture.[7] But this knowledge does not challenge the inescapable truth that the vast majority of those activities deemed worthy of the official record have been performed largely by and credited almost exclusively to male members of ruling classes.

As a coherent chronological and interpretive enterprise, women's history has been most successful with respect to the United States. The history of European women remains spotty, although the quality of discrete work is high. We should be hard pressed to write a consistent general history of European women, or even of the experience of women within a single European country. The history of English women seems rather more coherent than the history of many continental women, perhaps because national unity, precocious industrialization, and a visible and successful suffrage movement provide some obvious structure. But even in England, women's history has yet to secure a recognized place in the academy. And elite pretensions notwithstanding, social history and family history—whatever their merits and quality—do not provide adequate proxies for women's history. The continental countries that figure most prominently in historical scholarship have lacked strong national women's movements, at least until very recently, and have hardly been receptive to women's history as a discipline. Thus, despite excellent discrete studies, we lack coherent national histories of European women. For the moment, we make do with the *précieuses* of seventeenth-century France, the *Jüdischer Frauenbund*, Lyonnaise Protestants, Aleksandra Kollontai, Flora Tristan and the other identifiable groups and figures that particular scholars have studied.[8] Occasionally a work such as Richard J. Evans's *The Feminists* provides a comparative perspective. And the rich work on families, deviants and popular life, especially associated with the Annales School, offers passing insights on the experience of particular women. But even the most outstanding examples of this work, such as David Herlihy and Christiane Klapisch-Zuber's *Les Toscans et leurs Familles,* cannot properly be designated women's history. If work on inheritance and dowries has revealed much about the conditions of some women's lives, it has yet to be systematically integrated into a theory of women's history that directly addresses women's perceptions and experience.[9] And if writing the history of European women is difficult, to write the history of women in the rest of the world is more difficult yet, splendid monographs notwithstanding.

Even for the United States, the problems remain formidable. The most coherent picture to emerge so far is that of white Northeastern womanhood, with only sketches of white Southern and Western women. Black, Spanish-American, Chicana, Native American, Chinese-American women and others have yet to find a place in the standard accounts. Irish, Italian and Jewish-American women—as in lesser measure their Polish, Scandinavian, German, and Slav sisters—have achieved a foothold in historical consciousness thanks to the efforts of the new labour history. But to take only one small example, we know next to nothing about American women and Catholicism, much less about Catholic women's education. Northern women's evangelicalism has merited considerable attention, but that of Southern women, black or white, remains essentially unexplored. And if we are being taught to respect the strength and progressivism of the Women's Christian Temperance Union, we have no major modern study of the Young Women's Christian Association which rivalled it in numbers and influence and may have had a significant edge with respect to social reform on behalf of working women.[10] Withal, this partial catalogue of what we do not know is not intended as a reproach: the subject is young and thriving, and the gaps will be filled. Filling those gaps, however, will not automatically clarify the place of women's history in history.

Official History and Woman as 'Other'

The dominant tendency in American women's history has established a series of questions and hypotheses. The central debates concern the appropriate weight we should grant to personal and formal political achievements and values in women's lives; the importance of women's identification with the family; the social significance of women's *ad hoc* or informal powers within families or communities; the loss or gain in status for women attendant upon political or economic change (the American Revolution, industrialization), the changing nature and value of women's work. Scholars differ sharply on these and other questions. But despite disagreements, historians of women have tended to emphasize the distinctive attributes that differentiate the lives of all women from those of all men. They have drawn attention to the female life cycle—especially to recurrent and risky childbirth, but also to the particular experiences of youth and age, to the paucity of rites of passage, to women's special experience of medical practice. They have stressed the gap that separates most female lives from public events and have reminded us that the invention of reliable contraception has more decisively affected the lives of women than the majority of political revolutions.[11]

This line of thought leads towards a recognizable theory of women's history. It would, perhaps, be unfair to say that such a theory exclusively emphasizes the private character of female experience. It also points to the extension of women's private experience into the public realm in the wide range of activities referred to as social housekeeping. Recently, there has been a growing emphasis on the political significance of women's movements for social reform. Apparently, this emphasis derives from a general commitment to the significance of culture and gender as politics and a general commitment to minimizing the significance of class, including class differences among women. Obviously, serious attention to gender as a category of historical analysis obliges the historian, or indeed the social critic, to take full account of the role of gender in the elaboration of forms of political power— but hardly to substitute it outright for class. Much of the work that emphasizes gender to the exclusion of class still fails to confront the hard truth emphasized by Barbara Leslie Epstein: the legacy of domesticity may have empowered women to speak out on behalf of particular moral values and may have bequeathed them networks from which to construct movements and alliances, but it severely hampered their view of themselves, of their proper social roles and of their goals. It also ignores the class foundations of the varieties of domestic life and women's conflicting interpretations of public issues depending upon their class and ethnic origin. Thus, Carl Degler's discovery that the interests of the family and the interests of women's personal development were 'at odds' throughout the nineteenth and twentieth centuries falls woefully short of offering either a theory of women's history or a theory of women's place in mainstream history. Degler correctly identifies the paradox that the modern family and modern feminism emerged in the same historical period, but he wilfully ignores the class relations—the political economy and social relations—that are indispensable to understanding either. Degler, in fact, offers no challenge to the dominant theory of American women's history, but merely a specific synthesis of the monographic work on which that theory rests. Nor has this dominant theory been seriously challenged by the recent arbitrary attempts to broaden its purported political significance. An occasional study, such as Jacquelyn Dowd Hall's fine book on Jesse Daniel Ames, wisely bypasses the theory entirely in favour of setting forth the complexities of specific women's social action.[12] But as a rule, the theory that informs most work in American women's history implicitly accepts the dominant male view of women as 'the Other' and merely attempts to turn it to advantage. This view of women's history, which at its most rich and complex has indeed taught us much, does not necessarily challenge mainstream history. Or rather, it poses a challenge so extreme as to make interchange next to impossible.

The nearly universal exclusion of women from history as it has been written and taught has been no accident or mindless oversight. The best available evidence suggests that the great world-historical religions, like powerful and successful states, have systematized and extended the ubiquitous patterns of male dominance that pervade most societies. The same can be said of most formal institutions, including the modern professions, labour unions and political parties. In important ways, capitalism accelerated this process, as did, at least initially, the great bourgeois revolutions that consolidated its political foundations. Western imperialism exported it. And few socialist revolutions have done much to correct the trend. Precisely those institutions and groups most interested in producing histories as the record of their own rise and mission have reflected male intentions. The historical subject has, overwhelmingly, been male. In this perspective, history records man's escape from and triumph over the submerging claims of domesticity and nature (closely identified with the engulfing feminine). Man has made history by defining not-man as Other and then identifying his success with the triumph of universal values of justice and order.

With rare exceptions, women's history has addressed precisely what was left out of official history. Historians of women can, therefore, be tempted to reject all official history as irrelevant to female experience.[13] But this strategy, in its purest form, perpetuates many of the most pernicious myths of official history. For the strategy capitulates to official history's insistence upon the universal claims of female biology. The confrontation between women's history, as it has taken shape during the past decade, and mainstream history offers a special opportunity to rethink the basic premises that inform historical interpretation—but only if the confrontation engages both parties. Women, as members of one sex, but also members of all societies, must cultivate and take pride in that twoness of which DuBois wrote. They must also recognize that even their identification as a gender is itself an historical construction. The domination of women by men figures at the core of the domination of specific classes, races, ethnic groups, and peoples. It intersects with all forms of subordination and superordination and cannot be understood apart from them.

II. Gender Systems and Historical Analysis

Feminist scholarship has correctly insisted upon the social construction of gender. It is now widely accepted that all societies promote identities and roles taken to be appropriate to the genders and, normally, present those identities and roles as natural emanations of sexual difference. The relations between any innate biological difference and socially promulgated gender differentiation may be left aside for the moment; historians must accept the gender identities and roles that different societies assign to males and females as historical facts that require historical analysis. They must also recognize the characteristics ascribed to males and females as interrelated, as integral parts of a dominant gender system.[14] The primary theoretical implication of the confrontation between women's history and official history is this recognition of gender system as a primary category of historical analysis—as deeply ingrained in social and economic formations and the political institutions to which they give rise as class relations. The dominant gender system in any society delineates the authoritative versions of masculinity and femininity, the socially legitimated opportunities for living one's life as a male or a female. In addition, the gender system subsumes under gender differentiation much of the natural world and the varieties of human activities and experiences. The tremendous variation, across time and space, in the gender-specific allocation of forms of labour (tasks), attributes and moral responsibilities clearly demonstrates the mutability of gender systems. It is fruitless to look for a uniform oppression of women, or a universal form of male dominance. But it is necessary to search out and analyse the allocation of roles and identities between the genders in order to understand the dynamics of any social system.

Understanding the gender system as a critical feature of all social relations simultaneously inaugurates the essential restoration of women to historical process and moves us beyond the dead-end of attempting to establish sexual difference as an agent of historical causation. It enables us to understand women as full participants in the human struggle to survive and to triumph over nature in the sense of creating a distinctly human world. But we must also avoid jumping from the frying pan of ubiquitous sexual conspiracy into the fire of complacent functionalism. The female outrage that fuelled much of the early feminist scholarship and still informs some of it has forced us to question the purportedly natural assumptions that women did not figure in the great sagas of power because of their childbearing responsibilities in particular, or their biological destiny—read inferiority—in general. We have now learned—not exactly to our surprise, but nonetheless not without pain—that as a rule women were actively excluded from the corridors of power as well as from the halls of learning. But, however systematic the exclusion of women, the men who launched those activities were not primarily concerned with women at all: men chose to build states and fight wars in ways that may have been misogynist, but essentially, on the most historically significant level, they were primarily concerned with winning wars or building states. They acted as agents of classes and communities and as such, sought to expand the power of the community or class they represented.

This basic recognition of the complexity of human motivation and the interdependence of members of families, members of communities, and of classes themselves has encouraged historians of working peoples and oppressed ethnic and racial groups to look closely at the social, economic, and ideological bonds that link those with objectively opposed interests. The lines of argument are familiar. For example, working classes in advanced nations have frequently supported the imperialist policies of their leaders or laid down their lives in wars against their working-class brothers of other nations. Working people and oppressed groups have frequently acquiesced, at least to some extent, in ideologies that cast them as inferior members of the collectivity. Some groups of workers have accepted what we might, with the benefit of hindsight, call precarious and short-term economic gains in exchange for the objective weakening of the position of their class within society as a whole. Women committed to active social roles or to greater sexual freedom for themselves have opposed suffrage. Members of all such groups, including women, have at times sufficiently accepted the hegemony of the dominant ideology to accept its definitions of excellence as models for themselves.

Historians and social theorists have disagreed in their appraisal of such strategies. Not so long ago, it was fashionable in left circles to speak of the false consciousness of the working class. It was equally fashionable among Whig celebrants of the status quo to praise the wise espousal of individual mobility. The dominant tendency in American historiography and social thought has treated such painful compromises with things as they are as functional adaptation. Such functionalism effectively removes conflict, struggle and necessarily hard choices from historical process: society, like an organism, unfolds with its component members finding their appropriate niches. Except for the proliferation of jargon, it disconcertingly resembles Panglossian optimism or, perhaps, a beneficent utilitarianism.

Functionalism weighs heavily on women's history. For functionalists early paid attention to the reproduction of social values and institutions and to the special importance of the family in society. Fortified by their interests in economics, anthropology and psychology, functionalists willingly acknowledged the importance of family life—and indeed of women's roles—in the stabilization and reproduction of social relations and political cultures. Their thought invited the inclusion of female experience, but it had passed verdict on the meaning of that experience before the work even began. Women naturally fit into familial roles; their activities naturally complement those of their men; they naturally provide a nurturing climate for the inculcation of the young into their preordained adult roles. Furthermore, women's natural familial roles governed their access to the public sphere—to those economic, social and political roles that naturally accrued to men.[15] To the extent that this line of thought came to dominate family history, it provoked many historians of women to criticize sharply the identification of women and the family as a natural unit of study. In fact, even in Western European and American societies with their unusually high proportions of people never married, most people did spend most of their lives as members of families. And thanks to the inhospitability of the workplace, the constraints of the law, and the informally licensed violence against women who trespassed alone upon the public space, most women did find in the family not merely their principal arena of activity, but the major source of their social identity as well. But this simple association reveals little about the terms upon which women formed families of procreation, the powers they derived from family membership, or the relations between women and men within families. Nor does it reveal the extent to which families themselves were products of historical process—explicit political and ideological policies.

Family History Reconsidered

Families are not merely the fundamental unit of community, they are—or have been until very recently—the fundamental units of production and governance. With all our historical sophistication, it remains difficult to shake the model of the family as biological and affective unit of parents and offspring, perhaps augmented or extended by various kin. Yet anthropologists have demonstrated how many forms the family can take, and by now we should recognize that the critical historical development from the Western perspective has been the emergence of political and economic conditions that endowed individual paternity with the control of women and their offspring.[16]

Historians of medieval and early modern Europe, taking paternity for granted, have distinguished between family and household so as to separate out consanguineal and social relations. They have traced the winnowing away of the social chaff from the familial grain. They have especially associated changes in the affective and ideological representation of the family with changes in the socially prescribed role of women and with the new emphasis on motherhood and conjugal intimacy. In this complex and far from unilinear process, the wide variety of family and household forms in which women have participated has not represented a natural extension of an unchanging female role; rather, the family has constituted the primary arena in which gender systems have been reproduced and transformed. In this sense, placing women's history within history forces a substantive reinvestigation of the nature of family relations as gender relations—possibly gender conflict—within the context of social, economic and political relations.[17]

Just as the model of the natural nuclear family remains difficult to shake, so does the modern model of individualism. Against this standard of individual autonomy and responsibility we tend to weigh the indisputable dependence of women upon the family. A far more useful working assumption is the interdependence of all individuals in all pre-capitalist and most capitalist societies. The medieval peasant family, the Genoan artisan family, the American frontier family, the immigrant working-class family, the black share-cropping family, the modern French peasant family, the urban or rural working-class European family—all required the full participation of all family members. But the terms of participation varied considerably. Many historians, including, for example, Leonore Davidoff, Laura Oren and John Faragher, find significant asymmetry in either the contributions of men and women or the power and status taken to derive from their respective contributions. In short they find systematic oppression of women by men within the family. Others like Joann Vanek claim to find symmetry, albeit with difference, in the contributions of men and women to the domestic economy. Implicitly, Louise Tilly, Joan Scott, Tamara Hareven and others who emphasize the importance of family strategies would seem to agree.[18] In fact, the chances are excellent that the relative status and power of men and women within families wax and wane according to material conditions and ideological tendencies beyond the immediate control of family members, as well as according to the temperaments of those concerned.

For most of recorded history the family has mediated the economic, social, and political participation of individuals in the larger communities of which their families are part. But this mediation cannot be reduced to some minor adjustments. Dominant classes have normally promoted distinct family policies. The very model of family that we now so take for granted resulted directly from the determination of early modern state-builders to provide themselves with the most governable population possible. To this end, albeit in different ways, both the French and English monarchs promoted the definition of the family as a unit and the special authority of the father within the family. To achieve their ends, they mustered the force of law, emerging police, tax collectors and the public institutions they were attempting to put in place. To drive the lesson home, they long continued to rely upon an explicit patriarchal ideology to justify their own rule.[19]

This early modern patriarchy sought aid and comfort from much older practices and ideologies. But pious self-justifications notwithstanding, it was also attempting to inaugurate a newly comprehensive and ruthless form of government. Its fatherly tentacles sank deeper into the lives of disparate communities than tradition would ever have countenanced. To the men, the fathers of families whom it drew into its network, it offered the recompense of genuine rule over the women of their own families. But this new domestication of women came apace with the important, and frequently brutal, transformation of class relations, with the preparation of a traditional aristocracy for the responsibilities of capitalist agriculture, capital accumulation and rational self-governance.[20]

The patriarchal monarchs did their job too well. The classes they schooled in the discipline of rational governance rapidly decided to dispense with the

nominal father and assume responsibility themselves. The succession of bourgeois revolutions dismantled patriarchy in government—and frequently beheaded patriarchal monarchs to bring the lesson home. As I have argued
elsewhere, the theoretical justifications for this new interpretation of sovereignty as the emanation of the individual and his absolute property rights
took a necessary detour through familial relations, positing the equality of
man and wife within the family as the logical foundation for individual autonomy and representative government. The customs of the country, not to
mention economic transformation, militated against women realizing this
theoretical equality in practice. In fact, the repudiation of legally sanctioned, hierarchical class distinctions cost more than a few aristocratic
women the luxury of dabbling in court politics. The consolidation of capitalism, succeeded by the rationalization of economic relations and eventually industrialization, complemented the political developments in gradually
circumscribing their participation in all so-called public activities. The public defeat of patriarchy, its repudiation as a viable model of relations between
men, left men, if anything, a freer hand to rule their women at home. The
father-king is dead, long live the father.[21]

III. Women in the Age of Capital

Much recent work in social history and the history of women has clustered
around the transition to capitalism and the great bourgeois political revolutions—also variously described as industrialization, urbanization and
modernization. Throughout this work runs a steady debate about the improvement or deterioration wrought by these changes in the lives of women
and working people. As yet we have little work of a comparative nature and
little that links the political to the socio-economic changes. But even the
most cursory reading of the evidence reveals the disconcerting paradox that
the ostensibly great political and economic advances frequently trailed apparent or real losses for both women and workers. Perhaps the questions that
centre on better or worse, on loss or gain, may not be properly cast. The new
work is nonetheless furnishing the materials that will begin to permit us to
think about social systems in a more comprehensive fashion and to recognize the gender system and the division of labour by sex—in all their permutations of class and race—as central to any social system.

The contribution of the bourgeois-democratic revolutions to the social
and political individualism of women requires special mention. The bourgeois-
democratic revolutions cannot be fully understood independent of the capitalist social relations they consolidated. Like the ideology of bourgeois
individualism, capitalism—and especially industrial capitalism—potentially
offered a much greater measure of independence and of equality with men

than had previous class relations. Yet, many historians of women, like many historians of working people, have been led, by their opposition to the inequities of capitalism in practice, to romanticize life in pre-capitalist—and especially pre-industrial—societies. This romanticization has been marvellously encouraged by the sanctimonious and complacent hypocrisy of those who preach the upward and onward virtues of modernization and the triumph of the middle classes. Both sides of this heated debate tend to ignore the decisive implications of structural transformation. With respect to women, both capitalism and bourgeois ideology profoundly altered the nature of male dominance. Neither abolished it, and, in the short run, both may have intensified it, at least with respect to particular groups of women.

However complex the issues, it is essential to recognize that pre-bourgeois societies systematically favoured the subordination of women to men and the exclusion of women, as individuals, from public power, whereas bourgeois society offered women not merely a new model of individualism, but previously unimaginable possibilities for practical equality with men. Science, technology, and medicine increasingly reduced the physiological differences between men's and women's contributions to socially necessary labour to insignificance. Machines permitted women to do much the same work as men. Medical advances decreased the risk of death in childbirth and the risk of infant death, thereby decreasing the number of children a woman needed to bear to contribute to reproduction. The spread of contraceptive devices permitted women to limit their pregnancies without renouncing or curtailing their sexual relations. Urbanization offered women the possibility of surviving independent of a family or household. Modern schooling increasingly offered them access to literacy.

Despite, or perhaps because of, their potential contributions to female independence and equality, bourgeois ideology and capitalist social relations both raised massive barriers to female individualism. Both marshalled a formidable combination of custom and modern science to justify women's subordination; both invited the alliance of men across class lines to sustain it. New denigrations of female nature, like new celebrations of female needs for protection, informed the theory and practice of excluding women from full social and political participation. Over time many of these barriers fell before the determined struggles of women on their own behalf. Withal, the legacy of exclusion is so deeply embedded in our political, social and economic relations that women as a group look ever more like an oppressed and exploited economic class. It is reasonable to doubt that the advanced capitalist nations could now provide economic equality for their female populations, but their inability to do so results from their economic structure—from capital's need to extract surplus value—not from any necessary logic of the ideology of individualism. It should, however, make us thoughtful that, logic and promise notwithstanding, capitalism has derived such profit from the oppression of women. In practice, its special forms of male dominance helped to produce and reproduce those class relations which have served it so well.

The Bourgeois Construction of Gender

The term 'patriarchy' has plagued all attempts to describe the persistence of male dominance over women and children. It cannot fruitfully be extended beyond its specific historical manifestations. Simply to identify the rule of the father with paternal dominance within discrete families or households abstracts from the social and political relations that constitute different societies. Patriarchy is not merely a relation between men and women, but one between men and other men. And patriarchy evokes not merely the practices of domination, but their representation and legitimation as well. The norms of a patriarchal society in which sovereignty and authority are taken to derive from the innate rights of fathers and society as a whole is represented as a familial organization are in fundamental contradiction to those of a bourgeois society which prides itself on its rationalism and individualism—at least for its fully participating male members. Innumerable variations and gradations separate pure patriarchy from pure individualism. The early bourgeois societies sought to retain as many patriarchal vestiges as possible, at least with respect to the control of women and labour. They also cherished pious patriarchal metaphors to validate a domination increasingly divorced from patriarchal institutions. For the practice and ideology of absolute property and of citizenship were fundamentally at variance with those of traditional hierarchy and patriarchy. Even the modern slave system of the American South departed from traditional patriarchy in its special combination of outright ownership of labour with a new paternalistic ideology. In seigneurial systems, serfs were not owned and their servile status, transmitted by the father, not the mother, provided a safety valve against identifying their condition either with a thing that is owned or with an innate, biological destiny. And, as Linda Kerber has demonstrated, when American males consolidated their vision of individual autonomy in the concept of citizenship, they felt obliged to formulate a complementary concept of Republican motherhood rather than to rely upon older patriarchal notions of hierarchical dominance. As these examples and many others demonstrate, a distinctive bourgeois paternalism indisputably persisted in a variety of forms in all capitalist societies, and bourgeois law brought incalculable assistance to men's domination over their women. But we obscure more than we clarify in equating this paternalism and this dominance with patriarchy proper, as we do by conflating the forms of paternalism and dominance experienced by women in different countries and of different classes and races.[22]

Male assault upon formal patriarchy was usually accompanied by the elaboration of an explicit ideology of separate spheres. Much ink has flowed in recent years over the appropriateness of separate spheres as an accurate description of the sexual division of labour in bourgeois societies. Yet there is no doubt that the concept figured significantly in the self-representations of bourgeois societies. The problem lies not in the emergence of the ideology, but in the confidence that the representations and exhortatory prescriptions mirrored practice. Lower-class women assuredly did not have access to the material security that would have permitted the full cultivation of true womanhood and full-time motherhood that the literature advised. Even for well-to-do women, the removal of productive labour from the household was a long drawn-out process. The cleavage between home and market remained less than perfect. Changing patterns of work, consumption, leisure—like changing notions of time, the work ethic and individual identity—bound the two as much as they differentiated them. It remains, nonetheless, beyond dispute that the idea of separate spheres, however complex the reality, enjoyed important ideological status. It designated roles and invited their acceptance; it helped to legitimate the economic dependence of women upon men and the exclusion of women from the expanding worlds of politics, business, the professions and organized labour; it proposed a model of womanhood that paradoxically permitted a greater licence in the exploitation of women who did not enjoy freedom from labour-force participation; it cast a veil over the contradictions that divided women by race and class, and it afforded even privileged women no access to the experience of authoritative selfhood that for men was embodied in the notions of property, work and political responsibility.[23]

The concept of separate spheres has deep roots in the gender differentiation at the core of all world-views and social formations. Bourgeois society cannot, in this respect, be credited with inventing separate spheres, but it can be credited with promoting and generalizing the ideology of separate spheres as the custodian of displaced notions of hierarchy. It thus disembedded—to borrow, by analogy, from Karl Polanyi's discussion of the capitalist market[24]—gender difference. Where traditionally this difference had figured in all explanations of the world as it is, the very fact of difference became an ideological justification for collective male and class dominance in a society that claimed to draw its identity from the freedom of individuals. The pervasive division of labour by sex cut across class lines, which were increasingly subordinated to it, at least in official ideology. And since the division of labour by sex was taken to be a natural extension of gender identity, it tended to become wholly identified with the gender system that itself came to absorb older notions of hierarchy and dependence. In this respect, the representations of gender difference came to dominate the most

fundamental representations of social order. In particular, it came at once to
shape and be embedded in even the most scientific analyses of social and
economic life.

Elizabeth Fee, Charles Rosenberg, Carroll Smith-Rosenberg, Yvonne
Knibiehler and others have demonstrated that the anthropological and medical views of women arose as a product of larger ideological projects. The
discourse on female nature can be traced to the origins of modern anthropological and medical thought, but it attained maximum coherence and scientific hegemony towards the end of the nineteenth century, at about the
same time as did the parallel discourse on innate racial characteristics. From
the perspective of political science, Susan Moller Okin has recently argued
for the persistence of a functional view of women in political thought. Her
provocative work nonetheless eschews the specific historical development
of political and social thought and thus tends to slight the very special discourse about women that can be shown to pervade all modern political and
social theory.[25]

Reproductive Strategies and Class Struggle

The formidable role of economic discourse in shaping the perceptions and
practice of modern gender relations requires special mention. The science
of economics, with its roots in Political Arithmetik and Political Economy,
came of age with the extension of the capitalist mode of production. From
the outset, it provided the formal analysis of capitalism, the scientific self-
consciousness of capital and the social relations of production and reproduction it engendered. Understandably it tended to exercise its calculations
upon those activities and relations which lent themselves to calculation, especially the surplus produced by domestic units or the non-domestic buying
and selling of labour. For centuries such market activities had been the marginal by-products of the reproduction of the mass of agricultural society.
The triumph of the capitalist mode of production generalized and systematized these marginal activities. Between the twin poles of absolute property
and the buying and selling of labour-power, much of the fundamental economic life of society came under the aegis of market exchange and became
an integral part of the accumulation of capital. Hence, it became customary
to speak of market activity as productive. But the human participants in
the process no doubt saw it differently. Specifically, the labour of women—
although not only of women—was consistently classified as non-productive
if it did not command a wage: the grinding expenditure of human energy
and the usefulness of its products had nothing to do with the issue. The critical transformation occurred not so much from reproduction to production,
or from subsistence to market, but rather from the transformation of the

components of reproduction or subsistence into commodities. It was thus the source of reproduction or subsistence that changed. The wage gradually replaced the peasant holding or the individual shop as the cornerstone of reproduction. Only from the perspective of capital can wage-labour be called productive, and only because it generates exchange-value and surplus-value, not because of the inherent quality of its products. There is no criterion other than the participation in exchange-value and the production of surplus-value that would justify calling the labour that produces the loaf of Wonder Bread productive and that which produces a homemade loaf unproductive. The cultural and psychological by-products of this process include the sentimentalization of the homemade loaf and the attendant pressure on women to continue producing use-values in order to demonstrate their womanly qualities.

It is a measure of the success of capitalism as a world-view that its preferred distinctions between production and reproduction, subsistence and market, public and private, acquired such hegemony. It is a measure of the success of capitalism as a social system that so many political and economic institutions enforced these distinctions. For women, their relative exclusion from this process of commodification went hand-in-glove with their exclusion from full individualism. Only with the generalization of the capitalist mode of production did the purportedly natural relation between the family, as mediator of exchange- and use-values, and capital take shape.

Initially, women played a rather more important role in early industrial activity than has commonly been acknowledged. We have come to know a good deal about the migration of whole families into the mills. Only with the advent of a more mature industrial system were the respective patterns of labour-force participation for women and men sharply differentiated. This pattern reflects the wholesale transfer of the agricultural family unit to an industrial setting and its subsequent restructuring. It also presupposes the prior dislocation of the family from its agricultural holding. In other patterns, for example in France, the United States, and even Japan, agricultural families retained a hold on their agricultural moorings long after the family farm could support all of its members. Under these conditions, as Thomas Dublin has argued for the Lowell mill girls, unmarried daughters would likely be the most disposable members of the family work-force. Daughters, then, along with other indigent single women who risked becoming a charge on public resources, migrated or were assigned to labour in the new mills and factories. From the perspective of the rural division of labour by sex, they were following their gender-appropriate task of spinning (or, later, as in Marlhes, ribbon making) into the new place of work. From the perspective of employers, they seemed to promise a docile and tractable labour force.

Thus the early accommodation of the family to nascent industrial capital-ism was to be found in precisely that labour-force participation of women upon which both capitalists and workers would frown.[26] As factory work and wage-labour moved from a marginal or supplementary contribution to the livelihoods of increasing numbers of working people to their founda-tion, the wage-labour of working-class women was increasingly governed by the norms of the dominant culture, reinforced by the gender-specific structure of industrial capitalism. It took generations for the working class— and then only its dominant section—to establish its right to a male wage that would afford a viable family subsistence. Until that time, all members of the working-class family contributed to family income, although they tried their best to avoid the direct labour-force participation of married women.[27]

It has become common to ascribe the general absence of married women from the labour force to one or another family strategy. The arguments about the persistence of traditional values, childbearing and the need for the mother at home are familiar. We now also know, thanks to the work of Heidi Hartman, Claudia Goldin and others, that the workplace did not encourage female participation on equal terms with men or reward consistent labour-force participation with long-term increases in wages. Labour market seg-mentation reinforced, if it did not directly contribute to, working people's adherence to the standards of the ideology of separate spheres. Workers and bosses, however sharp their differences on other matters, concurred in dis-couraging the employment of married women: at least women at home spared class struggles over the control of women and their time. Yet those black women studied by Elizabeth Pleck apparently chose the role of work-ing mother in order to free at least some of their children for education in the interests of advancement in the next generation.[28]

The dominant patterns, in short, were neither necessary nor inherently functional. They represented a specific compromise between antagonistic classes at a specific historical moment. The experience of the working class and, hence, the reproductive strategies it adopted were structured by the development of capitalism as a mode of production. And, to the extent that a powerful association emerged between women, the domestic sphere, use-values and traditional values, that association itself was a product of capi-talism, not a hold-over from an earlier social order. But the consequences of this compromise still weigh upon women's access to economic equality with men. And the identification of separate spheres with the economic metaphors of production and reproduction as well as with the means by which economic value is calculated reaches to the centre of our collective perceptions and values, including our historical theories.

The Challenge of Women's History

We have learned much about women's social participation. Their labour, normally relegated to the category of use-values, permitted the operation of farms, the survival of working-class families and the forging of community institutions. Long before they received the vote, women joined actively in the political life of their communities and nations. They participated in strikes or supported strikers. They organized reform groups, circulated petitions, pressured politicians and legislatures, organized for suffrage and against lynching, campaigned for peace movements, labour legislation reform, and educational reform, and fought for temperance. Their charitable, missionary and club activities all carried political implications. Frequently working specifically for themselves and other women, they always worked for specific classes, communities, ethnic and racial groups or nations. The world we have inherited could not have been built without them, neither the bad in that world nor the good. They worked for all contending parties—for the Klan as well as against lynching.

Women's history demonstrates the relation of the officially powerless to the success of the powerful, but the contributions of women have not been much valued.[29] And there is a bitter irony in that commonplace observation. For in truth, the undervaluation of women has not only led to the slighting of women's participation in slave revolts, *jacqueries,* strikes and revolutions; it has also led to the slighting of their formidable contribution to the building of slave societies, the suppression of *jacqueries,* the consolidation of big business and the efforts at counter-revolution. Women did develop discrete values, frequently in conflict with those of the men of their own group and frequently in common with specific sensibilities of women of other groups. But the foundations of female values and self-consciousness lay in the tension between their exclusion from the public worlds of exchange-value and political power and the values they had developed within the interstices of the male-dominated world. The prevailing myth of woman-as-Other would encourage us to lump the wide range of women's experiences under the oppression of womanhood. But if we have learned anything, it must be that we must uncover the history of women in all its tragic complexity.

The history we know has been written primarily from the perspective of the authoritative male subject—the single, triumphant consciousness. Much history has, in fact, rested upon the determination to deny ambiguity, conflict and uncertainty. It has served to provide worthy pedigrees for individuals, rising classes, nations, cultures and ideologies. Whatever their differences, women share the experience of having been denied access to an authoritative self as women. The twoness of which DuBois wrote permeates women's experience. In this sense, women's history challenges mainstream history not to substitute the chronicle of the female subject for that of the male, but rather to restore conflict, ambiguity and tragedy to the centre of historical process: to explore the varied and unequal terms upon which genders, classes and races participate in the forging of a common destiny.

Notes

[The frequent use of periods in titles rather than colons reflects the house style at the *New Left Review,* as does the use of single rather than double quotation marks.]

1. W. E. Burghardt DuBois, *The Souls of Black Folk,* New York 1964, p. 15.

2. Ibid, pp. 16–17.

3. Joan Kelly, 'The Doubled Vision of Feminist Theory: A Postscript to the "Women and Power" Conference,' *Feminist Studies* [5, no. 1] (Spring 1979), pp. 216–27.

4. M. Z. Rosaldo, 'The Use and Abuse of Anthropology: Reflections on Feminism and Cross-Cultural Understanding,' *Signs* 5, No. 3 (Spring 1980), pp. 389–417, esp. 394.

5. See, among many, Michelle Z. Rosaldo & Louise Lamphere, (eds.), *Women, Culture and Society,* Stanford 1974; Rayna Reiter, (ed)., *Towards an Anthropology of Women,* New York 1976; Shirley Ardner, (ed.), *Perceiving Women,* London 1975, and *Defining Females—The Nature of Women in Society,* New York 1978; Ernestine Friedl, 'The Position of Women: Appearance and Reality,' *Anthropological Quarterly* 40 (1967), pp. 97–108; Susan Carol Rogers, 'Women's Place: A Critical Review of Anthropological Theory,' *Comparative Studies in Society and History* 20, No. 1 (1978), pp. 123–62; Lucienne Roubin, 'Male Space and Female Space Within the Provençal Community,' in R. Forster & O. Ranum, (eds.), *Rural Society in France,* Baltimore 1977; Françoise Zonabend, *La mémoire longue. Temps et Histoires au village,* Paris 1980. For recent works that emphasize the constraints on women's social roles, see, among many, A. Kuhn & A. M. Wolpe, (eds.), *Feminism and Materialism,* London 1978; Kate Young, Carol Wolkowitz and Roslyn McCullagh, (eds.), *Marriage and the Market. Women's Subordination in International Perspective,* London 1981; Monique Etienne and Eleanor Leacock, (eds.), *Women and Colonization. Anthropological Perspectives,* New York 1980; Maurice Godelier, 'The Origins of Male Domination,' *NLR* 127 (May–June 1981), pp. 3–17.

6. Natalie Zemon Davis, *Society and Culture in Early Modern France,* Stanford 1975; Olwen Hufton, 'Women and the Family Economy in Eighteenth-Century France,' *French Historical Studies* IX (1975), pp. 1–22, and her *The Poor in Eighteenth-Century France,* New York & London 1975; Mary Johnson, 'Old Wine in New Bottles: The Institutional Changes for Women of the People During the French Revolution,' in Carol R. Berkin and Clara M. Lovett, (eds.), *Women, War and Revolution,* New York 1980, pp. 107–44; Darlene Gay Levy and Harriet Branson Applewhite, 'Women of the Popular Classes in Revolutionary Paris, 1789–1795,' *loc. cit.,* pp. 9–36; Nicole Castan, 'La criminalité familiale dans le ressort du Parlement de Toulouse (1690–1730),' in A. Abbiateci, (ed.), *Crimes et criminalité en France sous l'Ancien Régime, 17e–18e siècles,* Paris 1971; E. P. Thompson, 'The Moral Economy of the English Crowd in the Eighteenth Century,' *Past and Present* 50 (1971), pp. 76–136.

7. Nancy Cott, *The Bonds of Womanhood,* New Haven 1977; Kathryn Kish Sklar, *Catharine Beecher. A Study in American Domesticity,* New Haven 1973; Carroll Smith-Rosenberg, 'The Female World of Love and Ritual,' *Signs* 1, No. 1 (Autumn 1975). See also, Nina Auerbach, *Communities of Women. An Idea in Fiction,* Cambridge (Mass.)

1978; Nina Baym, *Woman's Fiction. A Guide to Novels by and about Women in America, 1820–1870*, Ithaca & London 1978; Keith E. Melder, *Beginnings of Sisterhood. The American Woman's Rights Movement, 1800–1850*, New York 1977; Susan Phinney Conrad, *Perish the Thought. Intellect and Women in Romantic America, 1830–1860*, New York 1976. The favourable interpretation of women's bonds and values was sharply attacked, but the importance of their existence confirmed by Ann Douglas, *The Feminization of American Culture*, New York 1977. The more recent studies include, Ruth Bordin, *Woman and Temperance. The Quest for Power and Liberty, 1873–1900*, Philadelphia 1981; Mari Jo Buhle, *Women and American Socialism 1870–1920*, Urbana, Chicago, London, 1981; Carl Degler, *At Odds. Women and the Family in America from the Revolution to the Present*, New York & Oxford 1980; William Leach, *True Love and Perfect Union. The Feminist Critique of Sex and Society*, New York 1980; Winifred Wandersee, *Women's Work and Family Values 1920–1940*, Cambridge (Mass.) 1981; Estelle B. Freedman, *Their Sisters' Keepers. Women's Prison Reform in America, 1830–1930*, Ann Arbor 1981; Susan Ware, *Beyond Suffrage. Women in the New Deal*, Cambridge (Mass.) 1981; Mary Beth Norton, *Liberty's Daughters. The Revolutionary Experience of American Women 1750–1800*, Boston 1980. For a provocative, if overly rigid, attempt to assess women's responses to the constraints on them, see Lyle Koehler, *A Search for Power. The 'Weaker Sex' in Seventeenth-Century New England*, Urbana, Chicago, London 1980. Blanche Wiesen Cook, *Women and Support Networks*, New York 1979, makes a strong, explicit case for the specific role of female friendships as supports for single women acting in a world in which their male equivalents enjoyed the support of families.

8. Carolyn Lougee, *Le Paradis des Femmes*, Princeton 1977; Marion A. Kaplan, *The Jewish Feminist Movement in Germany. The Campaigns of the Jüdischer Frauenbund, 1940–1938*, Westport 1979; Barbar Evans Clements, *Bolshevik Feminist. The Life of Aleksandra Kollontai*, Bloomington 1979; Beatrice Farnsworth, *Aleksandra Kollontai: Socialism, Feminism, and the Bolshevik Revolution*, Stanford 1980; Cathy Porter, *Alexandra Kollontai: The Lonely Struggle of the Woman Who Defied Lenin*, New York & London 1980; Natalie Zemon Davis, *Society and Culture*; Dominique Desanti, *Flora Tristan. La femme revoltée*, Paris 1972; Jules-L. Puech, *La Vie et l'oeuvre de Flora Tristan*, Paris 1925; Laura S. Strumingher, *Women and the Making of the Working Class: Lyon 1830–1870*, St. Albans (Vt.) 1979; Edith Thomas, *Pauline Roland. Socialisme et féminisme au XIXe siècle*, Paris 1956, and her *Louise Michel*, Montreal 1980; Steven C. Hause and Anne R. Kenney, 'The Limits of Suffragist Behavior: Legalism and Militancy in France, 1876–1922,' *American Historical Review* 86, No. 4 (October 1981), pp. 781–806; Charles Sowerwine, *Les Femmes et le socialisme*, Paris, 1978; Jean H. Quataert, *Reluctant Feminists in German Social Democracy, 1885–1917*, Princeton 1979; Werner Thönnessen, *The Emancipation of Women. The Rise and Decline of the Women's Movement in German Social Democracy 1863–1933*, London 1973; Richard J. Evans, *The Feminist Movement in Germany 1894–1933*, London & Beverley Hills 1976; Karen Honeycutt, 'Clara Zetkin: A Left-Wing Socialist and Feminist in Wilhelmian Germany,' PhD Dissertation, Columbia University, 1975; Richard Stites, *The Women's Liberation Movement in Russia. Feminism, Nihilism, and Bolshevism, 1860–1930*, Princeton. 1978; Dorothy Atkinson, Alexander Dallin and Gail Warshofsky Lapidus, (eds.), *Women in Russia*, Stanford 1977. The literature on women in English history is now vast. Among many, see Barbara Kanner, (ed.), *The Women of England From Anglo-Saxon Times to the Present. Interpretive Bibliographical Essays*, Hamden 1979; Doris Stenton, *The English Woman in History*, London 1957; Martha Vicinus, (ed.), *Suffer and Be Still*, Bloomington & London 1972, and her sequel, *A*

Widening Sphere: Changing Roles of Victorian Women, Bloomington & London, 1977; Leonore Davidoff, *The Best Circles. Society, Etiquette and the Season,* London 1973; Ivy Pinchbeck, *Women Workers in the Industrial Revolution, 1750–1850,* London & New York 1930; J. Jean Hecht, *The Domestic Servant Class in Eighteenth-Century England,* London 1956; J. M. Beattie, 'The Criminality of Women in Eighteenth-Century England,' *Journal of Social History* 8 (Summer 1975), pp. 80–116; Sally Alexander, 'Women's Work in Nineteenth-Century London: 1820–1850,' in Juliet Mitchell and Ann Oakley, (eds.), *The Rights and Wrongs of Women,* Harmondsworth 1976; Angus McLauren, 'Abortion in England, 1890–1914,' *Victorian Studies* 20 (1977), pp. 379–400; Margaret Hewitt, *Wives and Mothers in Victorian Industry,* London 1958; Françoise Basch, *Relative Creatures. Victorian Women in Society and the Novel,* New York 1974; Vineta Colby, *Yesterday's Women: Domestic Realism in the English Novel,* Princeton 1974; Elaine Showalter, *A Literature of Their Own: British Women Novelists from Brontë to Lessing,* Princeton 1977; Mary Jacobus, 'Tess: The Making of a Pure Woman,' in Susan Lipschitz, (ed.), *Tearing the Veil. Essays on Femininity,* London 1978; Barbara Taylor, 'Religious Heresy and Feminism in Early English Socialism,' in Ibid.; Dorothy Thompson, 'Women and Nineteenth-Century Radical Politics. A Lost Dimension,' in *Rights and Wrongs of Women*; Anna Davin, 'Imperialism and Motherhood,' *History Workshop* 5 (Spring 1978), pp. 9–65; F. K. Prochaska, *Women and Philanthropy in 19th Century England,* Oxford 1980; Andrew Rosen, *Rise up Women!,* London 1974; David Morgan, *Suffragists and Liberals. The Politics of Woman Suffrage in Britain,* Oxford 1975; Silvia Franchini, *Sylvia Pankhurst 1912–1914, Dal Suffragismo alla Rivoluzione Sociale,* Pisa 1980; Pat Thane, 'Women and the Poor Law in Victorian and Edwardian England,' *History Workshop* 6 (Autumn 1978), pp. 29–51; Patricia Knight, 'Women and Abortion in Victorian and Edwardian England,' *History Workshop* 4 (Autumn 1977), pp. 57–69; Angus McLauren, 'Women's Work and the Regulation of Family Size,' Ibid., pp. 70–81; Frances Finnegan, *Poverty and Prostitution. A Study of Victorian Prostitutes in York,* Cambridge & New York 1979; Judith R. Walkowitz, *Prostitution and Victorian Society. Women, Class, and the State,* Cambridge & New York 1980.

9. Richard J. Evans, *The Feminists,* London 1977. For other examples of comparative work, see Ross Paulson, *Women's Suffrage and Prohibition: A Comparative Study of Equality and Social Control,* Glenview 1973; Marilyn J. Boxer and Jean H. Quataert, (eds.), *Socialist Women. European Socialist Feminism in the Nineteenth and Early Twentieth Centuries,* New York 1978; Jane Slaughter and Robert Kern, *European Women on the Left. Socialism, Feminism, and the Problems Faced by Political Women, 1880 to the Present,* Westport 1981; Joni Lovenduski and Jill Hills, (eds.), *The Politics of the Second Electorate. Women and Public Participation,* London 1981; Theresa McBride, *The Domestic Revolution. The Modernization of Household Service in England and France, 1820–1920,* New York 1976, and her 'The Long Road Home: Women's Work and Industrialization,' in *Becoming Visible: Women in European History,* ed. Renate Bridenthal and Claudia Koonz, Boston 1977; Leila J. Rupp, *Mobilizing Women for War. German and American Propaganda, 1939–1945,* Princeton 1978; Joan W. Scott and Louise A. Tilly, 'Women's Work and the Family in Nineteenth Century Europe,' *Comparative Studies in Society and History* 17 (1975), pp. 375–93; Pierre Fauchery, *La Destinée féminine dans le roman européen du dix-huitième siècle, 1713–1807; Essai de Gynécomythie Romanesque,* Paris 1972. For a critique of the Annales School's treatment of women's history, see Susan Mosher Stuard, 'The Annales School and Feminist History: Opening Dialogue with the American Stepchild,' *Signs* 7 (Autumn 1981), pp. 135–43. For some examples, among many, of

the new family history, see David Herlihy and Christiane Klapisch-Zuber, *Les Toscans et leurs familles: Une étude du catasto florentin de 1427,* Paris 1978; Lawrence Stone, *The Family, Sex and Marriage in England, 1500–1800,* New York 1977; Jean-Louis Flandrin, *Families in Former Times. Kinship, Household and Sexuality,* Cambridge 1979; Julius Kirshner and Anthony Molho, 'The Dowry Fund and the Marriage Market in Early Quattrocento Florence,' *The Journal of Modern History* 50, [no. 3] (1978), pp. 403–38; Andre Burguière, 'De Malthus à Max Weber; le mariage tardif et l'esprit d'entreprise,' *Annales E.S.C.* 27, Nos. 4–5 (July–October), pp. 1128–38; David Levine, *Family Formation in an Age of Nascent Capitalism,* New York 1977; Christiane Klapisch-Zuber, 'Zacharie, ou le père évincé: les rites nuptiaux en Toscane,' *Annales E.S.C.* 34, No. 6 (November–December 1979), pp. 1216–1243, and her 'Household and Family in Tuscany in 1427,' in *Household and Family in Past Time,* ed. Peter Laslett with Richard Wall, Cambridge & New York 1972, pp. 267–82; Robert Forster and Orest Ranum, (eds.), *Family and Society. Essays From the Annales,* Baltimore 1978; Diana Owen Hughes, 'Toward Historical Ethnography: Notarial Records and Family History in the Middle Ages,' *Historical Methods Newsletter* 7 (1974), pp. 61–71, her 'Domestic Ideals and Social Behaviour: Evidence from Medieval Genoa,' in *The Family in History,* ed. Charles Rosenberg, Philadelphia 1975, pp. 115–43, and her 'Kinsmen and Neighbors in Medieval Genoa,' in *The Medieval City,* ed., H. A. Miskimin, D. Herlihy, and A. L. Udovitch, New Haven 1977. Some of the more recent work on family and marriage is demonstrating the ways in which female dowries contributed to class relations. See especially, Diana Owen Hughes, 'From Brideprice to Dowry in Mediterranean Europe,' *Journal of Family History* 3 (1978), pp. 262–96; and Susan Mosher Stuard, 'Dowry Inflation and Increments in Wealth and Medieval Ragusa (Dubrovnik),' *The Journal of Economic History* XLI, No. 4 (December 1981), pp. 795–812.

10. For examples of the new labour history, see the various articles in R. Edwards, M. Reich, D. Gordon, (eds.), *Labor Market Segmentation,* Lexington (Mass.) 1975; and in Milton Cantor and Bruce Laurie, (eds.), *Class, Sex and the Woman Worker,* Westport 1977. For a general overview, see Alice Kessler-Harris, *Women Have Always Worked. A Historical Overview,* Old Westbury 1981; James J. Kenneally, *Women and American Trade Unions,* St. Albans (Vt.) 1978; Susan Estabrook Kennedy, *If All We Did Was to Weep at Home: A History of White Working-Class Women in America,* Bloomington & London 1979; Leslie J. Tentler, *Wage-Earning Women. Industrial Work and Family Life in the United States, 1900–1930,* New York & Oxford 1979. Many of the older studies are still valuable, e.g., Edith Abbott, *Women in Industry. A Study in American Economic History,* New York & London 1910; Elizabeth Beardsley Butler, *Women and the Trades. Pittsburgh, 1907–1908,* New York 1911. Among the many specialized studies, see Virginia Yans-McLaughlin, *Family and Community. Italian Immigrants in Buffalo, 1880–1930,* Ithaca & London 1971; Maureen Greenwald, *Women, Work, and War. The Impact of World War I on Women Workers in the United States,* Westport 1980; Karen Sue Anderson, *Wartime Women,* Westport 1981; David Katzman, *Seven Days a Week. Domestic Service in Industrializing America,* New York & Oxford 1978; Philip S. Foner, *Women in the American Labor Movement: From World War I to the Present,* New York 1980; Karen Beck Skold, 'The Job He Left Behind: American Women in the Shipyards During World War II,' in *Women, War and Revolution,* pp. 55–76; Ruth Milkman, 'Women's Work and the Economic Crisis; Some Lessons from the Great Depression,' *The Review of Radical Political Economists* 8, No. 1 (Spring 1976), pp. 73–97. On the YWCA, see Mary S. Sims, *The Natural History of a Social Institution—the Y.W.C.A.,* New York 1936; Elizabeth Wilson,

Fifty Years of Association Work Among Young Women, New York 1916; Elsie D. Harper, *The Past Is Prelude. Fifty Years of Social Action in the YWCA,* New York 1963; Sophonisba Breckinridge, *Women in the Twentieth Century. A Study of Their Political, Social and Economic Activities,* New York 1933, pp. 28, 56–57, 85, 260–70 *passim*; Helen Bittar, 'The Y.W.C.A. of the City of New York,' PhD Dissertation, New York University 1979.

    11. See, for example, Joan Hoff Wilson, 'The Illusion of Change: Women and the American Revolution,' in Alfred F. Young, (ed.), *The American Revolution, Explorations in the History of American Radicalism,* DeKalb 1976, pp. 383–446; or Gerda Lerner, *The Majority Finds Its Past,* New York 1979. For a sharp critique of some of the early writings on women and medicine, see Regina Morantz, 'The Perils of Feminist History,' *Journal of Interdisciplinary History* 4, No. 4 (Spring 1974)[: 649–660]. For a recent formulation of the differences between those who emphasize culture and those who emphasize politics in women's history, see Ellen DuBois, Mari Jo Buhle, Temma Kaplan, Gerda Lerner, and Carroll Smith-Rosenberg, 'Politics and Culture in Women's History: A Symposium,' *Feminist Studies* 6, No. 1 (Spring 1980), pp. 26–63. This debate appears in somewhat different form among women on the left who find patriarchy as important as, if not more important than, class relations in the oppression of women. See, for example, Lydia Sargent, (ed.), *Women and Revolution. A Discussion of the Unhappy Marriage of Marxism and Feminism,* Boston 1981; Batya Weinbaum, *The Curious Courtship of Women's Liberation and Socialism,* Boston 1978; Zillah Esenstein, (ed.), *Capitalist Patriarchy and the Case for Socialist Feminism,* New York 1978, and her *The Radical Future of Liberal Feminism,* London & Boston 1980. The debate becomes almost unrecognizable in the hands of Jean Bethke Elshtain, *Public Man, Private Woman. Women in Social and Political Thought,* Princeton 1981. Her broadside attack on such diverse figures as Nancy Chodorow, Myra Dinnerstein, Juliet Mitchell, Sheila Rowbotham, and the late Michelle Z. Rosaldo, among many, is presented in a tone that closes rather than opens debate. Her open red-baiting, founded on a pre-school reading of Marx and a caricature of contemporary Marxism, has made her fashionable in those liberal circles increasingly inclined to cold war politics. See Elizabeth Fox-Genovese, 'The Personal Is Not Political Enough,' *Marxist Perspectives* 2 (Winter 1979/80), pp. 94–113.

    12. Degler, *At Odds*; Barbara Leslie Epstein, *The Politics of Domesticity. Women, Evangelism and Temperance in Nineteenth-Century America,* Middletown 1981; Jacquelyn Dowd Hall, *Revolt Against Chivalry. Jesse Daniel Ames and the Women's Campaign Against Lynching,* New York 1974. Much of the debate within women's history had addressed the merits of suffrage as a goal of the women's movement and its value as an accomplishment. The strongest defence of the importance of politics is presented by Ellen DuBois, *Feminism and Suffrage. The Emergence of an Independent Women's Movement in America 1848–1869,* Ithaca & London 1978. See also her excellent edition, *Elizabeth Cady Stanton / Susan B. Anthony. Correspondence, Writings, Speeches,* New York 1981, esp. pp. 172–200, where she introduces Stanton's own sharp critique of the women's movement. Another part of the debate addresses the value of cross-class alliances among women, especially their value to working-class women. For a recent strong, if occasionally flawed defense of the discrete interests of working-class women and the failure of middle-class women to understand those interests, see Meredith Tax, *The Rising of the Women: Feminist Solidarity and Class Conflict, 1880–1917,* New York & London 1980.

    13. The most sophisticated statement of the position that official history has nothing to do with women's history is to be found in Joan Kelly-Gadol, 'Did Women Have a Renaissance?' in Bridenthal and Koonz, (eds.), *Becoming Visible.*

14. See, for example, Gayle Rubin, 'The Traffic in Women: Notes on the Political Economy of Sex,' in Rayna Reiter, (ed.), *Towards an Anthropology of Women*, [New York,] 1975. See also Carol MacCormack and Marilyn Strathern, (eds.), *Nature, Culture and Gender*, Cambridge 1980.

15. The most influential figure here has been Talcott Parsons. In addition to his many works, see Neil J. Smelser, *Social Change in the Industrial Revolution*, London 1959. Functionalism has become deeply ingrained in all modernization theory, as well as in the consensus view of American history. For one critique of the application of modernization theory to women's experience, see June Nash and Helen Icken Safa, (eds.), *Sex and Class in Latin America. Women's Perspectives on Politics, Economics, and the Family in the Third World*, South Hadley (Mass.) 1980.

16. Cf. Sanday, *Female Power and Male Dominance*; Etienne and Leacock, (eds.), *Women and Colonization*; Malia Stevens, 'Women, Kinship and Capitalist Development,' in Young, Wolkowitz and McCullagh, (eds.), *Of Marriage and the Market*; and, for a provocative theoretical discussion, Karen Sacks, *Sisters and Wives. The Past and Future of Sexual Equality*, Westport 1979. Also see Jack Goody, *Production and Reproduction*, Cambridge 1976.

17. Laslett, (ed.), *Household and Family in Past Time*; Peter Laslett, *Family Life and Illicit Love in Earlier Generations*, Cambridge, 1977; Flandrin, *Families in Former Times*; Jack Goody, Joan Thirsk, and E. P. Thompson, (eds.), *Family and Inheritance. Rural Society in Western Europe 1200–1800*, Cambridge, 1976; Margaret Spufford, *Contrasting Communities: English Villages in the Sixteenth and Seventeenth Centuries*, Cambridge 1974; Miranda Chaytor, 'Household and Kinship: Ryton in the late 16th and early 17th centuries,' *History Workshop* 10 (Autumn 1980), pp. 25–60; Françoise Zonnabend, *La mémoire longue*; Martine Segalen, *Mari et femme dans la société paysanne*, Paris 1980; Wolfgang Mager, 'Haushalt und Familie in protoindustrieller Gesellschaft: Spenge (Ravensberg) während der ersten Hälfte des 19 Jahr-hunderts—Eine Fallstudie,' in Neithard Bulst, Joseph Goy und Jochen Hoock, (eds.), *Familie Zwischen Tradition und Moderne*, Göttingen 1981, pp. 141–79; Levine, *Family Formation*; Keith Wrightson and David Levine, *Poverty and Piety in an English Village: Terling 1525–1700*, New York 1979; Alan Macfarlane, *The Origins of English Individualism*, Oxford 1978; Hans Medick, 'The Proto-Industrial Family Economy: The Structural Function of Household and Family During the Transition from Peasant Society to Industrial Capitalism,' *Social History* 3 (1976), pp. 291–315; Lutz Berkner, 'The Stem Family and the Development Cycle of the Peasant Household: An 18th-Century Austrian Example,' *American Historical Review* LXXVII (1972), pp. 398–418; Hans Medick and David Sabean, 'Family and Kinship: Material Interest and Emotion,' *Peasant Studies* 8, No. 2 (1979), pp. 139–60; F. Mendels, 'La Composition du ménage paysan en France au XIXe siècle: Une analyse économique du mode de production domestique,' *Annales E.S.C.* 33 [, no. 4] (1978), pp. 780–802; Christopher Clark, 'The Household Economy, Market Exchange and the Rise of Capitalism in the Connecticut Valley, 1800–1860,' *Journal of Social History* 13, No. 2 (Winter 1979), pp. 169–90; Rolla Milton Tyron, *Household Manufactures in the United States, 1640–1860*, New York 1966; Daniel Blake Smith, 'Mortality and the Family in the Colonial Chesapeake,' *Journal of Interdisciplinary History* VIII (1978), pp. 403–27; Crandall A. Shifflett, 'The Household Composition of Rural Black Families: Louisa County, Virginia, 1880,' *Journal of Interdisciplinary History* VI (Autumn 1975), pp. 235–60; Nancy Lou Oberseider, 'A Sociodemographic Study of the Family as a Social Unit in Tidewater, Virginia 1660–1776,' PhD Dissertation, University of Maryland 1975; Philip Greven,

'Family Structure in Seventeenth-Century Andover, Massachusetts,' *William and Mary Quarterly*, 3rd ser., 23 (1976), pp. 234–56; Lois Green Carr, 'The Development of the Maryland Orphans' Court, 1654–1715,' in Aubrey C. Land, Lois Green Carr, and Edward C. Papenfuse, (eds.), *Law, Society, and Politics in Early Maryland*, Baltimore 1977, pp. 41–62; Russell R. Menard, 'Immigrants and Their Increase: The Process of Population Growth in Early Colonial Maryland,' in Ibid., pp. 88–110; Lorena S. Walsh, 'Servitude and Opportunity in Charles County, Maryland, 1658–1705,' in Ibid., pp. 111–33; Allan Kulikoff, 'The Beginnings of the Afro-American Family in Maryland,' in Ibid., pp. 171–96; Thad W. Tate and David Ammerman, (eds.), *The Chesapeake in the Seventeenth Century. Essays on Anglo-American Society and Politics*, Chapel Hill 1979; Irene D. Hecht, 'The Virginia Muster of 1624/5 as a Source for Demographic History,' *William and Mary Quarterly*, 3rd ser., 30, No. 1 (January 1973), pp. 65–92; Elizabeth Anne Kuzenesof, 'An Analysis of Household Composition and Headship as Related to Changes in Mode of Production,' *Comparative Studies in Society and History* 22, No. 1 (1980) [: 78–102]; Harriet Friedmann, 'Household Production and the National Economy: Concepts for the Analysis of Agrarian Formations,' *The Journal of Peasant Studies* 7, No. 2 (January 1980), pp. 158–84; Gavin Wright, *The Political Economy of the Cotton South. Households, Markets, and Wealth in the Nineteenth Century*, New York 1978; Teodor Shanin, (ed.), *Peasants and Peasant Societies*, Harmondsworth 1971; Donald Bender, 'A Refinement of the Concept of Households: Families, Co-residence, and Domestic Functions,' *American Anthropologist* 69, No. 5 (October 1967), pp. 493–504; Rayna Rapp, Ellen Ross, and Renate Bridenthal, 'Examining Family History,' *Feminist Studies* 5, No. 1 (1978)[: 174–200]; Olivia Harris, 'Households as Natural Units,' in Young, Wolkowitz and McCullagh, (eds.), *Of Marriage and the Market*.

18. Leonore Davidoff, 'Mastered for Life: Servant and Wife in Victorian and Edwardian England,' *Journal of Social History* 7, No. 4 (1974), pp. 406–28; Laura Oren, 'The Welfare of Laboring Families: England, 1860–1950,' in *Clio's Consciousness Raised*, ed. Mary Hartman and Lois Banner, New York 1974; John Mack Faragher, *Women and Men on the Overland Trail*, New Haven 1979; Julie Roy Jeffrey, *Frontier Women: The Trans-Mississippi West 1840–1880*, New York 1979; Joann Vanek, 'Work, Leisure and Family Roles: Farm Households in the United States, 1920–55,' *Journal of Family History* 5 [, no. 4] (1980), pp. 422–31; Louise Tilly and Joan Scott, *Women, Work and Family*, New York 1978; Louise Tilly, 'Structures de l'emploi, travail des femmes et changement démographique dans deux villes industrielles: Anzin et Roubaix, 1872–1906,' *Le Mouvement sociale* 105 (1978), pp. 35–58, and her 'The Family Wage Economy in a French Textile City,' *Journal of Family History* 4, No. 4 (1979), pp. 381–94; Tamara K. Hareven, (ed.), *Transitions. The Family and the Life Course in Historical Perspective*, New York 1978. See Natalie Zemon Davis, 'Women in the *Arts Mécaniques* in Sixteenth-Century Lyon,' in *Mélanges en hommage de Richard Gascon*, ed. Jean-Pierre Gutton, Lyon 1979. Cf. also James R. Lehning, *The Peasants of Marlhes: Economic Development and Family Organization in Nineteenth-Century France*, Chapel Hill 1980; Deborah G. White, 'Ain't I A Woman? Female Slaves in the Antebellum South,' PhD Dissertation, University of Illinois at Chicago Circle 1979; Noralee Frankel, 'Workers, Wives, and Mothers: Black Women in Mississippi, 1860–1870,' PhD Dissertation, George Washington University 1982. Implicit functionalism normally accompanies a more or less explicit adherence to modernization theory and is fully compatible with an emphasis of women's appropriation of their own 'sphere.' See, for example, Nancy Cott, *Bonds of Womanhood*. For a critique of the use of modernization theory in women's history, see Richard Evans, 'Modernization Theory

and Women's History,' *Archiv für Sozialgeschichte* XX (1980), pp. 492–514; Elizabeth Fox-Genovese, 'Gender, Class, and Power: Some Theoretical Considerations,' *The History Teacher* 15, No. 2 (February 1982), pp. 255–76, and my 'Women and Work: A Preliminary Contribution to the Terms of the Discussion,' Fernand Braudel Center, *Working Papers*, Seminar I: 'Group Formation and Group Conflict in the Historical Development of the Modern World System' (March 1981). For more complex uses of the notion of family strategy, see Pierre Bourdieu, 'Marriage Strategies as Strategies of Social Reproduction,' in *Family and Society*, ed. Forster and Ranum, and his *Outline of a Theory of Practice*, Cambridge 1977; David Levine, *Family Formation*.

19. Among many, Ronald Trumbach, *The Rise of the Egalitarian Family. Aristocratic Kinship and Domestic Relations in Eighteenth-Century England*, New York 1978; James Traer, *Marriage and the Family in Eighteenth-Century France*, Ithaca & London, 1980, and his 'From Reform to Revolution: The Critical Century in the Development of the French Legal System,' *Journal of Modern History* 49, No. 1 (1977), pp. 73–88; Ralph Giesey, 'Rules of Inheritance and Strategies of Mobility in Prerevolutionary France,' *American Historical Review* 82, No. 2 (1977), pp. 271–89; James K. Sommerville, 'The Salem (Mass) Woman in the Home, 1660–1770,' *Eighteenth Century Life* I, No. 1 (1974), pp. 7–10; Janelle Greenberg, 'The Legal Status of Women in Early Eighteenth-Century Common Law and Equity,' *Studies in Eighteenth-Century Culture* IV (1975), pp. 171–82; Eleanor Searle, 'Merchet in Medieval England,' *Past and Present* 82 (1979), pp. 3–43; Emmanuel LeRoy Ladurie, 'A System of Customary Law: Family Structures and Inheritance Customs in Sixteenth-Century France,' in *Family and Society*, ed. Forster and Ranum; Lawrence Stone, *The Family, Sex and Marriage*; Jacques Lafon, *Les Époux Bordelais 1450–1550*, Paris 1972; Mervyn James, *Family, Lineage and Civil Society: A Study in the Society, Politics and Mentality of the Durham Region*, Oxford, 1974.

20. Gordon Schochet, *Patriarchalism in Political Thought: The Authoritarian Family and Political Speculation and Attitudes Especially in Seventeenth-Century England*, New York 1975; Robert Mandrou, *Magistrats et sorciers en France au XVIIe siècle*, Paris 1968; Jean Bodin, *The Six Bookes of a Commonweale*, Cambridge (Mass.) 1962; Julian H. Franklin, *Jean Bodin and the Rise of Absolutist Theory*, Cambridge 1973; Peter Laslett, (ed.), *Patriarchia and Other Political Works of Sir Robert Filmir*, Oxford 1949. See also, Pashal Larkin, *Property in the 18th Century, with Special Reference to England and Locke*, Cork 1930; Richard Sclatter, *Property: The History of an Idea*, London 1951; C. B. MacPherson, *The Theory of Possessive Individualism from Hobbes to Locke*, Oxford 1962; Michael Walzer, *The Revolution of the Saints*, New York 1973. Sheldon Wolin, *Politics and Vision* (Boston 1970), holds that politics ends with Locke. Cf. Marcel Garaud, *La Révolution et la propriété foncière*, Paris 1959; Marcel Garaud & Romuald Szramkiewicz, *La Révolution française et al famille*, Paris 1978; J. Portmer, 'Le Statut de la femme en France depuis la réformation des coutumes jusqu'à la rédaction du Code civil,' *Recueil Jean Bodin XII*, Brussels 1962, pp. 447–497, and 'La femme dans la législation royale des deux derniers siècles de l'Ancien Régime,' *Mélanges Petot*, Paris 1959, pp. 441–454; L. Abensour, *La Femme et le féminisme avant la révolution*, Paris 1923; Barbar Boons Diefendorf, 'Marriage and Patrimony in Sixteenth-Century France: The Families of the Paris City Councillors, 1535–1575,' PhD Dissertation, University of California at Berkeley 1978.

21. Elizabeth Fox-Genovese, 'Property and Patriarchy in Classical Bourgeois Political Theory,' *Radical History Review* IV, Nos. 2–3 (Spring–Summer, 1977), pp. 36–59 [reprinted in this volume, pp. 1–20]. Zillah Eisenstein develops similar ideas in *The Radical Future of Liberal Feminism*. Cf. Elshtain, *Public Man, Private Woman*; and R. W. K.

Hinton, 'Husbands, Fathers and Conquerors: I,' *Political Studies* 15 (1967), pp. 291–300, and 'Husbands, Fathers and Conquerors: II,' *Political Studies* 16 (1968), pp. 56–67. See also Richard Allen Chapman, 'Leviathan Writ Small: Thomas Hobbes on the Family,' *American Political Science Review* 69 (March 1975), pp. 76–90; and Mary Lyndon Shanley, 'Marriage Contract and Social Contract in Seventeenth Century English Political Thought,' *Western Political Quarterly* 32 (March 1979), pp. 79–91.

22. Linda K. Kerber, *Women of the Republic,* Chapel Hill 1980; Elizabeth Fox-Genovese and Eugene D. Genovese, *Fruits of Merchant Capital,* New York & Oxford [1983], especially Chapter 11, 'The Ideological Bases of Domestic Economy,' and Chapter 5, 'Poor Richard at Work in the Cotton Fields: A Critique of the Psychological and Ideological Presuppositions of *Time on the Cross*'; Marylynn Salmon, 'Equality or Submersion?' in *Women of America,* ed. Carol Berkin and Mary Beth Norton, Boston 1979, and her '"Life, Liberty and Power." The Legal Status of Women after the American Revolution,' in *Women, War and Revolution,* ed. Berkin and Lovett; Eugene D. Genovese, *Roll, Jordan, Roll* (New York 1974) uses both paternalism and patriarchy in referring to the slaveholders, usually paternalism for their relations with their slaves and patriarchy for their relations with their own women. Large plantations included productive and domestic life within a single sphere and the slaveholder presided over it all, with no significant checks to his will except the resistance of slaves and women. But even the largest plantations were embedded within a democratic system and even the wealthiest and most powerful planters engaged in democratic, rather than hierarchical relations with the other male members of their society. In this respect, as in so many others, the slave society of the American South constituted a hybrid society. This society may have fostered the persistence of what we might call domestic patriarchy, but it was not a full patriarchal society because of the nature of the relations among white men. This is not the place to resolve the question of terminology, but antebellum Southern society does constitute an important litmus test of the varieties of male dominance.

23. Leonore Davidoff, *The Best Circles,* and her 'The Separation of Home and Work. Landladies and Lodgers in Nineteenth- and Twentieth-Century England,' in *Fit Work for Women,* ed. Sandra Burman, New York, 1979; Barbara Welter, *Dimity Convictions,* New York 1976, especially chapters 1 and 2; Sklar, *Catharine Beecher*; Mary Ryan, 'A Women's Awakening: Evangelical Religion and the Families of Utica, N.Y., 1800–1840,' *American Quarterly* 30 (1978), pp. 602–23, her 'Femininity and Capitalism in Antebellum America,' in *Capitalist Patriarchy,* ed. Eisenstein, and her *The Cradle of the Middle Class, The Family in Oneida County, New York, 1790–1865,* Cambridge 1981; Gerda Lerner, 'The Lady and the Mill Girl,' in her *Majority Finds Its Past*; Catherine Hall, 'The Early Formation of Victorian Domestic Ideology,' in *Fit Work for Women,* ed. Burman; Neil Mc-Kendrick, 'Home Demand and Economic Growth; A New View of the Role of Women and Children in the Industrial Revolution,' in *Historical Perspectives. Studies in English Thought and Society in Honour of J. H. Plumb,* London 1974; Barbara Corrado Pope, 'Revolution and Retreat: Upper Class French Women after 1789,' in *Women, War and Revolution,* ed. Berkin and Lovett; Leonore Davidoff, Jean L'Esperance and Howard Newby, 'Landscape with Figures: Home and Community in English Society,' in *Rights and Wrongs,* ed. Mitchell and Oakley. Raymond Williams, *The Country and the City* (New York 1973), argues cogently that the vision of the country as a retreat from capitalism was nothing but a myth. The same is true for the home.

The dominant tendency in women's history has largely ignored the experience of black women, but see Sharon Harley and Rosalyn Terborg-Penn, *The Afro-American Woman.*

Struggles and Images, Port Washington (N.Y.) 1978; Angela Davis, *Women, Race and Class,* New York 1982; Alfred M. Duster, (ed.), *Crusade for Justice. The Autobiography of Ida B. Wells,* Chicago 1970; Anna Julia Cooper, *A Voice from the South by a Black Woman of the South* (1892) repr. New York 1969; Bonnie Thornton Dill, 'The Dialectics of Black Womanhood,' *Signs* 4, No. 3 (Spring 1979), pp. 543–55; bell hooks, *Ain't I a Woman. Black Women and Feminism,* Boston 1981; Joyce A. Ladner, *Tomorrow's Tomorrow,* Garden City 1972; Gerda Lerner, (ed.), *Black Women in White America. A Documentary History,* New York, 1963, and her 'Early Community Work of Black Club Women,' *Journal of Negro History* 59 (April 1974), pp. 158–67; Bert James Loewenberg and Ruth Bogin, (eds.), *Black Women in Nineteenth-Century American Life. Their Words. Their Thoughts. Their Feelings,* University Park (Pa.) 1976; White, 'Ain't I a Woman'; Frankel, 'Workers, Wives, and Mothers'; Catherine Davis Tilman, 'Afro American Women and Their Work,' *The A.M.E. Church Review* 11, No. 4 (April 1895), pp. 477–95. The dissertation in progress of Evelyn Brooks Barnett (University of Rochester) will address the ideology of separate spheres in the thought and practice of black women in the second half of the nineteenth century.

24. Karl Polanyi, *The Great Transformation,* New York 1944.

25. Elizabeth Fee, 'Science and the Woman Problem: Historical Perspectives,' in Michael S. Teitelbaum, ed., *Sex Differences. Social and Biological Perspectives,* Garden City 1976, pp. 175–223; Carroll Smith-Rosenberg and Charles Rosenberg, 'The Female Animal: Medical and Biological Views of Woman and Her Role in Nineteenth-Century America,' *Journal of American History* 60 (Sept. 1973), pp. 332–56; Carroll Smith-Rosenberg, 'The Hysterical Woman: Sex Roles Conflict in Nineteenth-Century America,' *Social Research* 39 (Winter 1972), pp. 652–78; Yvonne Knibiehler, 'La Nature Féminine au Temps du Code Civil,' *Annales E.S.C.* 31, No. 4 (July–August 1976), pp. 824–45; Sarah Kofman, *Aberrations. Le Devenir-Femme d'Auguste Comte,* Paris 1978; Susan Moller Okin, *Women in Western Political Thought,* Princeton 1979. Cf. Umberto Cerroni, *Il Rapporto Uomo-Donna Nella Civiltà Borghese,* Rome 1976; Lorenne M. G. Clark and Lydia Lange, (eds.), *The Sexism of Social and Political Theory. Women and Reproduction from Plato to Nietzsche,* Toronto 1979; Elizabethan H. Wolgast, *Equality and the Rights of Women,* Ithaca & London 1980. For a general view of many of these questions, see the recent special issue of *Signs,* separately published as, Catharine R. Stimpson and Ethel Spector Person, (eds.), *Women: Sex and Sexuality,* Chicago 1980.

26. Thomas Dublin, *Women at Work,* New York 1980; Bettina Eileen Berch, 'Industrialization and Working Women in the Nineteenth Century: England, France, and the United States,' PhD Dissertation, University of Wisconsin-Madison 1976; Shelby T. McCloy, 'Charity Workshops for Women, Paris, 1790–95,' *The Social Service Review* XI (1937), pp. 274–84; Yvonne Forado-Cuneo, 'Les Ateliers de Charité de Paris pendant la Révolution Française 1789–1791,' *La Révolution Française* 86 (1933), pp. 317–42; Gary B. Nash, 'The Failure of Female Factory Labor in Colonial Boston,' *Labor History* [20, no. 2] (1979)[: 165–88]; Mark Selden, 'The Proletariat, Revolutionary Change and the State in China and Japan, 1850–1950,' Fernand Braudel Center, *Working Papers,* Seminar I (February 1981); Lehning, *Peasants of Marlhes.*

27. See, among many, Tilly and Scott, *Women, Work and Family;* Michael R. Haines, 'Industrial Work and the Family Life Cycle, 1889–1890,' *Research in Economic History* 4 (1980); Michael Anderson, *Family Structure in Nineteenth-Century Lancashire,* Cambridge 1971; Frances Collier, *The Family Economy of the Working Classes in the Cotton Industry 1784–1833,* Manchester 1964; Lawrence A. Glasco, 'The Life Cycles and

Household Structure of American Ethnic Groups: Irish, Germans, and Native-Born Whites in Buffalo, New York, 1855,' *Journal of Urban History* 1 (1975), pp. 339–64; Daniel J. Walkowitz, *Worker City, Company Town. Iron and Cotton-Worker Protest in Troy and Cohoes, New York, 1855–84,* Urbana 1981; Bruce Laurie, *Working People of Philadelphia, 1800–1850,* Philadelphia 1980, pp. 11–12; Clyde and Sally Griffen, *Natives and Newcomers. The Ordering of Opportunity in Mid-Nineteenth-Century Poughkeepsie,* Cambridge (Mass.) 1978, pp. 228–54; Yans-McLaughlin, *Family and Community;* Jacob Mincer, 'Labor Force Participation of Married Women,' in Universities-National Bureau Committee for Economic Research, *Aspects of Labor Economics.*

28. Heidi Hartman, 'Capitalism, Patriarchy and Job Segregation by Sex,' *Signs* 1, No. 3, pt. 2 (1976), pp. 137–69, her 'The Unhappy Marriage of Marxism and Feminism: Towards a More Progressive Union,' *Capital and Class* [3, no. 2] (1979)[: 1–33], and her 'The Family as the Locus of Gender, Class and Political Struggle: The Example of Housework,' *Signs* 6, No. 3 (Spring 1981)[: 366–94]; Claudia Goldin, 'Female Labor Force Participation: The Origin of Black and White Differences, 1870 and 1880,' *Journal of Economic History* 37 (March 1977), pp. 87–108, and her 'The Work and Wages of Single Women, 1870 to 1920,' *NBER Working Paper Series,* No. 375 (1979); Edwards, Reich, Gordon, (eds.), *Labor Market Segmentation;* Martha Blaxall and Barbara Reagan, (eds.), *Women and the Workplace: The Implications of Occupational Segregation,* Chicago 1976; Valerie Kincade Oppenheimer, *The Female Labor Force in the United States. Demographic and Economic Factors Governing its Growth and Changing Composition,* Berkeley 1970; Elyce Jean Rotella, 'Women's Labor Force Participation and the Growth of Clerical Employment in the United States, 1870–1930,' PhD Dissertation, University of Pennsylvania 1977; Cindy Aron, 'To Barter Their Souls for Gold: Female Clerks in Federal Government Offices, 1862–1890,' *Journal of American History* 67, No. 4 (March 1981) [: 835–853]; Barbara Klaczynska, 'Why Women Work: A Comparison of Various Groups— Philadelphia, 1910–1930,' *Labor History* XVII (Winter 1976)[: 73–87]; Margery Davies, 'A Woman's Place Is at the Typewriter,' *Radical America* 8 (July–August 1974)[: 1–28]; Susan J. Kleinberg, 'Technology's Stepdaughters: The Impact of Industrialization upon Working Class Women, Pittsburgh,' PhD Dissertation, University of Pittsburgh 1973; Elizabeth Pleck, 'A Mother's Wages: Income Earning Among Married Italian and Black Women, 1869–1911,' in Michael Gordon, (ed.), *The American Family in Socio-Historical Perspective,* 2nd ed., New York 1978, and her 'The Two Parent Household: Black Family Structure in Late Nineteenth Century Boston,' *Journal of Social History* 6 (Fall 1972) [: 3–31]. Also see Katzman, *Seven Days a Week.*

29. Elizabeth Janeway, *The Powers of the Weak,* New York 1980.

Four

Women and Work

Work constituted the very fabric of the lives of most French women during the eighteenth century. At least ninety percent of them, from about the age of fourteen on, spent most of their waking hours engaged in one or another form of work, which contributed decisively to French economic life as well as to the survival of the majority of French families. But the divisions that crisscrossed French society also crisscross any modern attempt to identify a single model of women's work. If work normally designates hard, physical labor, it also encompasses a variety of tasks and responsibilities that ensure the functioning of the society as a whole. If estate management should be classified as work for men, so must household management be classified for women; if military service is classified as work for men, so must the suckling and rearing of infants be classified for women. Almost everywhere that masculine activity is designated as work, its female counterpart should also be so designated. Only at the very upper echelons, among the court nobility and the wealthy urban classes, do we find some evidence of a sexual division of labor that casts men in performing roles that might properly be labeled work (government or judicial office, banking or other financial and commercial services) while their wives and daughters led lives of genuine leisure.

During the eighteenth century, as previously, the work of women varied according to estate membership, level of income, and urban or rural residence. More dramatically, a woman's work varied according to whether it was performed within and for her family or in what we might call the public sector, for a wage. All of these distinctions and possible criteria for classification remain subject to innumerable exceptions and confusions. The work of a poor noble's wife might closely resemble that of a wealthy peasant's wife; the work of a *moyenne bourgeoise* or of the wife of a comfortable artisan might resemble both in being performed within the familial context while differing from them because of the different female tasks associated with urban and rural residence. The work of all these women would thus differ structurally from that of an urban servant or factory employee in not being performed for a wage; yet, in given regions, the tasks of all such women would likely include some measure of spinning, lace making, or other textile work. In many parts of the countryside, a female servant would perform for a wage tasks that she might have performed gratis for her own family.

In a very general way, it is possible to construct a taxonomy of women's work that identifies tasks, activities, and responsibilities especially associated with the female gender. In its broadest contours, such a taxonomy would delineate the association of women with such forms of work as infant care; food preparation and service; textile work, especially spinning; the washing of clothing and linens; various farm activities, such as poultry raising; and various forms of marketing. Nonetheless, according to region and to the economic structure of the household to which she belonged, a woman could perform any of an enormous range of tasks; the governing structural principle remained the sharp distinction between, and the complementarity of, the labor performed by the two genders.[1] Thus, however important, the associations of culture and practice—encoded in a legion of proverbs and betraying deep assumptions about the appropriate sexual division of labor—do not tell us enough. Throughout the eighteenth century, the heavy hand of tradition continued to govern the patterns of women's work, but the social and economic changes of the "long" eighteenth century that began as early as the 1660s made recognizable inroads in the lives of innumerable French women and their men. None of these changes revolutionized inherited behavior and norms, but, by the 1760s, with the *tournant des mentalités* of which Michel Vovelle writes, they had left a decisive mark on the lives of many. Their combined impact pointed toward those social, economic, and gender relations that would be inscribed in post-Revolutionary society.[2]

It is not yet possible to construct a complete picture of women's work in its remarkable diversity, much less in its variation by region and class. It would be more difficult yet to provide an accurate assessment of the specific contribution of women to French economic development in this period, although it has become inexcusable to neglect the indisputable presence of that contribution. Here, we merely delineate general patterns of change and continuity in the working lives of women in relation to French social and economic change as a whole. The scattered and uneven basic research precludes constructing a single, all-encompassing model; and, in all likelihood, the rich diversity of women's working experience would not lend itself readily to standardization in any case. But the general patterns are clear enough. The more difficult challenge lies in estimating the relations among random variation, quantitative growth, and abiding qualitative change. Did the working lives of any particular group of women change decisively during the century, and, if so, in what ways?

Notoriously, historians love to find traditional society, in all its reassuring stability, in the century that precedes the one they are studying. The tumultuous life of sixteenth- and early seventeenth-century France should protect us against the worst of those illusions. Economic growth did, nonetheless, mark the decades that succeeded the crisis of the late seventeenth century. The long eighteenth century included the eradication of genuinely killing famines and the inauguration of steady population increase. Notwithstanding the absence of precise figures, we can, with some confidence, assert that the twenty million subjects of Louis XIV had expanded to some twenty-six million. Eighteenth-century women may not have been bearing more children than their foremothers—and increasingly some would abandon those they did bear—but they raised more of those they had and kept them to adulthood, just as they were somewhat more likely to share their own adulthood with siblings, spouses, and familiar neighbors.[3]

The secular economic growth and rise in prices that, especially after 1730, accompanied this demographic push brought significant changes in French society as a whole. The persistent rigidity of French social and economic structures ensured a superficial consistency in an increasingly strained organization of French social and economic relations. French women of different social origins and different regions experienced those strains differently. Their working lives cannot be dissociated from the destiny of their regions and families of origin, as well as that of their conjugal families—or from an enforced or chosen unmarried status.

From the point of view of eighteenth-century commentators themselves, the great changes they had witnessed in their lifetimes were the frightening growth of luxury, the accelerated commercial pace, the increase in dangerous urban classes, the degradation of agriculture, the decline in population, the abandonment of traditional rural and familial mores, and the general erosion of an ordered, hierarchical society. These perceptions are more useful as indications of change than as precise descriptions of its character. Population was increasing; estates and even corporations, despite Turgot's edict of abolition (February 1776), remained in place; and, by and large, growth affected the countryside more powerfully than the cities (only Paris, Lyon, Marseilles, and Bordeaux exceeded 100,000 in population; while Nantes, Lille, and Rouen surpassed 50,000, and only fifty others reached the 10,000–50,000 range[4]).

In 1789, France remained an overwhelmingly rural society in which the twenty-one million odd peasants accounted for 85 percent of the total population. Genuine workers, in the sense of those fully dependent upon the buying and selling of their labor power, numbered only 1,200,000, or 4.6 percent of the population. The nobility of the sword and robe together constituted a scant 1.5 percent of the population, or 400,000 individuals, and the secular and regular clergy only 0.5 percent, or 130,000 individuals, of whom 50,000 may have been women. The bourgeoisie, accounting for a modest 8.4 percent of the total, consisted of some 2,300,000 heterogeneous members, but the bourgeoisie did represent society's most dynamic identifiable segment. Everywhere, its numbers were growing and its activities were expanding. The *petite bourgeoisie* grew with particular vigor and, increasingly, formed a distinct layer between the *peuple* and the older, "real" bourgeoisie.[5]

The spectacular growth of external commerce, together with the increasingly rapid pace of internal trade, accounted for much of this dynamism, just as it impressed contemporaries as the carrier of a revolution in behavior and mores. In social life, many were prepared to blame women for—or at least to associate them intimately with—the apparent disorder, much in the manner of those teeth-grinding theorists who today blame feminists for the supposed disaster provoked by a revolt against injustice. Luxury in particular and conspicuous consumption in general were taken to be specifically female failings. Mothers of all social classes were held accountable for their reluctance to nurse their own children. Horrified commentators portrayed the cities, Paris in particular, as dens of female vice and portrayed even convents as seedbeds of future luxury or debauchery. The dramatic increase in abandoned children was ascribed to the license of single women, especially domestic servants. Eager, if hard-pressed, administrators and inspectors of manufactures sought to harness disorderly single women to the discipline of royal manufactures, new factories, and *ateliers de charité*. In short, the representations of women in general and metaphors of rampant female sexuality in particular were repeatedly, if imperfectly, linked to the perception of social and economic change. This emphasis on women at risk, manifested in undisciplined female sexuality and taste for luxury, did at least call attention to important changes that were occurring in the lives of some women, even as it obscured the real character of most women's working lives.[6]

Early modern French prescription and practice identified women's work closely with the family economy operating under the authority of its male head—the woman's father, husband, brother, or son. Among the peasant majority, strong attitudes toward the sexual division of labor prevailed; women in peasant families performed what were taken to be traditional female responsibilities, including infant care, child rearing, food preparation, and the general care of the dwelling. Normally, they also had their special agricultural responsibilities, most frequently the raising of poultry but also the care of occasional dairy animals. In most parts of France, women engaged in spinning for the family's own clothing and, increasingly, for wholesalers. They might also participate in ribbon making or lace making. They were ordinarily responsible for doing laundry and for providing the family with water. All of this work could be, and commonly was, onerous. Considerable physical labor was required for such tasks as transporting water to meet the daily needs of families that could include eight or more members, not to mention *servantes* and *valets*. At harvest time, if not at other times as well, women could be drawn into the agricultural labor force. Peasant women could also engage in marketing the products of their poultry yards, the dairy, and a small vegetable garden; or they might run a small business of their own, such as a cabaret, a laundry or dyeing operation, or a butcher shop.[7]

In all instances, the status and economic opportunity of the rural woman were closely governed by those of her husband. Women's servile status disappeared with that of their men, but women, like their men, remained accountable for *lods et ventes, cens, corvées,* and other obligations that encumbered the holding. In addition, throughout most of France, by custom and by law, women were strictly subordinated to their husbands. The complex legal network that described their specific status varied from region to region and deserves extended study. As a general rule, however, the absolute state had contributed mightily, when and where it could, to reinforcing the powers of husbands and fathers. Although in regions such as the Comtat, Brittany, the Angoumois, and the Ile de France, rural wives might function and be recognized as *co-fermiers* with their husbands, they remained virtual servants in many others. The legal and social institutions that shaped woman's status were particularly important for her right to, or say in, the disposition of the fruits of her labor. But even where she retained some legally guaranteed economic rights, custom might still dictate forms of service and subservience, such as her serving meals to the men of the household and waiting to eat herself until they had done. Finally, the importance of the family unit in rural economic life made it virtually impossible for her to survive on her own. As in the city, widows inherited going concerns from husbands and continued on their own; but, even under these conditions, success normally dictated remarriage or the active collaboration of one or more sons or sons-in-law.[8]

Women's work, in this context, remained highly flexible and unspecialized, in some instances almost invisible. The carrying of water, to keep to the example, was designated as an occupation only in cities and then seemed to be performed largely by men. The special skills required for spinning, ribbon making, lace making, and the like could be highly complex, but they were normally practiced within the interstices of daily life, rather than as a profession that organized the daily allocation of time. As if in consonance with the informality of the practice, the induction into the skill was passed from mother to daughter as part of the female culture that also included special powers and knowledge associated with childbearing and the medicinal properties of herbs. Girls were, in this sense, slowly inducted into a way of life, rather than receiving an apprenticeship or even specific agricultural training. Even when they, like their brothers, went as servants to a neighboring family, their work would double that of the mistress of the holding in its diffuse character, rather than center on specific tasks. Also, they might occasionally be hired as unspecialized agricultural day laborers. This lack of specialization did not detract from the value of women's work in peasant society; many a proverb reminded young men that the first quality to seek in a prospective bride was her ability to labor.[9]

The work of women in early modern French cities mirrored that of the countryside in its structure, if not in its specific tasks. As Natalie Davis has insisted for the role of women in the *arts mécaniques* in sixteenth-century Lyon, women worked, within the prevailing constraints, "however and wherever they could . . . helping husbands and making anything from pins to gloves." No matter how high the praise they earned for their craft, "it usually remained within the world of their street, their *commérage,* their tavern, their kin—unpublished and unsung."[10] Within the world of corporations and guilds, women enjoyed scarcely greater opportunities for status and independence than they did among the peasantry. As wives and daughters, they retained the customary female responsibilities for the household and the early years of the new generation. In addition to this work, they participated in the crafts of their fathers, husbands, and sons. But they did not normally receive specialized apprenticeships, participate in *compagnonnage,* or receive a formal voice in the deliberations of the corporation. The dominant pattern remained that of a domestic and economic partnership—augmented by the dowry and based on artisanal property, including the man's skill and whatever real estate—in which the man governed and the woman assisted. A similar relationship prevailed among shopkeepers and *marchands.* Custom and law combined to promote asymmetrical relations between men and women within the family, but whatever the subordination of the wife, the work of both partners remained essential to success. The files of the intendant of Bordeaux for the 1770s contain requests from widowers and widows alike for pensions to assist them in caring for the numerous children that their bakery or carpentry shop could not support in the absence of their spouse.[11]

If participation in the family economy characterized the work of most urban women, the city nonetheless offered greater, and more rapidly expanding, opportunities than the country did for women to work outside the family economy. In fact, women's work related to the family economies as a series of gradations, rather than as a stark dichotomy. Women could work as assistants to their men in a single craft; they could work within the household at a different craft, contributing their income to the family pool; they could work outside the household to help support the family; and they could work in or out of the household to support themselves. Only in the last instance did their work contribute primarily to their own economic independence, rather than to the survival or prosperity of their family; and even then, women who lived at home invariably contributed something to the family pool. Girls who worked as employees or servants and retained all, or the major share, of their earnings for themselves normally did so to build a dowry that would permit them to marry. Women's work in the cities could follow any of these patterns, but it was more likely than in the country to offer some element of separation from the working lives of their men— through a different occupation, through the control of earnings, or both.

As a rule, the organized trades or *métiers* did not offer women significantly greater independence or status than did any other arena of French economic life. Women's position in the so-called mixed guilds, those that accepted female as well as male members, never matched that of their male counterparts. Conditions varied from city to city, but women could be found among the drapers, the weavers, the bakers, the fishmongers, the printers, the goldsmiths, the masons, and many others. Their participation in the guild depended upon its particular regulations; but, normally, their entrance depended upon succession from a husband or a father and, even then, did not guarantee them full rights. Printers' widows might continue the work of the shop and even retain journeymen, but they could not inaugurate a new piece of work. The widows of meat roasters and pastry makers did not even have the right to employ an apprentice. Women were not usually represented in the governing councils of the guilds, nor did they participate in the *compagnonnage*, except in the symbolic role of the *mère*, who welcomed and housed the participants in the *Tour de France* during their stay in a particular city.[12]

Some mixed guilds did allow women independent entry. Thus, the drapers and the hostelers of Dijon and the drapers and goldsmiths of Caen, like the grain merchants and fishmongers of Paris, were always referred to as *maîtres et maîtresses, marchands et marchandes, graniers et granières, apprentis et apprentisses*.[13] In these instances, the numbers of female participants seem to have ensured their recognition, if not their full equality. Without detailed local institutional histories, it remains difficult to account for this female presence systematically; but it is safe to assume, at least in the case of Paris and in the case of guilds in which marketing constituted an important element of the activity, that the inclusion of women reflected women's accepted marketing role.[14]

Finally, a few guilds remained purely female guilds. In Paris, only the seamstresses, the spinners, the lingerie makers, and the boutique keepers were of this number; and the same conditions probably existed in the provinces. If some of these female guilds enjoyed longstanding charters and privileges, others were of more recent origins. The seamstresses, for example, received their formal organization in 1675. Organized identically to the male corporations, the female corporations also required apprenticeships and entry fees and tended to restrict the position of *maîtresse* to the daughters of *maîtresses*. Like their male counterparts, these guilds elected juries to protect the integrity of the craft—that is, the monopoly of its exercise. Whatever the difficulties of their position within the guilds, women apparently favored that protection over unfettered economic competition; following Turgot's experiment with freedom, they welcomed the restoration of regulation.[15]

The very complexities of women's position in the corporations during the eighteenth century faithfully reflects their position in the economy and the world of work. That position obeyed the three dominant principles that had governed women's specific roles in the economy since time immemorial: the intimate association of women with a family economy that simultaneously exacted their full participation and their subordination, a gender system that prescribed cultural and social norms and behavior for women in general, and expediency. These principles also governed women's access to other forms of activity and employment within the urban economy.

The city had long offered women special opportunities as midwives, servants, laundresses, prostitutes, and hawkers or market women of various kinds. The services they performed, like the goods they offered for sale, were, in a general way, associated with what were taken to be the appropriate attributes of their sex. Thus, the casual labor, like the more regular wage labor, available to women largely derived from their crude sexuality, their association with clothing and textiles, their responsibility for cleanliness, and their special association with the provision of food. No one has yet advanced a systematic explanation for women's pervasive marketing activities, and space hardly permits one here. Women's market responsibilities in so many disparate societies—for example, those of West Africa and the Caribbean Islands—deeply contravene the tendency to seclude women within the home. Perhaps marketing the basic necessities of life was taken to be a natural extension of the women's domestic responsibilities. In any event, by the beginning of the eighteenth century, women pervaded the tortuous network of the urban market. Trafficking in everything from grain to fish, from flowers to old clothes, they hawked their wares or presided over their stands. Responsible, as consumers, for purveying the subsistence of their families, they came to view the markets in which they also sold as their special preserve. In this respect, the passionate and occasionally violent defense of the so-called moral economy by women in the years preceding and during the Revolution must be understood, at least partially, as an attempt to defend their specific social roles. Their participation in exchange, whatever its apparent independence from traditional constraints, represented merely a transformation of the work that guaranteed their fulfillment of their familial obligations.[16]

These general patterns of female work, which affected a majority of women, persisted throughout the eighteenth century, but economic growth did alter the working lives of significant numbers in a variety of ways. Despite the absence of full-scale agricultural revolution in the countryside and the persistence of weighty seigneurial dues, a long process of consolidation for some and fragmentation for others, including a significant assault on those common lands upon which the survival of so many poorer peasants depended, had been underway since the late seventeenth century. The net effect of these complex changes, including the emergence of commercialized agricultural production in some regions, was to sharpen distinctions of wealth and access to land among the non-noble agricultural classes. In regions like the Nord, so closely studied by Georges Lefebvre, an ever greater number, both absolutely and proportionately, of rural inhabitants could no longer rely upon an agricultural holding to provide secure foundations for the family economy. Under these conditions, women as well as men resorted to wage labor to round out their contribution to family survival. Much of this labor consisted of various forms of agricultural daylabor (*journaliers* and *journalières*) or, for women, of work as servants on wealthier farms. But pure agricultural work, in its manifold variety, could no longer support the growing, and sometimes excessive, rural population.[17]

Throughout the eighteenth century, the tentacles of merchant's capital sank deeper and deeper into the residually seigneurial countryside, binding country and city ever closer together. The results for women varied dramatically, but by the 1760s, it would no longer be possible to draw a sharp line between urban and rural experience. In the still largely isolated Auvergne, for example, holdings that could no longer support a family independently and provide for the dues and taxes it owed required an infusion of cash or, at the very least, additional means of support for some of the family members.

Auvergnat men took to the roads to seek work, venturing as far as Paris or northern Spain. Their women remained at home and managed the family holding, in the process taking on most of the agricultural labor traditionally designated as male. The work of the wives of seamen, as in Nantes, held family members and property together during their husbands' long absences. More commonly, women were the first to leave agricultural labor or even the family holding in order to supplement its resources. The growth and transformation of the textile industry, especially the introduction of new fabrics such as cotton and new technology, required the growing participation of nonguild labor. Such labor was entirely consistent with women's longstanding roles as spinners, and many continued to perform piecework in their own homes for pitiful sums. Others, as in Normandy, sought the factories of cities like Rouen and towns like Elbeuf. Sometimes they went as part of a family migration, sometimes on their own.[18]

The intensive commercialization of agriculture, especially viticulture, in the regions around Bordeaux and the remarkable growth of overseas commerce in the city itself combined to produce a soaring growth of the urban population, to which women of the adjacent regions contributed steadily. Commonly migrating as servants, women also went to a wide variety of other urban occupations, in particular those associated with the clothing and food trades. Many ended up as prostitutes; others accumulated sufficient dowries to marry and frequently remained in town as the wives of artisans or shopkeepers. In the 1780s, the *Journal de Guyenne* regularly carried advertisements for positions available and positions sought. Thus, one widow, forty-five years of age, "knowing how to read, write, sew, and iron laundry," sought a job as a governess; another wished to sell wine retail either from her house or from that of the proprietor. And a *modiste* sought to employ a "*demoiselle* who knows how to work in fashion and to whom wages in proportion to her talents would be offered."[19] Cissie Fairchilds has found comparable advertisements for servants in the "Affiches et annonces de Toulouse" in the same period. Nantes, for which Jacques Depauw has found evidence of a steady rise in illegitimate births, and which also experienced the dynamic impact of Atlantic trade, experienced the growth of a working female population, much of it unmarried.[20]

The examples could be multiplied, but, however varied the specific regional patterns, the growth of a female wage-labor force throughout the eighteenth century remains beyond dispute, as does the importance of the rural roots of urban female employment. The case of servants in general remains striking. Not merely did the growth of the urban bourgeoisie create a demand for more urban servants, perhaps especially the *bonne-à-tout-faire*, but changes in the payment of servants (wages were increasingly paid rather than noted as due), the rising cost of male servants, and the growth of urban work for men combined to promote what we might call the "feminization" of domestic service. Sometime during the 1760s, it is possible to discern the outlines of that nineteenth-century experience of domestic service as a way station for young women between their rural roots and their urban adulthood. The same period witnessed something of a decline in the notion of the servant as a member of a patriarchal family and a rising attempt to define and implement contractual relations between masters and servants.[21]

The influx of single women into the cities has frequently been held responsible, albeit with a range of explanations, for the rise in illegitimate births that characterized the eighteenth century. For whatever reasons, single women were at risk in the eighteenth-century urban market; but the coercive bedding of servant girls, however common, cannot alone account for abandoned children. It is difficult to apprehend statistically, but the abandonment of children by married, working parents remains indisputable. And this abandonment itself surely reflected new attitudes towards work and its fruits. We are glimpsing, in this practice, the beginnings of that dramatic and precocious control of fertility that would characterize nineteenth-century France. The link between child rearing and women's work emerges sharply from the consideration of wet-nursing. Whatever were taken to be the sins of luxury-seeking, irresponsible, upper-class women with respect to nursing their own offspring, the most numerically significant employers of wet nurses were working, urban mothers. Their labor was necessary to the family economy, and their occupations did not permit the casual combination of formal work and domestic responsibilities. Even when married and working for their families, urban women were increasingly tied to forms of work that structured the use of their time, rather than fitting into the interstices of their lives. The same economic growth that provided them with, and made them dependent upon, such work threw a web around their rural sisters, who turned to mercenary wet-nursing to supplement faltering rural family economies.[22]

Throughout the century, the burgeoning textile industry proved a principal employer of women. In addition to home work and proto-industrial employment as members of families, women served the emerging textile factories in considerable numbers. And where unemployed single women threatened to become a charge on public expenses, convents as well as government and charitable agencies created factory-like employment for them in such forms as the *ateliers de charité*.[23] The growth of the fashion industry provided employment for as many as thirty seamstresses in one place—Rose Bertin's famous dressmaking establishment—and was beginning to provide opportunities for them as shopgirls in fashionable boutiques. The links be-tween such activities and the larger network of the world of fashion are legion, including various levels of prostitution, acting, dancing, modeling for artists, and selling favors with flowers. Sébastien Mercier and Restif de La Bretonne may have overdrawn their pictures of the intertwining of luxury and female sexuality, but they were not entirely wrong. The urban economy was indeed fraught with danger for women.[24] But it also offered unprece-dented opportunity. Doubtless, few women matched the independent eco-nomic success of a Rose Bertin. Even where women, because they were single or widowed, might retain control of their earnings, they normally earned so much less than men that significant economic advancement was precluded. Servants could amass dowries only because their jobs, whatever the hazards, provided lodging and food. Other women increasingly had to provide for themselves. But the city at least offered precarious possibilities that the country did not, for in the cities women could find furnished rooms, lodging houses, and networks of other women, not to mention shops and taverns with prepared food. Women could, in short, live alone and struggle to survive.[25]

The most portentous economic and social changes of the eighteenth cen-tury directly marked the working lives of women. For the vast majority of women, their membership in a family economy and the prescribed roles of the dominant gender system continued to govern the work to which they would have access or be obliged to perform, as well as their independent control of the fruits of that labor. Expediency, however, modified these gov-erning principles in any individual case. During the late eighteenth century, women could be found in almost any kind of work, including in such male preserves as the mines and the precarious makeshift activities of scavenging and crime.[26]

As the contours of capitalist France took clear shape during the revolu-tionary decade, discernible guidelines emerged for the appropriate relation of women to work in a new society. At the lowest social levels, women would continue to work, when and where they could, for the makeshift family economies that would characterize the urban and rural worlds first of the laboring poor and then of the emerging proletariat. At the upper levels of society, women would be discouraged from participation in the extra-domestic world of work. Many bourgeoises would work with their husbands in family enterprises ranging from crafts, to shops, to restaurants, to full-scale businesses (we know that in the Nord, at least, women would manage factories); but all of these activities remained closely tied to family life and can be interpreted as an extension of women's role within the domestic econ-omy. As the professions took shape, they would exclude women. The law had always done so; but medicine, which took longer to develop a homo-geneous organization, would gradually lop off such female preserves as midwifery, even though the midwives had eagerly pursued their own pro-fessionalization throughout the eighteenth century. Education remained a special case, much complicated by the role of the religious orders.[27]

In important respects, the social, economic, and political changes of the eighteenth century resulted not from the experience of the masses of labor-ing women, which remained governed as much by expediency as by prin-ciple, but from the experience of upper-class women. As early as the late seventeenth century, Mme de Maintenon and Fénelon had proposed a new work ethic for the women of the lesser nobility. Their prescriptions had been developed in reaction to the excesses of the *précieuses,* who promoted a mix-ture of feminism, fashionable gallantry, female learning, luxury, and social mobility. In contrast, Maintenon and Fénelon emphasized modesty, frugal-ity, devotion, domesticity, and, yes, industry. Their vision of the appropriate female role meshed well with older notions of women's role in a family economy, but it broke ground in identifying work and self-conscious domes-ticity as fitting for upper-class women.[28] The steady rise of luxury and fash-ionable life throughout the eighteenth century discouraged the general adoption of their program, but the growing sense of a society gone wrong, especially as evinced in the irresponsible behavior of wealthy women, alarmed many.

In the wake of the Revolution, and with the emergence of a unified domi-nant class of urban and rural capitalist notables, the fears of license and unruly luxury merged with older notions of domestic order to produce a transformed model of domestic economy. This model, like the prototype of Maintenon and Fénelon, emphasized duty and work for women as wives and mothers of families. Buttressed by a capitalist economy and a systematic, bourgeois political economy, it unequivocally identified the domestic sphere as female. In this respect, the new domestic economy proffered a coherent model of women's work still governed by family needs (the paternalism of the *Code Napoléon*) and a dominant gender system, but it was newly recast as a universal model of appropriate female social contribution to which bour-geoises and noblewomen alike could adhere.[29] The model could also be taken to describe the time-honored practices of women in family economies firmly based in artisanal or peasant property and, in fact, owed much to them. In essence, it simply linked women's work to absolute property and male individualism; but in the process, it organized the tremendous variety of women's tasks and contributions under a generalized representation of female identity to which, with the gradual extension of industrialization, increasing numbers of French women could be invited to identify.

Notes

1. Jean-Marie Gouesse, "Parenté, famille et mariage en Normandie aux XVIIᵉ et XVIIIᵉ siècles. Présentation d'une source et d'une enquête," *Annales: économies, sociétés, civilisations* 27, nos. 4–5 (July–Oct. 1972): 1139–1154; François Lebrun, *La Vie conjugale sous l'ancien régime* (Paris: Armand Colin, 1975), esp. pp. 78–84; Yves Castan, *Honnêteté et relations sociales en Languedoc (1750–1780)* (Paris: Plon, 1974), esp. pp. 162–207.

2. Michel Vovelle, "Le tournant des mentalités en France, 1750–1789: la 'sensibilité' pré-révolutionnaire," *Social History* 5 (May 1977): 605–630.

3. Ernest Labrousse et al., *Histoire économique et sociale de la France,* vol. 2, *Des Derniers Temps de l'âge seigneurial aux préludes de l'âge industriel (1660–1789)* (Paris: Presses universitaires de France, 1970), pp. 23–84; Jean Meuvret, "Les crises de subsistance et la démographie de la France d'ancien régime," in his *Etudes d'histoire économique* (Paris: Armand Colin, 1971), pp. 271–281.

4. Among many, see Victor Riqueti, marquis de Mirabeau, *L'Ami des hommes* (Avignon: n.p., 1756); Chevalier de Cerfvol, *Mémoire sur la population dans lequel on indique le moyen de la rétablir & de se procurer un corps militaire toujours subsistant & peuplant* (London: n.p., 1768; Paris: EDHIS, 1973); Goyon de La Plombanie, *L'Homme en société ou nouvelles vues politiques et économiques pour porter la population au plus haut degré en France,* 2 vols. (Amsterdam: Marc Michel Rey, 1763; Paris: EDHIS, 1970); Edgar Faure, *La Disgrâce de Turgot* (Paris: Gallimard, 1961); Labrousse et al., p. 73; Roland Mousnier, *The Institutions of France under the Absolute Monarchy 1598–1789: Society and the State,* translated by Brian Pierce (Chicago: University of Chicago Press, 1979), pp. 472–473. The edict of August 1776, issued after Turgot's departure, modified but did not rescind his reform.

5. Labrousse et al., p. 607. For a rough estimate of female members of religious orders, see Léon Abensour, *La Femme et le féminisme avant la révolution* (1923, Geneva: Slatkine, 1977), pp. 263–264.

6. Louis Sébastien Mercier, *Tableau de Paris,* 8 vols. (Amsterdam: n.p., 1783); Nicolas Edmé Restif de La Bretonne, *Les Nuits de Paris* (Paris: Aux trois compagnons, 1947), or idem, *Le Paysan perverti* (Lausanne: Editions L'Age d'Homme, 1977); Jean Pierre Gutton, *La Société et les pauvres* (Paris: Editions des Belles Lettres, 1971), esp. pp. 438–466, and idem, *L'Etat et la mendicité dans la première moitié du XVIIIe siècle* (Lyon: Centre d'études foreziennes, 1973), esp. pp. 142–155; Shelby T. McCloy, "Charity Workshops for Women, Paris, 1790–1795," *Social Service Review* 11 (1937): 274–284; "Bureaux et ateliers de charité," *Oeuvres de Turgot et documents le concernant,* edited by Gustave Schelle, vol. 3 (Paris: Presses universitaires de France, 1919; Darmstadt: Blaschke & Ducke GmbH, 1972); Camille Bloch, *L'Assistance et l'état en France à la veille de la révolution* (Paris: Librairie Alphonse Picard & Fils, 1980).

7. Olwen Hufton, "Women and the Family Economy in Eighteenth-Century France," *French Historical Studies* 9, no. 1 (Spring 1975): 1–22; Restif de La Bretonne, *La Vie de mon père* (Paris: Editions Garnier, 1970). For excellent general overviews, see Martine Segalen, *Mari et femme dans la société paysanne* (Paris: Flammarion, 1980); and Françoise Zonabend, *La Mémoire longue. Temps et histoire au village* (Paris: Presses universitaires de France, 1980). See also Jean-Louis Flandrin, *Families in Former Times,* translated by Richard Southern (Cambridge: Cambridge University Press, 1979): esp. pp. 85–118.

8. Flandrin, pp. 118–145; Abensour, pp. 238–249; James Traer, *Marriage and the Family in Eighteenth-Century France* (Ithaca: Cornell University Press, 1980). See also

Gustave Fagniez, *La Femme et la société française dans la première moitié du dix-septième siècle* (Paris: Librairie universitaire J. Gamber, 1929), esp. pp. 135–203.

9. Gouesse, pp. 1146–1147; Segalen, pp. 23, 30; James L. Lehning, *The Peasants of Marhles* (Chapel Hill: University of North Carolina Press, 1980); Georges Lefebvre, *Les Paysans du nord pendant la révolution française* (Paris: Armand Colin, 1972), p. 277.

10. Natalie Zemon Davis, "Women in the 'Arts mécaniques' of Sixteenth-Century Lyon," *Mélanges Richard Gascon* (Lyon: Presses universitaires de Lyon, 1979)[, 139–167].

11. Davis, "'Arts mécaniques.'" Archives départementales de la Gironde, C 66, contains a series of requests mainly from 1774–1775, and C 84 contains a request from Veuve Gougère, *Boulangère,* February 1776. See also Maurice Garden, *Lyon et les Lyonnais au XVIIIe siècle* (Paris: Editions des Belles Lettres, 1970), pp. 275–353; Emile Coornaert, *Les Corporations en France avant 1789,* 2d ed. (Paris: Editions ouvrières, 1968); pp. 184, 190, 206; Madeleine Guilbert and Viviane Isambert-Jamati, *Travail féminin et travail à domicile: Enquête sur le travail à domicile de la confection féminine dans la région parisienne* (Paris: Centre national de recherches scientifiques, 1956), pp. 9–11; Mary Durham Johnson, "Old Wine in New Bottles: The Institutional Changes for Women of the People during the French Revolution," in *Women, War and Revolution,* edited by Carol R. Berkin and Clara M. Lovett (New York: Holmes & Meier, 1980), p. 108.

12. Abensour, pp. 184–191; Coornaert, *Corporations,* and idem, *Les Compagnonnages en France du moyen âge à nos jours* (Paris: Editions ouvrières, 1966), pp. 178–179.

13. Abensour, p. 189.

14. Johnson, pp. 109–110; Jeffrey Kaplow, *The Names of Kings. The Parisian Laboring Poor in the Eighteenth Century* (New York: Basic Books, 1972), esp. pp. 55–65. On the culture of the marketplace, see A. P. Moore, *The Genre Poissard and the French Stage in the Eighteenth Century* (New York: The Institute of French Studies, Columbia University, 1935). See also Jean Martineau, *Les Halles de Paris des origines à 1789* (Paris: Editions Montchrestien, 1960), esp. pp. 246–248.

15. Abensour, pp. 184–185. On the reaction to Turgot's edicts, see *Histoire générale de Paris: les métiers et corporations de la ville de Paris,* edited by René de Lespinasse and François Bonnardot (Paris: Imprimerie nationale, 1879), vol. 3, pp. 1–34. On male attitudes toward women's participation in corporations, see *Doléances des maîtres-ouvriers fabricants en étoffes d'or, d'argent et de soie de la ville de Lyon adressées au roi et à la nation assemblée,* edited by Fernand Rude (Lyon: Editions Fédérop, 1976), pp. 36–39.

16. Johnson, "Old Wine"; Darline Gay Levy and Harriet B. Applewhite, "Women of the Popular Classes in Revolutionary Paris, 1789–1795," in Berkin and Lovett, *Women, War and Revolution,* pp. 9–36; George Rudé, *The Crowd in the French Revolution* (Oxford: Oxford University Press, 1959); Olwen Hufton, "Women in Revolution, 1789–1796," *Past and Present* 53 (1971): 90–108.

17. Olwen Hufton, *The Poor in Eighteenth-Century France* (Oxford: Oxford University Press, 1974), esp. pp. 25–68; Lefebvre, pp. 277–298; Labrousse et al., pp. 487–497.

18. Hufton, *The Poor,* pp. 69–127; Nicole Castan, "La criminalité familiale dans le ressort du parlement de Toulouse (1690–1730)," in A. Abbiateci, et al., *Crimes et criminalité en France sous l'ancien régime (17e–18e siècles)* (Paris: Armand Colin, 1971), p. 95; Gouesse, p. 1148; Jeffrey Kaplow, *Elbeuf during the Revolutionary Period: History and Social Structure* (Baltimore: Johns Hopkins University Press, 1964), pp. 52–99; F. Mendels, "Proto-Industrialization: The First Phase of Industrialization," *Journal of Economic History* 32, no. 1 (March–June 1972): 241–261.

19. *Journal de Guyenne,* no. 22 (1787), 86, 87, and no. 25 (1787), 101.

20. Cissie Fairchilds, "Masters and Servants in Eighteenth-Century Toulouse," *Journal of Social History* 12, no. 3 (Spring 1979): 368–393, and her *Domestic Enemies: Servants and Their Masters in Old Regime France* (Baltimore: Johns Hopkins University Press, 1984); Jacques Depauw, "Amour illégitime et société à Nantes au XVIIIᵉ siècle," *Annales: économies, sociétés, civilisations* 27, nos. 4–5 (July–Oct. 1972): 115–182.

21. Fairchilds, "Masters and Servants." See also Achille Guillaume Le Bègue de Presle, *L'Economie rurale et civile, ou moyens les plus économiques d'administrer et de faire valoir ses biens de campagne et de ville* (Paris: Buisson, 1789), vol. 1, pp. 97–109, on the appropriate contractual relations between masters and mistresses and their servants. Madame Duplessy, corresponding with her newly married daughter, similarly offers advice on dealing with servants as employees (Bibliothèque de la ville de Bordeaux, MS. 1201, letters for the autumn of 1768).

22. See, among many, Claude Delasselle, "Les Enfants abandonnés à Paris au XVIIIᵉ siècle," *Annales: économies, sociétés, civilisations* 30, no. 1, (Jan.–Feb. 1975): 187–218; A. Lottin, "Naissances illégitimes et filles mères à Lille au XVIIIe siècle," *Revue d'Histoire Moderne et Contemporaine* 17 (1970): 278–322; François Lebrun, "Naissances illégitimes et abandons d'enfants en Anjou au XVIIIe siècle," *Annales: économies, sociétés, civilisations* 27, nos. 4–5 (July–Oct. 1972): 1183–1189; Cissie Fairchilds, "Female Sexual Attitudes and the Rise of Illegitimacy: A Case Study," *Journal of Interdisciplinary History* 8 (1978): 627–667; George D. Sussman, "The Wet-Nursing Business in Nineteenth-Century France," *French Historical Studies* 9, no. 2 (Fall 1975): 304–328, esp. 306–308. For an example of a working woman of the artisan class who sent her children to be wet-nursed, see the account of the mother of Pierre Samuel Du Pont de Nemours in *The Memoirs of P. S. Du Pont de Nemours Addressed to His Children,* edited and translated by Elizabeth Fox-Genovese (Wilmington: Scholarly Resources, 1984).

23. See note 6 above and Yvonne Forado-Cuneo, "Les Ateliers de charité de Paris pendant la révolution française 1789–1791," *La Révolution Française,* 86 (1933): 317–342, and 87 (1934): 29–123.

24. On Rose Bertin, see Abensour, p. 184, and innumerable contemporaneous memoirs such as Henriette Louise, baronne d'Oberkirch, *Mémoires de la baronne d'Oberkirch sur la cour de Louis XVI et la société française avant 1789,* edited by Suzanne Burkard (Paris: Mercure de France, 1970).

25. Roderick Phillips, "Women's Emancipation, the Family and Social Change in Eighteenth-Century France," *Journal of Social History* 12, no. 4 (Summer 1979): 553–568.

26. Hufton, *The Poor;* Porphyre Petrovitch, "Recherches sur la criminalité à Paris dans la seconde moitié du XVIII siècle," in Abbiateci et al., *Crimes et criminalité,* pp. 187–261; Arlette Farge, *Le Vol d'aliments à Paris au XVIIIe siècle* (Paris: Plon, 1974), esp. pp. 62–69, 116–122; "Filles publiques," Archives municipales de Bordeaux, FF 75.

27. Abensour, pp. 215–221, on the training of midwives and the competitive response of the surgeons; Madame Coutanceau, *Elèments de l'art d'accoucher en faveur des élèves sages-femmes de la généralité de Guyenne* (Bordeaux: M. Racle, 1784); *Une Femme d'affaires au XVIIIe siècle. La Correspondance de madame de Maraise, collaboratrice d'Oberkampf,* edited by Serge Chassagne (Paris: Privat, 1981). For women and education, see the essay by Samia I. Spencer[, "Women and Education," in *French Women and the Age of Enlightenment,* ed. Samia I. Spencer (Bloomington: University of Indiana Press, 1984), 83–96].

28. Carolyn Lougee, *Le Paradis des Femmes: Women, Salons, and Social Stratification in Seventeenth-Century France* (Princeton: Princeton University Press, 1976), pp. 173–208; J. C. Barnard, *Fénelon on Education* (Cambridge: Cambridge University Press, 1966).

29. Elizabeth Fox-Genovese and Eugene D. Genovese, "The Ideological Bases of Domestic Economy," in *Fruits of Merchant Capital* (New York: Oxford University Press, 1983); Barbara Corrado Pope, "Revolution and Retreat: Upper-Class French Women after 1789," in Berkin and Lovett, *Women, War and Revolution*, pp. 215–236; Margaret H. Darrow, "French Noblewomen and the New Domesticity, 1750–1850," *Feminist Studies* 5, no. 1, (Spring 1979): 41–65; Claire de Rémusat, *Essai sur l'éducation des femmes* (Paris: L'Advocat, 1824); Madame Gacon-Dufour, *Manuel de la ménagère à la ville et à la campagne et de la femme de basse-cour* (Paris: Buisson, 1805), and idem, *Manuel complet de la maîtresse de maison et de la parfaite ménagère* (Paris: Roret, 1826).

Five

Culture and Consciousness in the Intellectual History of European Women

The coming of age of European women's history has, during the past half decade, accelerated the pace of recovering women's presence, roles, and perceptions. This upsurge of feminist scholarship has resulted in much more attention to women by historians independent of feminist concerns.[1] Their work has expanded our knowledge of women's presence and behavior in previous societies and should force renewed attention to problems of theory, notably those that concern women's motivations and perceptions. For if feminism, in its many and ambiguous meanings, continues to influence historians of women, disagreements about feminist theory engender widely disparate interpretations of the lessons to be drawn from women's history. These disagreements emerge as all the more important since women's history seems to be changing from the history of feminism into feminist history.

Perhaps the single most refreshing recent development in women's history has been the resurgence of intellectual history. This work, by touching on the history of ideas of womanhood and gender relations as well as on the history of women's development of a distinctive discourse about themselves and their worlds, offers a new prism through which to consider the origins of modern feminism in particular and of women's thinking in general. It also highlights the theoretical controversies by bringing women's consciousness and opportunities for self-expression to the forefront. Above all, it offers

"Culture and Consciousness in the Intellectual History of European Women." *Signs* 12, no. 3 (Spring 1987): 529–47. Copyright 1987 by the University of Chicago Press. All rights reserved. Reprinted by permission of the publisher.

myriad opportunities to explore the interplay of gender and class struggles, the relation between experience and consciousness, and the complex and shifting roles of families, communities, and states in confining women's bodies and stunting their minds.

Women's intellectual history also depends heavily on the progress in social, political, and economic history. Neglect of the social dimension of women's oppression and of some women's privilege can lead to a premature emphasis on the importance of what women as a sex shared in contrast to what divided them by class. These separate realms of sex and class meet in gender, loosely defined as the social construction of sex. To consider their respective roles in the formation of women's consciousness requires equal attention to women's own narratives and to the dominant discourses to which women belonged or by which they were, in some sense, "colonized."

The most significant recent publications for women's intellectual history may well have been the translation of Christine de Pizan's *The Book of the City of Ladies,* the collection of Joan Kelly's seminal essays (especially the one on early feminist theory), and Caroline Bynum's *Jesus as Mother.*[2] While Kelly claims for modern feminist thought a rich, coherent, and continuous tradition that began four hundred years before the French Revolution, Bynum claims that a special tradition of female "mystical authorization" provided women with an alternative to clerical power in a period characterized by both greater ecclesiastical institutionalization and a growing sense of "man's likeness to God."[3]

The implications of Kelly's and Bynum's work contrasts sharply with that of Dale Spender's recent romp through four centuries of women's intellectual history. According to Spender's conspiratorial interpretation, men have generally silenced women and, when they could not, have suppressed evidence of women's voices. In so doing, men have ensured that male values are perceived "as the *only* valid frame of reference for society," and have prevented "women from sharing, establishing, and asserting their equally real, valid and *different* frame of reference, which is the outcome of different experience."[4] Clearly, men have largely retained a monopoly on the dominant culture, but Spender is saying that men silenced women because women's voices challenged or subverted men's view of the world, not merely because women would challenge men for place. This judgment rests on the correlative assumptions that women's intellectual work reflected a distinctive female culture and that the conflict between the sexes has dominated history. Thus Spender, like others, frequently lumps men's opposition to women under the general and ahistorical categories of misogyny or patriarchalism.

Misogyny can be found in all periods, all communities, all societies, and in many male texts.[5] Misogyny doubtless fuels much of the opposition to women's self-assertion but hardly constitutes an adequate theoretical explanation for women's oppression. For only the naive believe that oppressors must or even generally do hate those whom they oppress. Indeed, the greatest of the horrors are missed by those who fail to understand that hatred need not enter into oppressive relations at all. To emphasize men's hatred and fear of women is to personalize gender relations and detract attention from the various forms of sexism that characterize them. Nor is anything gained by homogenizing all forms of male domination as "patriarchy" and thereby obscuring the specific characteristics of such genuinely patriarchal societies as that of ancient Rome. Misogyny and patriarchy exist in, not outside of, history and must be used with precise reference to historical relations of genders and classes.[6]

Despite temptations to essentialism or ahistoricism, the best recent work in women's history explicitly or implicitly confirms the centrality of historical development to women's experience. Bynum's work links the forms and social acceptance of women's spirituality to the specific conditions of the High Middle Ages and demonstrates how institutional change affected women by excluding them from clerical roles but also by providing alternate opportunities for their agency. Her discussion of "Jesus as mother" arrestingly demonstrates how men's preoccupation with gender roles and relations shaped the dominant culture.

Donald Weinstein and Rudolph Bell also link changes in style and personnel of sainthood to changing social and economic conditions and challenge, at least for religious life, the view that women enjoyed a particularly high status during the Middle Ages that deteriorated with the urbanization of the fourteenth and fifteenth centuries.[7] Weinstein and Bell, like Bynum, stress the significance of the class base from which saints were drawn and argue that it expanded. Less sensitive than Bynum to women's transcendence of gender roles through mysticism, they argue that female sainthood remained closely tied to the prevailing views of appropriate female roles: women were especially likely to be healing and helping saints. They were also likely to embrace their vocations at the price of deep opposition from their families. Would-be saints refused food, mortified their flesh, and wrestled constantly with temptations that would allow them no peace. Their stories foreshadow those of Renaissance female intellectuals and of pious women such as Margery Kempe.

Bell more directly addresses the theme of women's relation to food in his *Holy Anorexia,* in which he argues that the self-starvation of such female saints as Catherine of Siena represented both a quest for personal autonomy vis-à-vis a dominant "patriarchy" and a war against bodily urges. His argument, which relies heavily on the intrinsically compelling modern literature on anorexia, at once highlights some previous women's attempts at self-control and slights the historically specific analysis of women's motivations.[8] Caroline Bynum, paying more attention to the culture from which these women's motivations emerged, argues conversely that their fasting represented a flight to, rather than from, physicality.[9]

Bynum sheds additional light on female vocations by showing that women who began their careers in convents as children, in contrast to those who began them as young women, manifested a special spiritual self-confidence and authority. Although she does not make the explicit connection, her work subtly confirms the insight of such women intellectuals as Christine de Pizan and Mary Astell that cloistered communities offered women essential support to attain excellence.[10] Both the women saints and the women mystics operated within the confines of the same discourse that feminist scholars today are finding in secular medieval courtesy books and literature.[11] We are beginning to get a picture of women's relation to the dominant model of womanhood, to the tension between elements of rejection and of acceptance. Perhaps the most arresting and detailed account of one young woman's search for identity within the confines of Renaissance society can be found in Judith Brown's *Immodest Acts*. Brown scrupulously explores the relations between a woman's motivations and the patterns of language and behavior in which her society allows her to express them.[12]

Women's possibilities for effective action varied according to time and class. The debate about putative changes in women's status, especially according to class, remains murky. Suzanne Wemple demonstrates that the weaker the state, the Church, and class organization, the more power upper-class Carolingian women enjoyed, although less as individuals than as members of families. As the family gained at the expense of the state, women gained. Carolingian promotion of the indissolubility of marriage increased not only women's prestige and security but also their subjection to their husbands. Retha Warnicke suggests that the power of English Catholic women similarly increased under Elizabeth, when Catholic households functioned as miniature parishes.[13]

In an early and influential article, Joan Kelly, noting a growing confinement of upper-class women in the Italian city-states, had queried whether the so-called Renaissance qualified as such for women.[14] Kelly's subsequent article on feminist theory reversed her earlier position and implicitly identified the emergence of a coherent body of feminist thought in the period that she had originally claimed was the seedbed of women's domestic confinement and the great downturn in women's status. The instructive contradiction between Kelly's two positions exposes as problematic the relations between ideological and social change for women and as even more problematic women's relation to hegemonic (male) culture. The Renaissance, the Reformation, and the rapid expansion of commerce have all been related to the growth of "individualism" in Western culture. But, as Bynum's work implicitly confirms, the growth of that (male) individualism tended to subject women to increased male authority within smaller families, even as it introduced at least the literate to a concept of individualism that permitted them a glimpse of a new imaginative universe in which they might figure as authoritative subjects.[15]

In practice, as Wemple and others demonstrate, women's intellectual and educational opportunities increased, albeit at a much lower level, in tandem with those of the men of their class. The rationale for educating women and the nature of the education they received constitute another matter. The incentives for educating women include the spread of Protestantism, the dissemination of the idea of the "mother-educator," and, eventually, the need for a minimally educated female labor force.[16] The history of women's education constitutes an important part of the history of women's intellectual life. But we know immeasurably more about the education of women following the rise of capitalism and the modern—especially the democratic—state than before, primarily because the systematic attempt to educate women emerged with them. In this perspective, Mary Astell's preoccupation with the education of elite women emerges as pivotal—however one judges her status as the "first feminist."[17]

Precapitalist European societies placed a low priority on educating women and actively discouraged women who sought educations or respect as intellectuals. Fine studies by Retha Warnicke, Betty Travitsky, Margaret King and Albert Rabil, and others confirm that during the Renaissance and Reformation some Italian and English women intellectuals pieced together educations with the assistance of devoted fathers, brothers' tutors, or helpful local clerics.[18] These studies also confirm that few if any women, even the most privileged, who alone had access to such opportunity, managed to acquire educations equal to those of the most learned men or managed to produce as much high-level work as those men. A disproportionate number of aspiring women intellectuals ended their lives in silence or illness, or in the paradoxically stimulating yet stifling intellectual atmosphere of the convents.

The personal histories of intellectual women compel subjective analysis, but many of the most accomplished women of the early period did not leave autobiographical accounts. Any impulses women might have had to chronicle their struggles presumably withered under the severe opprobrium attached to any authoritative female voice. In the occasional female autobiographical account, such as the *Book* of Margery Kempe, the woman

herself did not write but dictated, and she invoked the first person only because of a special, divine mission, not because of her own subjective worth.[19]
Significantly, religious vocations apparently provided the most compelling
justification for women's first-person narratives. However, it is not safe to
assume that they consciously invoked that calling as a subterfuge for individualistic self-assertion.

Whatever the complex motivations of female saints, many learned ladies
apparently sought recognition as what Simon Shepherd designates "warrior
women," even as they defied the conventions that normally circumscribed
the acceptable actions of their sex.[20] Despite a tradition of transvestism, most
extensively discussed by Marina Warner in her book on Joan of Arc, church
and secular leaders were quick to excoriate women who transgressed the
spirit of their sex, most notably those whom they denigrated as Amazons.[21]
But most women intellectuals, like most women saints, probably were less
intent on denying their sex than they were on challenging the limits imposed
on women. No doubt the models of women's strength changed in prebourgeois Europe just as the persistent misogynist attitudes assumed different
guises in different periods.[22] European culture, despite deep hostility toward
and mistrust of women, especially women's sexuality, recognized female
strength and even allowed for the possibility of positive female, as distinct
from male, strength. Further, as Hanna Pitkin has argued, even the most
sophisticated political theory took account of gender.[23] Early modern European women and men worked within a dominant discourse on gender, even
if they drew different conclusions from it. The Britomart of Spenser's imagination shares much with Christine de Pizan's models of female excellence.

The affiliation between Christine de Pizan's ideas and those of succeeding intellectual women is also emerging. However, tracing that transmission
from Christine to her successors and between women of different social
groups depends heavily on female literacy, and, since so few medieval women
were literate, the record remains spotty.[24] The men, notably clerics, who
produced the earliest models of European womanhood in hagiographic
accounts of the early medieval queens, invoked the most conventional categories of female domestic virtue and passed lightly over their heroines' threatening and unladylike political wheelings and dealings.[25] The domestic model
of female virtue that dominated male views of female excellence throughout
the Middle Ages and early modern periods influenced women's own ideas
and circumscribed their possibilities for effective action.[26]

Work by M. Wensky and Merry Woods on women in guilds, like that of
Barton Hacker on women and the military, taken in conjunction with the
fine essays in the collections edited respectively by Barbara Hanawalt and by
Lindsey Charles and Lorna Duffin, suggests that during the medieval and

early modern periods the growth of the state and of institutionalization tended to reinforce the power of men, as heads of families, over women and thus tended to promote the domestic confinement of women.[27] According to David Herlihy, smaller, more efficiently and domestically organized families appeared in various parts of Europe beginning in the late Middle Ages and "developed a distinctive set of relationships" characterized by the domination of the father.[28]

Joan Kelly's feminist tradition embodied women's early attempts to assimilate the new notions of individual excellence and subjective authority to their own sense of female excellence. The specific ways by which women transmitted these ideas require documentation, but whether there was overall a continuous development in feminist discourse may not be important. Clearly, as the conditions from which Christine's voice emerged recurred (with local differences), her claims for women also reemerged, and from the fifteenth century an increasing number of voices defended the claims of women as a sex. Whether they defended those claims in the language of individual political rights is another matter.

Kelly's linking of the "feminism" prior to 1789 to that of the modern period is troublesome. Judgment depends primarily on how we assess the relation between broad historical change and the history of ideas in women's history. It remains open to debate whether feminism should be primarily identified with the elite intellectual tradition that was indispensable to its emergence. Margaret Spufford's work on popular culture suggests, first, that female literacy was much more widespread in seventeenth-century England than indicated by the official statistics, which reflect only women's ability to sign their names; and, second, that the plays, ballads, and stories with which the women of the popular classes were familiar disseminated a variety of positive and negative images of women. But both popular and elite culture remained bound by the terms of the *querelle des femmes,* with its underlying assumptions of male superiority, until the eighteenth century.[29] Thus, Phyllis Mack shows that the success of women prophets during the English Civil War depended precisely on their being exceptional. For their contemporaries' acceptance of their vastly overreaching the bounds of the conventional women's role confirmed that role as normative.[30]

Women writers have long had to work within a dominant discourse and have had to struggle against a hostile ideology of womanhood and for a language of women's being. Susan Schibanoff has argued that Christine overcame the sense of self-alienation and self-hatred with which male theory swamped her by deciding that "her own feelings and thoughts about women . . . are more authoritative than the opinions of all the poets and philosophers she has studied" and by elevating "personal experience into a form of

wisdom higher than anything literacy and authority can offer."[31] Some subsequent women found a special relation to the dominant tradition without
so directly challenging it by "mothering" men's minds.[32] Nonetheless,
Schibanoff's remarks point to a tension within women's history that Christine did articulate. Christine inaugurated not only a tradition of women's
writing on behalf of the excellence of women—in the theoretical discourse—
but also a tradition of women writing women's stories. The two traditions
persist and also shape the ways in which we write our various versions of
women's history. But since the eighteenth century, perhaps earlier, they have
also tended to separate into objective and subjective, or structural and autobiographical, streams. The split, which has roots in the Renaissance and the
scientific revolution, crystallized in the triumph of capitalism and of the ideology of bourgeois individualism that were anchored by the great English
and French revolutions.

During the middle of the eighteenth century, as Rita Goldberg and others have argued, the dominant culture seems to have generated a new image
of woman—perhaps the first glacial shift since antiquity, although glimmerings appeared in England earlier. Genuine misogyny persisted but lost official standing and retreated into indirection. The prevailing images of shrew,
harlot, and Amazon gave way to the image of the romantic heroine and loving mother, quintessentially celebrated by Rousseau and Goethe. This model
accompanied the intellectual revolution of Enlightened thought and men's
new sense of themselves and their needs as individuals in a harshly competitive world; it proposed a new generalized view of women as members of a
species and a new view of female sexuality, the danger of which it whimsi-
cally denied or repressed. It extolled women as custodians of morality and
religion, now reduced to the virtues of the home. And it explicitly generalized not merely women's essence as sexual beings but women's social roles
as members of a gender as well. Although the new vision of women as
domestic beings had precedents, it differed in granting women dominion in
the home.[33]

This new view of women, as developed by men, did not grant women
full status as individuals. Susan Staves has perceptively observed that in the
British literature of the mid-eighteenth century, pity for "seduced maidens"
was lavished as much, if not more, on their fathers. And Mary Lyndon Shanley has argued that, as late as in the discussion of divorce in 1857, many men
regarded women's right to hold property as a threat to marriage because of
its implicit recognition of the existence of two separate minds. The gap between the newly favorable portrayal of women and the persisting, possibly
increasing, discrimination against women as social actors doubtless prompted
Mary Wollstonecraft's bugle call. It is hard to imagine Wollstonecraft's

language of rights independent of the broader culture that was proclaiming men's rights as individuals even as it also proclaimed women's submission.[34]

By the end of the eighteenth century women's literacy was substantially increasing, with a concomitant increase in women's writing for a distinctly female, as well as a mixed, public. The fiction that promoted the new model of woman offered women themselves a powerful vehicle for their own voices.[35] Katharine Rogers has argued that eighteenth-century British women's writings, including fiction, should be recognized as "feminist." By feminist she refers to women's writing of their own experience for other women and women's interest in telling and appreciating women's stories. In different ways, Mary Poovey and Judith Newman have insisted on women's growing ability to subvert images of female gentility and passivity—the image of the proper lady—by faithfully advancing their own experience as an implicit judgment on dominant male views of women.[36]

Women's ability to share their stories increased exponentially with the increase in women's literacy and the circulation of women's writings. But this burgeoning women's culture need not necessarily be equated with feminism. Basically, it derived from and perpetuated an essentialist view of women as a sex, even if it can occasionally move beyond it. Hilda Smith, writing about seventeenth-century intellectual and literary women, prefers to restrict feminism to the attempt to claim the benefits of rationalism for women and deplores the sentimentalization of women's writings in the eighteenth century.[37] Mary Wollstonecraft—and herein lies much of her force—drew on both the rationalist and the essentialist currents, but she added to them a structural and political dimension that distinguishes her thought from anything that came before.

The upper-class and especially the middle-class women who initially benefited from the new ideals of educated and domestic womanhood did not immediately pick up on either the political or the structural implications of Wollstonecraft's feminism. Some did, however, begin to connect ideas of women as a sex to ideas of women as a gender—to imagine that women's needs as women concerned social and political as well as personal relations and that claims for women would have to be made in the name of all women. Nonetheless, in general the class lines held firm, and even Elizabeth Gaskell, who sympathized with lower-class women, accepted and worked into her fictions the ideas of bourgeois political economy.[38]

By and large, during the late eighteenth and early nineteenth centuries, the political relay passed to working-class women and to sisters committed to their cause. Lower-class women responded energetically to the social and political transformations of the period, although scholars disagree about their goals and their views of themselves. So far, evidence about attitudes of active political and intellectual women, notably Owenites and Saint-Simonians, toward female sexuality exceeds that for working-class women. But even the scattered evidence leaves no doubt that women of the popular classes had their own ideas about women.[39]

Work on women in popular protests, working-class politics, and utopian socialist movements demonstrates that from the 1780s to the 1840s the implications of the French and industrial revolutions were worked out through a complex intermingling of old and new attitudes. Claire Moses and Barbara Taylor have drawn attention to the compelling visions of women's sexual and economic freedom advanced by the women of the Saint-Simonian and Owenite movements. Taylor makes large claims for Owenite socialist women's understanding (shared by some Owenite men) that the fight against capitalism, the bourgeoisie, and emerging industrialization constituted a fight against the sexual exploitation of women within the family. She ultimately agrees with the subjective interpretation of women's history as the chronicle of the struggle for women's personal liberation, although she scrupulously attends to the structural questions. Her conclusions differ from those of Moses, who emphasizes the structural foundations for women's protest, and differ even more from those of Dorothy Thompson and David Jones, who have carefully studied the Chartist women for whom Taylor barely veils her contempt.[40]

The Chartist women do, ultimately, constitute the best test for the roles and attitudes of women in popular social and political protest during the early nineteenth century. Thompson views their mobilization as evidence of the mobilization of whole communities against the onslaught of industrial capitalism and in favor of working people's participation in government. She and Jones both underscore Chartist women's commitment to the cause, their commitment to their rights as women, and their willingness in the end to fulfill prescribed women's roles if necessary to advance the cause. Malcolm I. Thomis and Jennifer Grimmet, in a valuable, if occasionally flawed, overview of women's roles in popular protest throughout the period, argue even more strongly that traditional notions of gender relations governed not merely women's own actions in popular protests but also men's occasional dressing as women to defend specific community rights associated with women's sphere.[41]

The impact of capitalism on women continues to provoke heated debate, especially for the industrial era. Feminist scholars like Joan Burstyn, Carol Dyhouse, and Deborah Gorham, who study women's education and the ideology of womanhood, emphasize the importance of the doctrine and practice of separate spheres, which they see as the distinguishing mark of women's experience under capitalism. Yet recent work has shown that the ideology of separate spheres flourished in the medieval and early modern periods, too,[42] and women's history suggests that if capitalism had any effect, it was slowly to undermine separate spheres by eroding their material foundations.

Confusion persists in great part because those societies in which separate spheres had the least justification insisted most firmly on their basis in biology and natural law. Societies in which women's competition for men's places was becoming a real possibility, if not yet a general practice, raised the doctrine of separate spheres to new ideological prominence. The more advanced the economy, the more likely the society was to advance an ideology of separate spheres to justify separate and unequal education for women and the exclusion of women from the emerging professions and political life. This ideology of female confinement strongly influenced women's intellectual and organizational efforts.[43] Martha Vicinus has sensitively explored the personal tensions and social limitations that plagued single women who sought psychological and economic independence within nineteenth-century British society.[44] Women prophets of female emancipation or female excellence (the two claims occasionally intertwined) drew on old dreams of ordered communities, new visions of communities of free individuals, and evangelical traditions. Some helped to lay foundations of subsequent feminist movements. Variously, they embodied the romanticism and transitional radical politics of their time.[45]

By mid-century, notwithstanding the defeat of these early struggles and dreams, bourgeois women's organizations began to promote women's rights. Except for recent work on France, contemporary scholars have not shown much concern for the topic of suffrage, partly because much has already been written and partly perhaps because of a growing disillusionment with institutional rights coupled with a growing interest in the more diffuse manifestations of sexism.[46] The debate over the relations between the organized feminist movement in general—notably the struggle for women's political rights—and a more diffuse "womanist" feminism nonetheless persists.[47] It may even be gaining a welcome new complexity thanks to Mary Jo Maynes's and others' renewed attention to the respective claims of gender and class in working-class women's perceptions of the salient obstacles to their own emancipation.[48] Also, biographies, such as Sheila Herstein's study of the idiosyncratic middle-class feminist Barbara Leigh Smith Bodichon, are increasing our understanding of the relations between personal motivations and political strategies.[49]

The experience of working-class women, like that of their middle-class sisters, confirms the tightening grasp of the doctrine of separate spheres as the model for gender relations and European society's growing preoccupation with sexual difference. The churches, the medical profession, and many conservative politicians and social theorists viewed women as unsuited for anything but marriage and motherhood. The discourse on sexuality intertwined with men's crass opposition to competition from women. The two are frequently difficult to disentangle but obviously concurred in viewing women's gender roles as inevitably dictated by their sexuality.[50] Nonetheless, at least some working-class women, as Juliane Jacobi-Dittrich argues, "refused to accept a role as victim of a male-dominated love life" and "developed personal and/or political goals for themselves."[51]

The tantalizing work on sexuality and social relations whets the appetite for more. Judith Walkowitz has built on her pioneering study of women's attitudes toward the relations between gender and sex to argue that the myth of Jack the Ripper was used, under the guise of protecting women against male violence, to intensify their domestic confinement. Alain Corbin has argued that the very regulation of "modern" French prostitution encouraged bourgeois men's fantasies of female sexuality independent of reproduction, thereby, he might have added, more stringently confining bourgeois women to their socially defined reproductive and asexual roles. By analogy, the popular fiction for women during this period also sought to bind women psychologically and imaginatively to their domestic identities.[52] Women themselves remained deeply divided. Did they want equal relations between the sexes through promotion of greater sexual freedom for themselves, or did they want less for men?

Not surprisingly, the twentieth century generated a massive increase in women's subjective testimony and with it an increase in the variety of women's voices. In particular, elite and intellectual women appear to have entertained more radical views, especially about sexuality and women's independence, than many of their less affluent sisters. Women who experienced the Great War as a liberation or who, like Rebecca West, vigorously pressed women's claims for independence differed significantly from Marie Stopes's middle-class correspondents who sought greater sexual pleasure for themselves, but only if it did not jeopardize a stable and companionate marriage. School girls meanwhile continued to read magazines that bombarded them with conventional models.[53]

All of the work on the twentieth century confirms that sexism, instead of receding with the triumph of modernity, may even have become more generalized and more difficult to locate in any single institution. The so-called sexual revolution may have loosened the grip of the nuclear family on female sexuality, but it is not clear that it significantly weakened sexism or acceptance of conventional gender roles. The Nazis viewed racism and the sexism it reinforced as twin poles of a comprehensive ideology of social order.[54]

The record shows both vast gains in the possibility for an independent existence for women and persistent hostility to that independence. The waves of feminism that punctuate the century also testify to women's own growing commitment to an ideal of personal liberation. Feminists continue to differ among themselves as to whether women most need formal rights equal to those of men or whether they need a cultural and psychological revolution. They differ over whether women's liberation will mean freedom to be like men or freedom to be more like women. Above all, they differ over what constitutes the authentic female voice. Here, the debate, which sets culture against politics, most sharply divides Marxist feminists and separatists, especially some of the new French feminists. As the recent work in European women's history demonstrates, we are far from clear about what we mean by women's culture, much less women's consciousness. To the extent that women have been "colonized," the dominant intellectual traditions have shaped their ways of thinking about themselves and the world. The language of feminism is heavily indebted to changes in the dominant culture and cannot be understood independent of them.[55] Women have drawn on their own experience to write their own stories, but always on the basis of their experience in a specific society. Even the ideal of personal liberation, which perniciously influences contemporary feminist theory, derives from the disintegration of European bourgeois (male) culture.

Temma Kaplan, writing of women's protests in Barcelona in the early twentieth century, has suggested that we adopt the term "female consciousness" as a substitute for the bankrupt categories of Marxism and feminism.[56] Her attempt to capture faithfully the experience of the working-class women she has studied commands an admiration that we should not confuse with acceptance of her theoretical suggestion. For women's consciousness does not derive exclusively from their biology or even from their everyday lives in the narrow sense. It also derives from their communities' and the larger society's models of womanhood, from structural opportunities for women as women and for working people as members of a class, from prevailing family and political relations, and more. On any given occasion, women may act out of their complex sense of their identities, rights, and responsibilities as women. But even then that sense will also derive from their sense of themselves as members of a class, a nation, and a larger culture.

Louise Tilly, who champions the social determination of women's experience, insists that women resist oppression or exploitation according to the same principles as men. They do not necessarily engage in the same kinds of resistance as men, but they, like men, will act in response to the possibilities that society shapes for them.[57] Her position follows logically from her commitment to social science and to the historian's presumed responsibility to aim for a rational and objective assessment of social structure and relations. She resoundingly castigates the flight from materialism into "feelings, attitudes, and unique symbolic acts" and warns against generalizing about the mentality of a group from the subjective experience of an individual. But Tilly's plea for a structural analysis that can explain how groups thought and felt ends in a misguided condemnation of the attempt to study psychological states. She counterposes social relations and psychological relations as if they were essentially incompatible.[58]

The new European women's intellectual history alerts us to the complex links between women's discourses and dominant (male) discourses. To be a woman in biology, sexuality, and everyday life lies at the core of any woman's experience of membership in a gender. But to be a woman in those ways is only the beginning, and even those ways are defined in a language fashioned by the others to whom women relate. Consciousness is, finally, a matter of language, as are political and social goals. And all three are also matters of political and social relations—of power and its abuses.

Notes

1. For a trenchant critique of the nonfeminist history of women, see Susan Mosher Stuard, "The Annales School and Feminist History: Opening Dialogue with the American Stepchild," *Signs: Journal of Women in Culture and Society* 7, no. 1 (Autumn 1981): 135–43. For recent review articles, see Joan Scott, "Women in History: The Modern Period," *Past and Present*, no. 101 (November 1983), 141–57; and Olwen Hufton, "Women in History: The Early Modern Period," *Past and Present*, no. 101 (November 1983), 125–40. This review primarily addresses works published in English since 1975. The references cited here only begin to do justice to the recent work.

2. Christine de Pizan, *The Book of the City of Ladies,* trans. Earl Jeffrey Richards, foreword by Marina Warner (New York: Persea Books, 1982); Joan Kelly, "Early Feminist Theory and the *Querelle des Femmes,* 1400–1789" (1982), reprinted in *Women, History, and Theory: The Essays of Joan Kelly* (Chicago: University of Chicago Press, 1984); Caroline Walker Bynum, *Jesus as Mother: Studies in the Spirituality of the High Middle Ages* (Berkeley and Los Angeles: University of California Press, 1982).

3. Bynum, 255.

4. Dale Spender, *Women of Ideas and What Men Have Done to Them from Aphra Behn to Adrienne Rich* (London: Routledge & Kegan Paul, 1982), 5.

5. See Ian Maclean, *The Renaissance Notion of Woman: A Study in the Fortunes of Scholasticism and Medical Science in European Intellectual Life* (Cambridge: Cambridge University Press, 1980). Compare Arlene Miller Guinsburg, "The Counterthrust to Sixteenth-Century Misogyny: The Work of Agrippa and Paracelsus," *Historical Reflections / Reflexions historiques* 8, no. 1 (Spring 1981): 3–28; and the subtle analysis of Patricia Crawford, "Attitudes to Menstruation in Seventeenth-Century England," *Past and Present*, no. 91 (May 1981), 47–73.

6. Sheila Rowbotham, "The Trouble with Patriarchy," in *People's History and Socialist Theory,* ed. Raphael Samuel (London: Routledge & Kegan Paul, 1981), 364–69; Susan Moller Okin, "Patriarchy and Married Women's Property in England: Questions

about Some Current Views," *Eighteenth-Century Studies* 17, no. 2 (Winter 1983/84): 121–38.

7. Donald Weinstein and Rudolph M. Bell, *Saints and Society: The Two Worlds of Medieval Christendom, 1000–1700* (Chicago: University of Chicago Press, 1982), 223.

8. Rudolph M. Bell, *Holy Anorexia* (Chicago: University of Chicago Press, 1985).

9. Caroline Walker Bynum, "Fasts, Feasts, and Flesh: The Religious Significance of Food to Medieval Women," *Representations,* no. 11 (Summer 1985), 1–25.

10. For a new study of Astell's life and ideas, see Ruth Perry, *The Celebrated Mary Astell: An Early English Feminist* (Chicago: University of Chicago Press, 1986).

11. Dianne Bornstein, *The Lady in the Tower: Medieval Courtesy Literature for Women* (Hamden, Conn.: Archon Books, 1983); Nikki Stiller, *Eve's Orphans: Mothers and Daughters in Medieval English Literature* (Westport, Conn.: Greenwood Press, 1980); and Peter Dronke, *Women Writers of the Middle Ages* (Cambridge: Cambridge University Press, 1984).

12. Judith C. Brown, *Immodest Acts: The Life of a Lesbian Nun in Renaissance Italy* (New York: Oxford University Press, 1986).

13. Suzanne Fonay Wemple, *Women in Frankish Society: Marriage and the Cloister, 500–900* (Philadelphia: University of Pennsylvania Press, 1981); Retha Warnicke, *Women of the English Renaissance and Reformation* (Westport, Conn.: Greenwood Press, 1983).

14. Kelly (n. 2 above).

15. For the misogynist treatment of Florentine women in their families of origin, see Christiane Klapisch-Zuber, *Women, Family, and Ritual in Renaissance Italy,* trans. Lydia Cochrane (Chicago: University of Chicago Press, 1985).

16. See Samia Spencer, "Women and Education," in *French Women and the Age of Enlightenment,* ed. Samia Spencer (Bloomington: Indiana University Press, 1984) [, 83–96]; Susan C. Karant-Nunn, "Continuity and Change: Some Effects of the Reformation on the Women of Zwickau," *Sixteenth Century Journal* 12, no. 2 (1982): 17–42; Linda L. Clark, "The Socialization of Girls in the Primary Schools of the Third Republic," *Journal of Social History* 15, no. 4 (Summer 1982): 685–98; Karen M. Offen, "The Second Sex and the Baccalaureate in Republican France, 1800–1924," *French Historical Studies* 13, no. 2 (Fall 1983): 252–86.

17. Perry (n. 10 above).

18. Margaret L. King and Albert Rabil, Jr., eds., *Her Immaculate Hand: Selected Works by and about the Women Humanists of Quattrocento Italy* (Binghamton, N.Y.: Medieval & Renaissance Texts & Studies, 1983); Warnicke; Betty Travitsky, comp. and ed., *The Paradise of Women: Writings by English Women of the Renaissance* (Westport, Conn.: Greenwood Press, 1981); Suzanne W. Hull, *Chaste, Silent, and Obedient: English Books for Women* (San Marino, Calif.: Huntington Library, 1982); and Hilda L. Smith, *Reason's Disciples: Seventeenth-Century English Feminists* (Urbana: University of Illinois Press, 1982).

19. See Clarissa W. Atkinson, *Mystic and Pilgrim: The Book and World of Margery Kempe* (Ithaca, N.Y.: Cornell University Press, 1983).

20. Simon Shepherd, *Amazons and Warrior Women: Varieties of Feminism in Seventeenth-Century Drama* (New York: St. Martin's Press, 1981). Also see Dianne Dugaw, "The Female Warrior Heroine in Anglo-American Balladry" (Ph.D. diss., University of California, Los Angeles, 1982).

21. Marina Warner, *Joan of Arc* (London: George Weidenfeld & Nicolson, 1981).

22. Christina Larner, *Enemies of God: The Witchhunt in Scotland* (Baltimore: Johns Hopkins University Press, 1981); Joy Deborah Wiltenberg, "Disorderly Women and

Female Power in the Popular Literature of Early Modern England and Germany" (Ph.D. diss., University of Virginia, 1984).

23. Hanna Fenichel Pitkin, *Fortune Is a Woman: Gender and Politics in the Thought of Niccolò Machiavelli* (Berkeley and Los Angeles: University of California Press, 1984). See also Arlene W. Saxenhouse, *Women in the History of Political Thought* (New York: Praeger Publishers, 1985).

24. Kelly, "Early French Feminist Theory," in *Women, History, and Theory* (n. 2 above). Also, see Diane Bornstein, ed., *Ideals for Women in the Works of Christine de Pizan* (Detroit: Michigan Consortium for Medieval and Early Modern Studies, 1981); Deborah A. Symonds, "The Re-forming of Women's Work and Culture: Scotland, 1760–1820" (Ph.D. diss., State University of New York at Binghamton, 1984); and Peter Taylor and Hermann Rebel, "Hessian Peasant Women, Their Families, and the Draft: A Social-Historical Analysis of Four Grimm Fairytales," *Journal of Family History* 6, no. 4 (Winter 1981): 347–78. For women's plays, which may have provided an important link between elite and popular women's ideas, see Fidelis Morgan, *The Female Wits: Women Playwrights on the London Stage, 1660–1720* (London: Virago, 1981).

25. Paula Stafford, *Queens, Concubines, and Dowagers: The King's Wife in the Early Middle Ages* (Athens: University of Georgia Press, 1983).

26. Judith Herrin, "Women and the Faith in Icons in Early Christianity," in *Culture, Ideology and Politics: Essays for Eric Hobsbawm*, ed. Raphael Samuel and Gareth Stedman Jones (London: Routledge & Kegan Paul, 1982), [56–83,] demonstrates that women especially defended icon worship because it could be carried on at home. Nonetheless, see Susan Groag Bell's argument for the transmission of culture through female—notably mother-daughter—networks, "Medieval Women Book Owners: Arbiters of Lay Piety and Ambassadors of Culture," *Signs* 7, no. 4 (Summer 1982): 742–68.

27. M. Wensky, "Women's Guilds in Cologne in the Later Middle Ages," *Journal of European Economic History* 11, no. 3 (Winter 1982): 631–50; Merry Wiesner Wood, "Paltry Peddlers or Essential Merchants? Women in the Distributive Trades in Early Modern Nuremberg," *Sixteenth-Century Journal* 12, no. 2 (1981): 3–13; Barton C. Hacker, "Women and Military Institutions in Early Modern Europe: A Reconnaissance," *Signs* 6, no. 4 (Summer 1981): 643–71; Barbara A. Hanawalt, ed., *Women and Work in Preindustrial Europe* (Bloomington: Indiana University Press, 1986); Lindsey Charles and Lorna Duffin, eds., *Women and Work in Pre-Industrial England* (London: Croom Helm, 1985); and my "Women and Work," in Spencer, ed. (n. 16 above) [reprinted in this volume, pp. 75–91]. See also Martha C. Howell, *Women, Production, and Patriarchy in Late Medieval Cities* (Chicago: University of Chicago Press, 1986); and Elizabeth Fox-Genovese and Susan Mosher Stuard, *Restoring Women to History: Western Civilization I* (Bloomington, Ind.: Organization of American Historians, 1983).

28. David Herlihy, "The Making of the Medieval Family: Symmetry, Structure, Sentiment," *Journal of Family History* 8, no. 2 (Summer 1983): 116–30. Compare Steven Ozment, *When Fathers Ruled: Family Life in Reformation Europe* (Cambridge, Mass.: Harvard University Press, 1983); and Miriam Chrisman, "Family and Religion in Two Noble Families: French Catholic and English Puritan," *Journal of Family History* 8, no. 2 (Summer 1983): 190–210.

29. Margaret Spufford, *Small Books and Pleasant Histories: Popular Fiction and Its Readership in Seventeenth-Century England* (Athens: University of Georgia Press, 1981); and, on the complex problems of literacy, see Rab Houston, "The Literacy Myth? Illiteracy in Scotland, 1630–1760," *Past and Present*, no. 96 (August 1982), 81–102.

30. Phyllis Mack, "Women as Prophets during the English Civil War," *Feminist Studies* 8, no. 1 (Spring 1982): 19–47.

31. Susan Schibanoff, "Comment on Kelly's 'Early Feminist Theory and the *Querelle des Femmes,* 1400–1789,'" *Signs* 9, no. 2 (Winter 1983): 324.

32. Ruth Perry and Martine Watson Brownley, eds., *Mothering the Mind: Twelve Studies of Writers and Their Silent Partners* (New York: Holmes & Meier, 1984).

33. Rita Goldberg, *Sex and Enlightenment: Women in Richardson and Diderot* (Cambridge: Cambridge University Press, 1984); Elizabeth Fox-Genovese and Eugene D. Genovese, *Fruits of Merchant Capital* (New York: Oxford University Press, 1983), chap. 11, "The Ideological Bases of Domestic Economy"; and Londa Schiebinger, "Skeletons in the Closet: The First Illustrations of the Female Skeleton in Eighteenth-Century Anatomy," *Representations,* no. 14 (Spring 1986), 42–82. Also, see the fine articles by Mary Lindeman, "Love for Hire: The Regulation of the Wet-Nursing Business in Eighteenth-Century Hamburg," *Journal of Family History* 6, no. 4 (Winter 1981): 379–95, and "Maternal Politics: The Principles and Practice of Maternity Care in Eighteenth-Century Hamburg," *Journal of Family History* 9, no. 1 (Spring 1984): 44–63. On England, see Caroline Davidson, *A Woman's Work Is Never Done: A History of Housework in the British Isles, 1650–1950* (London: Chatto & Windus, 1982); Irene Q. Brown, "Domesticity, Feminism, and Friendship: Female Aristocratic Culture and Marriage in England, 1660–1760," *Journal of Family History* 7, no. 4 (Winter 1982): 406–24; Sara Heller Mendelson, "Stuart Women's Diaries and Occasional Memoirs," and Patricia Crawford, "Women's Published Writings, 1600–1700," both in *Women in English Society 1500–1800,* ed. Mary Prior (London: Methuen, 1985); and Margaret George, *Surely We Know Them: Bourgeois Women in Seventeenth-Century England* (Urbana: University of Illinois Press, 1987).

34. Susan Staves, "British Seduced Maidens," *Eighteenth-Century Studies* 14, no. 2 (Winter 1980/81): 109–34; Mary Lyndon Shanley, "'One Must Ride Behind': Married Women's Rights and the Divorce Act of 1857," *Victorian Studies* 25, no. 3 (Spring 1982): 355–76.

35. See Domna C. Stanton and Jeanine Parisier Plottel, eds., *The Female Autograph* (New York: New York Literary Forum, 1984).

36. Katharine M. Rogers, *Feminism in Eighteenth-Century England* (Urbana: University of Illinois Press, 1982); Mary Poovey, *The Proper Lady and the Woman Writer: Ideology as Style in the Works of Mary Wollstonecraft, Mary Shelly, and Jane Austen* (Chicago: University of Chicago Press, 1984); Judith Lowdes Newton, *Women, Power, and Subversion: Social Strategies in British Fiction, 1778–1860* (Athens: University of Georgia Press, 1981). Also, see Nancy Armstrong, "The Rise of Feminine Authority in the Novel," *Novel* 15 (1981/82): 129–45; Nancy K. Miller, "Emphasis Added: Plots and Plausibilities in Women's Fiction," *Publications of the Modern Language Association* 96, no. 1 (January 1981): 36–48; and Judith Hinde Stewart, "The Women Novelists," in Spencer, ed. (n. 16 above).

37. Hilda Smith (n. 18 above). For one example of the essentialist current, see Bonnie G. Smith, "The Contribution of Women to Modern Historiography in Great Britain, France, and the United States, 1750–1940," *American Historical Review* 89, no. 3 (June 1984): 709–32. For a discussion of the pitfalls of essentialism, see Elizabeth V. Spelman, "Woman as Body: Ancient and Contemporary Views," *Feminist Studies* 8, no. 2 (Spring 1982): 109–32.

38. Simon Dentith, "Political Economy, Fiction and the Language of Practical Ideology in Nineteenth-Century England," *Social History* 8, no. 2 (May 1983): 183–99.

39. Thomas W. Laqueur, "The Queen Caroline Affair: Politics as Art in the Reign of George IV," *Journal of Modern History* 54, no. 3 (September 1982): 417–66.

40. Claire Moses, "Saint-Simonian Men / Saint-Simonian Women: The Transformation of Feminist Thought in 1830s' France," *Journal of Modern History* 54, no. 2 (June 1982): 240–67, and *French Feminism in the Nineteenth Century* (Albany: State University of New York Press, 1984); Barbara Taylor, *Eve and the New Jerusalem: Socialism and Feminism in the Nineteenth Century* (New York: Pantheon Books, 1983); Dorothy Thompson, *The Chartists: Popular Politics in the Industrial Revolution* (New York: Pantheon Books, 1984); David Jones, "Women and Chartism," *History* 68, no. 222 (February 1983): 1–21.

41. Malcolm I. Thomis and Jennifer Grimmet, *Women in Protest, 1800–1850* (New York: St. Martin's Press, 1982).

42. Joan Burstyn, *Victorian Education and the Ideal of Womanhood* (London: Croom Helm, 1980); Carol Dyhouse, *Girls Growing Up in Late Victorian and Edwardian England* (London: Routledge & Kegan Paul, 1981); and Deborah Gorham, *The Victorian Girl and the Feminine Ideal* (Bloomington: Indiana University Press, 1982). Compare M. Jeanne Peterson, "No Angels in the House: The Victorian Myth and the Paget Women," *American Historical Review* 89, no. 3 (June 1984): 677–708; Martine Segalen, *Love and Power in the Peasant Family: Rural France in the Nineteenth Century,* trans. Sarah Matthews (Chicago: University of Chicago Press, 1983); and Elizabeth Swain, "Faith in the Family: The Practice of Religion by the Gonzaga," *Journal of Family History* 8, no. 2 (Summer 1983): 177–89.

43. See Karen Offen, "Depopulation, Nationalism, and Feminism in Fin-de-Siècle France," *American Historical Review* 89, no. 3 (June 1984): 648–76. Also, see Claire Richter Sherman and Adele M. Holcomb, eds., *Women as Interpreters of the Visual Arts, 1820–1979* (Westport, Conn.: Greenwood Press, 1981).

44. Martha Vicinus, *Independent Women: Work and Community for Single Women, 1850–1920* (Chicago: University of Chicago Press, 1985). See also the highly polemical Sheila Jeffreys, *The Spinster and Her Enemies: Feminism and Sexuality, 1880–1930* (Boston: Routledge & Kegan Paul, 1986).

45. B. Taylor; Moses; Stanley Zucker, "German Women and the Revolution of 1848: The Case of Kathinka Zitz-Halein and the Humania Association," *Central European History* 13 (1980): 237–54.

46. Steven C. Hause with Anne R. Kenney, *Women's Suffrage and Social Politics in the French Third Republic* (Princeton, N.J.: Princeton University Press, 1984); Patrick K. Bidelman, *Pariahs Stand Up! The Founding of the Liberal Feminist Movement in France, 1858–1889* (Westport, Conn.: Greenwood Press, 1982); and Charles Sowerwine, *Sisters or Citizens? Women and Socialism in France since 1876* (Cambridge: Cambridge University Press, 1982).

47. See the essays in the section "Feminisms" of Ruth-Ellen B. Joeres and Mary Jo Maynes, eds., *German Women in the Eighteenth and Nineteenth Centuries: A Social and Literary History* (Bloomington: Indiana University Press, 1986), notably Richard Evans's restatement of his restrictive use of the term, "The Concept of Feminism: Notes for Practicing Historians," 247–58, and Hans Adler's plea to introduce religion as a serious aspect of the discussion, "On a Feminist Controversy: Louise Otto vs. Louise Aston," 193–214.

48. Mary Jo Maynes, "Gender and Class in Working-Class Women's Autobiographies," in Joeres and Maynes, eds., 230–46.

49. Sheila R. Herstein, *A Mid-Victorian Feminist: Barbara Leigh Smith Bodichon* (New Haven, Conn.: Yale University Press, 1986). See also Olive Banks, *The Biographical Dictionary of British Feminists* (New York: New York University Press, 1985).

50. Ellen Ross and Rayna Rapp, "Sex and Society: A Research Note from Social History and Anthropology," in *Powers of Desire,* ed. Ann Snitow, Christine Stansell, and Sharon Tompson (New York: Monthly Review Press, 1983), 51–73; Walter L. Arnstein, *Protestant versus Catholic in Mid-Victorian England: Mr. Newdegate and the Nuns* (Columbia: University of Missouri Press, 1982); Janet Sayers, *Biological Politics: Feminist and Anti-Feminist Perspectives* (London: Tavistock Publications, 1982). First-person accounts for working women remain sparse, but see *The Red Virgin: Memoirs of Louise Michel,* ed. and trans. Bullit Lowry and Elizabeth Ellington Gunter (University: University of Alabama Press, 1981); and Liz Stanley, ed., *The Diaries of Hannah Cullwick, Victorian Maidservant* (New Brunswick, N.J.: Rutgers University Press, 1984).

51. Juliane Jacobi-Dittrich, "The Struggle for an Identity: Working-Class Autobiographies by Women in Nineteenth-Century Germany," in Joeres and Maynes, eds., 343.

52. Judith Walkowitz, "Jack the Ripper and the Myth of Male Violence," *Feminist Studies* 8, no. 3 (Fall 1982): 543–74, and "Male Vice and Feminist Virtue: Feminism and the Politics of Prostitution in Nineteenth-Century Britain," *History Workshop,* no. 13 (Spring 1982), 77–93; Alain Corbin, "Commercial Sexuality in Nineteenth-Century France: A System of Images and Regulations," *Representations,* no. 14 (Spring 1986), 209–19; Martha Vicinus, "'Helpless and Unfriended': Nineteenth-Century Domestic Melodrama," *New Literary History* 13, no. 1 (1981): 127–43; Sally Mitchell, *The Fallen Angel: Chastity, Class and Women's Reading, 1835–1880* (Bowling Green, Ohio: Bowling Green University Popular Press, 1981); Carol A. Senf, "'Dracula': Stoker's Response to the New Woman," *Victorian Studies* 26, no. 1 (Autumn 1982): 33–50; and D. A. Miller, "*Cage aux folles*: Sensation and Gender in Wilkie Collins's *The Woman in White,*" *Representations,* no. 14 (Spring 1986), 107–36.

53. Sandra M. Gilbert, "Soldier's Heart: Literary Men, Literary Women, and the Great War," *Signs* 8, no. 3 (Spring 1983): 422–50; Jane Marcus, ed., *The Young Rebecca: Writings of Rebecca West, 1911–1917* (New York: Viking Press, 1982); Ellen M. Holtzman, "The Pursuit of Married Love: Women's Attitudes toward Sexuality and Marriage in Great Britain, 1918–1939," *Journal of Social History* 16, no. 2 (Winter 1982): 39–52; Kirsten Drotner, "Schoolgirls, Madcaps, and Air Aces: English Girls and Their Magazine Reading between the Wars," *Feminist Studies* 9, no. 1 (Spring 1983): 33–52; Atina Grossmann, "The New Woman and the Rationalization of Sexuality in Weimar Germany," in Snitow et al., eds., 153–71; Elisabeth Lenk, "Indiscretions of the Literary Beast: Pariah Consciousness of Women Writers since Romanticism," *New German Critique,* no. 27 (Fall 1982), 101–14.

54. Gisela Bock, "Racism and Sexism in Nazi Germany: Motherhood, Compulsory Sterilization, and the State," *Signs* 8, no. 3 (Spring 1983): 400–21. Renate Bridenthal, Atina Grossmann, and Marion Kaplan, eds., *When Biology Became Destiny: Women in Weimar and Nazi Germany* (New York: Monthly Review Press, 1985). See also Patricia Hilden, *Working Women and Socialist Politics in France, 1880–1914: A Regional Study* (Oxford: Clarendon Press, Oxford University Press, 1986), for the argument that men's views of women and men's roles, rather than women's, accounted for the failure of the French socialists to find an abiding place for women.

55. For a revealing example of this indebtedness, as well as a preliminary attempt to wrestle with it, see Alice Jardine, *Gynesis: Configurations of Woman and Modernity* (Ithaca, N.Y.: Cornell University Press, 1985).

56. Temma Kaplan, "Female Consciousness and Collective Action: The Case of Barcelona, 1910–1918," *Signs* 7, no. 3 (Spring 1982): 545–66.

57. Louise A. Tilly, "Paths of Proletarianization: Organization of Production, Sexual Division of Labor, and Women's Collective Action," *Signs* 7, no. 2 (Winter 1981): 400–417.

58. Louise A. Tilly, "People's History and Social Science History," *Social Science History* 7, no. 4 (Fall 1983): 471–72.

Six

Foreword to *Fanny Kemble*

Proud, high-spirited, and, withal, not entirely un-self-critical, Frances Anne Kemble embarked on August 1, 1832, with her father, Charles Kemble, the actor, for an acting tour of the United States in the hopes of restoring the family's fortunes. Kemble, always known as Fanny, had launched her career as an actress three years previously when she had made her debut as Juliet at Covent Garden with a similar object. Her success launched her career and temporarily helped her father, but did not solve the long-term problems. The American tour, which lasted from September 1832 to June 1834, brought the desired professional and financial success and, at its conclusion, Kemble's marriage to Pierce Butler, the heir to a great slaveholding fortune, who had assiduously courted her during her appearance in Philadelphia.

Throughout the tour Kemble kept a journal that she published in 1835 over the intransigent objections of her husband. The initial impetus for publication came from Kemble's determination to earn some money to provide for her beloved aunt, Dall (her mother's sister, Adelaide De Camp), who had accompanied her on the tour and been injured when a carriage overturned. Dall died as a result of those injuries, and the pressing need for money dissipated. Yet Kemble persisted in her plans for publication. Even after her husband deleted all proper names, knowledgeable contemporaries could, with little difficulty, recognize many of the people who figure in her pages. Pierce Butler strenuously objected to Kemble's frank and unflattering depiction of Americans and America. Undoubtedly, he objected to his wife's publishing at all. For as Mrs. Pierce Butler, Fanny Kemble had joined a world in which respectable married ladies did not normally write for publication.

Foreword to *Fanny Kemble: Journal of a Young Actress,* edited by Monica Gough, ix–xx. New York: Columbia University Press, 1990. Copyright 1990 by Columbia University Press. All rights reserved. Used by permission of the publisher.

Today, Frances Anne Kemble is best known as a writer for her celebrated *Journal of a Residence on a Georgian Plantation, 1838–39,* written during a brief stay on Pierce Butler's Sea Island plantations. That journal, published in 1863, constituted a deliberate intervention in the war against slavery, and perhaps a personal attack on the husband from whom she had acrimoniously parted. As a direct, personal testimony to the iniquities of slavery, and as a detailed account of everyday life on a slave plantation, it has ranked among the most widely influential accounts of the antebellum South.

Any close reader of the *Journal of a Residence,* especially one who also knows something of that Southern slave society which Kemble was indicting, cannot but recognize the extent to which she crafted her narrative for maximum polemical effect. Under the veneer of a straightforward account of ordinary life amidst slaveholders and slaves, she dramatically rendered scenes and encounters designed to represent the aspects of the system that most appalled her—notably, the unchecked power of the master, the assault on the spirit as well as the bodies of the slaves. Kemble unmistakably intended to juxtapose the hierarchy and dependence of slave society with the upstanding individualism and personal independence of free (bourgeois) society. From this contrast, Kemble herself emerges as the unswerving defender of the values of work, initiative, and individual responsibility.

Like the *Journal of a Residence,* this journal of Kemble's first visit to the United States, her twenty-two-month tour as an actress, properly belongs to the genre of travelers' accounts. But also like the *Journal of a Residence,* it must be recognized as something more. For, in depicting American society, Kemble was, however covertly, self-consciously depicting herself.

An accomplished actress and a skillful and graceful writer, not to mention a highly self-aware and politically astute woman, Kemble must be credited with multiple purposes in writing and publishing her journals. Not least, she must be credited with scrupulous attention to the representation of herself offered to public scrutiny. The problem of Kemble's self-representation commands particular attention because, by normal criteria, her journals did not focus—or focused only peripherally—on self-representation. Given the genteel and cultivated surface of travel narrative, the present journal in particular challenges us to mobilize all the strategies of reading that literary critics have been developing.

Stylistically, Kemble relies upon informality and apparent spontaneity to establish the tone and structure of her narrative. Embarking on an adventure, exploring a new world, she is simply keeping a record of people and places, manners and morals. She writes as if writing for herself alone. This strategy permits her, without apparent inconsistency, to write only of those objects, customs, and events that capture her attention. Although the pretense of providing a full chronicle provides the principal structure of the narrative, it remains a pretense—a useful stylistic convenience that relieves her of the obligation to impose a more artful narrative structure.

Throughout the journal a cluster of key events recurs frequently enough to afford the reader a sense of her daily life: meals, horseback rides, social gatherings, appearances at the theater. Beyond these, she most commonly writes of trips, outings, social events, or noteworthy people. Intermittently, she offers descriptions of particular places or scenery. And always she interpolates personal comments on weather, food, dress, behavior, literature. Occasionally, she offers arresting observations on the American scene, but, overall, she fails to provide the acute commentaries and telling judgments for which we still read Frances Trollope, Harriet Martineau, and even Kemble's own *Journal of a Residence,* to say nothing of Alexis de Tocqueville. As travelers' accounts go, this journal remains sufficiently impressionistic to permit us to wonder about its author's intentions.

Although we are accustomed to think of journals and diaries as essentially personal and even confessional, Kemble's steadfastly eschews the confessional mode. Here and there, she writes of her personal responses, but only of the most neutral: her responses to discomfort, her judgments of others' behavior, and once her personal experience of fear. Pierce Butler, whom she would marry in the very month (June 1834) in which the journal leaves off, figures with increasing frequency in it from 1833 on, but he receives no personal comment at all. Kemble does not even tell us that he is so constantly mentioned during its closing months because he has fallen in love with Fanny and has accompanied the Kembles on their tour, although she does, again without special comment, show that he accompanies her on unchaperoned expeditions. The reader is given no hint that he and Fanny are planning to marry.

Kemble remains similarly reticent on other personal matters, especially her own inmost feelings. Her journal, in this respect, does not belong to the recognized genre of confessional self-exploration. If anything, this uncommonly talented and poised twenty-three-year-old takes herself as given. Her journal of an actual journey never moves into the realm of metaphor—the journey to self-knowledge. She never confides in her readers, never entrusts us with her secrets. At most, she tersely notes that she did or did not act well on this or that evening.

Reticence notwithstanding, Kemble's journal is, in essential respects, a self-representation—or, a more correctly, a self-portrait. With three years of success as an actress behind her when she began this journal, Kemble could take herself for granted. Her journal would potentially be of interest because she was who she was—Fanny Kemble. She understandably felt no need to introduce herself to her readers. Nor presumably, did she feel any obligation to reveal her private thoughts. Her self-portrait was fashioned less in the interests of candor—much less self-revelation—than in the interests of a subtle and refined self-promotion. Not for her that wanton exhibitionism which would bare the private self to the public gaze. Rather, she sought to construct a public self-representation that would reinforce and enhance her already established reputation as an actress. And she realized her self-appointed task with consummate skill.

The narrator—or self—of Kemble's journal emerges as a cultivated, tasteful, and refined English observer of the American scene. Throughout the journal, Kemble makes scant reference to herself, says little that would remind her readers that she is an unmarried young woman of twenty-three. Her self-representation emerges primarily from her observations on and responses to others, and especially to American manners and morals. Her principal self-identification emerges from her contrasting England and America, from her abiding nostalgia for the England she has left. Although she regularly refers to her own performances at various theaters, she otherwise writes little of her position as an actress.

Kemble established herself as a recognized actress during a period in which it was just becoming acceptable for reputable women to perform in public. To be sure, her own aunt, the celebrated Mrs. Siddons, had paved the way in earning a reputation as a brilliant and highly respectable actress. But her success remained exceptional in an age in which most British actresses belonged to troupes that toured the country and enjoyed questionable reputations for morality. The bourgeois public reacted against what it increasingly perceived as eighteenth-century excesses of self-display. During Kemble's lifetime, the reaction took shape as full-blown Victorian domestic prudery and made women's public self-display yet more problematic. In several places, Kemble writes of the accomplishments of actors, notably her own father and Edmund Kean, in a manner that underscores the artistry and skill of their craft. But she mentions no other actresses at all. In a serious discussion of the best way to stage the witches' scene in *Macbeth,* she refers in passing to the actors who were (mis)playing them, thus, if unintentionally, reminding her readers that many female roles were still being performed by men.

Parts of the journal suggest that Kemble may have been concerned to establish the legitimacy of her own appearance on the stage and, especially, her own credentials as a respectable woman, although she never explicitly raises the issue. In fact, on more than one occasion she takes pains to underscore the artifice of the theatrical performance. She regularly comments on her own performance, sometimes judging it good, sometimes poor. She read-ily points out the absurd reality that underlies the illusion of the play, ridi-culing, for example, a performance during which a costume that was too small for her kept ripping as she moved. She ruthlessly dissects inferior and even comically bad renditions of *Romeo and Juliet,* the play in which she had scored her own first success, which she still loves, and cannot bear to have performed incompetently. In a more general way, she reflects that acting is the lowest of the arts—if it is indeed an art at all. Should it not, she wonders, thus undercutting her own status as an actress, more properly be viewed as a mere amusement?

In these and other ways, Kemble carefully refrains from taking herself as actress too seriously and subtly distances herself from the condition of actress. Yet she is fully capable of covertly defending the profession of acting as craft and even, implicitly, as art. In particular, she fiercely links acting to Shake-speare, the greatest embodiment of English literature. Time and again she refers to the beauty and genius of Shakespeare's plays, berating those who betray their sublime integrity by poor acting. She thereby covertly associates those who act them well with their intrinsic worth. Driving home the rela-tion between fine acting and literary genius, she forcefully opposes the idea advanced by one of her acquaintances that drama could best be rendered by having individuals recite key monologues in private social gatherings. Not possible, she fumes. Shakespeare so rendered would be Shakespeare denatured. Even his eternal lines depend for their full beauty and meaning upon the enactment of the entire play—the stage, the sets, the costumes, the actors.

Kemble's ambiguities and inconsistencies about acting doubtless testify to some uncertainty about her own status as a professional actress. The stud-ied objectivity with which she treats the topic in general and her own per-formances in particular further emphasizes the distance she seeks to establish between herself and her public role, as does her repeated association of the theater and acting with men. On her telling, her role as an actress represents nothing more or less than her practice of a craft. She never claims any spe-cial talent or consideration as a woman and so, by the same token, makes no apology for engaging in what some might view as unwomanly self-display.

The publication of this journal and other evidence confirm that Kemble harbored no serious doubts about her right as a woman to enter the pub-lic sphere. Her most cherished ambitions concerned writing for publication rather than acting, which she had taken up primarily to help her family's financial situation. Even before she went on the stage, she had written a play, *Francis I.* Most of her difficulties with her husband, Pierce Butler, apparently stemmed from her unwillingness to accept the subservient role of wife that he considered essential. Her determination to publish this journal gave rise to a protracted quarrel that was never smoothed over and that must be recognized as one of the contributing causes of their divorce. But the journal does not openly testify to Kemble's commitment to the independent rights of women, nor does it openly emphasize her personal claims to consideration and respect.

Kemble's standards for her personal merit lie not in her acting, nor even explicitly in her status as writer, but in her nationality, her culture, her breeding, her class, with her nationality invariably surpassing and informing the rest. Above all she is English. From first to last, England affords the standards by which she judges everything American. From first to last, England figures as the sign of everything she values.

Throughout the journal, Kemble evokes England as the talisman of her identity. In words disconcertingly similar to those of Robert Browning's "Home Thoughts from Abroad," she voices the nostalgia of the unwilling exile. Oh, to be in England! Oh, to enjoy the English spring! Oh, to smell an English flower! The condition of American roads evokes unflattering comparisons with those of England. The quality of American labor could not be worse; the bearing of American laborers could not be more provocative and insulting. The products of that labor are invariably inferior to English goods. (Thank goodness, Pierce Butler had the wit and consideration to bring some silver forks on the tour in upstate New York, "for the wretched two-pronged iron implements furnished by our host were anything but clean or convenient.") American horses lack any semblance of decent training, but then Americans do not really know how to ride. American women, although beautiful, are insufferably dressed and speak in shrill, grating voices. American men are, in general, hard-driving and coarse. The country's famed republican feeling amounts to a mixture of "impudence and vulgarity to be met with no where but in America." American violets and cowslips have no fragrance. Americans have no sense of that good home religion that anchors any respectable society—do not even regularly celebrate Christmas in the family circle. In short, America is replicating England in caricature, replicating the forms with none of the substance.

Kemble assuredly knew that in sharply criticizing American manners and morals she was establishing herself as superior to Americans. And the qualities in which she depicted herself as superior deserve attention. She understood the qualities of a good horse; she appreciated the fragrance of even the humblest flower; she had impeccable taste in fashion; she spoke in a cultured voice; she appreciated the quality of fine workmanship; she expected the appropriate deference from servants; she knew the difference between silver and iron; she knew, above all, what it was to be a lady. And should her readers mistake her deeper meaning, she insists on "what I have always thought most sacred," namely, "the dignity of woman in her own eyes and those of others." Kemble reserved her private responses for her protracted correspondence with her closest friend, Harriet St. Leger. In this journal, she offers us something else: a highly crafted portrait of herself as discriminating observer.

It is hard to believe that Kemble did not, from the outset, keep her journal with a public purpose in mind. As early as the initial trip across the Atlantic, she mentions that she read her journal to her fellow travelers, the Hodgkinsons. Doubtless her lifelong ambition to excel as a writer informed the care with which she recorded discrete incidents and observations. She frequently dwells upon her love for literature, notably Shakespeare and Byron. Washington Irving, whose work she much admired, evokes one of her few admissions of admiration for things American. Writing, in contrast to acting, unquestionably figured as one of the arts. Writing offered an enduring way to establish her own talent.

The superficially episodic and casual style of a journal also offered protection against the naked display of ambition. Presenting herself as observer rather than as protagonist, or even as author in the formal sense, shielded her from accusations of self-promotion or self-display. By the time that she committed her observations to print, she indisputably knew that many, beginning with her own husband, would not accept her protestations of innocence. She even noted that during her stay in Washington the natives had taken her talk as an insult to America and Americans: "All Washington was in dismay, and my evil deeds and evil words was town talk." But by the time she was revising the journal for publication, she was prepared to dismiss all objections as parochial and self-interested. Perhaps the pithiness of her comments on America did provoke narrow American resentment, but that was their problem not hers. She was already serving the larger interests of truth that she would yet more polemically serve in her *Journal of a Residence*. She was representing the excellence of English taste and, in so doing, representing herself as the embodiment of the English gentlewoman.

This journal concludes abruptly with Kemble's first glimpse of Niagara Falls. Earlier in the journal, she had approvingly reported a conversation with Noah Webster in which he had insisted that he would not try to describe Niagara—that no words could capture its grandeur. Nor does she herself try to do so. As they approached the falls, she was taken with "a perfect frenzy of impatience" so that she could have run the whole remaining way. When they actually arrived near the spot, she sprang from the carriage and rushed along the path "divided only by a thicket from the tumultuous rapids." In a minute, she had passed the thicket and "stood upon Table Rock. Trelawney [one of their traveling companions] seized me by the arm, and without speaking a word, dragged me to the edge of the rapids, to the brink of the abyss. I saw Niagara—Oh God! Who can describe that sight!!!" And so concludes the journal, leaving the reader with the self-consciously romantic picture of Fanny at one with one of the great manifestations of nature.

Fanny Kemble's depiction of her travels in America does not explicitly offer a representation of her internal journey to self-knowledge. One is even permitted to speculate that the published version reflects an uneasy compromise between the self that experienced those travels and the self that published their account. For during the years of the journal, Kemble was falling in love and deciding to marry. By the time she was revising for publication, her marriage was in trouble and her determination to publish was adding to other difficulties. Her representation of herself embodies something of both selves and, in attempting to compromise between them, emphasizes what she wished to be viewed as the constant features of her character. The journal, in this respect, offers a static rather than a dynamic self-representation. It also offers a remarkable, if oblique, glimpse of the mind of an extraordinary woman.

Seven

Feminism and the Rhetoric of Individual Rights, Part One

The defense of equal rights has historically constituted the bedrock of American political rhetoric, and one of its great strengths has consisted precisely in its abstraction from historically diverse conditions. But in our own time, the defense of equal rights can only be extended so far within our legal system. Increasingly, the women's movement is stretching the concept of rights well beyond its original meaning, and above all divorcing it from many, if not most, women's perceptions of their own lives and needs. In many respects, the feminist theorists who emphasize women's difference from men probably capture women's perceptions of themselves better than the feminist theorists who emphasize gender interchangeability. But neither set of arguments has translated easily into a persuasive political rhetoric for feminism.

The coming-of-age of academic, which is to say theoretical, feminism is incontestably a welcome development, not least because of its contribution to the intellectual ferment of our age. Nor are there necessarily grounds for complaint if that theoretical work, like other academic work, develops at some remove from the pressures and hurly-burly of day-to-day politics. As an intellectual enterprise, feminist theory deserves the same respect—and intellectual freedom—accorded to other intellectual enterprises. It is, nonetheless, probable that most feminist theorists hope that their work will, ultimately, have some repercussions in the world beyond the academy. And, indeed, impressionistic evidence strongly suggests that the dominant tendencies in feminist theory are influencing the ways in which women's issues are discussed at large. Under these conditions, it seems fair to scrutinize the underlying assumptions and practical implications of that theory and, especially, to ask how successful it has been in developing a political rhetoric.

Criticism and abstraction—what others call dialectics or theory—come easily to academics. They are what we do. All of us, myself included, find it easy to think of feminist theory as a sustained argument or discussion with our predecessors and contemporaries. More often than not, in short, we argue about each other's arguments, and as we do, we tend to move further and further from the women to whom the original arguments purportedly referred.

In the hands of some, the pursuit of theory focuses primarily on the rejection or reversal of the so-called male values of universalism, rationality, and logic, which are charged with having silenced women. In the hands of the more sophisticated, notably such feminist legal theorists as Jennifer Nedelsky and Martha Minow, the pursuit of theory has resulted in a sharp and nuanced critique of our inherited conceptions of rights (or what Minow calls the concern with boundaries) and to a new emphasis upon "difference" as central to any viable conception of human justice.[1] But even these thoughtful arguments, with their explicit concern for the immense variety of specific human experience, reveal the inescapable limitations of theoretical work. For, from a policy perspective, it would be child's play to reconcile the emphasis on diversity with conservative social policies that insist upon the primacy of the discrete individual—and upon that individual's responsibility for his or her destiny. This, indeed, is the irony of postmodernism.[2]

As a general rule, feminist theorists have tended to gravitate to an insistence upon the significance of the concrete as against the abstract. They have, that is, tended to evoke the immediacy of women's experience in order to expose and combat the ways in which men's theoretical abstractions deny it. Hélène Cixous, for example, insists upon the overriding significance of women's bodies.[3] Margaret Homans underscores women writers' embeddedness in the pre-symbolic—in the ordinary business of everyday life.[4] Carol Gilligan argues that women's sense of morality derives from their assessment of the best way to resolve specific conflicts.[5] Feminist theory abounds with arguments that women, in some way, are closer to nature, closer to the tending of specific bodies, closer to life as it is lived in specific bodies than are men. The tendency of much feminist theory to associate women with the claims of the concrete or empirical does not, of course, make it any less theoretical and, in many instances, any less abstract. But it does signal a problem, namely the difficulty of constructing a dialectical, or abstract, theory of an empirical reality that is presented as defying all previous (male) dialectics. This problem is compounded by feminist theorists' understandable temptation to reason about woman in the abstract, even when invoking the plural, women.

The full measure of this temptation can only be grasped by recognizing the extent to which feminist theorists view their project as, in some measure, one of loosening the stranglehold that man—or men—have maintained on human possibilities and prestige, from earning a living to running the public world to representing the deity. Most feminist theory almost inevitably defines itself in some way against prevailing non-feminist theories, which it frequently defines as male, or against prevailing institutions, cultures, and customs, which it frequently labels patriarchal. This focus on male power and norms has led feminists to represent the resistance to their goals as monolithic, whether they call that resistance man, men, or patriarchy. And if the enemy is a monolith, does it not follow that its victims are, in some way, united?

In recent years, feminist theorists have increasingly attempted to break out of these traps by insisting upon the compelling claims of race, class, and ethnicity—insisting, that is, upon the aspects of women's lives that may divide rather than unite them. Today they are even moving beyond those categories to emphasize the claims of difference itself, although not all feminist theorists are always rigorously clear about whether difference means the difference between women and men, the differences among women, or some complex combination of both. The choice among those three readings of difference matters—and has serious consequences for feminist theory and politics. But that is another discussion. Here, I only wish to suggest that even when feminist theory has most strenuously emphasized women's association with the diversity of life as it is lived in different bodies, and even when it has most vociferously attacked what it views as the male predilection for abstraction, it has itself tended to privilege dialectical over rhetorical modes of thinking.

Let me anticipate the predictable objections. Yes, we do have a feminist rhetoric—of sorts. The most compelling slogans of the sixties and seventies, such as Robin Morgan's felicitous "sisterhood is powerful," come to mind. Linda Gordon's "woman's body, woman's right" has proved, if anything, more enduring. Examples abound. But it seems to me that the most influential examples of feminist rhetoric have propounded generalizations, or even abstractions. Feminist rhetoric has primarily emerged from exigencies of feminist struggles. From Mary Wollstonecraft's resounding vindication of the rights of woman to Angelina Grimké's denunciation of the similarity between the condition of women and that of slaves, feminist rhetoric has been closely linked to the perceived struggle for women's rights. But the struggle for women's rights itself remains closely tied to the habits of mind and behavior that many feminists claim to oppose. And if feminists are on to something in suggesting that women are different from men but also differ among themselves, then our inherited language of rights may not afford the basis for a persuasive feminist rhetoric. Grounding feminism in the language of rights may, in fact, amount to refusing the challenge to create a service-able, pragmatic, and flexible feminist rhetoric at all.

Listen to Angelina Grimké, writing in the nineteenth century of the rights of women and slaves. "The investigation of the rights of the slave," she wrote to Catharine Beecher in 1836, had led her to a better understanding of her own:

> I have found the Anti-Slavery cause to be the high school of morals in our land—the school in which human rights are more fully investigated and better understood and taught, than in any other. Here a great fun-damental principle is uplifted and illuminated, and from this central light, rays innumerable stream all around. Human beings have rights, because they are moral beings: the rights of all men grow out of their moral nature; and as men have the same moral nature, they have essentially the same rights. These rights may be wrested from the slave, but they can-not be alienated: his title to himself is as perfect now, as is that of Lyman Beecher: it is stamped on his moral being, and is, like it, imperishable. Now if rights are founded in the nature of our moral being, then the mere circumstance of sex does not give to man higher rights and respon-sibilities, than to woman. To suppose that it does, would be to deny the self-evident truth, that the "physical constitution is the mere instrument of moral nature." To suppose that it does, would be to break up utterly the relations of the two natures, and to reverse their functions, exalting the animal nature into a monarch, and humbling the moral into a slave; making the former a proprietor, and the latter its property. When human beings are regarded as moral beings, sex, instead of being enthroned upon the summit, administering upon rights and responsibilities, sinks into insignificance and nothingness. . . .[6]

Grimké has a rhetoric, or at least she is, in the popular sense, rhetorical: the purpose of her letter is to argue for the rights of women and slaves, which she defends on moral grounds. In this single paragraph, she uses the word "rights" six times and the words "moral" or "morals" eight. She evokes fundamental principles and self-evident truths. She contrasts rights that are wrested with those that are alienated, insisting that the alienation of human rights is impossible since they are grounded in the moral nature that all men—a designation that she takes to include women and slaves—share. In a skillful maneuver, she divorces rights from material being (one interpretation of nature) and human law, thus reducing sex and legal status to accidents of circumstance and abstracting from the specific conditions of legal dependence that she opposes. Her argument confusingly assimilates the anatomical characteristics of women's bodies and the legal condition of slaves to a single notion of injustice.

Grimké insists that political justice must be grounded in and informed by a divinely sanctioned, internal, and immaterial truth. This conviction influences the nature and structure of her argument. Thus, although she refers to concrete, substantive phenomena such as high schools and property, and to specific events such as the American Revolution, she immediately transforms the substantives into tropes. Grimké ends by claiming for women and slaves an absolute human right that consists exclusively in the opposition to the restriction of freedom—the constraints of monarchy and of human property. In the struggle for individual rights, history, politics, and society dissolve in a dazzling stream of light that implicitly emanates from God Himself, leaving souls to stand naked before the bar of divine justice. Although the goal of the struggle for freedom—human rights—is unabashedly formulated in the language of history and politics, the rhetoric skillfully evokes concrete referents only to transform them into abstractions.

Grimké does not specify the positive content of the rights she evokes, but it is safe to assume that, not being so presumptuous as openly to pit the rights of women and slaves against God's intentions, she had narrower social, political, and legal rights in mind. In fairness, it is clear enough that what she intended by rights was self-determination—equal prerogatives and legal standing with free white men. But she may well have lacked confidence that those concrete goals would move others to action. Her rhetorical strategy even suggests that she believed the opposition to specific changes in condition (married women's property rights, emancipation, or manumission) was so intransigent that she would do better to wage the struggle on the terrain of moral abstractions than on that of specific political reforms. Whatever her motivation, it is clear that she was determined to harness her own interpretation of God's intentions to the cause of securing human rights for women and slaves. To this end, she mobilized a rhetoric that primarily relied upon abstractions and tropes that conflated finite political rights with the liberation of the human soul. She and other antislavery feminists, most notably Harriet Beecher Stowe, regularly turned to concrete referents to evoke responses of pity and horror to the oppressed condition of women and slaves, but when it came to evoking positive goals, more often than not they fell back on abstractions.[7]

Their silence with respect to the specific goods they were struggling for is understandable. In their time, as in our own, the most powerful justification for opposing hierarchy lay in the doctrine of rights. That doctrine, as it developed in the seventeenth and especially the eighteenth centuries, above all embodied a struggle against authority. (There are limits to what you can do to me.) Originating in a series of political struggles against hierarchical governments, the doctrine of rights understandably assumed a political form. In time and place, the defense of individual political rights was literally revolutionary, but it was also limited. And the victors of revolutions normally moved rapidly to inscribe rather stringent limitations in the law of their lands. But in defending individual rights, however narrow their intentions, the political revolutionaries unleashed a powerful trope the implications of which radically exceeded their own limited goals. Not least was their own emphasis on defense of individual rights as a struggle against unlawful tyranny, and their evocation of nature to defend that revolt left a portentous legacy.

From the social contract to the evocation of human rights the emphasis has so insistently fallen on the defense of individual rights as natural—or in Grimké's case, divine—as to permit the speculation that the proponents of those rights above all protest any restrictions on the freedom of the individual. In fact, most successful defenders of individual rights have expected the constraints of history and society to obtain. The "customs of the country," to borrow John Locke's evocative phrase, rarely tumble as rapidly as governments. The hold of one generation on the next proves more intractable than Grimké's rhetoric or moral equality would concede. Sex is more than a mere circumstance. And even attributes and institutions, which may logically appear but circumstantial, have a wondrous way of constraining the absolute freedom of individuals.

The origins of the women's movement of the 1960s and 1970s, like that of the mid-nineteenth century, intertwined with a pressing struggle to improve the condition of African Americans. Like the civil rights movement, the women's movement mobilized a language of freedom, rights, and solidarity. As the movement developed, the language of rights came to exercise an ever wider sway over feminist thought. But, as Ethel Klein has argued, most women actually came to the movement—or to feminism—more from a sense of personal grievance than from a desire for justice in the abstract.[8]

We should not draw that distinction between personal grievance and a sense of abstract justice too sharply, but it does help to explain many feminists' mounting frustration with the practice—and eventually even with the language—of equal rights. Initially, and with telling polemical force, women could argue that they had been excluded from the rights enumerated in the United States Constitution, notably equality before the law. But as the barriers to equal rights began to fall, many women found their situations less improved than they had hoped, and some women found them worse.[9] Not surprisingly, some feminists began to express some disillusionment with the rhetoric of equal rights. Some argued that the very conception of equal rights derived from men's experience and, accordingly, could not adequately address women's specific disadvantages and grievances. Some began implicitly to extend the language of equal rights beyond its solid legal foundations, frequently toward an ideal of liberation. And many—women whom feminists do not as a rule take seriously—probably began to doubt that the language of rights held any promise for women, whom they saw as primarily needing protection.

The growing disillusionment, which began to be expressed during the mid-1980s in the wake of the defeat of the ERA, was, significantly, accompanied by a stream of works that began to call attention to women's differences from men. From Carol Gilligan's insistence that women speak in a different voice than men, to Sara Ruddick's insistence that women engage in a distinct "maternal" thinking, feminist theorists began to stake out their claim that women's personal experience yields a markedly different vision of the world and its proper ordering than men's.[10] These theorists have, in effect, countered Angelina Grimké's claim that sex is a mere circumstance with the claim that sex is of considerable, perhaps essential, importance. But, and this is my main point, their claim has not led them seriously to revise the substance of the discussions of feminist political strategy. They have, that is, uneasily combined the emphasis on the difference between women and men with an emphasis on the rights of women as individuals.

In a recent essay, Nicki Hart highlights the problems even as she tries to fashion a fresh theoretical perspective on them. "Women," Hart insists, "are not the same as men."[11] Women bear children; men do not. Building on this obvious biological fact, Hart mounts a sweeping challenge to contemporary social theory, notably against what she calls anti-essentialist feminism. Mainstream academic feminism, she charges, has willfully discounted women's procreative labor and assumed that the road to female "liberation" necessarily leads through full incorporation into the capitalist labor market. In so doing, it has disregarded the true needs and desires of the vast majority of women.

The core of Hart's argument lies in her contention that procreative labor constitutes "the material and substantive" foundation of women's subordination. Late capitalist society has stripped away the cultural justifications for male domination, exposing its naked materialist character. Women remain the second sex because of their capacity to bear children. The bearing and rearing of children, rather than sex per se, accounts for most of the difference between men's and women's earnings. (Single women, to all intents and purposes, earn as much as their male peers.) In Hart's view, feminists have erred in pointing to systemic bias against women in the labor market, including labor market segmentation, as the primary source of women's oppression. Their theories have, in other words, abstracted from the substance of women's oppression.

Of course Hart is right on the main point: women's reproductive capacities—their irreducible differences from men—cannot simply be collapsed into existing theoretical models. Here we have what is becoming widely formulated, especially among academic socialist feminists, as the "equality-difference" dilemma. How, that is, can a humane society protect women's difference as women without curtailing their access, as individuals, to equality?[12] Hart primarily departs from those who evoke a general sense of sexual, psychological, and ethical difference in focusing on procreation as a specific form of labor and in denying that women's equal participation in the labor market offers an adequate solution to women's economic inequality. She is, in this respect, mainly attacking those socialist feminists who continue to defend the goal of establishing women's functional equality—virtual interchangeability—with men. Yet, in one essential respect, Hart does break decisively with those she is criticizing. For she never criticizes their underlying individualist premises, notably the persisting devotion to "equality." To follow her argument to its logical conclusion is to acknowledge women's rights as individuals to bear and rear children at public expense.

Admittedly, Hart moderates the individualistic implications of her argument by attending more closely than most to the all-too-frequently unacknowledged gap in the experience and goals of women of different classes and races, insisting that women who lack the opportunity to pursue careers find a deep source of personal fulfillment in motherhood. She could further have strengthened the argument about women's commitment to motherhood had she noted that many professional women are also showing an unforeseen preference to stay home with their children.[13] Experience suggests that many mothers feel a special bond to their infants, and a special satisfaction in sharing and guiding their early development. But not all women enjoy caring for small children, and some abuse them. Even the most devoted mothers may crave some respite from caring for very young children, including an opportunity to engage in some work outside the home that permits them to interact with other adults. But the main problem with Hart's argument remains vagueness about who is to pay for procreative labor and on what terms.

Hart's defense of motherhood would find warm support among many conservatives, who invariably combine the defense of motherhood with a passionate defense of the family. But Hart herself says nothing of families, much less of fathers. Her silence strongly suggests that she views motherhood as a woman's individual right that society must respect and, especially, support. Historically, specialization in procreative labor has normally depended upon an individual man's ability and willingness to pay for it. Men have paid women to be mothers. And when men have been unwilling or unable to do so, women have tended to have abortions, commit infanticide, abandon or give up their children for adoption, or struggle along the best they could. Today, the proliferation of divorce, as Hart notes, has virtually liberated men from the obligation to support women and children. The collapse of what many view as repressive sexual norms, combined with the improved standards of health and nutrition, has liberated children to have children. The growing acceptance of single motherhood is virtually liberating men from any stake in children at all.

It is one thing to agree that children do constitute the primary resource of society and a pressing matter of public concern. It is another to agree (and some do not) that the immediate care of a small group of children by a single individual may constitute the optimal means of preparing them to participate effectively in an advanced technological society. But neither of these propositions necessarily leads to the conclusion that the biological mother, independent of the biological father, should be entitled to perform that labor at public expense. And if we could accept this conclusion, how would we then decide upon the private, or individual, rights that mothers should enjoy? How, in other words, are we to conceptualize women's private rights as mothers? The strongest argument for the public subsidy of childbearing and childrearing lies in the claim that they constitute our most valuable social resource and, hence, our most pressing social responsibility. But might that argument not also entail the corollary that the public, which supports the children, has some interest—even rights—in the conditions of their bearing and rearing? Hart's unwillingness to consider such questions reinforces the impression that she remains bound by the premises of individualism, which she simply wishes to extend to women's control of children. She seems, in short, to be claiming that women as mothers have an individual right to raise and control the children they bear without the interference of the children's fathers or the society that supports them. She thus (however unintentionally) binds the protection of motherhood to the narrowest view of individual rights and social atomization. She thus sketches a position that, at its most macabre, could be taken as a defense of the rights of mothers even over the "rights" of children.[14]

Like other celebrants of women's difference, Hart in the end does not seriously challenge the status quo. Her program reduces to the plea to support biological mothers for a period of specialized mothering, thus reinforcing rather than criticizing the atomized individualism grounded in the capitalist market into which our social institutions are collapsing. And, by implicitly building upon the experience and values of middle-class American women, it denies the yet more difficult experience of women of different classes and races. However much impoverished women need support for themselves as mothers, that support would arguably be almost useless without equal support for the communities into which their children will be born.[15] Surely it is relevant that the United States ranks lowest among all industrialized nations in the social support and services it provides for children. Surely the radically different experience of women in Eastern Europe should make us thoughtful about any programs to support women's mothering that do not take some account of the context within which the mothering occurs.[16] Surely to simply treat children as women's private concern is to risk that society in general, not to mention men in particular, will resist paying taxes for their support.

Notwithstanding Hart's attempt to ground feminist theory in the substance of women's lives and to raise questions of policy, she remains, finally, imprisoned by the language of rights and the premises of individualism. At the heart of her rhetoric, in other words, lies a dangerous contradiction. For it seems to me that the last decade of feminist politics—if not its entire recent history—has revealed that, for a significant number of American women, not to mention women in Zambia, Croatia, Egypt, Iran, or elsewhere throughout the world, feminist rhetoric does not capture their imaginations and loyalties—it is not about their lives and their dreams.[17] So, if Klein is correct that many women have been drawn to gender politics, if not to feminism, by personal experience, what has gone wrong?

Long ago, Aristotle argued that the disposition of "present and definite issues" often involves "love, hate, or personal interest." It belongs to rhetoric, Aristotle insists, to mobilize those feelings—"to discover the real and apparent means of persuasion, just as it belongs to Dialectic to discover the real and apparent syllogism."[18] According to Aristotle, rhetoric "may be defined as the faculty of discovering the possible means of persuasion in reference to any subject whatever."[19] "The function of Rhetoric, then, is to deal with things about which we deliberate, but for which we have no systematic rules; and in the presence of such hearers as are unable to take a general view of many stages, or to follow a lengthy chain of argument."[20] Rhetoric consists in acts of proper presentation and persuasion, although, Aristotle allows, there is a branch of rhetoric that rests on the conviction of moral superiority and the assumption that you can browbeat others into submission. But ideally rhetoric should be a subtle—even, I might suggest, a narrative—form of argument rather than a form of polemics.

Arguably, contemporary feminism has failed to develop a persuasive rhetoric, a convincing story. There are many, like Angelina Grimké, who draw upon a sense of moral superiority to make their case, but they are demonstrably failing to win votes and even followers. Many feminists celebrate women as nurturers but have developed no rhetoric of reproduction—have idealized mothers but have not devised a way of rewarding reproduction. We have lost the rhetoric of sacrifice, sainthood, heroism, *agape*. The list could be extended, but I think my point is clear. Many women remain convinced that feminism is not about their lives.

Rhetoric, in contrast to dialectics, is inherently referential and requires a commitment to thick description. To persuade women—not to mention men—of the validity, usefulness, and morality of feminist goals, we need to cast those goals in a plausible rhetoric that takes account of women's needs in relation to our society. Today the persistence of the language of equal rights has, ironically, deprived us of a coherent political rhetoric. It has, especially, dampened much of the confidence of the liberal feminism of the 1970s and is leading, or has already led, to a bifurcation between an emerging conservative feminism and a paralyzed socialist feminism. For those of us for whom this alternative is uninviting, the solution must be to write a new story, a story about women's lives, not women's rights. To sketch in the elements of the plot will be my intent in Part Two of this essay.

1. Jennifer Nedelsky, "Reconceiving Autonomy: Sources, Thoughts, and Possibilities," *Yale Journal of Law and Feminism* 1, no. 1 (Spring 1989): 7–36; Martha Minow, *Making All the Difference: Inclusion and Exclusion in American Law* (Ithaca, N.Y.: Cornell University Press, 1990).

2. Much of postmodernism lends itself to a very conservative praxis. For a chilling fictional example of the dystopian possibilities, see Margaret Atwood, *The Handmaid's Tale* (New York: Fawcett Crest, 1987).

3. Hélène Cixous, "Laugh of the Medusa," *Signs* 1, no. 4 (Summer 1976): 875–93.

4. Margaret Homans, *Bearing the Word: Language and Female Experience in Nineteenth-Century Women's Writing* (Chicago: University of Chicago Press, 1986).

5. Carol Gilligan, *In a Different Voice: Psychological Theory and Women's Development* (Cambridge, Mass.: Harvard University Press, 1982).

6. Angelina Grimké, "Letters to Catharine Beecher, Letter XII," in *The Feminist Papers: From Adams to de Beauvoir*, ed. Alice Rossi (New York: Bantam Books, 1973), 320–21.

7. Harriet Beecher Stowe, *Uncle Tom's Cabin, Or, Life Among the Lowly*, ed. Ann Douglas (New York: Penguin Books, 1981; orig. ed., 1852).

8. Ethel Klein, *Gender Politics: From Consciousness to Mass Politics* (Cambridge, Mass.: Harvard University Press, 1984).

9. Leonore J. Weitzman, *The Divorce Revolution: The Unexpected Social and Economic Consequences for Women and Children* (New York: Free Press, 1985); Sylvia Ann Hewlett, *A Lesser Life: The Myth of Women's Liberation in America* (New York: William Morrow, 1986). For a recent polemical critique of this position, see Susan Faludi, *Backlash: The Undeclared War Against American Women* (New York: Crown, 1991).

10. Gilligan, *In a Different Voice*; Sara Ruddick, *Maternal Thinking: Toward a Politics of Peace* (Boston: Beacon Press, 1989). Both Gilligan's and Ruddick's arguments first appeared as journal articles in 1980.

11. Nicki Hart, "Procreation and Women's Rights—Part I" and "Procreation and Women's Rights—Part II," *Contention* 1, nos. 1 and 2 (1991)[: 89–104, 65–88]. My critique of Hart is developed at greater length in my "Procreation and Women's Rights: A Response," *Contention* 1, no. 3 (1992)[: 217–25].

12. In *Feminism Without Illusions: A Critique of Individualism* (Chapel Hill: University of North Carolina Press, 1991), I have attempted to explore some of the implications of this dilemma; see, e.g., 156–58. See also, Cass R. Sunstein, ed., *Feminism and Political Theory* (Chicago: University of Chicago Press, 1990).

13. See, for example, Suzanne Gordon, *Prisoners of Men's Dreams: Striking Out for a New Feminine Future* (Boston: Little Brown and Company, 1991), and Felice N. Schwartz, "Management Women and the New Facts of Life," *Harvard Business Review* 67, no. 1 (January/February 1989): 65–76.

14. On the problems of attributing "rights" to children, see Elizabeth H. Wolgast, *The Grammar of Justice* (Ithaca, N.Y.: Cornell University Press, 1987).

15. See, for example, William Julius Wilson, *The Truly Disadvantaged: The Inner City, the Underclass, and Public Policy* (Chicago: University of Chicago Press, 1987); Deborah Prothrow-Stith, with Michaele Weissman, *Deadly Consequences* (New York: HarperCollins, 1991).

16. See, for example, Francine du Plessix Gray, *Soviet Women: Walking the Tightrope* (New York: Doubleday, 1990); and the review by Tatyana Tolstaya, *New York Review of Books*, 31 May 1990, pp. 3–7.

17. See, for example, the nuanced discussion in Leila Ahmed, *Women and Gender in Islam: Historical Roots of a Modern Debate* (New Haven, Conn.: Yale University Press, 1991).

18. Aristotle, *The Art of Rhetoric*, vol. 22 of *Aristotle in Twenty-Three Volumes*, trans. John Henry Freese (Cambridge, Mass.: Harvard University Press, 1982), 13.

19. Aristotle, *The Art of Rhetoric*, 15.

20. Aristotle, *The Art of Rhetoric*, 23.

Eight

Feminism and the Rhetoric of Individual Rights, Part Two

Notwithstanding the momentous changes of recent decades, the rhetoric of feminism, as I argued in Part One, has remained tied to the rhetoric of equal rights from which it originally derived. Not surprisingly, feminists' insistence on the rhetoric of equal rights, with its implied message that women aspire to equality as individuals with men, has powerfully influenced perceptions of feminism among opponents as well as supporters. Conservatives have had no difficulty in caricaturing the feminist story of the strong, independent woman and contrasting it, unfavorably, to the more traditional story of the fulfilled domestic woman who especially delights in the satisfactions of motherhood.[1] Most feminists, however, continue to defend women's rights as the rights of individuals who must be free of the encumbering roles that have shackled women's opportunities in the past.

The possibilities of conservative feminism, however much derided in most academic circles, should not be underestimated, although the project faces considerable difficulties, notably the assumption that, in the world of no-fault divorce, marriage and motherhood can still be counted on as a career. Conservative feminism nonetheless benefits from many women's persisting sense that marriage and motherhood simultaneously offer a measure of security in a dangerous world and the satisfactions of a calling that includes a large dose of service. In our times, the vision has become deceptive but, as in many instances, the power of the vision has outlived the probability of realizing it. We would be rash indeed to ignore or dismiss with contempt the considerable numbers of women who would prefer a secure marriage with a partner who provided a reasonable standard of living to the insecurities attendant upon going it alone.

The problem with the conservative position derives from most conservatives' commitment to an ad hoc political economy grounded in the defense of the maximum freedom of the market.[2] For, at an accelerating rate, our postmodern economy has been destroying the family wage that permitted a worker to support a wife and children on a single paycheck. At least since World War II, the national and, increasingly, the global economies have been systematically warring against precisely those traditional values that conservatives claim to defend. The contradiction between political economy and social ideals leaves conservatives vulnerable, especially on the fate of women and children.

With the collapse of the world socialist movement, feminists, notably socialist feminists, face problems that are, if anything, more acute than those of the conservatives. To be sure, socialist feminists have, as a rule, resolutely refused to be socialist. Well before the collapse of the world socialist movement, American socialist feminists were expending considerable energy in demonstrating their serious doubts about—even hostility to—Marxism, and in developing a position that incorporated aspects of both radical feminism on the one hand and historical materialism on the other.[3] According to Alison Jaggar socialist feminism differs from radical feminism in resisting the temptations of idealism and biologism, and from Marxism by fundamentally revising the entirety of traditional Marxist analysis. Socialist feminists remain primarily committed to overcoming "all forms of alienation but especially those that are specific to women." For them, women's subordination has been ubiquitous throughout history and characterizes all aspects of the relations between women and men, not just economic relations, and not just in contemporary capitalism.[4]

Socialist feminists have thus attempted to argue that the subordination of women to men constitutes a discrete system of oppression that exists parallel to and, in some measure, independent of the subordination of workers to employers. As Iris Young has pointed out, this "dual systems" theory has always been fraught with tension.[5] But since the collapse of the communist regimes in Eastern Europe, discussions by socialist feminists of the theory of production have virtually disappeared. Most socialist feminists continue to flirt with uneasy support for some form of welfare state, but without grounding their programs in a comprehensive political economy. Their commitment to personal liberation has, moreover, led them to strengthen, if anything, their underlying commitment to a radical individualism. As a result, socialist feminist views, shorn of potentially embarrassing political and economic policies, have become virtually indistinguishable from the left wing of the Democratic Party and especially from the mainstream of the National Organization of Women. In this respect, their language of personal liberation has intertwined with a more conventional language of rights, with the specific referents of rights left as vague as Angelina Grimké left hers. The predominant message nonetheless remains that women's difference from men must not be allowed to jeopardize women's rights as individuals.

Significantly, some of the most important U.S. Supreme Court cases that have defended the differential treatment of women and men, notably *Muller v. Oregon* (1908) and *Hoyt v. Florida* (1961), have done so on the ground of women's family roles as well as—or even instead of—the ground of physical difference. In *Muller,* the Court found that grounds for protecting a woman from too long hours of labor lay in her "physical structure and a proper discharge of her maternal functions. . . ."[6] In *Hoyt,* the Court found grounds for relieving women from obligatory service on juries in the fact that notwithstanding the "enlightened emancipation" of women from many restrictions and protections that had previously kept them from full participation in community life—again, this in 1961—"woman is still regarded as the center of home and family life."[7]

Today, many feminists vociferously attack the constraints that traditional family roles impose upon women, and some even argue that the family constitutes women's primary oppressor. It nonetheless seems significant that the most vehement critiques of the burdens that family life and maternal functions impose upon women have come at the precise moment at which 1) those burdens were lessening relative to previous historical periods, and 2) the family was crumbling, primarily because of men's abandonment of it.[8] Today, it is fair to say that the feminization of poverty correlates directly to single motherhood or female-headed households. Certainly, many feminist scholars insist that the best way to rectify women's economic vulnerability does not necessarily lead through a restoration of the "traditional" family, in which women are at high risk of physical and psychological abuse.[9] For such feminists, women might well be better served by policies that permitted them to attain independence as individuals.

Since the 1960's, the women's movement has relied heavily on a language of freedom and rights, even, and perhaps especially, when it has sought to take account of the differences between women and men. It is, nonetheless, not clear that a rhetoric that emphasizes women's rights as individuals and denounces men as the main source of women's oppression will strike all women as adequate to their situation. And it is even possible that a rhetoric that proclaims motherhood—or the decision to terminate a pregnancy—as woman's absolute individual right or entirely her private concern may strike some women as not merely misguided but threatening.[10]

Nowhere are the problems associated with the defense of women's interests as a matter of individual right clearer than in the debates over abortion. The defense of woman's right to choose to have an abortion has been squarely grounded in the rhetoric of absolute individual right and in the related rhetoric of privacy.[11] At its most extreme, the defense of this position evokes the Declaration of Independence, suggesting that a woman's right to freedom and equality as an individual supersedes all other considerations. Thus, even as many feminists are increasingly insisting upon the differences between women and men, they reinforce feminism's political commitment to individualism.

A woman's right to have an abortion, which has emerged as the litmus test for most feminists as for most of those who strongly oppose feminism, underscores the contradiction in applying the conception of individual right indiscriminately in the defense of women's difference and women's equality. Consider the implications of the claim that abortion is an absolute right. Is the argument, in Angelina Grimké's sense, that sex is a mere circumstance? Is the right to abortion intended to free women from the consequences of their own sexuality? There are those who would argue that that is precisely what it is intended to do: to free women to engage in sex in the manner of adolescent men—i.e., without responsibility for the consequences. Such arguments lead into the treacherous and conflicted realm of personal morality. It is hard to dispute that, for our society, women's sexuality still evokes complicated feelings, not least among women themselves. From this perspective, the debate over abortion appears, at least in part, as about that sexuality and as a part of a larger struggle to free women from men's control. But the defense of what we might call "no fault" sex is only the less significant part of the story.

The other, and more troubling, part concerns the attempt to free women from their own reproductive capacities—from their ascribed and frequently self-proclaimed special responsibility for and connections to children in particular and human life in general. The struggle for the freedom to choose an abortion is primarily being waged at law. Most feminists want women to enjoy the legal right to choose—to make a private personal decision. But it seems fair to ask: what story do the laws that the feminist movement seeks to defend or implement tell us about women—and about our society? From some perspectives, a rather depressing story of women as free and autonomous, even isolated, agents—a story worthy, in its way, of Margaret Atwood's *The Handmaid's Tale*. It is a story of women for whom pregnancy and childbearing constitute unacceptable emotional and economic burdens, not least because these women are so disconnected from society, including their sexual partners and families, that they cannot safely be held to consult anyone else about their decisions. It is a story of young women, still legal minors, for whom consultation with parents means risking physical and sexual abuse. It is a story about women who are so uncertain of themselves that they cannot be asked to postpone their decisions for as little as twenty-four hours. It is a story about daughters and wives for whom incest and rape are a predictable cause of pregnancy. More depressing yet, a woman's individual right to abortion will not solve any of the problems that lead feminists to believe that women need that right, and may even result in further diminishing men's increasingly fragile sense of responsibility for reproduction.

The story told by our laws is one of desperate loneliness and anomie that is very difficult to reconcile with the prevailing feminist stories about women's special sense of interconnectedness and responsibility. On the face of it, the intrinsic connections between a woman's absolute individual right to abortion and maternal thinking, or women's special sense of morality, are elusive. Some, notably Carol Gilligan, have recognized the problem and attempted to defend a woman's choice to have an abortion as the product of a complex assessment of the respective claims of the living and the not-yet-born.[12] Such arguments lead easily into arguments about quality of life—what world would the woman be bringing the baby into? Robert Goldstein has drawn upon the psychoanalytic discussions of the symbiotic relation between mother and child to defend abortion. How, he would ask, could we condemn a child to come into the world without being able to count on that mother love which is essential to its survival?[13]

The arguments from quality of life for women and children command attention. But they are empirical rather than abstract arguments and, as such, exist on a different plane from the argument for abortion as a woman's absolute individual right. For the defense of abortion is not grounded in an empirical assessment of the situation of particular women. If it were, it would have to be cast as an argument that, under determined conditions, a woman should not be required to carry a fetus to term. Such an argument would, however, presumably require certification on the part of some group that the inauspicious conditions indeed prevailed. And those who defend abortion as a woman's absolute individual right apparently do not trust any representatives of society at large—even members of their immediate families, ministers, judges, or doctors—to make such a determination fairly.

Theoretically and intuitively, it seems difficult, if not impossible, to reconcile any argument for absolute individual right with an argument for binding connection among two or more individuals. And, if so, then we need to acknowledge that the arguments for absolute individual right are—as they always have been—metaphors for, or abstractions from, a much more complex human reality. In defending abortion on the grounds of absolute individual right, feminists are—however inadvertently—adapting to women's purposes precisely that individualism and abstraction which they so mistrust in men. In this perspective, they are, at the very least, falling into a serious theoretical inconsistency. More important, they are not offering a positive alternative to the social atomization and family breakdown that have made the right to abortion seem so compelling.

One of the strengths of feminist thinking, in fact, consists in precisely the emphasis on human interconnectedness which the argument from absolute individual right seems to deny. Sadly, most feminists have not followed the logic of that insight to its full conclusions. Rather than arguing for the interdependence of all members of families, communities, and societies, they seem (and I emphasize the "seem") simply to be arguing that women's experience endows them with a superior form of understanding. And if that is all that is meant by women's speaking in a different voice, then it is understandable that they attribute the sense of interconnectedness to individual women's minds rather than to society as a whole. For if society really is as intradependent as women picture it, then society has claims upon all of its members—all individuals—and absolute individual right must be recognized as a fiction.

Another great strength in feminist thinking lies in the value that women are supposed to attribute to life in all of its diverse manifestations. If women are indeed the nurturers of life and the tenders of sick and dying bodies, then they, above all others, must understand the claims of the weak and the dependent. Such an understanding is difficult to reconcile with the insistence that women have an absolute individual right to terminate developing life at will. And if they have the right in the case of pregnancy, why should they not also have it in the case of the handicapped, the elderly, and the terminally ill? In each instance, the implied argument is that one individual has a right to determine quality of life for another individual. Here, the predictable response would be that a fetus cannot be considered a human life in the same sense as a person outside the womb. But that argument requires explicit attention to the quality of life that the fetus embodies, which feminists in general have been reluctant to do.

No, feminists do not usually defend the right to abortion on the grounds that women have a right to kill babies. To the contrary, the more sophisticated invariably argue that women who refrain from carrying fetuses to term are above all concerned with the proper care of babies. Yet even those who show most concern in this regard normally rely upon individualist arguments

that assume, when they do not openly assert, that there may be conflict between the quality of life for the mother and for the potential baby. The underlying assumption is that for a woman to develop her full potential, she must
be free from the burden of an unwanted, or unplanned, child. In this respect,
the logical conclusion of the individualist argument is the recognition of
conflict between the interests of two individuals, and the assertion that a
woman has a right to put her individual interest first.

Such assumptions, even when not openly stated, seem to derive from the
belief that women have, for centuries, been forced to live out roles that men
have imposed upon them. In this thinking, the role of mother and the
responsibility for children becomes another male ploy to keep women in their
place. There is, accordingly, a certain perverse logic in the view that to free
themselves from men's domination women must reject everything that men
have imposed on them. Yet in accepting this view of individual freedom,
women remain hostage to the most robust aspect of Western male thought—
the emphasis upon individualism. Indeed, the view that women have a radically different view of the world than men—that women are, for example,
especially nurturing—also derives from the tradition of male individualism
that has cast woman as the "other." But then so does the view of those who
oppose abortion on the grounds that the fetus has an individual right to life.

The language of individual rights is simply inadequate to the situation of
a pregnant woman, and rather than trying to distort it to fit one or another
position, we would do better to accept its inadequacy to this exemplary situation as an indication of its inadequacy to capture the complexities of the
relations among human beings—to tell the stories of human beings' lives. It
is also inadequate to the unique dependence of a fetus. Rather than continuing to speak of the rights of life, which perpetuate the illusion of individual right in another guise, might we not better think simultaneously of the
sanctity and the social context of life?

In our time, neither scripture nor science clearly suffices to offer us an
absolute definition of life in the abstract. Some Americans do insist that either
scripture or science does so, but if we consider human life as a continuum
from birth to death, the lines of its beginning and end are blurred. And,
across the continuum, social resources play a decisive role. Thanks to medical technology for which society pays, premature babies, who as recently as
twenty years ago would not have survived, now live, as do people who would
have died of heart or kidney failure. Most of us find it difficult to accept that
any single individual take the life of another individual. Usually we call such
willful taking murder. Some people oppose capital punishment, even for
those who have been convicted of murder, on the grounds that it demeans
our sense of ourselves as a civilized people. Yet we remain understandably

loathe to admit that innumerable factors resulting from social interdependency impinge upon any definition of life.

With respect to abortion, this means that many of those who most resolutely oppose abortion are also those who are most prepared to let babies, once they have been born, die, or live at a level of social deprivation that should demean our sense of ourselves as a civilized people and should assuredly challenge any complacent claim to respect the right to life. The right to life means nothing without the means to sustain it, and even a commitment to the sanctity of life is difficult to defend without some consideration for social context.

James Boyd White has suggested that law is most usefully understood not as a "system of rules, but as a branch of rhetoric . . . as the central art by which community and culture are established, maintained and transformed."[14] In this perspective, Mary Ann Glendon has argued that the laws on abortion in the United States are working to create a society of atomized individuals. In fact, we stand effectively alone among industrialized nations in defending and combating abortion on the grounds of absolute individual right, just as we stand effectively alone among industrialized nations in failing to enforce a social context that can truly value and support reproduction. Not surprisingly, we also rank first among industrialized nations with respect to personal violence.[15]

American society, with its special commitment to individualism, has long confided to women primary responsibility for the values that embody our humanity, but for which we are unwilling to pay: nurture, care, patience, self-sacrifice. Today, at least some women are saying that they cannot assume those responsibilities without some support—saying, that is, that they must be able to assure their own survival. Other women refuse to accept that shattering of dreams—refuse, that is, to accept that the essence of our humanity can be reduced to individual right or a market transaction. Abortion has emerged as the central issue that divides them, and as the central metaphor for the nature of our society.

Neither the story of radical individualism nor that of traditional domesticity meets the needs of our present situation, although both have figured in American women's self-perceptions and in the language of feminism. Today the unthinkable has come to pass. The vast majority of American women have effectively been freed from the constraints—and protections—of domesticity. Most will still be married at some point in their lives, but few, if any, can safely assume that marriage will assure their livelihood and that of their children. Feminism has drawn its principal rhetorical force from naming what should no longer be done to women: women should no longer be excluded from equal pay for equal work; be excluded from the most prestigious and remunerative occupations; be subject to physical abuse; be harassed; be compelled to shoulder the burden of our humanity at the price of self-immolation. And feminism has couched these demands in the rhetoric of individual rights, when these demands might better be understood as the responsibility of an equitable society.

This rhetoric exudes an indisputable power, especially in insisting that women, too, are human beings who deserve the opportunity to prove their capabilities and who cannot be excluded from the full status of worker and citizen. But the rhetoric falters in projecting new stories of women's lives and new visions of women's possibilities. Throughout the nineteenth, and even the early twentieth, century, many women endowed their roles as wives and mothers with the aura of a calling. In retrospect, we may choose to emphasize the ways in which they were oppressed, but in time and place many of them embraced their fates, on their own terms and for their own reasons. And they forged a rhetoric peculiarly their own, insisting upon the special worth and responsibilities of their mission. Among innumerable others, Augusta Jane Evans, in her novel *Beulah,* reminded her readers of the wife's "holy work of love" in bringing her husband to religious faith and their children to responsible adulthood. Marriage, Evans insisted, was "the beginning of a new course of duties," and she told us that her heroine, Beulah, "was conscious of the power she wielded, and trembled lest she fail to employ it properly."[16]

The American women's movement, in the beginning, forcefully insisted upon the special qualities that women bring to public life, and drew upon them to justify women's rights. This strand, which became known as social feminism, promised that the public representation of women's values would create a better, more humane society for all.[17] Even today, there are those who argue that women's distinct experience, notably as mothers, has instilled in them a practice, and attitudes of attentive care, that could significantly contribute to the public good.[18] But, perhaps understandably, in an age of cynicism, we have, collectively, failed to develop a new narrative of female heroism that preserves an older sense of a special female calling to bind up the wounds of the world and attend to the next generation. We have, in effect, bought into the male narrative of power and insisted that, no longer willing to be its victims, we must, in self-defense, claim it as our own. As a narrow story of self-preservation it may serve, but as a blueprint for the future it fails woefully.

The question remains, can women be requested or required to shoulder the burden of our humanity alone? It is a lot to ask. It may be impossible. None of us has the perfect story, and in any case our times call for new stories that acknowledge the inescapability of our common life and of our interdependence. Abortion, perhaps more than any other issue, demonstrates how much we need a collective discourse of problem solving, a practical ethics. Feminists need stories that can lead women to feel compassion for one another's vulnerability and hard choices, to show respect for one another's different assessments of our common situation. The defense of individual right does not adequately capture women's stories and cannot adequately ground a feminist rhetoric. We need to recognize that we have no rights independent of responsibilities and that society must recognize its obligation to permit us to meet our responsibilities.

To capture women's imaginations and loyalties—to be politically effective —feminists must develop a political rhetoric that addresses ordinary women's goals for their own lives. And unless I am very much misguided, most women still place personal happiness and some measure of economic security high on the list. Most women, in other words, would like the opportunity to be wives and mothers as well as to receive equal pay for equal work and to be free of harassment in the streets and on their jobs. Many, perhaps most, women would also like to be able to terminate a pregnancy in specific cases, and much more. But not all of those goals fit easily into existing models of equal rights, and many women intuitively sense that the mere defense of equal rights distorts, or abstracts from, their stories of their own lives.

The defense of equal rights has generated a powerful political rhetoric, which from the days of Thomas Jefferson to our own has continued to exercise a powerful hold over men's imaginations. But that rhetoric has unabashedly served to create a convincing narrative of men's initiative and independence. Today it is open to question whether such rhetoric still convincingly refers to men's lives and possibilities. Be that as it may, a narrative that has rested upon assumptions about women's secondary status cannot easily be refurbished to meet their needs as citizens and workers. Nor can its rhetoric capture the complexities of their lives. But a usable narrative of women's lives might provide a rhetoric that could capture the interdependencies of all individuals. As George Orwell insisted:

> What is above all needed is to let the meaning choose the word, and not the other way about. . . . When you think of something abstract you are more inclined to use words from the start, and unless you make a conscious effort to prevent it, the existing dialectic will come rushing in and do the job for you, at the expense of blurring or even changing your meaning.[19]

It is time to ask ourselves whether the words we are using do justice to our meaning—whether they tell the stories we want to tell.

Notes

1. Susan Faludi, *Backlash: The Undeclared War Against American Women* (New York: Crown, 1991). See also my contribution to the debate over Katherine Kersten's defense of conservative feminism in *Policy Review*: "Conservative Feminism and Economic Reality —a Response to Katherine Kersten," *Policy Review,* no. 57 (Summer 1991): 83.

2. Traditional, notably southern, conservatives will privately admit to doubts about the freedom of the market, which ineluctably erodes all of the community values they cherish, but have been trapped into its acceptance by their alliance with the national Republican Party since the Reagan years.

3. Alison M. Jaggar, *Feminist Politics and Human Nature* (Totowa, N.J.: Rowman & Allanheld, 1983), esp. 9–12. See also Rosemarie Tong, *Feminist Thought: A Comprehensive Introduction* (Boulder and San Francisco: Westview Press, 1989), 173–93. See also my "Socialist-Feminist American Women's History: A Perspective," *Journal of Women's History* 1, no. 3 (Winter 1990): 181–210.

4. Jaggar, *Feminist Politics,* 12, 132–43, passim, esp. 136, 143.

5. Iris Young, "Socialist Feminism and the Limits of Dual Systems Theory," *Socialist Review* 10, nos. 2–3 (March–June 1980) and, for her more recent views, *Justice and the Politics of Difference* (Princeton: Princeton University Press, 1990).

6. Cited in Susan Gluck Mezey, *In Pursuit of Equality: Women, Public Policy, and the Federal Courts* (New York: St. Martin's Press, 1992), 14.

7. Cited in Mezey, *In Pursuit of Equality,* 15.

8. See Diana Pearce, "Welfare Is Not *for* Women: Why the War on Poverty Cannot Conquer the Feminization of Poverty," in *Women, the State, and Welfare,* ed. Linda Gordon (Madison: University of Wisconsin Press, 1990), 265. Pearce has drawn her data from U.S. Bureau of the Census, *Money Income and Poverty Status of Families and Persons in the United States: 1988,* series p-60, no. 165 (1989). See also Sara E. Rix, ed., *The American Woman 1990–91: A Status Report* (New York: W. W. Norton, 1990), 394. For a general perspective, see, among many, William Julius Wilson, *The Truly Disadvantaged: The Inner City, the Underclass, and Public Policy* (Chicago: University of Chicago Press, 1987); Deborah Prothrow-Stith, with Michaele Weissman, *Deadly Consequences* (New York: HarperCollins, 1991); Lenore J. Weitzman, *The Divorce Revolution: The Unexpected Social and Economic Consequences for Women and Children* (New York: Free Press, 1985); Sylvia Ann Hewlett, *A Lesser Life: The Myth of Women's Liberation in America* (New York: William Morrow, 1986). For a recent polemical critique of this position, see Faludi, *Backlash.* For a conservative view of the problems, see Allan C. Carlson, *Family Questions: Reflections on the American Social Crisis* (New Brunswick, N.J.: Transaction Books, 1988).

9. Gordon, *Women, the State, and Welfare,* e.g., 23; Carole Pateman, *The Sexual Contract* (Stanford: Stanford University Press, 1988).

10. For a thoughtful perspective on these issues, see Kristin Luker, *Abortion and the Politics of Motherhood* (Berkeley and Los Angeles: University of California Press, 1984). See also, Faye D. Ginsburg, *Contested Lives: The Abortion Debate in an American Community* (Berkeley and Los Angeles: University of California Press, 1989); Rosalind Pollack Petchesky, *Abortion and Woman's Choice: The State, Sexuality, and Reproductive Freedom* (New York: Longman, 1984).

11. For the historical background, see Linda Gordon, *Woman's Body, Woman's Right: A Social History of Birth Control in America* (New York: Grossman, 1976).

12. Carol Gilligan, *In a Different Voice: Psychological Theory and Women's Development* (Cambridge: Harvard University Press, 1982).

13. Robert D. Goldstein, *Mother-Love and Abortion: A Legal Interpretation* (Berkeley: University of California Press, 1988).

14. Cited by Mary Ann Glendon, *Abortion and Divorce in Western Law* (Cambridge: Harvard University Press, 1987), 8.

15. Prothrow-Stith, *Deadly Consequences.*

16. Augusta Jane Evans, *Beulah,* new edition, with an introduction by Elizabeth Fox-Genovese (Baton Rouge: Louisiana State University Press, 1992).

17. Nancy Cott, "What's in a Name?: The Limits of 'Social Feminism,' or Expanding the Vocabulary of Women's History," *Journal of American History* 76, no. 3 (December 1989): 809–29; Naomi Black, *Social Feminism* (Ithaca: Cornell University Press, 1989).

18. Mary O'Brien, *The Politics of Reproduction* (Boston: Routledge & Kegan Paul, 1981); Sara Ruddick, *Maternal Thinking: Toward a Politics of Peace* (Boston: Beacon Press, 1989); Jean Bethke Elshtain, *Women and War* (New York: Basic Books, 1987).

19. George Orwell, "Politics and the English Language," in *A Collection of Essays* (New York: Harcourt Brace Jovanovich, 1946).

Nine

The Legal Status of
Families as Institutions

Historically, our legal tradition has seen a fundamental contradiction between the family and the individual, or, to put it differently, has preferred to
treat the family as a corporate unit rather than as a collection of isolated individuals. This preference accounted for Blackstone's assertion,

> By marriage, the husband and wife are one person in law: that is, the very
> being or legal existence of the woman is suspended during the marriage,
> or at least is incorporated and consolidated into that of the husband:
> under whose wing, protection, and *cover*, she performs every thing.
> . . . Upon this principle, of an union of person in husband and wife,
> depend almost all the legal rights, duties, and disabilities, that either of
> them acquire by the marriage.[1]

By the same token, the children born into a family were expected to fall
under the authority of its head. The family, in other words, was taken to constitute a unit with a legal personality that transcended and subsumed the
individual rights of its constituent members.

The subordination of individual rights within the family was never complete. Husbands were not legally represented as owning their wives or their
children—although they were known to sell one or the other. In principle,
our tradition insisted upon a difference between family members and slaves,
although early advocates of women's rights were wont to emphasize the
similarity, arguing that married women, effectively, should be viewed as

"The Legal Status of Families as Institutions." *Cornell Law Review* 77 (1992): 992–96.
Copyright 1992, Elizabeth Fox-Genovese. All rights reserved. Used by permission of the
Cornell Law Review.

slaves.[2] Instructively, Southern slaveholders also evoked the similarities between family members and slaves, not to protest the subordination of married women, but to emphasize the humanity of slavery as a social relation.[3]

The conjugal, or nuclear, family of our tradition has always coexisted uneasily with notions of individual rights and responsibilities, but until recently the heavy hand of what Locke called "the Customs or Laws of the Countrey"[4] obscured the full measure of the conflict. The issue surfaced during the discussion of married women's property rights in New York state during the mid-nineteenth century. Traditionalists opposed such rights on the ground that they would inevitably disrupt Blackstone's vision of the partners to a marriage as embodied in one person—the husband. Advocates of women's rights supported these rights on the ground that married women should indeed be recognized as separate persons—and be properly equipped to protect themselves against their husbands' possible abuse or malfeasance. In the event, reform of married women's property rights primarily resulted from the efforts of a third group, which sought not to further the independence of women, but rather to bring greater consistency to the law of property and to conform that law to the social and economic realities of the developing capitalist economy.[5]

The debates over the property rights of married women foreshadowed a continuing debate over the rights of women as individuals—that is, women's natural rights. Many of those who favored the persisting subordination of women within families did so because they favored a view of the family as an island of traditional hierarchy within a swirling sea of capitalism and individualism. It is, nonetheless, instructive to note that many of those who most staunchly supported the traditional concept of the family came to oppose the persistence of slavery, which many of them perceived as both a moral outrage and a fetter on economic development.

The issue might be seen as a difference over the appropriate composition of families. The emancipation of the slaves effectively ensured the triumph of a very narrow conception of family and, however unintentionally, paved the way for the recognition of the family as little more than a contractual union of free individuals. Intuitively, many of us would insist upon the distinction between wives and children since the former first enter into the union voluntarily whereas the latter are born into it and spend many years in a state of physical as well as economic dependence.[6] But our own times sadly reveal that the tensions between the freedom of individuals fundamental to the market and the family as a corporate unit also affect the status of children.

But questions remain. How should we think about the individual rights and responsibilities of family members? Does the family legally constitute something more than the sum of its constituent parts? To insist upon the family as a moral or social unit will not suffice without a clear—and implicitly corporate—legal status. The arguments against untoward (however untoward is defined) state interference in family affairs normally assume the existence of an intact family. I do not wish to engage such questions as whether parents who are Christian Scientists have the right to deny medical care to a child with leukemia or meningitis. Rather, I wish to raise the question of whether the arguments apply with equal force in cases of divorce or other forms of family disintegration. Are there legal grounds for denying an abused spouse or child recourse against the abuser? Do we not assume that family members have rights as individuals? And, if we do, what legal constraints do we place upon their independent relation to the polity and the market?

The point at issue is whether family members are held accountable for behaving towards other family members as they would be obligated to behave toward any other individual or whether they are held accountable for behaving in certain ways toward other family members because of their special status as family members. Generally, this question has been framed as an inquiry into the power of fathers over other family members. Since the nineteenth century, and at an accelerating rate during the twentieth, the extreme forms of paternal power have come under increasing criticism and legal restriction. But the dismantling of that power has not led to new conceptions of the family as a corporate unit. Thus, the conception of the family as a group of individuals has followed naturally from the rejection of the view that the family's corporate identity was invested in the powers of its head. Tellingly, this rejection has also led to arguments that the concept and legal prerogatives of family relations should be extended to different groupings of individuals.

Until very recently, most people would have considered marital rape a contradiction in terms. If there is marriage, then there cannot be rape—although there may be an unacceptably violent exercise of marital rights. Today, many people assume that individual rights override marital rights—that behavior that is unacceptable if two people are not married is also unacceptable if they are married. The same could be said of child abuse. American society has always attributed some rights to members of families. Unlike early Roman society, we have never given fathers the right to kill their offspring with impunity. Even slaveholders were not legally allowed to kill their slaves on a whim.[7] But we have, at law, and especially in sentiment, granted special rights to the heads of households or families on the premise that their responsibility for family well-being entitled them to broad discretion in the exercise of their authority.

It is difficult, if not impossible, to separate the discussion of the family from the discussion of marriage. The movement for women's political and economic equality with men has primarily targeted women's traditional subordination within the family. In attempting to free women from that subordination, supporters of women's rights, have, however inadvertently, contributed the destruction of the last vestiges of the family's corporate status. But opponents of women's rights and defenders of the family have failed no less woefully by not providing a new conception of the family as a corporate unit. Thus, discussions of women's and children's rights as members of family units invariably focus on what Elizabeth Wolgast has called "wrong rights"—their rights as autonomous individuals.[8] I would argue that a revitalized view of the family requires a new conception of its corporate identity. Such a conception must simultaneously allow for women's full participation as parents and for both parents' binding economic responsibility to their children.

If we are to defend the rights of families as units, then perhaps we should begin by endowing them with some greater measure of permanence and a more binding mutual responsibility than that granted by a normal contract. Perhaps parents should be denied the right to divorce until their children have attained their majority or are economically self-sufficient. In the case of intolerable unhappiness, a husband and wife could separate but would not be allowed to remarry or to assume economic responsibility for another family. In pre-Revolutionary France such a separation was known as the separation of bed and board.

To be sure the enforcement of a married couple's binding economic responsibilities to each other and their children would require the cooperation of the federal government, but that is another debate. For the moment, permit me to conclude by reasserting that any serious discussion of families and individual responsibilities must begin with attention to the legal status of the family as an institution. A simple return to fathers of their historical power as heads of families will not suffice.

Notes

1. I William Blackstone, "Of the Rights of Persons," in *I Commentaries of the Laws of England,* 430 (Univ. of Chicago Press ed., 1979) (1765) (citations omitted).

2. *E.g.,* Angelina Grimké, "Letters to Catharine Beecher, Letter XII," in *The Feminist Papers: From Adams to de Beauvoir,* 320–22 (Alice S. Rossi ed., 1973). For the general use of the metaphor, see Blanche Glassman Hersh, *The Slavery of Sex: Feminist-Abolitionists in America,* passim (1978).

3. For the general use of the metaphor, see Elizabeth Fox-Genovese, *Within the Plantation Household: Black and White Women of the Old South,* 101 (1988).

4. John Locke, "The Second Treatise of Government," in *Two Treatises of Government* § 82 (Cambridge University Press 1960).

5. Norma Basch, *In the Eyes of the Law: Women, Marriage, and Property in Nineteenth-Century New York* (1982).

6. For an insightful discussion positing that individual rights for children are "wrong rights," see Elizabeth Wolgast, *The Grammar of Justice,* 28–38 (1987).

7. On the law of slavery, see Mark V. Tushnet, *The American Law of Slavery: Considerations of Humanity and Interest* (1981) and Eugene D. Genovese, *Roll, Jordan, Roll: The World the Slaves Made* (1974).

8. See supra note 6, at 28–38.

Ten

Difference, Diversity, and Divisions in an Agenda for the Women's Movement

Today, as in the past, the women's movement in the United States primarily reflects the experience and aspirations of white, middle-class women. The growing rhetorical attention to the differences among women of different classes, races, and ethnicities has changed little of substance. Of course much depends upon the way in which we define the "women's movement." If the term is taken to include the myriad of national, local, and neighborhood organizations, which act in the name of women, it implies considerable diversity, openness, and internal conflict. Women display extraordinary courage and ingenuity in acting in defense of their and their families' interests. But if the women's movement is broadly taken as more or less synonymous with "feminism," it must be recognized as considerably more homogeneous, exclusive, and unrepresentative of the majority of American women, including those who care most deeply and immediately about "women's issues." Feminism has generated its own complexities and divergent tendencies but mostly within the academy.

Historically, the women's movement has always divided into the two broad tendencies of "women's rights" and what Naomi Black calls "social feminism" (Black 1989). The first tendency focused on the struggle for women's rights in an attempt to promote women's equality with men and culminated in the long campaign to secure the ERA [Equal Rights Amendment]. The goals of this movement have been fundamentally white and middle-class and have rested on the assumption that what was good for one woman would be good for all women. Social feminism, in contrast to equal-rights feminism, has grown from an acceptance of women's differences from men and a determination to work for women's specific interests as the social feminists defined them. Like equal-rights feminists, social feminists demonstrated their share of class and racial bias and exclusivity, occasionally even supporting reactionary political movements (Blee 1991).

The women's movement is now at a crossroads. During the past decade, difference has replaced equality as a central concern of feminist theory. In part, this shift reflects a growing awareness that the early easy assumptions of similarities among women and their needs masked the variations of women's experience by race and class (as well as nationality). In part, it reflects an uncomfortable recognition that equality with men has continued to elude women or failed to satisfy their needs. Although these two sets of attitudes towards difference intertwine, they do not necessarily reinforce each other, much less yield a clearly unified women's movement. At the most basic level, women of different classes and races do not necessarily agree about the measure of equality between women and men [that] the women's movement should struggle for. And women assuredly do not agree about the significance of differences among women themselves. Thus, a white, middle-class, career woman may easily say that she does not believe in discrimination among women according to race and class and, nonetheless, assume that superior education should help to determine the selection of leaders. Or she may just as easily oppose social policies to benefit poor women which would significantly increase her own tax burden.

The Problem of Difference

Academic theorists who stress difference are trying to work their way through the complex overlapping of different kinds of difference, mainly by arguing for a "decentering" which abolishes the implicit norm that makes others different. Does not the very idea of woman as "different" presuppose an idea of man as the norm? Martha Minow, in particular, has convincingly argued that difference presents us with a dilemma (Minow 1990). To recognize difference is effectively to stigmatize those who are labeled as different. To emphasize the difference between women and men is implicitly to accept men as the norm and to accept the male view of women as differing from that norm. In Minow's view this perspective inevitably results in the drawing of boundaries which disadvantage those perceived as different. We cannot, she insists, escape the dilemma unless we recognize difference as a relationship which implicates both parties. How, she asks, "can historical discrimination on the basis of race and gender be overcome if the remedies themselves use the forbidden categories of race and gender? Yet without such remedies, how can historical discrimination and its legacies of segregation and exclusion be transcended?" (Minow 1990: 47). To complicate matters further, the dilemma of difference between women and men has tended to universalize a model of woman which obscures differences by race and class among women themselves.

This project, which directly challenges any notion of hierarchy, has been extended to differences among women (and men) by race and class. If white middle-class women are no more normative than poor black women, then the significance of difference understood as departure from the norm collapses. We are all different from one another. Furthermore, we all belong to different categories of difference. Some of us are women, but also black and rich. Where, in this case, does our primary allegiance lie? With our gender, our race, or our class? This line of thought logically leads to the conclusion that all categorizations are invidious, especially if they lead to judgments about the allocation of social resources.

The academic attack on that notion of difference, which implies a stable norm, primarily concerns questions of personal respect. Who are you to treat me as in some way lesser simply because I am different—that is, not you? The argument and sensibility are, at their core, radically individualistic: each of us deserves the same respect as any and every other, there are no legitimate grounds to discriminate among any of us, least of all because of attributes such as gender, race, or class. But if such arguments have opened interesting philosophical questions, their practical implications for political and social movements have as yet received little sustained attention. Iris Young's (1990) work embodies the main attempt to engage the practical implications of these questions. In practice, political and policy agendas are normally cast with respect to individuals or groups. Either each individual should receive the same treatment, regardless of personal attributes, or some individuals should receive different treatment because of personal attributes which identify them as members of a group. And, in this thinking, some attributes are taken to outweigh or erase others. Thus, our affirmative-action policies do not exclude some African Americans because their income exceeds a certain arbitrary line. It is possible to have attended elite schools throughout one's life and still benefit from opportunities that were initially designed to assist those who, presumably because of the color of their skin, had been barred from specific educational or employment opportunities.

The very idea of a woman's movement implicitly assumes that at least some differences between all women and all men have greater significance than the differences among women, or at least sufficient significance to justify the design and implementation of policies for all women. Women may need and deserve to be men's equals as citizens (voters) and, nonetheless, need and deserve some special status because they are women. Yet even feminists would not necessarily agree upon the reason women merit special consideration. Some would argue that women are different from men in ways which matter, normally ways which pertain to biology or sex. Others would argue that women are in no essential way different from men but have suffered from a history of oppression which makes them (at least for the moment) different in their command of a variety of salient resources. These two groups may forge a tactical alliance to defend, for example, affirmative-action programs for women, but they will continue to disagree theoretically on the justification for such programs. They will, accordingly, disagree about the ultimate role of equality and difference in the long-term agenda of a woman's movement.

As a general rule, the entire effort of the women's movement has been to redress the disadvantages women have historically suffered, and continue to suffer, as a result of their being women. The underlying argument nonetheless persists: were women disadvantaged because they were different, or because they were (brutally) excluded from equality? Recent debates over specific issues have clearly demonstrated that the mere recognition of difference does not guarantee justice or security for women and may even be invoked to deny them opportunities (Williams 1982). The case brought by the Equal Employment Opportunity Commission against Sears Roebuck chastened feminists by revealing the ways in which arguments for women's differences from men could be used to bar women from the most prestigious and best-paying jobs.

In the Sears case, the salient issues concerned women's purported preferences for some kinds of work over others and can, accordingly, be seen as broadly historical and cultural. In the soul-searching which followed in the wake of the Sears case, many feminists began to question the wisdom of invoking difference in matters of policy. In effect they reasoned that Sears had won the case by virtue of the argument that women, for a variety of reasons including risk and schedules, preferred not to work in commission sales. The Sears argument depended heavily on statistical reasoning: most women who had been given the opportunity to enter commission sales had chosen not to. But the decision which purportedly reflected most women's choices also reinforced the norms that excluded statistically atypical women from pursuing new opportunities (Scott 1988; Haskell and Levinson 1988, 1989; Fox-Genovese 1991). Such policy questions as these depend upon some ability to generalize and impose choices. They thereby challenge the women's movement to reflect upon its agenda.

At the time, most feminists agreed in opposing Sears' policies and joined in excoriating Rosalind Rosenberg, who served as expert witness for Sears. But, in the aftermath, it has become clear that the issues will not go away. The most complex and hotly contested issues concern the desirable consequences of women's reproductive capacities and "traditional" childcare responsibilities. Where can we draw the line between biological difference and social equality? Should pregnancy be treated like a disability, thus entitling women equal access to benefits available to all other workers? Does the defense of "maternity leave" benefit women or further imprison them in traditional roles, which they may not have wanted in the first place? Do parental or family-leave policies help to free women from stereotypical roles, or perhaps further disadvantage women who do not have husbands with whom to share the responsibilities?

The debate over women's participation in the military underscores the complexities with a vengeance. During the war in the Persian Gulf we were inundated with images of bereft children whose mothers had been called to active duty overseas. Some women in the Gulf were pregnant. Do we really want to separate mothers from their small children? Do we really want pregnant soldiers in a battle zone? And what of women's roles in the military? Should they, for example, have the right to participate equally with men in combat—and to receive equal pay for doing so? Many still recoil at the idea of any woman's participation in armed combat. Others insist that, in the case of a volunteer army, women, including mothers, are very likely to depend upon the incomes they receive from the military or want to develop their careers. As individuals, they should be allowed to make their own choices, to enter into contractual relations with which society has no right to interfere.

It should be obvious that women's roles in combat still have an over-determined symbolic significance. Even without direct participation in combat, women increasingly serve in dangerous and exposed military roles, notably in supplying troops at the front. The risk of death is arguably no (or not significantly) greater in the one case than in the other. Some would even argue that the support services bear the greater risk because they are not armed to defend themselves against attack. Yet there has been little public outcry against the risks women incur in serving at or just behind the front in non-combat roles. Clearly, there remains a deep tendency in the culture which rejects the image of women as soldiers—a role that has traditionally been viewed as quintessentially male. And since we know that the public, however uneasily, tolerates the separation of incarcerated mothers from their children and does not even notice the separation of some working women, notably immigrants, from their children, it is reasonable to argue that, in the case of the military, the emphasis ultimately falls on excluding women from equality rather than on protecting their difference.

And yet it remains possible that the case of the military dramatizes the role of the mother as much as it dramatizes that of the male warrior. It remains possible, in other words, that the instinct to exclude mothers of young children from combat, even when we tolerate high risk to other mothers of young children, embodies noble as well as self-serving tendencies. Or, to put it differently, do we best serve women's interests by defending the right of mothers to serve in combat or by insisting that no mothers should be separated from their children? It is hard to say. But this much we know: the successful defense of the right of mothers to serve in combat will do nothing to restore incarcerated women or migrant women workers to their children and is very likely to make their separation from those children more generally acceptable.

Similar questions arise in the recent case (Johnson Controls) of women's right to choose to work at high-paying jobs which endanger a foetus they may be carrying. That case, like the question of *maternal* leave, has sharply divided feminists. Many find the question of children troubling, although if we think of women only as individuals we have no grounds to interfere. We can argue that men can and should share equally in the responsibilities of child-rearing, but they cannot share equally in child-bearing. Yet we have, as a rule, failed to develop policies which protect women as child-bearers (as different from men) which do not also penalize them as individuals (as similar to men). As individuals, women should not be excluded from the most prestigious and remunerative work. But then, they should not be entitled to special privileges either. The question remains: do we collectively choose to view pregnant women, or even the mothers of infants, only as individuals among other individuals? That question should be separable from women's equal opportunity and obligation to serve, in some capacity, in the armed forces. But it is only separable if we, as a society, have policies which defend mothers' economic condition and professional prospects. Those are matters of public policy. And in the absence of appropriate policies we can only leave individual women to wrestle with conflicting claims alone.

Thinking Differently about Difference

Minow's work, like that of other feminist legal theorists, challenges us to think differently about difference in order to avoid certain traps in the continuing struggle for equality. Her thought, in this respect, has much in common with those who insist upon the importance of appreciating diversity. Women, who have suffered the burdens of difference, should be especially sensitive to the burdens it inflicts on others. Culturally, this position enjoins us to respect the individuality and traditions of others. Politically, it poses more difficult problems.

The continued existence of a women's movement in our time depends upon the agreement that women do share some characteristics which differentiate them from men. If not, women's interests would, as Marxists long argued, collapse into general social and political struggles. The vitality of a women's movement in our time depends upon the recognition that women are also divided by class and race. If women do not believe that they share some important interests with other women, there is no reason for them to organize as women, no reason for them not to define their primary struggle as one of class or race. But to deny the divisions among women by class and race is willfully to ignore the real challenge of feminist politics in our time, which cannot completely escape the legacy of the dream of equality.

Strictly speaking, equality evokes a mathematical relation—the two sides of an equation—and hence quantity rather than quality. Seen in this light, equality appears abstract and unrealistic. We do not expect women to be strictly equal to men in the sense of completely interchangeable with them. But then we do not expect men to be strictly equal to each other. Knowing that human attributes cannot be measured with mathematical precision, we expect all individuals to display a certain variability. But if we can accept variations in culture and personality, what about resources and, beyond resources, power?

Recent experience suggests that if women do need the protection of legal equality, they need more than that. Legal equality can help to guarantee women equality of opportunity but, since it does not create a "level playing field," it cannot guarantee them equality of results. Child-bearing, sexual harassment, and acquaintance rape all suggest, as many feminists are coming to recognize, that sexual or biological asymmetry cannot simply be legislated away. Our inherited (male) model of autonomous individualism is proving incapable of meeting women's needs. Indeed, the pursuit of autonomous individualism for women is increasingly exposing the limitations of the model for society as a whole.

Originally, equality was implicitly and explicitly taken to mean equality of opportunity. Today, disillusion with equality of opportunity runs so deep that many people have come to mistrust a wide variety of purportedly objective standards, such as standardized intelligence or aptitude tests, which were taken to guarantee equality of opportunity to people of different classes and races. Manifestly they did not. Yet even those who most sharply criticize the model of equality of opportunity have been loathe openly to criticize the individualistic principles on which it rests.

In *Feminism Without Illusions* I have argued that to escape the dilemma of equality versus difference women need a conception of equity which rests on the notion of individual right as grounded in society rather than as prior to it. The argument is not, as some have taken it to be, an attack on individualism, which does anchor our conceptions of individual rights and responsibilities. Rather, the argument rests on the assumption that we enjoy those rights and bear those responsibilities not because of innate attributes but because we are social beings: society, not nature, has endowed us with rights and is entitled to hold us accountable for meeting the attendant responsibilities (Fox-Genovese 1991, 1992a, 1992b).

Specifically, women's most pressing problems are social and economic in the broad sense and can never be adequately addressed on the basis of innate or presocial individual right. From this perspective, the differences among women of different classes and races emerge as especially important and potentially devastating. Although few of us like to discuss it openly, the grim possibility remains that the needs of middle-class (especially but not necessarily exclusively white) women could be met at the expense of poor women. For, notwithstanding the debilitating effects of abiding racism and the growing threat of ethnic tribalism, the most pressing issues remain economic. As our troubled economy makes abundantly clear, secure jobs which include the essential benefits of health care have emerged as the basic, and increasingly elusive, condition of a decent life—the functional equivalent of industrial workers' "family wage" or, before it, independent property in a farm or workshop which could support a family (May 1982).

Easy access to abortion, which many women passionately defend and which has virtually become the litmus test of feminism, can solve a woman's immediate problem of pregnancy, but cannot diminish most of the miseries that led her to become pregnant in the first place. At best, access to abortion will permit a poor woman to re-engage the dreary struggle for a more promising future without the encumbrance of a child, but it will not necessarily improve her education or her job prospects, provide her with medical insurance, or increase the likelihood that she will marry. And access to abortion does nothing for the poor woman who chooses to keep her child. Yet feminists, who claim to speak in the name of the women's movement and emphasize society's responsibility to accommodate women's lives and values, continue to defend abortion on the grounds of absolute individual right. The rhetoric in which the debate over abortion has been cast merits attention, for in discussing that which is most peculiarly personal and female (the ability to bear a child), it has drawn primarily on the public language of rights—

that is, the language of (male) citizenship (Fox-Genovese 1992a, 1992b). Although some feminist scholars (Vogel 1990; Young 1987) argue in favor of this treatment of equality and difference.

In effect, that rhetoric casts the reality of difference in the language of equality, thereby collapsing the one into the other. Something similar is occurring with respect to sexual harassment and acquaintance rape. In each of these cases, the argument seems to be that women have a right to be free of the consequences of their sexuality—their difference. Yet normally the political and policy discussions do not emphasize the theoretical complications; they focus on concrete objectives. Women must have access to abortion; women must be free of all forcefully imposed sexual attentions. In the measure that these issues have taken pride of place in the most visible agenda of the women's movement, they have tended to influence the discussions of other issues as well.

The radical individualism which informs so much feminist theory and thought has, willy-nilly, led middle-class spokeswomen for the women's movement to emphasize the issues which divide women from men, at the expense of the issues which divide women against one another. Poor women, indeed, have as much experience of male bullying and even brutality as middle-class women. The relations between women and men in the African American and Hispanic American communities are, if we can credit the reports, conflicted and strained. But even after all allowances have been made and caveats filed, it is safe to say that most poor women, both white and women of color, are more concerned with social and economic problems than they are with the "war between the sexes." We have no reason to doubt that many of them remain committed to establishing and sustaining marriages and families as one of the strongest bulwarks against economic insecurity. They may even remain attached to some aspects of "traditional" women's roles, if only because they know they will never be able to afford the kind of care for their children which can substitute for their own attention.

Ruth Sidel (1990) has argued that large numbers of young women of different classes and races have recently come to share a particularly female vision of the classic American dream. These young women have grasped the idea of themselves as future career women (presumably in the manner of *LA Law*) and in classic individualistic fashion are embracing the vision of financial equality. Other young women, Sidel reminds us, tend to cling to a more conservative vision of themselves as primarily future wives and mothers. Still others perceive themselves as "outsiders"—as fundamentally alienated from both the dream of professional success and the vision of traditional domesticity. Although there is some tendency for these attitudes to cluster by class, the correlation is far from absolute, and examples of each can be found in every class.

These divisions among young women mirror the complex divisions among women in American society at large. Normally, the women's movement does not much attend to the neo-traditionalist group, frequently viewing them as enemies of women's needs and progress. For the neo-traditionalists, women's best protection still lies in their assumption of inherited female roles and their dependence upon men. Nor has the women's movement seriously attended to the outsiders whose attitudes, in extreme cases, border on despair or nihilism. Ironically, the women's movement may not even fully encompass the complicated attitudes of the aspiring new professionals, many of whom are reconsidering the relations between career and family, frequently in order to emphasize the latter. In my judgment, for the women's movement to coalesce and succeed in its goals, it must attempt to engage the imaginations of all these young women—or at least to engage what they see as their most acute problems.

These different groups of women differ in their aspirations for their lives or even in whether they hope for anything at all. Within the groups, women differ according to temperament, talent, and family background. They nonetheless all share some general problems, notably how to provide for themselves, and possibly their children, in a world in which men cannot necessarily be obliged or even enticed to support them. The neo-traditionalists may be least likely to recognize their situation, but even as they affirm their commitment to "traditional" values and roles, they know, on some level, they are at risk. To reach such women, the women's movement needs to respect their values and desire to hold men accountable for wives and families. Frequently, neo-traditional women do work, are active in political movements, do engage in a variety of activities outside the home. They simply refuse to define themselves by their independence. If the women's movement could begin by listening respectfully—even if not in agreement—to the neo-traditionalists who oppose abortion, we would have made a beginning.

A Different Agenda

Conversations with poor African American and Hispanic American women, who would not dream of calling themselves feminists, have convinced me that they understand and are deeply committed to women's issues, beginning with women's need for "independence."[1] But they do not recognize feminism, or even a more diffuse women's movement, as having any relevance to their lives. Most do not even associate feminism with the social programs and services they, as women, most desperately need.

The lives of these women, and others across class and racial lines, nonetheless confirm that the women's movement potentially constitutes the cutting edge of a thorough reconsideration of the very notion of public policy and national priorities. In a society in which women must overwhelmingly rely upon their own earning power, they still earn 63 cents for every dollar earned by a man. And, in the measure that this figure represents an improvement over the 59 cents to every male dollar which women earned a few years ago, it represents growing equality between women and men in the worst-paying, least secure jobs of the service sector—McDonald's or the supermarket check-out counter—and, in lesser measure, in the more prestigious middle-class professions.

Attempts to redress this inequality have led members of the women's movement variously to support affirmative action and comparable worth. Both policies have registered some successes, both have left something to be desired. Affirmative action, which originated in the individualistic conception of equality of opportunity, has probably been most effective for women at the upper end of the income scale, although even there it has not successfully cracked what is known as the "glass ceiling." Comparable worth has primarily benefitted female public-sector employees from clerical workers to civil servants. A broad extension of the principles of comparable worth could potentially lead to a vast increase in economic security for women, but would certainly constitute a massive challenge to the principles of the free market. Moreover, the unlimited extension of comparable worth on the existing basis of re-evaluating forms of work traditionally ascribed to women would inescapably perpetuate traditional stereotypes of women's roles, risking the kind of stigmatization that Minow warns against.

In ways which both are and are not similar, the feminist campaigns against sexual harassment and acquaintance rape uneasily combine the goals of ensuring women's equality with men and protecting their difference from men. But, above all, both campaigns draw the battle lines squarely between women and men and thus, perhaps unintentionally, reinforce the individualist tendencies of middle-class feminism. Tellingly, both campaigns have drawn heavily upon the language of rights to make their claims: "Women have a right to be free of . . . ," in contrast to "Society has an obligation to protect women against . . ." Both reinforce the impression that feminism seeks to free women from the consequences of their sex in order to make them truly equal competitors with men. But competition between women and men may be precisely what women disadvantaged by race and class can least afford—and perhaps even what they least want.

The experience of disadvantaged women suggests that if the women's movement is to avoid the pitfalls of the dilemma of equality versus difference, it must recast women's issues as social issues in contradistinction to individual or even sexual issues. In this perspective, the agenda for the women's movement should emphasize health care, daycare, education, and benefits for part-time workers. Surely none of us needs reminding that the burdens of health care fall disproportionately upon women, who still assume primary responsibility for the care of the young and the elderly. And even if we believe that, ultimately, men should share that responsibility equally with women, it is unlikely that the best way to encourage them to do so is to cast them as competitors, much less as enemies. Does it not make more sense to provide the kind of social supports women so desperately need on the assumption that support and respect for the work women have traditionally done might encourage men to share in it?

Above all, the women's movement should acknowledge that it is presumptuous to fight battles about women's and men's "roles" in the name of women whose own preferences in the matter have not been consulted. Arlie Hochschild has argued that, with respect to household responsibilities, working-class men are, if anything, more likely than middle-class men to pitch in and help with whatever needs doing with no regard to "traditional" gender roles (1989). For such people gender roles are not the issue, although they may well adhere to conventional representations of those roles. As men's and women's activities within families change, and especially as men spend more time in caring for children, the representations of the roles may also change. Certainly severely disadvantaged women who, more often than not, have no resident men to share their burdens, need assistance in bearing their burdens more than they need debates about men's and women's roles.

Traditional assumptions about gender do play an important and debilitating role in the allocation of medical resources, however. The women's movement has pioneered in criticizing the inherent sexism of much medical thinking and care. As Carol Tavris has recently argued in some detail, most medical research and treatment remain fixated on the seventy-kilogram man, with such shocking results as the exclusion of mammography from most health-insurance coverage, low funding for breast cancer research, and an alarming tendency among male physicians to advise hysterectomies with wanton abandon (1992). In addition, as Tavris convincingly maintains, too many women's understandable responses to the circumstances of their lives, notably economic dependence, are reconstructed by mental-health professionals as illness or disorders which require protracted care. Men's problems must be dealt with, whereas women's illness must be stabilized through endless hours of group therapy which make the woman feel better about herself while leaving her circumstances unchanged. In Tavris's view the process amounts to little more than trapping a potential adult in a state of perpetual adolescence.

At this point a feminist campaign for national health policies would have to include close attention to the national allocation of medical resources. One might, for example, imagine a national system of health-care delivery which included the equivalent of a five-year national service for all prospective doctors. Such a system would help to ensure adequate medical care in impoverished rural areas and in inner-city emergency rooms. It could also ensure an adequate supply of obstetricians/gynecologists. A national policy might also include some rationing of health services, especially the more expensive and least effective, as the state of Oregon has done. A national health policy might even include the perpetuation of private insurance plans, perhaps in conjunction with some national insurance. It is, in other words, possible to imagine a variety of plans, no one of which need be biased according to gender no matter how much it might be biased according to income.

Health care in particular raises the question of benefits in general. It is common knowledge that the United States lags behind all other developed countries in its provision of support to its citizens. Countries like France and Canada provide family allowances to ease the burdens of raising children. Many countries provide guaranteed maternity leave and comprehensive day-care systems (Kamerman and Kahn 1978). In many instances, for example France and Israel, the various supports for child-rearing originated as populationist incentives. Traditionally, such pronatalism has reflected a concern for quantity of population, with a special eye to military security. It has also regularly figured as a favorite target of feminists, who tend to view pronatalism as a sinister plan to keep women barefoot and pregnant. There is, however, no reason not to adopt a pronatalism which promotes quality, in terms of health, education and well-being, rather than quantity, just as there is no reason to assume the bearing of children must always oppress, or disadvantage, women.

The question of quality of population leads directly to the question of childcare. The women's movement should promote a comprehensive, national policy of childcare, including parental leave, on the grounds that only such a policy can adequately recognize children as a social rather than a private responsibility. The defense of a national childcare system implies nothing about the form such a system could take and does not even imply that an effective system need be either uniform throughout the country or run by the federal government and staffed by federal employees. There is no reason why the women's movement cannot lead the way in considering a variety of forms of childcare and, in so doing, help to generate new support for childcare workers.

Good childcare services are expensive. In Atlanta, in the fall of 1992, several daycare centers were closing because the cost of meeting federal standards was forcing them to charge more than many parents could afford. As the costs presumably continue to rise, more centers will raise their rates or close, leaving the poorest working women unable to pay for the daycare they need in order to go to work. At the same time, childcare workers, who themselves are normally poor women who lack specialized skills, need to make a decent wage. The more childcare is professionalized, the more expensive it will become. The women's movement should be responsible both to the needs of working mothers and to the needs of childcare workers, who are very likely to be women and who are also working mothers. In a negative regard, the lessons of health care are instructive. The United States spends a larger proportion of its GNP on health care than other developed nations, provides those who are insured—or can pay—with as good or better health care than any other nation in the world, and still has a larger proportion of its population without adequate health care than any other developed nation.

As with the care of young children, so with education. None of us needs reminding of the deplorable state of most of our system of public education. Education, in a variety of ways, brings to the surface class and race differences among women themselves. There is no use pretending the solutions will be easy, but if the women's movement does not confront the problems directly, women of all classes and races will live with the consequences. Here again, the primary responsibility of the women's movement may well lie in encouraging the discussion of policies among feminists, rather than assuming there could be no difference of opinions and priorities. Can there or should there be a "feminist" position on multiculturalism, bilingual education, special education, local control, the teaching of math and science to girls, and all the rest? Not until the women's movement begins to recognize these issues as questions for discussion will we begin to develop coherent policies on women's position in society.

As the question of education confirms, the issues which most seriously affect women also affect men, however differently. As a number of feminist theorists have argued, all women and men exist and define themselves in specific historical situations and as members of specific social groups (Spelman 1988; Fox-Genovese 1988). In any given instance, group membership, notably by race and class, may more powerfully affect women's needs than their sex—at least in relation to the larger society. In our society, education constitutes the gateway to future economic prospects. Most dramatically, those with a college degree earn on average $16,000 more a year than those without one.

This perspective should help us to recognize the singular importance of a comprehensive policy of benefits for all workers. Many women who cling to traditional roles are, at least in part, clinging to the tangible, if precarious, security of their husbands' incomes, but especially their benefits. Women still comprise the majority of part-time workers who, notoriously, receive no benefits at all. Thus, espousing a policy of full benefits for all part-time workers should rank high on the economic agenda of the women's movement.

Conclusion

Any inclusive agenda for the women's movement must begin with comprehensive economic and social policies. In emphasizing economic issues I am not for a moment underestimating the pervasive aspects of sexism, which many feminists regard as primary. Without doubt, reproductive issues in particular and sexual issues in general will rank high on most women's agenda for the next decade and beyond. With no intention of trivializing the importance of these issues, I do believe that the economic issues take priority, if only because enforced economic dependence and lack of social support for the bearing and rearing of children decisively color the way in which the issues are perceived.

Women invariably understand reproductive and sexual experiences within a complex cultural and social matrix. Even the decision of whether to carry a pregnancy to term depends at least in part upon the network of support available, as well as upon religious and cultural values. The extreme tendency to argue for women's absolute reproductive rights as individuals cannot be divorced from the context which confronts most women with the necessity of dealing as individuals with a free market. Were women guaranteed a panoply of social and economic rights simply by virtue of their membership in society, they might be more willing to see child-bearing and child-rearing as social rather than individual activities.

As things now stand, women are more often than not penalized for being female individuals. The main tendency in the women's movement has, understandably, been to attempt to strengthen women's position as individuals. However understandable, that strategy has inevitably encouraged the heightened consciousness of differences—and even divisions—among women. Without doubt, some of the emphasis on difference derives from a commitment to value the traditions of one's own people and community. But some of it also comes from a frightening awareness of competition for scarce resources. In this respect, the theoretical writings about difference have failed to engage the depressing specter of possibly serious divisions among different groups, including different groups of women. If equality of opportunity has not benefitted all women relative to men, it assuredly has not benefitted all women relative to each other. Indeed, equality of opportunity, whatever its limitations, has probably benefitted some women not merely at the expense of other women, but also at the expense of the men upon whom other women in some measure depend.

Iris Young has argued that "where social group differences exist and some groups are privileged while others are oppressed, social justice requires explicitly acknowledging and attending to those group differences in order to undermine oppression" (1990: 3). But how are we to establish the salience of membership in more than one group. Are we to identify African American women primarily by gender, race, or class? Many African American feminists, like Beverly Guy-Sheftall, insist that the distinct character of African American feminism derives from attention to all three (1989). Normally, however, the attempt to establish policy priorities requires a decision about which war to fight first and about whom to take as allies. And, as Bette Dickerson's analysis conveys, this issue of alliances has been particularly problematic for leaders of African American women's organizations.*

A greater measure of economic justice will not automatically eradicate differences of gender, race, or class. It assuredly will not guarantee economic equality among women, although it may well promote a greater measure of economic equality between women and men within specific social groups. But then, it has never been clear that the majority of middle-class feminists have ever seriously wanted genuine economic equality among women. The point of a modicum of economic justice is not to level all economic distinctions, but to provide some combination of supports and incentives which will permit women some prospect of decent survival (Jencks 1992). This much at least is certain: if society fails to provide all women with a reasonable opportunity to help themselves, alone or with their families, we are likely to find ourselves increasingly divided.

In proposing an agenda of social and economic policies, I have tried, as a white, middle-class feminist, to take account of the needs of women of other classes and races. But I know full well that whatever my efforts, I cannot experience their situation from the inside; I can, however, be purposefully conscious of my own location at the intersection of gender, race, and class.† The white, middle-class women's movement has a long and ambiguous history of trying to act well towards women of different classes and races. Sadly, it has all too frequently fallen into the mode of lady bountiful. The assumptions of universalism and essentialism have permitted elite women to speak and act in the name of all women as if their success would unambiguously benefit others. We cannot be sure that it will. We cannot even be sure that some women's victory against gender discrimination will not result in the intensification of other women's experience of discrimination by

* Bette J. Dickerson, "Ethnic Identity and Feminism: Views from Leaders of African American Women's Associations," in *Color, Class and Country: Experiences of Gender,* ed. Gay Young and Bette J. Dickerson (London: Zed, 1994), 97–114.

† Kathryn B. Ward, "'Lifting as We Climb': How Scholarship by and about Women of Color Has Shaped My Life as a White Feminist." In *Color, Class and Country: Experiences of Gender,* ed. Gay Young and Bette J. Dickerson (London: Zed, 1994), 199–217.

gender, race, or class. In this perspective, it seems abundantly clear that if we are to have even the semblance of a comprehensive or inclusive women's movement, the leadership of that movement must reflect women's different backgrounds and goals.

Women's issues have emerged as central to the health and vitality of American society, yet their very centrality confronts any women's movement with unprecedented challenges. The vast majority of American women share needs for health care, daycare, education, and benefits for part-time work which transcend their differences of race and ethnicity and, in some measure, their differences of class. But the challenge of implementing and financing policies of this kind and on this scale reveals not merely the differences, but the divisions among American women. The most pressing agenda of the women's movement is to understand the magnitude of this challenge and to engage it in ways which might possibly negotiate the deep cultural, ideological, and economic divisions among the millions of women whose future prospects are at stake.

Note

1. These conclusions come from interviews I have conducted for my book-in-progress, *What Do We Want for Our Daughters (And Our Sons)*, which became "*Feminism Is Not the Story of My Life.*"

References

Black, Naomi. 1989. *Social Feminism.* Ithaca, N.Y.: Cornell University Press.

Blee, Kathleen M. 1991. *Women of the Klan: Racism and Gender in the 1920s.* Berkeley: University of California Press

Fox-Genovese, Elizabeth. 1988. *Within the Plantation Household: Black and White Women of the Old South.* Chapel Hill: University of North Carolina Press.

Fox-Genovese, Elizabeth. 1991. *Feminism Without Illusions: A Critique of Individualism.* Chapel Hill: University of North Carolina Press.

Fox-Genovese, Elizabeth. 1992a. "Feminism and the Rhetoric of Individual Rights, I & II," *Common Knowledge* 1 (1 & 2) [reprinted in this volume, pp. 120–31 and 132–43].

Fox-Genovese, Elizabeth. 1992b. "Feminist Rights, Individualist Wrongs." *Tikkun* 7 (3): 29–34.

Guy-Sheftall, Beverly. February 1989. "Women's Education and Black Women's Studies." Paper presented at the annual meeting of the Southeastern Women's Studies Association, Emory University, Atlanta, Georgia.

Haskell, Thomas, and Sanford Levinson. 1988. "Academic Freedom and Expert Witnessing: Historians and the Sears Case." *Texas Law Review* 66: 1629–59.

Haskell, Thomas, and Sanford Levinson. 1989. "On Academic Freedom and Hypothetical Pools: A Reply to Alice Kessler-Harris." *Texas Law Review* 67: 1591–1604.

Hochschild, Arlie, with Anne Machung. 1989. *The Second Shift.* New York: Viking Penguin.

Jencks, Christopher. 1992. *Rethinking Social Policy: Race, Poverty, and the Underclass.* Cambridge, Mass.: Harvard University Press.

Kamerman, Sheila B., and Alfred J. Kahn, eds. 1978. *Family Policy: Government and Families in Fourteen Countries.* New York: Columbia University Press.

May, Martha. 1982. "The Historical Problem of the Family Wage: The Ford Motor Company and the Four Dollar Day." *Feminist Studies* 8: 399–424.

Minow, Martha. 1990. *Making All the Difference: Inclusion, Exclusion, and American Law.* Ithaca, N.Y.: Cornell University Press.

Scott, Joan Wallach. 1988. "Deconstructing Equality-Versus-Difference: Or, the Uses of Poststructuralist Theory for Feminism." *Feminist Studies* 14: 33–50.

Sidel, Ruth. 1990. *On Her Own: Growing Up in the Shadow of the American Dream.* New York: Viking.

Spelman, Elizabeth. 1988. *Inessential Woman: Problems of Exclusion in Feminist Thought.* Boston: Beacon Press.

Tavris, Carol. 1992. *The Mismeasure of Woman.* New York: Simon and Schuster.

Vogel, Lise. 1990. "Debating Difference: Feminism, Pregnancy, and the Work Place." *Feminist Studies* 16: 9–32.

Williams, Wendy. 1982. "The Equality Crisis: Some Reflections on Culture, Courts, and Feminism." *Women's Rights Law Reporter* 7: 175–200.

Young, Iris Marion. 1987. "Difference and Policy: Some Reflections in the Context of New Social Movements." *University of Cincinnati Law Review* 56: 535–50.

Young, Iris Marion. 1990. *Justice and the Politics of Difference.* Princeton: Princeton University Press.

Eleven

Contested Meanings

*Women and the Problem of Freedom in the
Mid-Nineteenth-Century United States*

I.

Having lived amid the men with the guns in Alfred, Georgia, Paul D., the male protagonist of Toni Morrison's novel *Beloved*, knew that under slavery you protected yourself by loving small. Under those conditions, you "picked the tiniest stars out of the sky to own. . . . Grass blades, salamanders, spiders, woodpeckers, beetles, a kingdom of ants. Anything bigger wouldn't do. A woman, a child, a brother—a big love like that would split you wide open in Alfred, Georgia." Paul D. knew exactly what Sethe meant when she told him that she had to get her children to freedom before she could truly love them: "to get to a place where you could love anything you chose—not to need permission for desire—well now, *that* was freedom."[1] As those who have read *Beloved* know, Sethe defended her freedom to love her own children—to call them hers and to call herself a mother—by murdering her second daughter, the "crawling already?" baby, whom she posthumously named Beloved after a word that moved her in the funeral service.

For Paul D. and Sethe, freedom above all meant what Orlando Patterson calls "personal freedom," the freedom which, "at its most elementary, gives a person the sense that one, on the one hand, is not being coerced or restrained by another person in doing something desired and, on the other hand, the conviction that one can do as one pleases within the limits of that other person's desire to do the same." Personal freedom thus means the "power to do as one pleases, *insofar as one can*," in contrast to sovereignal freedom, which Patterson defines as "the power to act as one pleases, regardless of the wishes of others."[2] The notions of personal and sovereignal freedom have both been central elements in the Western tradition of freedom, which, in Patterson's view, also includes a notion of civic freedom—in his words, "the capacity of adult members of a community to participate in its life and governance." Further, the practice of civic freedom implies the existence of some kind of political community with "clearly defined rights and obligations for every citizen," although not necessarily a full political democracy.[3]

Notwithstanding Patterson's analytic care in defining what he calls the constitutive elements in the "uniquely" Western chord of freedom, the specific meaning of freedom remains elusive, primarily because of a widespread assumption that each of us knows what it means and a scarcely less widespread tendency to think of it in relation to our own experience. Yet those who have written most passionately about freedom have been those who simultaneously believed themselves entitled to it and deprived of it. Thus, perhaps as often as not, freedom has been claimed—and implicitly defined—in the heat of struggles against oppression or tyranny. In the modern West, freedom has preeminently been understood, as the implicit tension between Patterson's volumes respectively entitled *Slavery and Social Death* and *Freedom* suggests, as the antithesis of slavery, which, in the first instance, means an absolute or existential rather than contingent condition.[4]

The absolute antithesis between freedom and slavery is a distinctly modern phenomenon, born of the era of the American, French, and Haitian revolutions when political struggles toppled the traditional embodiments of sovereignal authority, replacing them with new models of civic freedom justified by and grounded in the sovereignal freedom of individuals.[5] Prior to the eighteenth century, Western societies were more likely to understand freedom as contingent and personal, and many were likely to separate the internal or future freedom of the Christian from the more limited freedoms that accrued to those of different stations in the world. Patterson argues that the genius of St. Paul lay in conjoining a vision of internal freedom that even slaves might enjoy to a vision of God's sovereignal freedom in which those who were saved might ultimately participate. In contrast, the genius, if we may call it that, of the great bourgeois revolutions was to transfer sovereignal freedom from God or the absolute monarch to the individuals who composed the polity.

The logic of this translation commands attention, especially since it is cutting such a wide swath in our own time. Following the lead of Thomas Hobbes and John Locke, eighteenth-century political theorists and revolutionaries reworked the notion of sovereignty, repudiating the sovereignal authority of monarchs whose trampling of the prior freedom of individuals they condemned as illegitimate. Sovereignty, they insisted, derived from the individual, who sacrificed some portion of his freedom upon entering into society. The principle of the individual's sovereignal freedom necessarily remained intact, if only because it was theoretically essential to the legitimation of governments. But its practical exercise was never assumed to be absolute. The sovereignal freedom of individuals in theory was thus checked by respect for the personal freedom of others in practice. The notion of civic freedom embodied this compromise between the competing sovereignal freedoms of the individuals who comprised the polity.

In practice the implementation of individual sovereignty, even in the early democratic republics, proved considerably less than universal, contrary to modern assumptions. In the United States, slaves, women, and even some men of insufficient property were excluded from active political participation, although all enjoyed some of the benefits of membership in a society that recognized the claims of civic freedom. But the most stalwart defenders of freedom, especially those from the South and including the Virginia political luminaries, automatically assumed that the citizenship of individual men was grounded in households whose members they represented in the polity and for whose well-being they assumed responsibility. Thus indirectly all free women and men participated in the life of the republic and enjoyed the protection of its laws even if they did not participate directly in its governance. Slaves enjoyed many fewer benefits from their residence within the United States, of which, according to the Dred Scott decision, they could not be considered citizens; but even slaves enjoyed the protection of some laws. For the great majority of the signers of the Declaration of Independence and the Constitution, these unequal political relations were grounded in Christian doctrine, which acknowledged the concept of stewardship and mediated participation in civic freedom.

Yet as Adam Seligman, following John Dunn, has recently argued, the early Lockean conception of individualism, and hence individual freedom, did not break radically with the previous and still pervasive religious vision of governance and political obligation.[6] In effect, Locke transferred the source of obligation and responsibility from the public arena to the interstices of the self (these are my words, not those of Seligman or Dunn). This move rested upon a separation between public and private that the early modern patriarchalism of a Robert Filmer or James I would not have acknowledged.[7] That separation, and the attempt (which concerns Seligman) to mediate it through the concept of civil society, decisively shaped the development of the idea of individualism.

In complex and shifting ways, the idea of individualism depended upon some combination of the related ideas of freedom, equality, reason, universalism, and autonomy—each of which, with the possible exception of autonomy, already had a history of its own. The novelty of individualism, in other words, lay less in the intellectual traditions upon which it drew than in its attempt to combine and rework them. In time and place, individualism's most radical innovation doubtless lay in its claims about the nature of political sovereignty, which it ascribed to independent (male) individuals rather than to a single sovereign who embodied in his (or occasionally her) person the ultimate, although in practice rarely unconditional, political will of the polity as a whole.[8]

The lingering death of old habits and attitudes long ensured that the political claims of individual freedom would be restricted to selected members of the polity, notably, those men who owned sufficient property to be deemed to have a direct stake in its governance. Yet even as political individualism restricted its benefits in practice it cultivated a more generous rhetoric of freedom and equality that invited the identification of those who lacked the attributes to claim political individualism for themselves. In that generosity lay the mainspring of its powerful hegemony, even among those who did not yet benefit directly from it. Thus political regimes grounded in the commitment to individual freedom presided over most of the history of modern slavery.[9]

I am well aware that I have shifted from the evocation of individual freedom to that of political individualism. I have done so with malice aforethought, for the shift captures the frequently unacknowledged tension at the heart of modern notions of freedom. Today, most of us find it virtually inconceivable to speak of personal freedom without simultaneously speaking of civic or political freedom: that is, the freedom to participate in the shaping of the laws and institutions that structure our public lives. Our difficulty in this regard elides the public and private and exposes our tendency to see civic freedom as a combination of personal and sovereignal freedom. Our difficulty is new. Until very recently, the modern conception of civic freedom, and the political individualism upon which it rested, coexisted with a persisting corporatism that recognized the personal freedom of people who did not participate directly in civic freedom.

II.

The experience of women in general and of slave women in particular challenges any simple understanding of the meaning of freedom in the history of the American republic. When the Founders said that all men were created equal, they meant all human beings—male and female, black and white.

They held that view as honestly as they believed that women were unsuited for political participation and as honestly as they accepted slavery. And they were in no contradiction at all. They did not agree that all people were equal, except in the equal worth of their respective versions of humanity—that is, in the equality of their souls before God—and in their innate sense of right and wrong, which therefore made each person responsible for his or her acts. In our own time, the meaning of freedom has been stretched to cover many more conditions, relations, and individuals than the original architects of American freedom ever intended and has especially, if irrationally, conflated freedom and equality. As a result, one may discern a growing tendency to reinterpret civic freedom from the perspective of personal freedom and, at the extreme, to push the meaning of personal freedom toward sovereignal freedom. In the process, we risk the loss of the Founders' assumption that practical freedom inescapably implied a recognition of coexistence—of limits and of responsibilities.

The Christian (specifically Calvinist) aspect of Locke's influence upon their thought commands attention. In working from a Calvinist conception of the equality of human souls before God, Locke was decisively separating equality from freedom in its permissive or anarchistic implications. The equality of souls lay in their equal subordination to God's dominion, which is to say in their individual responsibility to a higher authority. Hence the freedom of individuals lay in their ability to choose sin over virtue—to defy God's authority and pay the predictable price. The equality and freedom of political life exercised a much more restricted sway and primarily concerned the equal stake in sovereignty and governance shared by propertied male individuals, who were enjoined to represent the interests of their households of dependents.

During the antebellum period, American women did not directly participate in civic freedom, although we may safely assume that they all identified in greater or lesser measure with the message of personal freedom that pervaded the young nation's political ideals. Most undoubtedly still understood personal freedom primarily in terms of Christian teachings, to which they turned for guidance about their relations with and responsibilities toward others.[10] Many also, without seeing any contradiction, embraced significant elements of the emerging language of civic freedom. Thus during the 1830s, female mill operatives in Lowell turned to the revolutionary tradition to justify their opposition to their employers. Identifying themselves as "daughters of freemen," they insisted,

> *Let oppression shrug her shoulders*
> *And a haughty tyrant frown,*

And little upstart Ignorance,
In mockery look down.
Yet I value not the feeble threats
Of Tories in disguise,
While the flag of Independence
O'er our noble nation flies.[11]

There is no mistaking the young women's determination to claim the promises of American independence as peculiarly their own. In a second protest poem, another of their number drove the point home, and in so doing signaled yet more radical implications of the message of freedom:

Oh! isn't it a pity, such a pretty girl as I—
Should be sent to the factory to pine away and die?
Oh! I cannot be a slave,
I will not be a slave,
For I'm so fond of liberty,
That I cannot be a slave.[12]

The women operatives of Lowell belonged to a literate culture. For them, political language, like the language of the Bible in which they were immersed, linked formal literate culture to their personal situation. They had grown up hearing and reading the words that helped them to define their own identities. For them, the simple assertion that you, the boss, cannot do this to me, the woman worker, could best be rendered in the political language that defined the status of male citizens. But in borrowing that language, they were claiming it for their own identities. By the same token, they modified the culture from which they were borrowing. In particular, as they moved from the positive assertion, I too am free, to the negative assertion, I cannot be a slave, they gave new meaning to the common metaphor of slavery as the antithesis of freedom. During the 1840s and the 1850s, any number of women who sought to improve their own condition would insistently exploit the metaphor.

The metaphor of slavery as the antithesis of freedom resonated powerfully among the early proponents of women's rights, many of whom had already been active supporters of abolition.[13] The best-known vignette is that of the young Elizabeth Cady Stanton, who attended the World Anti-Slavery Convention in London with her husband only to find that the women would not be recognized as delegates—and were not allowed to address the assembly nor even be seated with the men. The outraged Stanton found it "pitiful to hear narrow-minded bigots, pretending to be teachers and leaders of men, so cruelly remanding their own mothers, with the rest of womankind, to absolute subjection to the ordinary masculine type of humanity."[14] Sitting through the proceedings, she and Lucretia Mott turned their thoughts to the plight of women. Mott had little faith in "the sincerity of abolitionists who, while eloquently defending the natural rights of slaves, denied freedom of speech to one-half the people of their own race." These self-styled philanthropists would have been appalled at the thought that women might be physically harmed, but "the crucifixion" of women's "pride and self-respect, the humiliation of the spirit, seemed to them a most trifling matter."[15] Walking home from the last session, Stanton and Mott resolved that immediately upon their return to the United States they would "form a society to advocate the rights of women."[16]

At that meeting, which was eventually convened in Seneca Falls, New York, in 1848, Stanton presented an impassioned defense of women's equal right to the freedom that men enjoyed. She did not reject women's special maternal and domestic responsibilities, but insisted that so long as women were degraded and oppressed, women could not meet those responsibilities and the nation would languish in its current state of "moral stagnation." Men commonly objected that "if the principles of freedom and equality" she advocated were put into practice, the harmony of domestic life would be destroyed. To the contrary, she countered, "there can be no true dignity or independence where there is subordination to the absolute will of another, no happiness without freedom." And as for women's role as mothers in shaping the character of young men, "So long as your women are slaves you may throw your colleges and churches to the winds."[17]

Stanton, who modeled the convention's Declaration of Sentiments on the Declaration of Independence, nonetheless insisted that the meeting was not intended to discuss only the details of social life. She and her colleagues were not proposing to petition the legislature "to make our husbands just, generous, and courteous, to seat every man at the head of a cradle and to clothe every woman in male attire."[18] She and her colleagues had assembled to discuss their civil and political rights and wrongs, "to protest against a form of government, existing without the consent of the governed—to declare our right to be free as man is free, to be represented in the government which we are taxed to support."[19] She thus focused directly upon civic freedom: the right of women to participate in the governance of the polity in which they lived and to which they paid taxes. And her Declaration of Sentiments began with the precise language of the Declaration of Independence, including "We hold these truths to be self-evident," but it modified the content by substituting for the "all men" of the original, "all men and women are created equal."[20]

Stanton did not restrict herself exclusively to civic freedom, for, in her view, man's presumption toward woman vastly exceeded her simple exclusion from political participation. "He has made her, morally, an irresponsible being," by allowing her to commit crimes with impunity, provided they be committed in the presence of her husband. He has deprived her of education and, in the church as well as the state, restricted her to a subordinate position. He has distorted public sentiment by assigning to her a different code of morals than that which obtains for man. In sum, "He has usurped the prerogative of Jehovah himself, claiming it as his right to assign for her a sphere of action, when that belongs to her and to God." Thus has man not merely disfranchised but degraded women by attempting in every means at his disposal "to destroy her confidence in her own powers, to lessen her self-respect, and to make her willing to lead a dependent and abject life."[21]

In that time and place, most Americans perceived Stanton's demand that women participate equally in civic freedom through the exercise of the franchise as unacceptably radical. But, as we may appreciate, the true radicalism of her Declaration lay in her insistence that men, in their relations to women, had arrogated sovereignal freedom to themselves, thereby demeaning and degrading women as autonomous individuals. Here is where the metaphor of freedom as the antithesis of slavery came powerfully into play. For Stanton, in evoking the cost to women of the deprivation of freedom under which they lived, borrowed heavily from eighteenth-century evocations of slavery as debilitating dependence. In so doing, she suggested that the deprivation of freedom had endowed women with the psychology of slaves, coloring their entire relation to the world. Thus, although in her speech to the convention she insisted that she did not intend to transform men's and women's roles, her passionate denunciations of the ways in which deprivation of freedom had distorted their respective characters betrayed an underlying perfectionist desire to refashion radically many aspects of the world.

Stanton neither mentioned nor protested against biblical teachings about women's subordination. She betrayed no inclination to attack religion, which she believed supported her cause. Her complaints lay with the men who had assumed the position of God and closed church leadership to women. Her strategy effectively divorced revealed religion from its institutional manifestations in the world, leaving it to women to claim the essence of religion for themselves. In this spirit, she exhorted her listeners to live as they should and feel their individual accountability to their Maker. She wished woman to know that her spirit was "fitted for as high a sphere as man's." She wished woman to "live *first* for God, and she will not make imperfect man an object of reverence and awe." Only thus would woman learn that her dependence must be upon God, her true happiness must derive from accomplishment of her duty. "Thus will she learn the lesson of individual responsibility for time and eternity."[22]

Stanton's thinking about the direct relation of the individual soul to God very much resembled that of the abolitionists with whom she and many other advocates of women's rights had worked. Like them, she was essentially arguing that the dictates of individual conscience took precedence over the teaching of ministers or even the Bible. The radicalism of this position lay in the claim that the freedom of the Christian included the right—for some, the obligation—of the individual Christian to define the meaning of freedom. Toward the end of her life in such writings as "Solitude of the Self" and *The Woman's Bible,* she openly advocated an emancipation and self-determination for women that challenged all institutional and ideological barriers. Women's freedom required a liberation from the artificialities of law and custom that, in freeing them, would transform society.[23]

III.

If Stanton began with the intention of claiming civic freedom for women, her reflections upon the implications of women's experience of "enslavement" led her to the conviction that women's emancipation required something akin to sovereignal freedom. To be sure, she did not write as if she were claiming for women the uncontested freedom to tell others what to do. Identifying the condition of women with that of slaves, she more modestly claimed that men had no right to tell women what to do. In practice, she would assuredly have acknowledged the legitimacy of a personal freedom that permitted women to do as they chose insofar as they could without encroaching upon the similar freedom of others. In theory, however, she focused exclusively upon what she believed women needed in order to rid their own minds of the crippling habits of dependency and compliance. We may be permitted to doubt that her goals could have been realized without serious cost to the freedom to which men had become accustomed, or, more important, without cost to the prevailing conception of freedom in society as a whole.

No less than Stanton and her colleagues, Southern slaveholding women understood the power of the association between abolition and freedom for women, but they rejected its implications. In practice, the vast majority supported slavery, which they recognized as an essential foundation for their own position as ladies. Life amid slaves caused them no end of frustrations, but it afforded them a freedom from household labor that they valued highly. More often than not, they viewed their own difficulties in supervising slaves as, in large measure, the consequence of their own weakness of character. They would commonly rail that this or that slave was lazy, uppity, or unruly; they would complain that all slaves were impossible; they might even express doubts about whether the ownership of slaves was good for women's or men's character. But when they turned to their diaries and journals they usually prayed for the strength and maturity to live up to their responsibilities by governing their slaves properly.[24]

Theoretically, most slaveholding women regarded slavery as a legitimate, indeed divinely sanctioned, social system. And those who thought about the theoretical justifications for slavery knew that the biblical justification for the subordination of slaves to masters was grounded in the prior justification for the subordination of women to men.[25] Louisa S. McCord, a formidable intellectual and polemicist who was more interested in economic theory than theology, readily intervened in public debates on the slave trade, the diversity of races, and the difference between white and black slavery.[26] A passionate defender of free trade, McCord paid more attention to the laws of economics than the laws of God. A passionate defender of Southern independence, including Southerners' right to hold slaves, she fully understood the claims of freedom. But she impatiently rejected the notion that they should be applied to women individually.

McCord never doubted the personal and intellectual capacities of gifted women (among whom she surely counted herself); she never denied that some women might chafe at being restricted to their allotted sphere. Of course women may suffer from "*compression,*" as may men. Who, at one time or another, does not? "Human cravings soar high. Perhaps there is no human being, not born in a state of imbecility . . . who does not suffer, or fancy that he suffers, from compression."[27] But she remained convinced that women's physical weakness necessitated male protection, which, in her view, justified women's social dependence upon men. Suppose, she suggested, that one were to pit an individual woman against an individual man, "in a direct state of antagonism, by throwing them into the arena together, stripped for the strife." Suppose one were to say to the man that this woman differs in no essential respect from himself, that she is "your equal and similar, possessing all rights which you possess, and (of course she must allow) possessing none others." What, in such a contest, would become of the woman's physical weakness? For McCord, the answer was clear: The woman would lose and the world become a "wrangling dog kennel."[28]

McCord unhesitatingly lumped the defense of women's individual rights with abolitionism, socialism, and all the other pernicious -isms that threatened to unravel the legitimate social fabric. The triumph of -isms would turn the world into a topsy-turvy nightmare—"a species of toothache, which, by some socialistic, communistic, feministic, Mormonistic, or any such application of chloroform to the suffering patient, may be made to pass away in a sweet dream of perfection."[29] The freedom that McCord, like many other slaveholding women, cherished was the freedom of their country, in which they believed themselves to participate. Freedom, in other words, adhered to the collectivity and, accordingly, to those who belonged to it. Their knowledge that not all members of the collectivity enjoyed an equal measure of personal freedom did not shake their confidence in the conception. And even McCord attacked the proclivity of Stanton and her colleagues to present religion as purely a matter of individual conscience. Such a perfect "democratic system," she scathingly noted, can only result in the deposition of God Himself, "by reducing *His* influence to a *single vote*," which in turn will result in the reversal of ranks until a militant proponent of women's rights (she had Harriet Martineau in mind) might ultimately "prefer (as some . . . recent works seem to suggest) to have it decided that she is *Le Bon Dieu* himself."[30]

When McCord and other pro-Southern women wrote of tyranny, they were invariably attacking the tendency of Northerners, especially those whom they called Black Republicans, to reduce the South to a state of subjugation.[31] In this respect, they interpreted the mounting calls for the freedom of slaves and of women as a direct attack upon the freedom of their society and hence upon their own freedom. In their minds they were defending a viable concept of civic freedom against a host of arrogant and presumptuous folks who were demanding the extension of sovereignal freedom to all. They worried that such challenges threatened the very concept of civic freedom, and they especially worried that these claims of sovereignal freedom directly defied God's law.[32]

At the close of the antebellum period, Augusta Jane Evans, who harbored serious doubts about the effect of slavery upon women's character, published a novel, *Beulah,* in which she searchingly explored the problem of women's freedom. Her protagonist, Beulah Benton, loathes the very idea of dependence in any form. Reproaching a friend who tries to convince her that a woman's heart has special needs, Beulah retorts, "What was my will given to me for, if to remain passive and suffer others to minister to its needs? Don't talk to me about woman's clinging, dependent nature. You are opening your lips to repeat that senseless simile of oaks and vines; I don't want to hear it; there are no creeping tendencies about me."[33] Like Louisa McCord, but yet more thoroughly, Evans enters the lists against the Northern drift toward a religion grounded only in the individual conscience. Evans represents Beulah's seduction by the forces of skepticism, singling out the Emersonian temptation to confuse the individual with God. Eventually, Beulah regains her faith and with it her ability to love. At the novel's close, she has married the guardian whose offers of adoption and financial support she had previously brushed proudly aside. Evans did not intend Beulah's marriage to signal her repudiation of a woman's legitimate claims to personal freedom; she did intend it to signal her willing repudiation of illegitimate claims to sovereignal freedom. Beulah's greatest strength lies in her unmediated relation to God; but that very relation includes acceptance of God's law, which assigns different social and civic positions to women and men.

IV.

By the close of the antebellum period, literate white women in the United States had mounted a serious contest over the meaning of freedom, especially as it applied to themselves. Northern antislavery and women's rights women frequently evoked the plight of black slave women as emblematic of the disorder and abuse wrought by the deprivation of freedom, but most of them also harbored a strong dose of racism that made them less than empathetic with black women's position.[34] Proslavery Southern women for their part might easily express deep devotion to a specific slave or deplore the tendency of white men to consort with slave women sexually. But, in general, neither group fully understood the situation and feelings of slave women, if only because they had great difficulty in viewing that situation as essentially similar to their own. The vast majority of white Southern women saw the possible emancipation of the slaves as a direct threat to themselves and the stability of their society. White, antislavery Northern women favored emancipation on principle, but since they normally did not know or live among any significant number of African-Americans, their convictions in this regard largely remained abstract.

Throughout the antebellum period, black slave women harbored and developed their own distinct conception of freedom, which began, and sometimes ended, with their own release from bondage. Knowing slavery from the perspective of the slave, they had no doubt that it constituted the antithesis of freedom. They lived with the everyday indignities and frequently the pain of being subject to the will of another and being (sometimes harshly, sometimes brutally) disciplined if they refused to comply. In everyday life, their lack of freedom meant that their persons and their time were largely at the disposal of their owners. Whether working in the fields or in the house, they followed the orders of masters, mistresses, overseers, and even capricious, undisciplined children. They were expected to do as they had been told, and if they did not they could expect to be punished.[35]

The more serious consequences of their enslavement, as many of them understood, nonetheless lay elsewhere. Slavery deprived women and men of the freedom to enter into legally sanctioned, binding marriages. It deprived them of the freedom to determine their children's futures, and frequently of the possibility of keeping their children with them. The absence of freedom disastrously curtailed, although never completely foreclosed, their ability to build their own churches and community institutions, their ability to provide their children with a literate education, even their ability to enforce their preferred visions of male and female roles. Slavery demonstrably limited their individual and collective mobility, but it no less portentously limited their individual and collective stability. At the extreme, it pitted each of them individually against the sovereignal freedom of the master—the power of his will over their lives.[36]

The worst case of the isolated slave who struggled in solitary combat against the will of an overbearing master did occur, but it was not the norm. The real horror of that absolute opposition between freedom and slavery as embodied in the master and the slave respectively lay precisely in its defining the outer limits—the logical possibilities—of slavery as a social system. In practice those possibilities were not realized, or only realized episodically. The majority of African-American slaves in the United States did not suffer the "social death" that Orlando Patterson sees as the essence of all forms of slavery.[37] Patterson's view implies an existential interpretation of slavery as the absence of freedom and hence of social connection, much as black is described as the absence of color. Considering slavery from an analytic perspective, Patterson views it as an absolute, which, in effect, means as the antithesis of sovereignal freedom.

The point is not that African-American slaves lacked civic freedom and endured severe restrictions upon their personal freedom. On both counts, they did. But they did not live in the kind of chaotic limbo that the total deprivation of all elements of freedom would imply. Some significant portion of the lives of most slaves was ordered as if they did enjoy at least some freedom. The notion that slavery in the United States should be viewed as a total institution, analogous to Nazi concentration camps, has been discredited primarily because historians of the slave community have not found that the majority of slaves were reduced to Sambos or Uncle Toms.[38] To the contrary, historians have found compelling evidence of a vigorous culture and strong familial or community bonds among slaves who had the wit to hide much of their independent life as a people from the eyes of their owners.[39]

Slave women developed their own patterns of everyday resistance to ease their oppression, finding countless ways to take possession of their tasks, to take pride in their skills, to provide small advantages for themselves and their children, to run off for brief periods to carve spaces of quiet and privacy out of their lives. They developed sophisticated techniques that pushed many a mistress to the brink of distraction because a task would be left undone, done too slowly, or not done in the prescribed way. Former slave children fondly recollected the time their mothers found—frequently at night—to make special food or clothes for their families, to instruct their children, or to worship in secret with other slaves. Here and there, narratives by former slaves or accounts by whites provide glimpses of passionately independent women whom no man could handle. Frequently these women were depicted as being of recent African origin, which they may or may not have been. But the convention of associating fierce, unbreakable independence with recent African origins suggests much about the attitudes of the majority of slaves. For these women whom none could handle were not merely represented as being cut off from whites, but from other members of the slave community as well. If only by contrast, the figure of the indomitable, independent African woman, who recognized no law other than her own will, reminds us that the majority of slaves did see themselves as members of a community that was bound together by shared conventions and practices, if not by formal laws.

The conventions and practices that ordered the lives of the majority of slave women derived from both African and American traditions and took from both sources a recognition of interdependence. As Patterson has argued, the Western conception of freedom was unique, so we should not expect the slaves to have derived it from their African past.[40] In this perspective, their unambiguous opposition to slavery might best be understood as precisely a rejection of slavery rather than a defense of freedom per se. The African societies from which the slaves were torn recognized neither individualism nor private property in the modern Western sense. African traditions and practices derived from a worldview that emphasized the importance of family, lineage, and collective effort. African societies also practiced slavery, but not usually the chattel slavery that was practiced in the United States. African slavery could be brutal, but conceptually it tended to be expressed in ideologies that emphasized the inequality and interdependence among people and the interdependence of the material and spiritual worlds.[41]

Southern proslavery ideology shared many of these features, especially the emphasis upon hierarchy and interdependence. Thus as Southern paternalism took shape it rested upon a commitment to the reciprocal, if unequal, rights and responsibilities of slaveholders and slaves, who belonged to a single household. Slaves were the first to understand and defend what they took to be their rights within this context, notably their rights to regular periods or days of rest and their claim upon some of the goods of the household. Among the black and white women, the slaves' sense of their rights frequently took the form of a cook's understanding that she was entitled to a certain amount of white flour or some other delicacy for her own family or a maid's understanding that she was entitled to some share of her mistress's cast-off clothing. More often than not, a female slave who ran off to the woods for a day or two—not the same as running away—or dawdled while completing an errand believed that she was acting within the rules of reciprocity, which is to say within her rights.

To invoke paternalism in this sense is emphatically not to invoke benevolence, for paternalism rested on violence and could wear a brutal face. It is, however, to underscore the ways in which slaveholders and slaves, however unequally, collaborated in creating and sustaining a sense of their mutual rights and responsibilities. And, more often than not, a slave's exercise of his or her "rights" required that a master or mistress meet his or her "responsibilities." Accordingly, both parties to this relation felt that they had claims upon one another that could not easily be encompassed by the individualist language of freedom. Both sides, to be sure, were aware of the language; both applied it to some aspects of their respective situations. But neither relied upon it entirely in their relations among themselves.

For the slaveholders—to risk simplification—the language of freedom applied to the public or civic realm of politics and governance in which male heads of households participated, and women, children, and slaves did not. For the slaves, following the Haitian Revolution, it also applied to a public realm the laws of which enforced their enslavement.[42] We know that countless slaves enthusiastically embraced the signs of civic freedom, and the Fourth of July became such a favorite day for them that even slaveholders, who in other situations remained remarkably blind to the evidence of their slaves' independent wills, tempered their rhetoric in public speeches. National independence was one thing, but the possible meanings that slaves might give to invocations of individual liberty and equality were entirely another.

The more literate and sophisticated slaves understood the issues perfectly. In 1852, Frederick Douglass openly reproached a white audience in New York City for their wanton appropriation of words that should belong to all. "What," he queried, "to the American slave, is your Fourth of July?" A day, he answered his own question, "that reveals to him, more than all the other days in the year, the gross injustice and cruelty to which he is the constant victim." Withal, he insisted, he was "not wanting in respect for the fathers of this republic," whom he acknowledged as "brave" and "great men." Thus, however disadvantageous the position from which he, as a former slave, was bound to regard them, he would unite with whites "to honor their memory."[43]

But the slaves' growing understanding that freedom was a status to which they, as a people and as individuals, might aspire and even fight for, did not overnight revolutionize their political perceptions. Knowing themselves to be slaves, their first understanding of freedom normally focused directly upon their determination to reverse their condition. Or to put it differently, they readily thought of freedom as, indeed, the antithesis of the enslavement they knew. It was in this spirit that countless slaves sought to claim for themselves the benefits of the civic freedom to which they knew they were entitled. But their understanding of the specific content of that civic freedom—what they expected it to mean in everyday life—was considerably more complex. They continued to adhere to concepts of social and political relations that derived from their African traditions and that were, in some measure, reinforced by their own determination to shape their experience as members of slaveholding households.

V.

Emancipation represented the political triumph of the Northern conception of freedom, which most Northerners presumably understood in the sense of civic freedom. Only a few leaders, most notably Thaddeus Stevens, insisted that the freedmen would require a sustained period of economic experimentation and political dictatorship to prepare them to overcome the legacy of slavery and participate in a republican polity. In the prevalent view, emancipation had simply freed former slaves to take their place as independent members of the polity. To decree the slaves' freedom was not, however, the same as its implementation. And, as the early claims on behalf of women's rights might have suggested, the inclusion of those who had previously been denied civic freedom might well raise questions about personal and sovereignal freedom as well. Radicals like Thaddeus Stevens understood that freedom without the means to sustain it might prove a mixed blessing at best, but they lost the fight for those forty acres and a mule that the majority of slaves believed would establish their position as independent farmers. The ultimate failure of Reconstruction to effect economic democracy and provide substantively for the former slaves left slaves and slaveholders to negotiate the new meaning of freedom as best they could, beginning with the meaning of free labor. The Freedman's Bureau played an important role, especially in the case of agricultural labor, frequently defending the freedpeople's interests, sometimes mediating between freedpeople and planters or landlords. But even at its best, it exercised only a limited sway over the full scope of former slaves' lives and even over their relations with their former masters and mistresses.[44]

For Northerners, it seemed natural that emancipation pre-eminently meant the implementation of the freedom of labor that lay at the center of Republican ideology and policies.[45] Freedpeople must work in order to live; employers must pay workers for their labor. But nothing, least of all labor, was that simple. In the event, sharecropping and tenancy proved much more common than agricultural wage labor throughout the South during the latter decades of the nineteenth century, but the regions such as the sugar parishes of Louisiana in which wage labor did prevail reveal much about both sides' attitudes toward the meaning of freedom. In the sugar parishes, both planters and freedpeople viewed postbellum labor through the prism of their relations under slavery. Thus while both sides were willing to capitalize on the advantages of free labor, neither side was willing to forego the advantages that paternalism had afforded them.[46] Freedpeople, for example, saw no inconsistency in drawing wages for their labor and continuing to demand that the planter provision their animals or grant them access to his animals and tools. Planters, for their part, had no patience with the notion that they should absorb the cost of labor and continue to respect traditional rights and prerogatives. If freedom had arrived, so be it. But they had always viewed the freedom of the labor market as the very antithesis of their own paternalistic relations with labor, and if the market had triumphed, then paternalism had no further claims upon them. Their clear-sightedness on this aspect of their new labor relations did not, however, prevent them from expecting their laborers to put in extra hours during the harvest season. And so it went, with neither side being prepared to adjust to the full implications of market relations.

Some planters, who sought to regulate the lives of their laborers as fully as possible, instituted prohibitions against leaving the plantation without a pass, drinking, gambling, and even the use of "bad language." Freedpeople understandably viewed such attempts as a direct assault upon the essence of their freedom, which lay in their ability to do as they saw fit. At the same time, freedpeople frequently recognized the importance of discipline to efficient collective labor, and they assuredly recognized that the wages they received for that labor gave them greater autonomy than they had ever known.[47] That very autonomy became another source of friction as workers in the sugar parishes of Louisiana, for example, were known to collect their monthly wages and take off for the city until they had been spent. Planters retaliated by attempting to withhold the wages until the end of the growing season, but freedpeople protested that this practice compromised their freedom, the essence of which lay in their ability to leave the plantation as they chose.[48]

If planters had difficulties in negotiating the meaning of free labor with freedmen, their difficulties with freedwomen were greater yet. Throughout the South freedwomen, with the full support of their men, sought to withdraw from field labor entirely and, if possible, from domestic labor in the houses of others as well. Freedwomen's aversion to field labor had appeared during the war and grew steadily thereafter. Even when freedwomen did agree to work in the fields, notably during harvests or other demanding seasons, planters complained that they never put in the full time required. In regions in which tenancy took hold, planters usually attempted to make contracts depend upon the willingness of freedwomen to participate in the labor.[49]

The reasons for freedwomen's resistance to paid labor for whites were many, but high among them ranked the commitment of both freedmen and freedwomen to the creation of their own families and households. It is widely known that countless former slaves responded to emancipation by formalizing marriages that under slavery had had no legal standing.[50] Shortly after the end of the war, one articulate freedman had exhorted a group of his fellows, enjoining them to recall that "The Marriage Covenant is the foundation of all our rights."[51] For both freedmen and freedwomen, the solemnization of marriages represented the premier sign of their ability to shape their own and their children's lives, to claim the essential promise of civic freedom, namely, the formal link between their public and private lives. For many former slaves, this was no empty formality, but the official recognition of their participation as a people in civil society. Each former slave might feel the lure of individual freedom, but most recognized that, even as individuals, freedpeople above all required the structure of families, churches, and schools to build a possible future for their people.[52]

For freedpeople, the corporate or institutional units of marriage, family, churches, and schools lay at the core of the meaning of freedom, but did not always come easily. They had to be defended not only against the claims of former slaveholders and a new class of landowners who were accustomed to the power to dispose of the labor of slaves as individuals, but against the hostility of a larger white community that could not easily stomach the prospect that former slaves would be their equals in Southern society. Although the most visible struggles normally occurred between individuals, many of those apparently personal struggles turned less on the individual case than on the consolidation of institutions, beginning with nuclear families, that grounded the place of freedpeople as free members of society. Thus a planter who sought to secure the labor of a married woman in his fields or his house was not merely laying claim to her as an individual, he was directly challenging her role as wife and mother and her husband's prior claim to her loyalty and labor.

Clearly most freedwomen concurred with their men that their first responsibility should be to their own families and that the freedom of the community would benefit from their willing assumption of the domestic roles against which Northern proponents of women's rights were beginning to protest. We would be naive to assume, however, that all freedwomen slipped naturally into their new roles. Slavery had mightily conspired to treat slave women as individuals, at the cost of their responsibilities as wives and mothers. Slavery had assuredly not been entirely successful in this regard, but it took a heavy toll. In consequence, it is not surprising that freedwomen were inclined to fight for a measure of personal (including sexual) freedom, on the understanding that the meaning of freedom would have to include their own right to do as they pleased.[53] Thus for freedwomen, every bit as much as for freedmen, embedded in the meaning of freedom lurked a wrenching contradiction between stability and mobility.

Stability dictated that freedwomen recognize some limitations on their personal freedom in the interests of the cohesion of the African-American community. And many seem to have agreed to those limitations on the understanding that they helped to define and safeguard women's roles as wives and mothers. Both African and American traditions valued those roles highly, especially that of mother, and one of the most widely recognized failures of slaveholding paternalism, as many slaveholders themselves worried, lay in its tendency to violate them.[54] During Reconstruction and thereafter, if we may believe African-American writers, women willingly associated their own propriety as wives and devotion as mothers with the respectability and "uplift" of the African-American community as a whole.[55]

No matter how fully freedwomen understood the importance of stability, many continued to flirt with the lure of mobility. Their experience of slavery, no less than that of freedmen, had predisposed them to understand freedom as a direct and ultimately personal repudiation of the power of slaveholders to dispose of their time, their labor, and their persons. The freedom to love a husband or children included the recognition of obligation to others. It may well have represented the essence of personal freedom in the sense of doing as one wished within the limits of another's desire to do the same, but in the context of intimate personal relations the limits of the other person's desire to do the same normally included foregoing freedoms that, without those relations, one might have properly enjoyed. Thus a mother who, under slavery, might well have felt entitled to run off, leaving one or more children to be cared for by others, would, precisely by virtue of having gained the freedom to define herself as a mother, lose the freedom to come and go at will. And in fact, even as slaves few women were willing to abandon their children.

VI.

For better or worse, slavery had bequeathed to freedwomen a sense of themselves as individuals that profoundly colored their understanding of the meaning of freedom and influenced the ways in which they redefined their relations with their world. Not long after Appomattox, Mary Jones overheard a discussion about the meaning of freedom between the cook and house-maid who had recently been her slaves. Kate and Flora dwelled especially upon their desire to own gold watches, bracelets, and chains, presumably seeing such items as fitting external signs of their new status.[56] Nor were they alone in their ambitions. Countless freedwomen challenged their former mistresses directly by assuming the airs and attire of ladies, notably parasols and veils. The challenge struck home. One officer of the Freedman's Bureau reported that the freedwomen's wearing of veils had so offended young white women that for a time they refrained from wearing veils themselves.[57]

One may readily savor the satisfaction the freedwomen got from the response of the white ladies, but the deeper significance, like that of the young white ladies' response, lay in its exposure of the symbiotic ties that bound many black and white Southerners together in a struggle of wills as fierce as any that their respective men experienced. Many former slavehold-ing women experienced emancipation as a devastating blow, even when they also claimed relief at being rid of the responsibility of supervising and car-ing for slaves. Mary Boykin Chesnut, in concluding her celebrated diary, captured the feelings of many when she grimly wrote, "I do not write often now—not for want of something to say, but from a loathing of all I see and hear. Why dwell upon it?"[58]

Initially, slaveholding women resisted the obvious truth that their for-mer slaves wanted to be free. Mary Chesnut, for example, confessed herself "daunted" when, in 1865, her friends the Martins left Columbia "and their mammy, the negro woman who had nursed them, refused to go with them."[59] But even those who acknowledged the freedpeople's desire for free-dom had great difficulty in understanding what freedom meant to them. One after another complained in her diary about problems with the former slaves who had chosen to remain, but who now expected to be treated like the free laborers they were. Ella Gertrude Clanton Thomas had an especially difficult time in coming to terms with those of her former slaves who stayed; Cather-ine Edmonston expressed relief at being free of the responsibility for hers.[60] But whatever a white woman's response, she might easily confuse the freed-people's departure, or even their decision to remain on new terms, with her own increased domestic burdens. From her perspective, their freedom meant her enslavement: what she bemoaned as unprecedented burdens, former slave women embraced as new, if uncertain, opportunities.

When former slaveholding women evoked their own enslavement, as many did, they frequently conflated the emancipation of their slaves with the Northern victory, thus reading their personal enslavement as a specific case of the enslavement of their society. As a seventeen-year-old, Emma LeConte reflected in her diary upon the terror of Sherman's approach and his destruction and pillaging of Columbia, South Carolina. She wrote proudly of still feeling unconquered, but of hating the Yankees more than ever, viewing the very name Yankee as "a synonym for *all* that is *mean,* despicable and abhorrent."[61] In a similar spirit, Amelia Gayle Gorgas wrote that although she loved her home state of Alabama, she dreaded "to reside there while the present state of the negroes remains unsettled—indeed I do not feel as if it were my state or country while we are ground under the heel of Yankee despotism."[62] Shortly thereafter, Elizabeth Kilcrease in Georgia wrote to a friend to bemoan the loss of her slaves and to share the remark of another of her friends who claimed, "I have lost my religion since the Yankees set my negroes free." Doubtless, Kilcrease commented, "this has been the experience of many Southern women."[63]

Such women were wont to understand freedom primarily as civic freedom —the freedom and order of their own society. They understood full well that religious and secular proslavery ideology were as one in linking the justification of slavery to the subordination of women, and they were accustomed to acceding to limitations upon their own freedom as necessary to a social order they valued highly. But as Elizabeth Kilcrease suspected, her friend was not alone in losing her faith in the wake of the Yankee victory. Emancipation forced Gertrude Thomas to recognize "how intimately my faith in revelations and my faith in the institution of slavery had been woven together." And her faith was shaken. For a time she doubted God, the truth of revelations, everything. "When I opened the Bible the numerous allusions to slavery mocked me."[64] Sarah Hine expressed the despondency of many when she wrote to a friend that white Southerners "share nothing on earth to look forward to, we have no future, no country, we are slaves to the will of others."[65]

For such women the world had indeed ended, or at least been turned upside down. And if they did not initially devote much thought to the implications of the defeat for their personal freedom, many gave considerable thought to its implications for the freedom of their former slaves. Lenora Clayton, for example, claimed sincere concern for the fate of the freedpeople, but doubted they were ready for freedom. Finding free labor more efficient than slave labor, she had no further interest in defending slavery, but she nonetheless believed that "the priceless boon of freedom is what few, if any [former slaves] comprehend."[66] And Laura Comer noted in her diary, "Freedom has fallen so suddenly upon the negro as to completely upset his equilibrium & turn his head."[67]

Women like Laura Comer might have been shaken to discover that freedwomen's ideas of freedom had much in common with what white women wanted for themselves. Eliza Andrews, however, began to understand the issues fairly rapidly. When Andrews's maid Charity first informed her that she had selected the name of Tatom and should henceforth be referred to as Mrs. Tatom, Andrews was amused. She nonetheless reflected that the freedpeople seldom, if ever, took the names of their owners when selecting what they called "their entitles." Presumably, she noted, since the name of the owner had been given to them in slavery, they wished "to throw off that badge of servitude. Then, too, they have notions of family pride."[68] Thus did Andrews implicitly acknowledge that the expression of family pride through the choice of one's own name represented an important sign of freedom. Although, however paradoxical it may seem, some freedpeople did take their former owners' names for precisely the same reason.

The most intense struggles between white and black women over the appropriate meaning of freedom occurred within households as both tried to come to terms with the meaning of free labor in the domestic context.[69] Former slaveholding women were loathe to be reminded that their former slaves now had families of their own to which they returned at night. Former slave women predictably insisted that these families represented their most important obligations. And how could a good wife and mother deny another good wife and mother's most sacred obligations? White mistresses found even apparently small signs of their free servants' independence almost unbearable, for they served as constant reminders of the independence of those whom they had been accustomed to view (however preposterously) primarily as extensions of their own will.

As paid workers, freedwomen found innumerable ways to remind their mistresses of their independence, if only by pretending not to understand instructions, working slowly, or leaving tasks undone. To make matters worse, free maids and housekeepers, like free male agricultural workers, rarely agreed that their wages evened accounts between them and their employers. Determined to preserve the aspects of paternalism that had benefited them, they insisted upon the mistress's obligation to provide them with cast-off clothing, a "servant's pan" of food for their family, or even personal assistance at times of emergency.[70] These practices challenged elite white women's own notions of freedom and frequently resulted in an accommodation between mistress and servant that preserved important elements of the more personal relations of paternalism. The white women took less kindly to freedwomen's determination to establish themselves on an independent footing and, above all, to ensure the social and economic advancement of their children. Gertrude Thomas did not miss the point. She raged at the idea that, while her own sons worked in the fields, the sons of freedwomen attended school.[71]

Throughout the former slave states, whites moved steadily toward depriving freedpeople of as much of the economic mobility and independence normally associated with freedom as possible. Whether by attempting to bind laborers to plantations through tenancy, sharecropping, and the payment of annual (rather than weekly or monthly) wages, or by attempting to deny them such attributes of economic freedom as the free participation in markets, whites sought to ensure the economic marginalization and continuing subordination of blacks.[72] These restrictions affected freedwomen in distinct ways. Should, for example, the everyday struggles between mistress and maid get out of hand, the maid would find herself vulnerable to accusations of theft, burglary, and poisoning, which she might not deserve. Freedwomen who delighted in the public display of clothing, or were simply out of an evening, might also find themselves jailed for "public disorder" or "drunkenness." Whites further sought to regulate the hours in which freedpeople could conduct commerce in order to curtail the independent markets that had sprung up in the wake of emancipation. Such restrictions were especially resented by freedwomen who frequented the markets in quest of calico, foodstuffs, and jewelry.[73]

Freedwomen struck back against the restrictions upon their freedom with all of the weapons at their disposal and more than a few ended in jail for their pains. Normally, their conflicts were with whites, but some fought bitterly against other freedpeople as well. Like freedmen, they had taken from slavery a fierce determination to be able to go where they pleased and do as they chose. Having endured enslavement, they were quick to believe that freedom must indeed mean its opposite. On more than one occasion, they behaved as if they sought to establish a sovereignal freedom that, in their view, mirrored and reversed the freedom enjoyed by their former owners. But their most radically individualistic interpretations of freedom normally coexisted with a fierce commitment to establish a viable claim to civic freedom for their people, even if that meant putting their own ambitions on hold. Among the many tragedies of Reconstruction and thereafter was the determination of Southern whites to forestall that participation in civic freedom and, indeed, economic freedom as well.

The costs on both sides ran high. For the freedpeople, they included a denial of civic freedom that frequently sent many individuals on a counterproductive quest for a freedom that recognized no legitimate limits; for the whites they included the crippling conviction that their own freedom depended upon the brutal oppression of others. Both parties to the struggle remained convinced that the interdependence of genuine personal and civic freedom could only be understood as a war.

VII.

By the end of the 1860s, the Thirteenth, Fourteenth, and Fifteenth Amendments had transformed the meaning of freedom in the United States by extending personal and civic freedom to the former slaves, although not until fifty years later did women acquire the basic civic freedom of suffrage. And not until the 1960s were the gains that the amendments had so broadly sketched fully assured to the descendants of slaves. By the time the civil rights movement reopened the struggle for full personal and civic freedom for African-Americans the possible meanings of freedom had radically expanded, and the emergence of a new wave of the women's movement would expand them even further. As these struggles broadened to include more groups who believed their freedom to be curtailed, they increasingly tended to cast their claims in terms of individual rights, not merely to participation in civic freedom, but to a more generalized freedom from a broad range of oppressions—with the definition of oppression, as Elizabeth Cady Stanton's writing presaged, subject to steady expansion.

Ironically, as the substance of slavery receded ever further into the past, the legacy of slavery as the antithesis of freedom cast a lengthening shadow. Many of those who felt themselves in some way excluded from the full promise of American freedom were increasingly tempted to cast their claims in absolute terms. Freedom, in this view, indeed meant the antithesis of slavery, but the antithesis of an absolute, existential slavery that very much resembled Patterson's conception of social death. And as the insistence of the claims mounted, the deep lessons of American slavery were dissipated in the shadowy reaches of fragile memory.

American slavery had been a violent, brutal system of social relations in which the lives of slaves were largely at the mercy of the slaveholders, who all too frequently abused their power. But American slavery never reduced African-American slaves to things, and rarely, if ever, to fully isolated and disconnected individuals. To believe otherwise is to deny the record of the heroic effort of African-American slaves to wrest from adversity the elements of personal dignity, mutual loyalty, and family and community solidarity. More, it is implicitly to identify freedom with a sovereignal freedom that inherently denies the freedom of others. That that tendency to favor sovereignal freedom existed, we know. It is all too human for those who have suffered oppression to seek to turn the tables on their oppressors by whatever means lie to hand. But the costs of acting on that tendency are high, and the effort itself usually proves self-defeating. Thus, in *Beloved*, Sethe attempts to explain to Paul D. how she killed her daughter by explaining to him what freedom meant to her. Maybe, she muses, she could not love her children "proper in Kentucky because they wasn't mine to love." School-teacher, in attempting to return Sethe and her children to slavery, threatened that freedom, and Sethe "couldn't let her nor any of em live under school-teacher." Cornered, she defended their freedom: "I took and put my babies where they'd be safe."[74] Yet, as Toni Morrison unmistakably cautions us, to kill a child in the defense of freedom is, whatever else it may be, the murder of a "crawling already?" baby.

Freedom has always been contested: such is its nature. Throughout most of Western history, most people have understood freedom to be preeminently internal, a matter of the individual soul's relation to God—which is to say, not of this world. In the measure that they have understood freedom to be of this world, they have preeminently understood it as a quality that pertained to corporate groups or collectivities, which were frequently represented by one or more individuals who acted in the name of the freedom of the group. Our modern world has increasingly transformed freedom into an individual right to be claimed and realized precisely in the world. But the very broadening of freedom's possible meanings has inevitably made those meanings the object of a steadily escalating contest of individual wills, with decreasing attention to the public good. With supreme historical irony, the escalation of demands for individual freedom now threatens the very survival of freedom itself.

Notes

1. Toni Morrison, *Beloved* (New York, 1987), 162.

2. Orlando Patterson, *Freedom, vol. 1: Freedom in the Making of Western Culture* (New York, 1991), 3–4.

3. Ibid., 4.

4. Orlando Patterson, *Slavery and Social Death: A Comparative Study* (Cambridge, Mass., 1982).

5. Patterson, *Freedom*, 322, following David Brion Davis, *The Problem of Slavery in Western Culture* (Ithaca, N.Y., 1966), notes that not until the eighteenth century did the Church recognize an incompatibility between internal freedom and external slavery. See also, David Brion Davis, *The Problem of Slavery in the Age of Revolution, 1770–1823* (Ithaca, N.Y., 1975); Eugene D. Genovese, *From Rebellion to Revolution: Afro-American Slave Revolts in the Making of the Modern World* (Baton Rouge, La., 1979); Elizabeth Fox-Genovese, *Feminism Without Illusions: A Critique of Individualism* (Chapel Hill, N.C., 1991).

6. Adam B. Seligman, *The Idea of Civil Society* (New York, 1992), 23. John Dunn, *The Political Theory of John Locke* (Cambridge, Mass., 1969).

7. Robert Filmer, *Patriarchia and Other Political Works*, ed. Peter Laslett (Oxford, 1949); Elizabeth Fox-Genovese, "Property and Patriarchy in Classical Bourgeois Political Theory," *Radical History Review* 4, nos. 2 and 3 (Spring/Summer 1977): 36–59 [reprinted in this volume, pp. 1–20]; Gordon J. Schochet, *Patriarchalism in Political*

Thought: The Authoritarian Family and Political Speculation and Attitudes Especially in Seventeenth-Century England (New York, 1975).

8. For a fuller discussion of these issues, see Fox-Genovese, *Feminism Without Illusions.*

9. Elizabeth Fox-Genovese and Eugene D. Genovese, *Fruits of Merchant Capital: Slavery and Bourgeois Property in the Rise and Expansion of Capitalism* (New York, 1983).

10. See, for example, Elizabeth Fox-Genovese, "Religion in the Lives of Slaveholding Women of the Antebellum South," in *That Gentle Strength: Historical Perspectives on Women in Christianity,* ed. Lynda L. Coon, Katherine J. Haldane, and Elisabeth W. Sommer (Charlottesville, Va., 1990), 207–29.

11. *The Man,* Feb. 22, 1834, quoted in Thomas Dublin, *Women at Work: The Transformation of Work and Community in Lowell, Massachusetts, 1826–1860* (New York, 1979), 93.

12. Harriet Hanson Robinson, *Loom and Spindle; or, Life Among the Early Mill Girls* (New York, 1898), 84, quoted in Dublin, *Women at Work,* 98–99.

13. Ellen Carol DuBois, *Feminism and Suffrage: The Emergence of an Independent Women's Movement in America, 1848–1869* (Ithaca, N.Y., 1978), 32, insists that women's dissatisfaction with their position was as much cause as effect of their participation in the antislavery movement. See also Blanche Glassman Hersh, *The Slavery of Sex: Feminist Abolitionists in America* (Urbana, Ill., 1978).

14. Elizabeth Cady Stanton, *Eighty Years and More: Reminiscences, 1815–1897* (New York, 1971; orig. ed., 1898), 81.

15. Ibid., 82.

16. Ibid., 83.

17. Elizabeth Cady Stanton and Susan B. Anthony, *Correspondence, Writings, Speeches,* ed. Ellen Carol DuBois (New York, 1981), 34–35.

18. Ibid., 31.

19. Ibid.

20. Elizabeth Cady Stanton, "Declaration of Sentiments," in *The Concise History of Woman Suffrage: Selections from the Classic Works of Stanton, Anthony, Gage, and Harper,* ed. Mari Jo and Paul Buhle (Urbana, Ill., 1978), 94–95.

21. Ibid., 95.

22. Stanton and Anthony, *Correspondence, Writings, Speeches,* 33.

23. *Concise History of Woman Suffrage,* 311. Elizabeth Cady Stanton and the Revising Committee, *The Woman's Bible,* Pts. I & II (Seattle, 1974; orig. ed. 1898).

24. Elizabeth Fox-Genovese, *Within the Plantation Household: Black and White Women of the Old South* (Chapel Hill, N.C., 1988); Fox-Genovese, "Religion in the Lives of Slaveholding Women."

25. Elizabeth Fox-Genovese and Eugene D. Genovese, "The Divine Sanction of Social Order: The Religious Foundations of the Southern Slaveholders' World View," *Journal of the American Academy of Religion* 55, no. 2 (June 1987): 201–23, and our "The Religious Ideals of Southern Society," *Georgia Historical Quarterly* [70] (1986)[: 1–17], repr. in *The Evolution of Southern Culture,* ed. Numan V. Bartley (Athens, Ga., 1988).

26. L. S. M. [Louisa S. McCord], "Carey on the Slave Trade," *Southern Quarterly Review* 25 (January 1854): 115–84; L. S. M., "Diversity of the Races: Its Bearing upon Negro Slavery," *Southern Quarterly Review* 19 (April 1851): 392–419; L. S. M., "Negro and White Slavery—Wherein Do They Differ?" *Southern Quarterly Review* 20 (July 1851):

118–32. For a general discussion of McCord, see Fox-Genovese, *Within the Plantation Household,* 242–89.

27. L. S. M. [Louisa S. McCord], "Enfranchisement of Women," *Southern Quarterly Review* 21 (April 1852): 324–25.

28. L. S. M. [Louisa S. McCord], "Woman and Her Needs," *DeBow's Review* 13 (September 1852): 275, 268.

29. Ibid., 268.

30. L. S. M., "Enfranchisement of Women," 330.

31. Augusta Jane Evans to Mary Howard Jones, November 26, December 4, 1860, Benning/Jones Collection, Chattahoochee Valley Local & Oral History Archives, Columbus College Library, Columbus, Georgia. See also, Elizabeth Fox-Genovese, "To Be Worthy of God's Favor: Southern Women's Defense and Critique of Slavery," *32nd Annual Fortenbaugh Memorial Lecture* (Gettysburg College, 1993).

32. Jamie Stanesa, "Dialogues of Difference: Personal Identity, Social Ideology, and Regional Difference in American Women Writers, 1850–1860," Ph.D. diss., Emory University, 1993; and Elizabeth Moss, *Domestic Novelists in the Old South: Defenders of Southern Culture* (Baton Rouge, La., 1992).

33. Augusta Jane Evans, *Beulah,* ed. Elizabeth Fox-Genovese (Baton Rouge, La., 1992; orig. ed., 1859), 116. See my introduction for a fuller discussion of these issues in the novel.

34. For free African-American women's perceptions of Northern white women's racism, see Harriet E. Wilson, *Our Nig; or, Sketches from the Life of a Free Black, In a Two-Story White House, North. Showing that Slavery's Shadows Fall Even There, by "Our Nig."* ed. Henry Louis Gates, Jr. (New York, 1983; orig. ed., 1859) and Harriet Jacobs' correspondence in Harriet Jacobs, *Incidents in the Life of a Slave Girl: Written by Herself,* ed. Jean Fagan Yellin (Cambridge, Mass., 1987). Cf. Jean Fagan Yellin, *Women and Sisters: The Antislavery Feminists in American Culture* (New Haven, Conn., 1989).

35. Fox-Genovese, *Within the Plantation Household;* Eugene D. Genovese, *Roll, Jordan, Roll: The World the Slaves Made* (New York, 1974); Deborah Gray White, *Ar'n't I a Woman? Female Slaves in the Plantation South* (New York, 1985).

36. Fox-Genovese, *Within the Plantation Household,* esp. 372–96. See also Peter Kolchin, *Unfree Labor: American Slavery and Russian Serfdom* (Cambridge, Mass., 1987).

37. Patterson, *Slavery and Social Death.*

38. Stanley Elkins, *Slavery: A Problem in American Life* (Chicago, 1959); Ann J. Lane, ed., *The Debate Over Slavery: Stanley Elkins and His Critics* (Urbana, Ill., 1971).

39. Genovese, *Roll, Jordan, Roll;* Lawrence Levine, *Black Culture and Black Consciousness: Afro-American Folk Thought from Slavery to Freedom* (New York, 1977); Herbert G. Gutman, *The Black Family in Slavery and Freedom, 1750–1925* (New York, 1976); Fox-Genovese, *Within the Plantation Household.*

40. Patterson, *Freedom.*

41. See G. A. Hopkins, *An Economic History of West Africa* (New York, 1973); Ester Boserup, *Women's Role in Economic Development* (London, 1970); Claire C. Robertson and Martin A. Klein, eds., *Women and Slavery in Africa* (Madison, Wis., 1984); and, for the general problem of the relation between African and Western culture, Kwame Anthony Appiah, *In My Father's House: Africa in the Philosophy of Culture* (New York, 1992).

42. Genovese, *From Rebellion to Revolution.*

43. Quoted in Ibid., 132–33.

44. On the general response to the destruction of slavery and the emergence of free labor during the war, as captured in the papers of the Freedman's Bureau, see the volumes in the series *Freedom: A Documentary History of Emancipation, 1861–1867,* Ira Berlin, Barbara J. Fields, Thavolia Glymph, Joseph P. Reidy, and Leslie Rowland, eds., ser. 1, vol. 1, *The Destruction of Slavery* (New York, 1985); Ira Berlin, Thavolia Glymph, Steven F. Miller, Joseph P. Reidy, Leslie Rowland, and Julie Saville, eds., ser. 1, vol. 3, *The Wartime Genesis of Free Labor: The Lower South* (New York, 1990); and Ira Berlin, Steven F. Miller, Joseph P. Reidy, and Leslie Rowland, eds., ser. 1, vol. 4, *The Wartime Genesis of Free Labor: The Upper South* (New York, 1993).

45. Robert W. Fogel, *Without Consent or Contract: The Rise and Fall of American Slavery* (New York, 1988); Eric Foner, *Free Soil, Free Labor, Free Men: The Ideology of the Republican Party Before the Civil War* (New York, 1970).

46. John Rodrigue, "Raising Cain: From Slavery to Free Labor in Louisiana's Sugar Parishes, 1862–1880," Ph.D. diss., Emory University, 1993, 340. On the general problems, Gerald David Jaynes, *Branches Without Roots: Genesis of the Black Working Class in the American South, 1862–1882* (New York, 1986); Joseph P. Reidy, *From Slavery to Agrarian Capitalism in the Cotton Plantation South: Central Georgia, 1800–1880* (Chapel Hill, N.C., 1992); William Cohen, *At Freedom's Edge: Black Mobility and the Southern White Quest for Racial Control, 1861–1915* (Baton Rouge, La., 1991).

47. Rodrigue, "Raising Cain," 199–200; Jaynes, *Branches Without Roots.*

48. Rodrigue, "Raising Cain," 244.

49. Ibid., 329–30; Noralee Frankel, "Workers, Wives, and Mothers: Black Women in Mississippi, 1860–1879," Ph.D. diss, George Washington University, 1982.

50. See, for example, Gutman, *The Black Family in Slavery and Freedom.*

51. Ira Berlin, Joseph P. Reidy, and Leslie S. Rowland, eds., *The Black Military Experience,* ser. 2 of *Freedom: A Documentary History of Emancipation, 1861–1867* (New York, 1982), 672–73.

52. See, for example, James D. Anderson, *The Education of Blacks in the South, 1860–1935* (Chapel Hill, N.C., 1988).

53. Nicholas Lemann, *The Promised Land: The Great Black Migration and How It Changed America* (New York, 1991), esp. 21–24.

54. Fox-Genovese, *Within the Plantation Household;* Jacqueline Jones, *Labor of Love, Labor of Sorrow: Black Women, Work, and the Black Family from Slavery to the Present* (New York, 1985). On slaveholders' concern that slavery did not respect slave marriages, see Fox-Genovese, "To Be Worthy of God's Favor"; Bell Irvin Wiley, "The Movement to Humanize the Institution of Slavery During the Confederacy," *Emory University Quarterly* 5 (Dec. 1949): 207–20; Bell Irvin Wiley, *Southern Negroes, 1861–1865* (New Haven, Conn., 1938), 168–72; Clement Eaton, *A History of the Southern Confederacy* (New York, 1961), 237–38; Calvin H. Wiley, *Scriptural Views of National Trials* (Greensboro, N.C., 1863); John Berrien Lindsley, "Table Talk," Dec. 10, 1861, May 8, 1862, John Berrien Lindsley Papers, Tennessee State Library and Archives.

55. Frances Ellen Watkins Harper, *Iola Leroy; or, Shadows Uplifted* (New York, 1988; orig. ed., 1892); Pauline E. Hopkins, *Contending Forces: A Romance Illustrative of Negro Life North and South* (New York, 1988; orig. ed., 1900); Claudia Tate, *Domestic Allegories of Political Desire: The Black Heroine's Text at the Turn of the Century* (New York, 1992), for instance, 149; Elizabeth Fox-Genovese, "To Write the Wrongs of Slavery," *Gettysburg Review* [2] (Winter 1989): 63–76.

56. Mary Jones to Mary Jones Mallard, November 17, 1865, in Robert Manson Myers, ed., *The Children of Pride: A True Story of Georgia and the Civil War* (New Haven, Conn., 1972), 1308–9.

57. Sidney Andrews, *The South Since the War* (New York, 1969; orig. ed., 1866), 187. See also Leon Litwack, *Been in the Storm So Long: The Aftermath of Slavery* (New York, 1979), 6, 116, 245, 315.

58. C. Vann Woodward, ed., *Mary Chesnut's Civil War* (New Haven, Conn., 1981), July 26, 1865, 834.

59. Ibid., February 16, 1865, 715.

60. Ella Gertrude Clanton Thomas Diary, Perkins Library, Duke University. An edited and somewhat cut version of the diary has been published as *The Secret Eye: The Journal of Ella Gertrude Clanton Thomas, 1848–1889,* ed. Virginia Ingraham Burr (Chapel Hill, N.C., 1990); Beth G. Crabtree and James W. Patton, eds., *The Journal of a Secesh Lady: The Diary of Catherine Ann Devereux Edmondston, 1860–1866* (Raleigh, N.C., 1979). See also, W. Maury Darst, ed., "The Vicksburg Diary of Mrs. Alfred Ingraham (May 2– June 13, 1863)," *Journal of Mississippi History* 44 (May 1982): 148–79.

61. Earl Schenck Miers, ed., *When the World Ended; the Diary of Emma LeConte* (New York, 1957), 66. See, in general, Elizabeth Fox-Genovese, "Diaries, Letters, and Memoirs," *Encyclopedia of the Confederacy,* Richard Current et al., eds. (New York, 1993) [, 470–78].

62. Amelia Gayle Gorgas to Joseph Gorgas, July 29, 1865, Gorgas Family Papers, University of Alabama, Tuscaloosa. See also, Mary Tabb Johnston with Elizabeth Johnston Lipscomb, *Amelia Gayle Gorgas: A Biography* (University, Ala., 1978).

63. Elizabeth Kilcrease to Clara Barrow, November 30, 1865, Barrow Family Papers, University of Georgia, cited by Mary Margaret Johnston-Miller, "Heirs to Paternalism: Elite White Women and Emancipation in Alabama and Georgia," Ph.D. diss., Emory University, 1994.

64. Ella Gertrude Clanton Thomas Diary, October 8, 1865. See also, Fox-Genovese, "Religion in the Lives of Slaveholding Women of the Antebellum South."

65. Sarah Hine to Charlotte Branch, February 10, 1866, Margaret Branch Sexton Papers, University of Georgia, cited by Johnston-Miller, "Heirs to Paternalism."

66. Lenora Clayton to Mary Ann Cobb, November 7, 1865, Howell Cobb Papers, University of Georgia.

67. Laura Beecher Comer Diary, July 1, 1865, in Anne Kendrick Walker, *Braxton Bragg Comer: His Family Tree from Virginia's Colonial Days* (Richmond, Va., 1947), 115.

68. Eliza Frances Andrews, *The War-Time Journal of a Georgia Girl,* ed. Spencer Bidwell King, Jr. (Macon, Ga., 1960), 346–47.

69. On the postbellum relations between elite women and their slaves, see Johnston-Miller, "Heirs to Paternalism."

70. For a full discussion, see Ibid. On the early-twentieth-century remains of these practices, see Voloria Mack-Williams, "Hard Workin' Women: Class Divisions and African-American Women's Work in Orangeburg, South Carolina, 1880–1940," Ph.D. diss., State University of New York, Binghamton, 1991.

71. Ella Gertrude Clanton Thomas Diary.

72. Mary Ellen Curtin, "The Human World of Black Women in Alabama Prisons, 1870–1900," in *Southern Women: Hidden Histories,* Virginia Bernhard, Betty Brandon, Elizabeth Fox-Genovese, Theda Purdue, eds. (Columbia, Mo., 1994) [, 11–30]. See also

Louis P. Ferleger, "Share-cropping Contracts and Mechanization in the Late-Nineteenth-Century South," *Agricultural History* 67, no. 3 (Summer 1993): 31–46, and his "Farm Mechanization in the Southern Sugar Sector After the Civil War," *Louisiana History* 23, no. 1 (Winter 1982): 21–34.

73. Curtin, "Human World."

74. Morrison, *Beloved*, 163–64.

Twelve

Feminism, Children, and the Family

Feminism originated and has developed as a demand for equality between women and men. Admittedly, the feminist commitment to equality has followed a sinuous road, not least because a variety of obstacles to full equality has periodically led some feminists to emphasize the differences between women and men that appear to make equality on male terms an elusive goal.[1] But when all the caveats are filed, the claims to equality nonetheless remain paramount, notwithstanding significant and sometimes unarticulated differences among feminists over whether equality should mean equality of opportunity or equality of results.[2] Arguably, most women are today struggling not for the equality demanded by feminists but for equity and fairness in the distribution of burdens.[3] The rhetoric of equality therefore distorts the issues.

Feminists' stated and unstated commitments to equality cast a long shadow over the relations among feminism, children, and the family.[4] From the start, some feminists argued that the so-called patriarchal family was itself the primary source of women's oppression and the primary obstacle to their liberation.[5] And even those who do not judge the family so harshly nonetheless tend to single out family responsibilities as a formidable obstacle to women's equality with men.[6] The proposed feminist solutions to this problem have gone in many directions, arguing for the transformation of male consciousness,[7] a new division of labor within the family (joint-parenting),[8] and a variety of state supports for working women or parents.[9] I hardly need to rehearse the objections to these and similar proposals for this audience. Suffice it to say that no equalization of men's and women's domestic responsibilities will be possible without considerable private and social cost. With this difficulty in mind, it seems useful to reconsider the problem itself.

In its initial stages, feminism primarily articulated a revolt by women against men. After all, men with their many freedoms and prerogatives made an easy target. More importantly, few women were prepared to admit openly that children constituted the real object of their attack or, to put it differently, the real constraint upon their equality with men.[10] And since I intend sharply to attack the feminist tendency to rebel against responsibility for children,[11] it is all the more important to understand that children do indeed account for a significant portion of women's inequality with men.[12] To be blunt, more often than not, children make and keep women poor, especially when the women have sole responsibility for them.[13] And since almost one-fourth of all children live only with their mothers,[14] it should be clear that any complacent assumption that mothers should just assume time-honored domestic responsibilities and stay home with their kids fatuously misses the point. Any consideration of feminism's attitudes toward children and the family must, accordingly, take into account these social and economic realities.

In fairness, however, it is not clear that these are the realities that immediately concern the most visible feminists. These feminists represent the group of upscale—affluent, well-educated, and primarily white—women who have fixed their own ambitions upon careers comparable to those of the most successful men.[15] These are the women who have pioneered in turning women's work within the home into servants' work—women who expect others to do their cleaning, care for their kids, and take on all the other drudgery of keeping life going.[16] (Conservatives are entitled to laugh and recall the old saw that socialism is a system in which everyone has servants.) No doubt, these women's incomes benefit their families, but not by the full amount of the income, for a significant portion of that income supports their own clothing, manicures, meals out, and travel—all of the signs of prestige and freedom that women who spend most of their time with kids cannot justify and usually cannot afford.

Arguably, many elite career women could choose to stay home without significant cost to their families' well-being. Many other women cannot; with rare exceptions, single mothers must work or go on welfare; many poor married women must also work.[17] The problem of choice falls the hardest on working-class and lower-middle-class women who cannot earn enough to replace the quality of the care they give their children, but who know that if they do not work their children may lose the opportunity to attend college. Most women wrestle with difficult choices about how best to meet their family responsibilities.[18] Even if many legitimately enjoy the opportunity to spend some time at work as well as at home, their work usually has more to do with necessity than with self-fulfillment.[19] Their problems should top the list of our agenda for social policy, if only because they reappear in sinister form in the statistics about teen crime, pregnancy, and suicide.[20]

Their problems are not those with which feminism has most directly concerned itself. Indeed, they are not those which feminists normally like to discuss at all. For buried in the private anguish of ordinary women who weigh hard choices lies the notion that the leading feminist premises about what women should want may mask a more complex and dangerous reality. Feminism has, above all, been driven by the determination to free women from the constraints under which they suffer, notably their biology.[21] This determination surfaces in the defense of the right to abortion as a fundamental right. In *Planned Parenthood of Southeastern Pennsylvania v. Casey,*[22] the Supreme Court effectively confirmed the logic of the feminist position in this regard, arguing that "[t]he ability of women to participate equally in the economic and social life of the Nation has been facilitated by their ability to control their reproductive lives."[23] The Court thus assumed that women are, by choice or necessity, independent economic agents who must be able to provide for themselves. It further assumed what most people have always known, namely that in important respects, the interest of women as individuals and the interests of children are at odds.[24] To be a fully autonomous individual—a player—women must be free not to bear children.

Societies have always coerced or cajoled women into finding a compelling interest in the care of children, and most elite women throughout history have not performed the work of caring for their own children.[25] This recognition does not negate the competing truth that women have generally had a deep personal interest in their children and a special sense of responsibility for them.[26] But, it should force us to acknowledge the complexity of the issue and to recognize the ways in which the failures of our social policies, beginning with no-fault divorce, have opened the door to feminist claims about women's primary need for independence and equality—their need not to be left at home with the kids.

Our most powerful rhetoric about the responsibilities and satisfactions of motherhood derives from a period in which men were normally held to the economic support of wives and children.[27] Those days are gone. Nor will newly draconian support policies for absent fathers bring them back. Feminists are uncomfortable with the claim that children do better with both fathers and mothers, even when they insist that fathers should share equally in the responsibilities of parenting.[28] We are not required to share these self-serving illusions. If we are to encourage mothers to put children first, we must encourage fathers and especially employers and public policies to do the same.

If feminism has not been friendly to children, most employers have not been either.[29] Pregnancies, breast feeding, chicken pox, recurring earaches, and even homework are antithetical to the norms of smoothly running organizations—and, in fairness, we should acknowledge that many firms cannot easily meet the attendant costs. Child-friendly solutions such as extended pregnancy leaves, job security for child-raising employees, and the rest can prove expensive, as can on-site daycare and job training for poor single mothers.

But, if we are serious about our commitment to children, we must find ways to solve these problems. The commitment to solutions does not oblige us to swallow reigning feminist and liberal-statist pieties and agree to an endless expansion of bureaucracy and state intervention. When feminism assumes that women must be liberated from their responsibilities to children in order to attain justice for themselves, it implicitly invites the conclusion that women who choose to have children may fairly be held responsible for them in the way that all individuals are held responsible for their "choices." Or, to put it differently, a mindless view of equality between women and men puts children at high risk. And if we uncritically accept the upscale, careerist feminist agenda, countless numbers of women will also suffer.

Our society has cut women lose from the secure pursuit of devotion to children.[30] The tension that always existed between the interests of women and the interests of children has erupted into a war in which women, to meet their purported responsibility to perform the moral work of society—the work for which the rest of us are unwilling to pay—are asked to sacrifice their own prospects not merely for glory and renown but for minimal security and equity.[31] We will not begin to define the appropriate relations among women, children, and family until we transcend both the feminist insistence upon equality and the conservative celebration of domesticity as usual. Only when we recognize that both an unattainable equality and a punitive inequality deepen the antagonism between the needs of women and children will we begin to imagine a model of equity that may serve the needs of both.

Notes

The form of citation in these endnotes is replicated from the original.

1. *See* generally Carol Gilligan, *In a Different Voice* (1982); Ellen DuBois, "Illusions Without Feminism," *The Nation*, Jan. 20, 1992, at 57–60 (review of Elizabeth Fox-Genovese, *Feminism Without Illusions* (1991)) (both discussing differences between men and women and resulting inequalities).

2. The issue is illustrated by the question of whether women should fight for "maternity leave," implying equal opportunity for women to work, or for "parental leave," symbolizing an equal sharing of parental responsibility by fathers. *See* Elizabeth Fox-Genovese, *Feminism Without Illusions,* 56 (1991).

3. Virginia Sapiro, *Women in American Society,* 410 (1994). As one commentator has noted, women who do not seek a feminist version of substantive equality "would find it intrusive and counterproductive for government" and law to try to effect it. Cass R. Sunstein, "Feminism and Legal Theory," 101 *Harvard Law Review* 826, 836 (1988) (review of Catharine A. MacKinnon, *Feminism Unmodified: Discourses on Life and Law* (1987).

4. *See, e.g.,* Joan C. Williams, "Gender Wars: Selfless Women in the Republic of Choice," 66 *N.Y.U. L. Rev.,* 1559 (1991) (discussing the working mother and abortion and arguing that "mothers who pursue their own self-interest are often condemned as selfish.") For a discussion of the impact of feminism on the family as a corporate unit rather than a collection of individuals, see Elizabeth Fox-Genovese, "The Legal Status of Families as Institutions," 77 *Cornell L. Rev.* 992–996 (1992) [reprinted in this volume, pp. 144–48].

5. *See, e.g.,* Simone de Beauvoir, *The Second Sex,* 444 (Vintage Books 1989) (1952) (labeling marriage "obscene in principle"); Kate Millett, *Sexual Politics,* 25–26 (1970) (arguing that patriarchy is a social constant, keeping women from political or social power).

6. *See* Barbara Ehrenreich, *The Hearts of Men: American Dreams and the Flight from Commitment,* 100–02 (1983) (reviewing feminist arguments against housekeeping by married women).

7. *See, e.g.,* Fox-Genovese, *supra* note 2, at 3–4; Casey Miller & Kate Swift, *Words and Women,* ix–x (1977).

8. *See, e.g.,* Virginia Held, "The Obligations of Mothers and Fathers," in *Mothering: Essays in Feminist Theory,* 7 (Joyce Trebilcot ed., 1984) [hereinafter *Mothering*] ("we may have urgent reasons to turn the parenting done by fathers and mothers into entirely similar activities.").

9. *See, e.g.,* Ehrenreich, *supra* note 6, at 177 (arguing that, for women to enter the workforce, they will need child care); Maria O. Hylton, "'Parental' Leaves and Poor Women: Paying the Price for Time Off," 52 *U. Pitt. L. Rev.* 475, 518 (1991) (arguing that parental leave legislation as currently constituted is inadequate and actually burdens women).

10. *See, e.g.,* Betty Friedan, *The Feminine Mystique,* 194–95 (20th anniversary ed. 1983) (1963) (explaining that the double duty of children and work does not adversely affect working mothers).

11. *See, e.g.,* Fox-Genovese, *supra* note 2, at 82; Jeffner Allen, "Motherhood: The Annihilation of Women," in *Mothering, supra* note 8, at 315, 316.

12. *See* Lenore J. Weitzman, *The Divorce Revolution: The Unexpected Social and Economic Consequences for Women and Children in America,* 275–76 (1985) (demonstrating how divorced women with children experience significant economic loss); M. Rivka Polatnick, "Why Men Don't Rear Children: A Power Analysis," in *Mothering, supra* note 8, at 21, 28–29, 33–34 (discussing the demands that children place on a mother's time).

13. Sapiro, *supra* note 3, at 433; *see also* Weitzman, *supra* note 12, at xi–xii.

14. In 1990, about 73% of children in the United States lived with both parents, 21% lived with their mother only, and 3% lived with neither parent. Sapiro, *supra* note 3, at

387. For a discussion of the difficulties of mothering and work, see Maxine L. Margolis, *Mothers and Such: Views of American Women and Why They Changed,* 46–47 (1984).

15. Fox-Genovese, *supra* note 2, at 28–29 (citing Elizabeth V. Spelman, *Inessential Woman: Problems of Exclusion in Feminist Thought* (1988)).

16. *See* Fox-Genovese, *supra* note 2, at 22 (arguing that feminism eases the passage of privileged middle-class women into the public sphere).

17. Laura A. Davis, "A Feminist Justification for the Adoption of an Individual Filing System," 62 *Cal. L. Rev.* 197, 209 (1988); *see also* Sapiro, *supra* note 3, at 388.

18. *See* Weitzman, *supra* note 12, at 319 (observing that the children of divorced working mothers rarely receive compensatory care from other family members).

19. Sapiro, *supra* note 3, at 431, 435, 437.

20. *See id.* at 438; Donna Gaines, *Teenage Wasteland,* 7 (1992) (discussing teen suicide); *see generally* Alex Kotlowitz, *There Are No Children Here* (1991) (tracing the lives of two children in a housing project over two years).

21. *See, e.g.,* Allen, *supra* note 11, at 315 (calling for women to "evacuate" motherhood). For a discussion of the pernicious effect of "phallocentrism" in public institutions, see Christine A. Littleton, "Reconstructing Sexual Equality," 75 *Cal. L. Rev.* 1279 (1987).

22. 112 S. Ct. 2791 (1992).

23. *Id.* at 2797.

24. *See* Polatnick, *supra* note 12, at 35 (arguing that a mother's duty to subordinate her personal objectives to the needs of others is not a path to power and success).

25. *See* Elizabeth Fox-Genovese, *Within the Plantation Household,* 16–17, 98 (1988) (discussing elite ante-bellum women who did not care for their own children).

26. *See* Sara Ruddick, *Maternal Thinking,* 70 (1989) (discussing the preservative love of mother for child).

27. *See* Margolis, *supra* note 14, at 33–39 (providing examples of nineteenth-century rhetoric concerning motherhood).

28. *See* Barbara D. Whitehead, "Dan Quayle Was Right; Harmful Effects of Divorce on Children," *The Atlantic,* Apr. 1993, at 47–48 (noting that any discussion of the superiority of two-parent families provokes angry protest).

29. *See, e.g.,* Hylton, *supra* note 9 (arguing that unpaid leave is inadequate for the needs of families and that the costs are passed on to poor workers).

30. For a critique of this cutting loose, see F. Carolyn Graglia, "The Housewife as Pariah," 18 *Harv. J.L. & Pub. Pol'y* 509 (1994).

31. *See* Fox-Genovese, *supra* note 4, at 995 (arguing that the family could be strengthened by denying parents the right to divorce, or at least the right to remarry and assume economic responsibility for another family, until their children are self-sufficient).

Thirteen

Beyond Autonomy

Sex, Repression, and Violence against Women

Reflecting upon the relation between the individual and society, Freud concluded that civilization was grounded in repression, notably the repression of sexuality.[1] He acknowledged that the imperatives cost individuals dearly and frequently resulted in neurosis. But whatever the costs, he never doubted that both individual achievement and an orderly life for society necessitated repression. Today, *Civilization and Its Discontents* is viewed more as a period piece than as a template for our times, but those who diminish its significance are deluding themselves. For Freud's underlying insight about the importance of individual restraint to a tolerable common life increasingly becomes more compelling.

Freud understood repression primarily as the process of internalization through which individuals enforce social norms and prohibitions by making them their own. And he understood repression as especially characteristic of Western European bourgeois culture, which imposed a strict sexual code upon its members. But most societies, including those without the West's predilection for internalization and individual guilt, have subjected sexuality to strict moral codes, which normally include some effort to protect the virginity of unmarried women, prohibit adultery, and hold men accountable for the children they father. In this respect, most societies have encoded sexuality in a binding web of conventions and prohibitions designed, implicitly or explicitly, to protect women against men's propensity for sexual irresponsibility and even violence. Thus—again, in most societies—women have fallen under the protection of the men of their family, lineage, or group, who have frequently been authorized to discipline women who defy that protection.

Freud belonged to the lineage of secular intellectuals who, from the Enlightenment until the mid-twentieth century, attempted to understand and analyze the patterns and dynamics of Western bourgeois culture. Like Smith, Marx, Weber, and Durkheim among many, he sought to reconcile and explain the relations of the individual—understood as the center of consciousness and experience—to the collective behavior of what Nietzsche called "the herd."[2] In this spirit, Freud's analysis of repression and its social function bound the individual to the work of civilization through self-direction or self-censorship. Having identified sexuality as the driving force of human life, he explored the ways in which life in society—civilization—dictated its channeling and containment.

Times have changed. Where previously women were assumed to be protected by men, they are now assumed to be battered, raped, and murdered by them. What was once taken to be normative is now taken to be hypocritical, and what was once taken to be aberrant is now taken to be typical. And the extensive literature on violence against women suggests men's violence against women is preeminently sexual. From here, it has been but a short step to the claims of many feminists that modern women are the victims of a "rape culture."[3]

The violence is, in fact, not new. Women have always lived under the shadow of male violence, much of which has targeted women's sexuality. Warfare, no doubt, affords the most obvious examples. As the recent horrors in Bosnia have painfully reminded us, invading armies often rape the women they encounter, and the heroes of any military conflict are as likely as the villains to treat women of the opposing side as fair game. Sometimes, they even treat women on their own side similarly, especially if the women are of a different class, race, region, or ethnicity. When Sherman marched through Georgia, his troops frequently raped the slave women on whose behalf they were presumably fighting. At the Charles Colcock Jones plantation, the Yankees threatened the slave women with physical assault and rape. One soldier attempted to drag Sue, by the collar of her dress, into her room. From then on, Sue slept in the big house. Mary Jones noted in her diary that the soldiers "were so outrageous at the Negro houses, that the Negro men were obliged to stay at their houses for the protection of their wives; and in some instances they rescued them from the hands of these infamous creatures."[4] Those Yankee soldiers may well have also assaulted poor white women, though evidence is hard to come by. We are thus left with the uncomfortable conclusion that Yankee "liberators" most freely expressed their violent proclivities against black and perhaps lower-class white women rather than against their political enemies.

Warfare offers an extreme case of the general tendency for men to engage in sexual violence against women whom they perceive as external to their own social and familial circles. The violence of privileged men against poor women runs like a raw scar throughout the historical record. Even if we should not fully credit the medieval practice of *droit du seigneur* (the right of a lord to have sexual relations with a peasant bride before her own husband did), we would do well to consider the logic that the image of it embodied. Control of other men's women, including entitlement to their sexuality, has frequently served as an indelible marker of class relations. In claiming a suzerainty or access with respect to the women of other men, superordinate men have powerfully etched their own superior standing in the minds of subordinates. In such instances the main object of the violation emerges not as the woman's sexuality per se, but rather as the confirmation of unequal social relations among men. A man who cannot protect his woman against the advances of another man is not that man's peer.

This reading of an intent that has informed innumerable acts of sexual violence against women woefully fails to take account of the experience of the specific woman against whose body it was directed. From her perspective, the purpose of the violence mattered little. What mattered was the way in which it was accomplished and its consequences for her—pain, indignity, humiliation, rage, and possibly an unmerited disgrace in the eyes of precisely the men against whom it was directed and who should have eased her misery. But if the intent does not matter, then violence against women ultimately has no history and may only be understood as random acts of nature, much like powerful Southern thunderstorms. For violence against women to be acknowledged as a moral or political problem, it must be understood not merely in relation to the intentions, conscious or unconscious, of those who perpetrated it, but in relation to its standing as a criminal assault against an individual woman. It must have a history understood in terms other than those of the law of the jungle or the perennial war between the sexes. It must, in other words, have a history that treats the violation of women's bodies as one individual's unacceptable attack upon another individual.

Before we cheerfully reconstruct history through the lens of our contemporary assumptions about male violence against women as purely an individual matter, we might profitably consider both its context and the elements that have composed it. It has become a historical commonplace, first advanced with special glee by the abolitionists, who delighted in affirming their own superiority to the South and Southerners, that the slave South teemed with sexual violence against slave women. No doubt such violence did occur.

It may even have occurred frequently, although our evidence as to its incidence is far from robust. We do know that violence was endemic to the slaveholding South: a rural, frontier society in which white men carried guns and, when they felt themselves provoked, were quick to use them or challenge the offender to a duel.[5] As a socially stratified, slaveholding society grounded in rural households over which a white man normally presided, the antebellum South incurred a high risk that the powerful would abuse their power.[6] That most did not do so is beside the point. The possibility was always there, and defense against its realization required a high standard of self-discipline on the part of the slaveholders, who did not always live up to their own ideals. This was another example of what Marc Bloch, evoking early medieval Europe, called a face-to-face society in which people, especially men, were more likely to deal directly with others than to turn to mediating institutions, including the law.[7]

For the slaves, Southern violence took the specific form of physical punishment of adult workers by other adults. Slave women, especially if they worked in the fields, ran the same risks of physical violence as the men, but, as Harriet Jacobs insisted, they also lived under the shadow of a violence peculiarly their own.[8] Vulnerable as workers, they were also vulnerable as women. And some of the violence they risked as workers could take sexual form, even when their sexuality was not the issue, or was so only indirectly. One of the great horrors of slavery lay in its tendency to breed sexual violence among the slaves as well as between masters and slaves. Our knowledge that today rape and other forms of sexual abuse are more likely to occur within social groups than against those of other social groups should lead us to expect this pattern. But we tend to resist it, presumably because we find it easier to believe that the men who exploit women's labor or oppress them socially also abuse them sexually.

Historians have been especially alert to evidence that slaveholding men treated the sexuality of slave women as theirs for the taking, and the ample evidence of interracial children testifies to a certain amount of interracial sex. Some slaveholders sustained continuing sexual relations with their slave women, sometimes establishing them as mistress of the household, sometimes manumitting and marrying them. Many more slaveholding men engaged in—or compelled—occasional sexual relations with slave women. Adolescent boys seem to have been especially given to this kind of passing sexual adventure, and some of them may have engaged in similar relations with slave boys, although almost no one then or since has talked about it.

Some, perhaps many, of these encounters took the form of rapes, but the truth is that we do not know. The white sources are predictably scanty, and even former slaves were reticent. From time to time, we catch glimpses, as in the case of David Dickson, one of the wealthiest planters in Georgia, who had sex with a thirteen-year-old slave, Julia Frances Lewis, who bore him a daughter, whom he adored and pampered.[9] According to the descendants of that daughter, Amanda America Dickson, Dickson forced himself upon the young Julia Lewis, who made him pay for it the rest of his days by ruling his household with an iron hand. The story, in its ambiguities, captures the larger ambiguity of much about interracial sexual relations under slavery. Given the evidence, however sketchy, of strong and abiding attachments, we have no grounds for assuming that, even if the story of Julia Lewis Dickson was atypical, slave women were invariably the passive and unwilling victims of these sexual attentions. There were always some women who understood the possibilities of turning sexual relations with slaveholding men to advantage, if only in the small ways that eased everyday life in a slaveholding household. There must always have been some who were physically or emotionally attracted to a specific white man, just as there were always some white men who were attracted to a specific slave woman. And finally, some of the sexual violence suffered by slave women from men was perpetrated by slave men.

One of the most gruesome accounts I know of violence against a slave woman details the actions of a black driver who had been instructed by his owner that he might beat a recalcitrant field slave, provided he did not hurt the baby she was carrying. So the driver dug a hole in the ground, put the woman in it, and covered her about to her arm pits, strapping her hands above her head. Then, he took "de long bull whup an' he cuts long gashes all over her shoulders an' raised arms, den he walks off an' leabes her dar fer a hour in de hot sun." Predictably, the flies and gnats were drawn to her wounds, and the sun exacerbated the pain. Then, "de driver comes out wid a pan full of vinegar, salt an' red pepper an' he washes de gashes." Whereupon, according to Analiza Foster, the former slave, who was recalling the incident, "he digs her up, but in a few minutes she am stone dead."[10] Analiza Foster knew of no worse story, but she reckoned there were plenty as bad.

Let us risk a speculation about this driver's motivations. His violence may, at least in part, have been triggered by the master's concern to protect the woman's unborn child, which evoked the masters' overriding interest in slave women's reproductive capacities. Modern analyses of violence against women underscore the frequency with which men's brutality targets women's sexuality and reproductive capacity; slave men were no exception, and the black driver's violence surely responded in part to a feeling of impotence, of inability effectively to "protect" slave women's vulnerability—or to monopolize and control their sexuality. Slave women, for their part, seem frequently to have assumed that, in the absence of such protection or control, their sexuality was theirs to dispose of and defend as best they could. And the record is clear that they did not take what they deemed excessive or illegitimate violence lightly. Many suffered or died for their resistance, and frequently they resisted with a violence that matched the violence to which they were subjected.[11] From time to time, slave women would singly or as a group confront an abusive overseer, returning blows as good as they got. No few even took on brutal masters or mistresses.

A significant number traded violence with fellow slaves. The point emphatically is not to suggest that the violence of slaves erased that of slaveholders and overseers, much less exonerated it, but simply that the effects of pervasive and corrosive violence are pervasive and corrosive. At the tragic extreme, those effects could, as Toni Morrison has evoked in her novel *Beloved,* lead slave women to turn against their own born or unborn children.[12] And when the tragedy of unfettered violence reaches those proportions, we have moved beyond normal considerations of responsibility and blame.

The case of slave women suggests some of the complexities of any consideration of the moral and historical problem of violence against women, and it sheds a disquieting light on the problems of violence against women in our own time. From the moment we label violence against women aberrant, pathological, or simply criminal, we necessarily imply a standard of normality. The historical record provides little comfort to those who would define all violence against women as abnormal. One is hard pressed to find examples of societies in which men do not beat women more frequently than women beat men, although men normally beat other men more frequently than they beat women. The problem for feminists—or simply for advocates of women—lies in how we define a baseline of normality. Many, if not most, societies have morally and legally sanctioned a father's or husband's right, perhaps obligation, to chastise the women who fell to his "protection," and to chastise them with a measure of physical force if need be. Beginning in the mid-seventeenth century, however, British and American law has tended to disallow husbands' beating of wives, and specific communities have, on their own, tended to shame and isolate men who engage in what the community viewed as excessive violence against their wives.[13] Standards of normality with respect to violence against women have changed recently at a dizzying rate. Few, if any, societies before our own time would have thought to label a husband's insistence upon his right to have sex with his wife as rape. Such changes have accompanied no less rapid changes in our standards regarding human rights in general. In one area after another, modern societies no longer sanction forms of behavior that as recently as a half-century ago they would barely have thought to question.

In large measure, the changes in standards may be attributed to a growing recognition of the rights of groups who have previously been excluded from many, if not all, aspects of the exercise of power. As these groups, notably women, have moved into direct participation in society, they have tended to insist that the protection that had purportedly sheltered them was nothing but a thinly disguised form of exploitation. The growing willingness to name violence against women as aberrant has included a growing determination to name much customary treatment of women as violent. Both tendencies have been facilitated, if not fueled, by the decomposition of bourgeois culture that has included not merely the disintegration of domestic institutions, but the breathtakingly rapid divorce of sex from morality.[14]

This conjuncture suggests that, even if we agree that our times have encouraged a decisive increase in the labeling and reporting of violence against women, we may also be dealing with an increase in its incidence. If we are confronting an absolute increase in violence against women, then we must at least entertain the possibility that we are looking at something more than the eternal manifestation of the physiological differences between the sexes, or even men's inherent propensity to violence. The positive aspect of this conclusion would be that we are confronting a historical development that should, in principle, be subject to modification. But its more sobering aspect would be that the developments associated with the increasing emphasis upon individualism, personalism, and rights that so many applaud may be precisely the historical developments that are producing the accelerated violence that most—if not all—of us deplore.

Above all, we must face the inescapable conclusion that if there has been an increase in violence against women, it has occurred in tandem with the "liberation" of women's sexuality from the stranglehold of male control. Traditionally, men too frequently resorted to violence to signify and reinforce their control of female sexuality, which they have tended to view as simultaneously their prerogative and responsibility. Their mere enunciation of this control effectively denied the individuality of women, who were defined by their membership in a group. Women, in return for their acceptance of that membership, received as much protection as the men of their group could enforce vis-à-vis the men of other groups. Certainly, for most women that protection was never absolute and for many it counted for little. Our recognition of the pervasive violence that laced the protection has led many, especially feminists, to argue that it must be recognized for the naked domination it was. But feminists have tended to repudiate the domination of women as women (members of a group) in the name of individualism and, especially, individual rights. In a painful irony, their defense of women's individuality has uncritically embraced the ideology of Nietzsche's modern herd and has thereby dissolved women into the larger group of undifferentiated individuals and invalidated any special consideration for their sexual vulnerability.

Notes

1. Sigmund Freud, "Civilization and Its Discontents," in *The Standard Edition of the Complete Psychological Works of Sigmund Freud,* 24 vols., ed. James Strachey (London: Hogarth Press, 1966–74), 21:64–145.

2. See Randall Havas, "Individualism and Herd Morality: Nietzsche's Commitment to Community," [*Common Knowledge* 4, no. 3 (1995): 20–34].

3. Emilie Buchwald, Pamela R. Fletcher, and Martha Roth, eds., *Transforming a Rape Culture* (Minneapolis: Milkweed Editions, 1993); Catharine MacKinnon, *Toward a Feminist Theory of the State* (Cambridge: Harvard University Press, 1989).

4. Robert Manson Myers, ed., *The Children of Pride: A True Story of Georgia and the Civil War* (New Haven: Yale University Press, 1972), 1238–39.

5. Bertram Wyatt-Brown, *Southern Honor: Ethics and Behavior in the Old South* (New York: Oxford University Press, 1982).

6. Elizabeth Fox-Genovese, *Within the Plantation Household: Black and White Women of the Old South* (Chapel Hill: University of North Carolina Press, 1988).

7. Marc Bloch, *Feudal Society,* 2 vols. (Chicago: University of Chicago Press, 1961).

8. Modernized sensibilities tend to find even the support of moderate corporal punishment unacceptable—to wit, the American response to the caning of an American youth in Singapore. The slaveholders, fully cognizant of Northern distaste for their system, were wont to counter that the violence of the early industrial system vastly exceeded anything they would tolerate. As the vigorous debate over the standard of living of British workers during the early Industrial Revolution suggests, these balance sheets remain difficult to draw. It nonetheless appears that the life expectancy of slaves in the antebellum South exceeded that of factory workers in Manchester during the same period. Robert W. Fogel and Stanley L. Engerman, *Time on the Cross: The Economics of American Negro Slavery,* 2 vols. (Boston: Little, Brown, 1974). Harriet Jacobs, *Incidents in the Life of a Slave Girl: Written by Herself,* ed. Jean Fagan Yellin (Cambridge: Harvard University Press, 1987).

9. Kent Anderson Leslie, "Amanda America Dickson: An Elite Mulatto Lady in Nineteenth-Century Georgia" in *Southern Women: Histories and Identities,* ed. Betty Brandon, Virginia Bernhard, Elizabeth Fox-Genovese (Columbia: Univ. of Missouri Press, 1992), 74–75.

10. Analiza Foster, *North Carolina Narratives,* vol. 14, pt. 1, 312–13, in George Rawick, ed., *The American Slave: A Composite Autobiography,* 19 vols. (Westport: Greenwood, 1972).

11. Fox-Genovese, *Within the Plantation Household,* e.g., 317–19.

12. Toni Morrison, *Beloved* (New York: Knopf, 1987).

13. Elizabeth H. Pleck, "Wife Beating in Nineteenth-Century America," *Victimology: An International Journal* 4 (1979): 71; and *Domestic Tyranny: The Making of Social Policy Against Family Violence from Colonial Times to the Present* (New York: Oxford University Press, 1987).

14. Richard Posner, *Sex and Reason* (Cambridge: Harvard University Press, 1992); Elizabeth Fox-Genovese, "Beyond Transgression: Toward a Free Market in Morals," *Yale Journal of Law and the Humanities* (1993)[: 243–64].

Fourteen

Women and Equality

Promise or Deception?

Surely one of the great curiosities of the late twentieth century must be that our political culture congratulates itself for having rejected all intellectual and moral justifications of inequality, except—with growing bad faith—inequality of wealth. Yet, proverbially, the repressed return. Claims of illegitimate inequality haunt us at every turn, and inequality of wealth seems to do nothing but grow. Toward the end of *The Pursuit of Equality in American History,* J. R. Pole wryly notes, "Equality had proved to be an infinitely more complex subject than it had seemed to most of its exponents and devotees of earlier generations."[1] Our own times have more than confirmed his observation, especially with respect to the equality of women.

I.

When Mary Wollstonecraft, a contemporary of Thomas Jefferson, entered the rights of woman on the revolutionary agenda of the late eighteenth century, she portentously cloaked women's status in the emerging political language of individualism, if only by assimilating it to the explosive and unambiguously political language of the rights of man.[2] That she did not actually demand political representation for women does not mitigate the implications of her appeal, but it did augur some understandable confusion. As Pole states, Wollstonecraft's primary concern remained to claim for women an intellectual and moral independence equal to that of men. She never claimed that women and men were, in other respects, identical, but simply that manners and morals, rather than nature, should be credited with women's indisputable proclivity for fashion and frivolity. Women, she believed, should be treated as serious, accountable beings, who were fully capable of intelligent reflection upon themselves and society.

In retrospect, we may recognize that Wollstonecraft was drawing upon a venerable Christian tradition of holding each soul accountable for its own relation with God. That tendency within Christianity always coexisted with tolerance, indeed enthusiasm, for a myriad of inequalities between women and men, variously justified by Scripture and nature, but Christianity could never forsake its fundamental tenet that, like every human being, women were responsible for their sins and rewarded for their virtues—that women must cultivate personal relations with God. Throughout the medieval and early modern periods, specific women, notably Christine de Pisan, had drawn upon this tradition to defend women's intrinsic capacity for excellence.[3] At an accelerating rate during the seventeenth and eighteenth centuries, a few women and even fewer men had begun to expand the tradition to include women's intellectual capacities, and perhaps even intellectual equality to men, on the grounds that, as one put it, "in mind there is no sex at all." So when Wollstonecraft wrote, the problem of women's spiritual and intellectual equality with men was not entirely new.

Wollstonecraft innovated by adopting the language of politics and, more significantly, of radical politics to call attention to her message. The full significance of her strategy may best be understood if we recognize that the results of the French Revolution, from which she borrowed, included the overthrow of the ascriptive inequalities of legal estates and the virtual identification of man and citizen with its implied claim that human beings are inherently political beings. The possible implications for women of Wollstonecraft's formulation were thus twofold: first, that women, in all their social and personal diversity, could be subsumed under the essential category of woman; and second, that women, as naturally endowed with rights, might also be seen as political beings. And although Wollstonecraft did not herself press the political implications of her claims, her successors would not take long to do so. Her evocation of the universal woman, however, had more immediate significance, if only by counterpoising women as a group to men as a group and demanding equality between them.

Wollstonecraft wrote during the dusk of a world in which differences of power and prestige among women might well be as significant, if not more so, than those between women and men within social groups and the dawn of a world in which all women, regardless of social position and resources, were equally excluded from public positions. The imaginative division of the world between public and private—male and female—spheres, which was emerging in Wollstonecraft's Britain and triumphed in Western societies after her death, provided the context within which subsequent advocates of women's rights read her words. And their experience of systematic legal exclusion or disadvantage on account of their sex in turn led most of them to shape their discussions of women's rights as a claim for women's equality with men. Some, to be sure, turned to the ideology of separate spheres to celebrate women's difference from men, but even they, sooner or later, were normally drawn to demand equal political rights for women, if only to permit them to defend their distinct morality in the public sphere. Both groups of women activists, moreover, accepted virtually without question the assumption inherent in Wollstonecraft's use of the singular "woman," namely, that women, by virtue of their sex, shared similar interests.

In retrospect, we may see that Wollstonecraft's most important legacy was simultaneously to erase possible inequalities among women from the discussion and implicitly to tie the defense of women's rights to the defense of the equality of women and men. Above all, Wollstonecraft, much in the manner of her male peers, successfully generalized her own experience to cover the experience of all women. A century after Wollstonecraft's death, when the political defense of the rights of woman had become an active struggle, the tensions between their justification on the grounds of "equality" and on the grounds of "difference" had surfaced in forms that Wollstonecraft might never have imagined. Both tendencies in what was finally being called "feminism" could nonetheless be traced to her assumptions about woman as a universal category.

When, during the mid-1970s, I began to teach *A Vindication of the Rights of Woman,* I was astounded by how contemporary the students found it and how easily they assimilated it to their own experience. It was as if, during these two centuries, nothing had changed. Their sense of the immediacy of Wollstonecraft's voice apparently derived from their conviction that she, like them, wanted the freedom to combine womanhood and professional accomplishment and that, like them, she wanted to respect herself and enjoy the respect of others. They especially responded to her conviction that women were reared to think and behave like girls rather than independent individuals. They instinctively understood her claim that women's dependence derived from things they did to themselves as well as things that were done to them. And they embraced her plea, "Let woman share the rights and she will emulate the virtues of man; for she must grow more perfect when emancipated, or justify the authority that chains such a weak being to her duty."[4]

In retrospect, it seems clearer to me than it did at the time that Wollstonecraft's immediacy in large part derived from her uncanny ability to

convey the psychological nuances of one woman's response to her situation—to personalize women's disadvantages in a way that invited students'
personal identification. But that immediacy also derived from the pervasive
radicalism of her politics. For although she refrained from detailing specific
reforms, she did insidiously suggest that, at some time in the future, "all will
be right."[5] And by all being right, she clearly meant that women like herself,
notably women intellectuals, would be equal to the men of their group. Her
reluctance to make specific proposals inevitably suggested that "equality"
was an abstraction, even as her sensitive evocation of women's feelings about
their own inequality suggested that the essence of equality lay less in political institutions than in women's feelings about themselves.

II.

The struggle for the passage of the Equal Rights Amendment (ERA) during
the 1970s and the early 1980s placed the issue of women's equality squarely
on the national agenda, even as it exposed persisting doubts among Americans as to whether absolute equality between women and men was possible
or even desirable. The failure of the amendment gave victory to the skeptics,
but simultaneously fueled a piecemeal struggle that would, within a decade,
effectively transform the meaning of equality in ways that few were willing
to acknowledge candidly.[6] The ERA itself was simple enough, claiming only
that "Equality of rights under the law shall not be denied or abridged by the
United States or by any State on account of sex" and providing that Congress should have the power to enforce the provisions of the article.

 The ERA, which had originally been proposed in 1923 by Alice Paul and
the Woman's Party, effectively claimed to extend and guarantee the fundamental promise of American citizenship to women, namely, the uncontested
enjoyment of the full rights of a citizen. Its insistence upon the Congress
as the ultimate guarantor of those rights was especially significant, in that it
seemed to bind women as equal players into the political life of the country.
The promise of the ERA lay in its extending to woman the rights that the
American political tradition had long granted man. As Raoul Berger argued,
if the equality of women as a group was not acknowledged as a matter of
natural law, their interest would continue to require repeated judicial intervention.[7] Even before the amendment's defeat, however, it was becoming
clear that the most radical feminists were unlikely to settle for this abstract
equality of opportunity. In the end, what feminists above all retained from
the struggle to pass the ERA was the conviction that women's goals should
be expressed and defended as "rights." They thus borrowed prestige and
legitimacy from the language of politics even as they increasingly turned to

the Supreme Court—the least democratic of our institutions—to secure the validation of their goals.

The turn to the courts to secure women's equality had begun before the defeat of the ERA, notably with the campaign to establish and defend abortion rights. *Roe* v. *Wade* had not itself been explicitly drafted in the language of equality, but had defended the availability of abortion under the rubric of the right to privacy.[8] In the wake of the defeat of the ERA and mounting conservative challenges to *Roe*, feminists were increasingly drawn to describe abortion as a fundamental right, analogous to those enunciated in the Declaration of Independence.[9] During the same years, affirmative action, which had originated to guarantee equality of opportunity, was increasingly defended as a means of securing equality of outcome.

For feminists, the most sobering affirmative action battle was probably *Equal Employment Opportunity Commission* v. *Sears, Roebuck & Co.*, for that case exposed the abiding tension between difference and equality in women's situation and divided feminist scholars and activists in an acrimonious debate.[10] The case served as a disillusioning reminder that the evocation of sexual difference was a two-edged sword that could easily be turned against women. Few, however, drew from their unpleasant brush with the dangers of difference an unambiguous commitment to equality of opportunity. At the extreme, postmodern feminists, notably Joan Scott, unilaterally repudiated the artificial dichotomy between difference and equality as invidious and illegitimate, because that dichotomy "denies the way in which difference has long figured in notions of equality and it suggests that sameness is the only ground on which equality can be claimed."[11] But even feminists who did not initially follow Scott into the thickets of postmodernist theory began to look for ways to promote equality without repudiating all vestiges of sexual difference.

Notwithstanding a strong current in feminist theory that actively celebrated women's difference from—and, frequently, superiority over—men, few feminists who paid any attention to women's situation in society and the economy were willing to repudiate the notion of equality entirely, and many embraced it enthusiastically. As in the time of Alice Paul, those most likely to defend equality were primarily concerned with the situation of elite professional women whose lives most closely resembled those of the men of their class and for whom "joint-parenting" and the availability of high-quality child care effectively negated the irreducible physiological differences between women and men. Even these feminists demonstrably benefited from programs to enforce affirmative action and punish sexual harassment, but they nonetheless tended to believe that undue emphasis on the differences between women and men would hinder, rather than advance, their professional prospects.

Feminist reluctance to emphasize the significance of sexual difference derived from fear of the ways in which the "protection" of women's difference could result in their exclusion from desirable opportunities such as military combat, hazardous industrial work, or even, as in the *Sears* case, commission sales. Similarly, many feminists opposed provisions for maternal leave on the grounds that it reinforced the notion that women were naturally responsible for children, thereby reinforcing the identification between women and reproduction. As the battle over *Roe* persisted into the early 1990s, many of the arguments for the availability of abortion increasingly emphasized women's right to be freed from their reproductive capacities. But these and related concerns about the ways in which difference might penalize women did not necessarily lead most feminists into an unambiguous defense of equality.

Most feminists persisted in a vague feeling, much like Wollstonecraft's, that women labored under the legacy of their historical subordination, which adversely affected—even precluded—their ability to compete on an entirely equal footing with men. Most, also like Wollstonecraft, were loathe to argue that nature had disadvantaged women relative to men, for that admission would effectively undercut the hope for equality in the future. But they were willing, if not eager, to endorse a variety of measures that would compensate for men's long-standing oppression of women in public and private relations. In this spirit, some feminists supported affirmative action initiatives that strongly resembled quota systems; others supported comparable worth; while still others, primarily on college campuses, supported a variety of speech and behavior codes.

By the early 1990s, some feminists were becoming nervous about a growing tendency among some women to promote so-called victim feminism. In popular books, first Katie Roiphe and then Naomi Wolf opened broadsides against women who were claiming ever more official protection for their purported sexual vulnerability, notably with respect to acquaintance rape. Roiphe, especially, offers a merciless picture of young victim feminists who were terrified of the sexual adventures with which they regularly flirted and who would turn morning-after regrets about consensual sex into formal charges of abuse.[12] In different ways, Roiphe and Wolf both suggest that it is high time for feminists to grow up and take responsibility for their lives, rather than turning to increasingly paternalistic institutions to protect them.

Even feminists who are most hostile to any emphasis on the significance of sexual difference have, nonetheless, refrained from attacking all manifestations of affirmative action out of hand; and very few, even of those who are most enthusiastic about sexual equality, have insisted that women should simply be left to fend for themselves in the world that men have created. Virtually all feminists, in other words, remain attuned to one or another way in which women and men are not equal, and virtually all of them are happy to see persisting inequalities redressed—if need be, by the police, the Congress, or, especially, the courts. So, even as differences about the most salient forms of inequality and about appropriate remedies persist, feminists continue to harbor an uneasy feeling that equality remains an elusive goal.

III.

Feminists' sense that equality keeps slipping through women's fingers betrays, among other things, a pervasive disagreement about the meaning of equality. Many feminists, eschewing the view of both left-wing radicals and right-wing traditionalists, scornfully dismiss equality in the sense of equality of opportunity as a bad joke, and some even see a malicious male conspiracy. The postmodernists' attack on the bad faith embedded in the implicit understanding of equality as "sameness" resonates among growing numbers of frustrated feminists who must constantly grapple with the knowledge that women are neither identical to men nor, as Western culture had traditionally held, their opposites. Notwithstanding the cogency of their critique, it, no less than the view it attacks, rests upon its own dubious assumptions.

At the core of much feminist theory, notably its postmodern variants, lies an unexamined assumption about the relation between politics and personal psychology or, to put it differently, politics and the subjective self. This assumption dangerously conflates what Charles Fried, in another context, has called "an effect of the principle" with "the principle itself."[13] Fried is protesting the limitations that many campuses have imposed on the First Amendment right of liberty of speech in the name of protecting the sensibilities of those unrestricted free speech might disparage and who might accordingly tend to be silenced by it, thereby losing their freedom of speech. As Fried insists, the argument is specious, and the policies enacted in its name are decisively altering the quality of intellectual exchange on many campuses. The ideological origin of the conflation of content with result is hardly a secret, although somehow we are compelled not to notice. But who does not know that this very conflation was the bedrock of Stalinism, which bluntly proclaimed that a reactionary result proved reactionary intent? That doctrine was, we might recall, the foundation for the charge that since the victims of the great purge trials had advocated policies objectively favorable to fascism, they were thereby proven to be fascists. Yet some feminists, notably Catharine MacKinnon, apparently oblivious of the ghastly history of her preferred doctrine, defend restrictions of male speech as necessary to women's freedom to speak, and any number of "multiculturalists" have done the same.[14]

The defense of freedom of speech, like other principles of liberty and democracy, depends upon an assumption about equality, namely, that the rules of free speech operate in an arena in which those who observe and benefit from the rules meet in some sense as equals. The defense of free speech is compatible with the assumption that those who benefit from it will also observe some minimal standards of manners or civility and respect other relevant laws. Free speech, in other words, has not normally been taken to legitimate the willful shredding of the arena in which it operates. Understood in this way, the principle of free speech adheres to a community rather than to individuals per se. Obviously, individuals exercise the right of free speech, but they do so because of their membership in a polity that has embraced free speech as a principle. Free speech and other liberties derive from community consensus and agreement, not from natural law; they are political, not natural, rights. Inequality among individuals should not affect their freedom of speech since they are indeed equal in their right to exercise it.

It has become a commonplace that uniform, abstract principles do not favor all individuals equally. Laurence Tribe, for example, has insisted that the right of free speech does not operate neutrally with respect to unions and corporations and must be understood as allocational rather than distributional.[15] Thus he argues that the tendency to see First Amendment rights as applying to society as a whole inevitably obscures the inequalities that prevent all people from benefiting equally from those rights. The received wisdom that to those that have shall be given obtains in countless situations of formal equality. But it does not logically follow that because formal equality may easily benefit the powerful more than the weak, especially when the unequally distributed power is economic or social, equality must ipso facto be repudiated as a principle. The hard truth remains that the principle of equality does not normally produce equality of effect. Nor is it clear that society would be freer or materially better off if it did.

As a political principle, equality has traditionally abstracted from the countless palpable inequalities that differentiate individuals. Were we to start with the attributes of individuals, we should be forced to acknowledge that the principle of equality is no principle at all, but a deceptive myth. No two individuals are, or ever will be, equal. But this fundamental truth has hardly escaped the attention of many political theorists who have defended the principle of equality as a cornerstone of modern democratic polities. It accordingly seems probable that most political theorists have accepted the principle of political equality as a worthy fiction, even as they have acknowledged that it is unlikely to alter substantial inequalities of temperament, character, talent, and material advantages. Nor does their provisional acceptance of the principle mean that they have not probingly criticized its failure to promote substantive equality in practice. Indeed, in our own time, political theorists have paid increasing attention to what equality means or does not mean.

One thing remains clear. In our time, at the level of general perception, equality means, above all, personal equality among individuals. It has become unacceptable to define anyone with reference to difference lest such reference be, in some way, disparaging or demeaning. Thus, in a fit of macabre humor, my husband has taken to referring to our dog and cats as "species-challenged persons." I fear that campus speech codes confirm that these are no laughing matters. But it is difficult not to suspect that even the fanatical attention to the signs of personal worth—self-esteem as it is known—themselves mask a deeper concern.

Presumably, we would not be witnessing such obsessive concern with personal status were status itself not up for grabs. Having discredited all rationales for difference in status, we have condemned ourselves to a society ordered by the vagaries of the market. At issue in most of the discussions of equality is economics, but since few are willing to talk openly about money, we talk about everything else. Difference figures prominently in these discussions, but primarily as a rationale for compensating for the presumed liabilities it imposes upon individuals. In our highly technical, global economy, adequate incomes increasingly depend upon jobs that require intellectual certification, normally one or more university degrees, and, in the United States, that carry benefits as well. Under these conditions, successful completion of a university degree amounts to a meal ticket. Broad recognition of this necessity has resulted in growing pressure on universities—again, especially in the United States, where so many universities are expensive—to grant students degrees almost independent of the quality of the work they perform.

Unfortunately, universities apparently find it more convenient, not to mention less expensive, simply to grant inadequately prepared students degrees than to make the effort to prepare them to earn them. This procedure invites angry denunciations of traditional standards, and even entire subjects, as sexist or racist or whatever. And if the university concurs that, for example, chemistry or seventeenth-century English literature are inherently hostile to women, whose self-esteem and comfort they do not foster and whose personal identification they do not invite, the university thereby frees itself of the obligation to educate women in those subjects without jeopardizing its sense of its own mission. All the university need do is transform its mission from the obligation to offer a demanding education into the responsibility to ensure the comfort of very different kinds of students. But the comfort of celebrating one's difference really means the equality of receiving the degree with its promise of employment. Thus the principle of education ends by being subordinated to the effect of the degree. And thus does the unspoken concern with economic equality shape our discussion of such principles as freedom of speech.

The ambiguities that reach fever pitch on university campuses in some measure pervade affirmative action programs beyond the university as well. As Stephen Carter has argued in *Reflections of an Affirmative Action Baby,* the issues defy easy solution.[16] In many instances, affirmative action programs have genuinely opened opportunities to individuals who would have been barred from them through prejudice, not through lack of talent. But as is widely recognized, affirmative action programs may easily slide into abuses that result in the dilution of requirements for members of specific groups, or even in the wholesale repudiation of requirements. These practices receive theoretical justification from postmodernists who argue that standards are inherently suspect because they inescapably embody the interests and experience of those who have designed them. Since, they argue, we all view the world through the prism of our own experience, the pretense that we may abstract rational or universal standards from that partial and self-interested experience cannot be sustained.

One would think that this postmodern argument must lead to a critique of equality, if not to a justification of inequality, but apparently, such candor would be asking too much. For at the core of the postmodern agenda lies a fierce commitment to impose equality of condition more or less by fiat. And this determination leaves no doubt that, in our time, equality has decisively shifted from equality of opportunity to equality of result, just as the defense of equality has moved from the elimination of barriers to their imposition.

IV.

As the pursuit of equality is increasingly taken to dictate the neutralization of the differences among individuals, the list of salient differences has increasingly grown. But even as the legally suspect differences multiply, differences of race and sex retain special significance. The arguments about race command extensive discussion; but, with all due respect to race, it is plausible to argue that the differences that derive from sex are of primary theoretical and practical significance in any consideration of equality. Common sense would suggest that men and women are not and never will be equal in the strict sense of identical, if only because of their respective bodies. But common sense would no less forcefully suggest that there is a rapidly shrinking number of things that men do that women cannot also do, frequently as well,

sometimes better. In an expanding sphere of life, the salient inequalities between any given man and any given woman may have little or nothing to do
with sex but, rather, with native intelligence, organizational skills, concentration, determination, ambition, whatever.

This being the case, it would seem reasonable to allow individual women
to compete directly with individual men for jobs, scholarships, raises, pro-
motions, and all the rest. Many feminists, however, argue that men, notably
in the case of such public arenas as work and politics, continue to enjoy an
unfair advantage over women that must be redressed. Although we are far
from perfect agreement about the nature of the advantage, the most common views include men's continuing numerical preponderance in most
public arenas, men's propensity to take sexual advantage of women, men's
comparative freedom from domestic responsibilities, or simply the residual
attitudes of many supervisors toward women. Each of these presumed male
advantages has given rise to policies and regulations that will, it is hoped,
level the playing field to ensure greater equality between women and men.
And whether one approves or disapproves of the various measures, it is difficult not to concur that their imposition has resulted in a reduction of individual liberty.

Feminists do not invariably concur, for, normally, they believe that some
reduction in men's liberty must occur if the liberty of women is to increase.
Thus, they might argue, there has not so much been a reduction in liberty
as a redistribution. They are wrong, both theoretically and practically, for
attempts to regulate people's behavior and expression, however nobly intended, are manifestations of a social engineering that does limit public liberty. But many feminists do not much worry about reductions in liberty that
are intended to protect victims against their alleged oppressors. In criticizing this victim feminism, Naomi Wolf enthusiastically argues that it is high
time for women to claim their rightful place as accountable adults and to
relinquish a victim identity that only demeans them. I largely agree with her.
But whatever one's position on women's ability to compete directly with
men, the more serious issue remains the danger that the policies to protect
women poses to the nature of the polity.

As a rule, feminists are reluctant to attribute women's disadvantage in
the worlds of work and politics exclusively, or even primarily, to their sexuality, preferring to focus upon the long history of women's systematic subordination. In other situations, however, women's sexual difference moves
to center stage. In recent years, for example, women's sexual vulnerability
has been taken to justify speech and behavior codes that will protect women
from its consequences—that is, will equalize results. Take the case of acquaintance rape, which has recently attracted so much attention in the United

States and the United Kingdom. Notwithstanding pro forma acknowledgments that women can rape and batter men, it has proved virtually impossible to discuss acquaintance rape as if women and men were sexual equals. The very essence of acquaintance rape consists in the assumption that a man has, through physical advantage, forced a woman to have sex against her will. Buried in this assumption lies the primary assumptions that men are sexual predators, women sexual victims, and each will always behave according to his or her nature. In different ways, both Naomi Wolf and Katie Roiphe vehemently insist that these assumptions dangerously perpetuate the sexual ideology that relegated women to the stewardship of men on the grounds that without male protection they would inevitably fall victim to sexual abuse.

Wolf and Roiphe, in effect, are arguing for sexual equality between women and men, at least in the sense of taking responsibility for one's own sexuality. Neither underestimates the gravity of rape as a crime, but both deplore victim feminists' tendency to view all sexual relations between women and men as a form of rape.[17] Surely, they protest, that is not what we have been fighting for. Sex is fun for women, and on the occasions in which a woman has had too much to drink, fallen into bed with a man, and awakened the next morning with a hangover and a gnawing sense of regret, she should take responsibility for her own actions and write the evening off to experience. To assuage one's personal regrets by accusing the man of rape demeans the woman and trivializes the crime of rape, including acquaintance rape.[18]

Wolf and Roiphe applaud the emergence of a world in which women have earned the right to sexual freedom, which they take to mean that women have finally achieved at least a measure of sexual equality with men. Their argument does not mean that women and men are sexually identical, nor does it deny the possibility that men may impose sex upon women by force. It simply assigns to women individual responsibility for their own sexuality. Writing out of the marrow of a class and professional world in which women compete directly and often successfully with men, they are warning other accomplished women of the cultural elite that if this micromanagement nonsense does not cease, women will end up being protected out of their most rewarding opportunities and may well lose the freedom to compete with other women as well. They belong, in other words, to the small but growing number of women who are prepared to fend for themselves rather than risk having others tell them what they may and may not do. And Wolf, who candidly admits to enjoying the amount of money she makes, openly celebrates capitalism as the royal road to individual success.

Wolf's frankly hedonistic position perhaps reveals more than she intends. For the combination of her opposition to victim feminism—she prefers power feminism—and her celebration of capitalism implicitly confirms that the point of various regulations, even those on sexual behavior, is ultimately to promote equality of outcome. And although Wolf delights in using her money to help others, she no less clearly delights in the control that allows her to decide whom to help. Thus, while she calls herself a humanitarian leftist, it seems unlikely that she wishes to promote leveling among individuals. She is committed to an equality of opportunity that is entirely compatible, indeed depends upon, the principle of liberty.

Those whom she calls victim feminists favor curtailment of liberty in principle precisely to ensure leveling between women and men. Regulations and codes such as those that now prevail at Brown University, Antioch College, and elsewhere impose strict standards on the behavior of male students, thus limiting their liberty presumably to increase the liberty of their female peers. Roiphe mercilessly mocks such codes, as she does marches to "take back the night" and young women's public confessions of their experiences of rape. In her view, rape is now being invoked to describe the give-and-take of relations between young women and men in an age of sexual freedom. Roiphe delights in sexual adventure, much as Wolf delights in her ability to earn money. My conversations with young women suggest that many have not adjusted as effortlessly as she to the world of sexual liberation. But many of those who do not want to play the game have absorbed enough to want to go to the party. They cannot take a lighthearted view of acquaintance rape, for the possibility haunts them. For, unsure of their own desires and resilience, they have difficulty in saying yes. And the more difficult they find it to say yes, the more difficult they find it to say no. No, they do not, at least with respect to sex, want to be treated as young men's equals, if that means playing by young men's rules. They also do not want to miss out on all of the fun.

Roiphe falls wide of the mark in insisting that all young women should welcome sexual adventure. Manifestly, many do not. Indeed, many, if my sources are reporting accurately (and I have no reason to believe that they are not), still want "relationships" much more than they want sex, and they only want sex if it is softened by a relationship—if the young man wants to talk meaningfully to them over breakfast. And some young women still remain virgins by choice, without manifesting any signs of neurosis. I am more than prepared to believe that young women's dreams of relationships are at least as worthy of respect as the dreams of the young women who delight in sexual adventure. But I remain astonished, perhaps thereby betraying my own generation, that they think that the way to realize those dreams is to go, scantily clad, to a party at which they drink more than usual, return to a young man's room, pet heavily, and then exercise their right to just say no. No matter how they have behaved, they emphatically have the right to say no; and no matter how they have behaved, the young man who fails to respect it is no gentleman. But a rapist?

Obviously, everything depends upon how one defines "rapist," and I should be the last to begrudge young women maximum protection. But I remain uncomfortable with the scenario. There was a time when fathers, brothers, dress codes, and curfews used to provide that protection, but women have righteously rejected all of the above as illegitimate—dare one say, patriarchal—restrictions on their independence and equality. In those bad old days, protection was privately provided by families and institutions that acknowledged their in loco parentis responsibilities while trying not to infringe upon the principle of liberty. Today, a significant number of feminists, rejecting such private infringements upon women's liberty, want to restrict the principle of liberty instead. But it is hard to believe that we gain by tying women's right to equality to their right to behave as if they wanted sexual adventure when they do not. Would it not be better to encourage them to exercise prudence in their choice of where they go and how they dress, thereby taking responsibility for themselves? No one has the right to force them to do so, but doing so would spare them traumatic encounters. And, possibly, it would even enhance their self-esteem.

The sexual inequality between women and men cuts to the heart of our discussions of equality in the abstract, but does not exhaust them. For it is conceivable that should women determine to protect what we recognize as our own vulnerabilities, including the ways in which most of us differ from men—that is, to assume responsibility for our own sexuality—we could, by our own initiative, do what fathers and brothers have traditionally done for us, namely, remove ourselves from situations that expose those vulnerabilities. Those who fancy sexual adventure could pursue it, prepared to take occasional knocks. Those who do not could look for relationships in more propitious circumstances.

V.

Sexuality increasingly figures at the center of the feminist imagination, but, if truth be told, it is not the most difficult issue. Feminists, after all, are the first to insist that rape is not about sex but about power. Difficulties persist in drawing hard-and-fast lines between rape as a crime and men's tendency to abuse their physical advantage, but the police and the courts are making steady progress in this regard; and if rape convictions still fall woefully short, they are increasing.[19] Thus even as we acknowledge that men and women are not sexually equal in the sense of sexually identical, we may imagine a world in which they share equal access to a principle of sexual freedom and take personal responsibility for its effects in their own lives.

Women's reproductive capacities are another matter entirely. Tellingly, neither Wolf nor Roiphe dwells upon children. Yet the ability to bear children and the disproportionate responsibility for rearing them decisively jeopardize women's equality with men. Many feminists nonetheless reject the notion that women's reproductive capacities should receive special protection, precisely on the grounds that the continuing association with children seems to condemn women to inequality.[20] The logic of this argument obviously points to freeing women from children, although few admit as much in so many words, much less discuss how the freedom should be effected in practice. We may nonetheless assume that an unarticulated desire to free women from children accounts for some of the passion of feminist rhetoric about women's right to choose to have an abortion. Feminist defenses of abortion are regularly cast in the language of equality—for women to be equal, they must have the right to sever their traditional association with reproduction. And in *Planned Parenthood of Pennsylvania* v. *Casey,* the Supreme Court effectively concurred.[21]

In *Casey,* the Supreme Court sustained pro-choice advocates' insistence upon abortion as a necessary guarantee of women's equality, but moved the emphasis from sexual equality to the equality of participation in the economy. The Court thus effectively argued that women must not be hindered from providing for their own economic support. *Casey* implicitly retreated from the logic of affirmative action and equalization of economic effects by defending the principle of equality of access to economic freedom. This position logically throws support for the children women choose to have back upon women themselves, with no guarantee of assistance from society, or even from the children's fathers.[22] Thus the many pro-choice activists who bitterly denounced the decision seem to have missed its significance, which was, unambiguously, to confirm a woman's right to choose to have an abortion.

In the light of *Casey,* the right to choose to have an abortion may be understood as an effort to remove women's reproductive capacities from discussions of women's equality with men and thus to strengthen the commitment to the principle of equality independent of its possible effects. Notwithstanding some feminist objections, it is reasonable to argue that with respect to women as individuals, the benefits of defending equality in principle, understood to mean equality of opportunity, outweigh the dangers of attempting to engineer equality of results—to argue that the best, and most just, way to defend equality is to defend it as an abstract principle that we do not expect to produce equality of results. Equality thus reduces, or is elevated, to equality of political and economic rights—the equal right to political and economic participation.

Since the time of Mary Wollstonecraft, and at an accelerating rate in our own time, many, including feminists, have insisted that equality of political rights easily reduces to a sterile formality in societies in which economic and social resources are unequally divided. But the attempts of feminists and others to rectify social and economic inequalities through curtailing liberty in principle present no less serious dangers. The arguments that the rights of entire groups of "victims" require the curtailment of liberty in principle are especially dangerous because the members of those groups are not socially and economically equal, or even comparable. As a result, a curtailment of liberty in principle may, in the end, benefit only a minority of the group, leaving the majority as—or more—socially and economically impoverished than ever. If, in other words, liberty in principle is to promote the effect of greater economic equality, then we must discuss the issue in economic terms without regard to sex, race, or ethnicity.

Should such a discussion occur, it would be reasonable to argue that greater economic equality benefits society as a whole and hence justifies curtailment of the liberty that society enjoys, although counterarguments are also strong. In contrast, it is less easy to argue that society as a whole benefits by favoring some groups of its members over others simply to rectify inequalities in presumed personal attributes and resources. No more than in the past will acceptance of the principle of equal opportunity guarantee equality among the various members of society, although in a democracy like our own, it may well be the best guarantee of maximum liberty for society and its members. Since the French Revolution first invoked the rights of man and the citizen, it has been clear that absolute liberty and absolute equality would never be compatible. The goal of democracies, in their various ways, has been to strike the best possible balance between liberty and equality.

With respect to women as individuals, the balance between liberty and equality remains fragile and an abiding source of controversy. The case of children exposes it as a farce, for neither liberty nor equality obviously benefits children for whom adult rights are, to borrow the words of Elizabeth Wolgast, "wrong rights."[23] Yet the protection of children's vulnerability, like provision for their health and education, should be a preeminent concern of society as a whole. Reproduction stands alone in any consideration of justice, for without reproduction, a society wills itself to destruction. Society must, in one way or another, protect its own reproduction, which means exempting that reproduction from the principles that govern relations among consenting adults. The struggle to ensure women's equality as consenting adults has, however unintentionally, opened the question of who participates in reproduction and, accordingly, benefits from its privileged status.

Historically, social reproduction has been taken to include the biological participants in it: mother, father, child. Recent decades have effectively— many would say, disastrously—released men from that association, thereby undoing in one stroke the work of centuries. The logic of feminism might seem to portend the release of women from it as well. If that logic triumphs, children will be left to depend upon the whims of individuals or to fend for themselves, unless we decide to treat them all as wards of society. If women are released from their traditional association with reproduction, they will thereby remove the main obstacle to their equality with men—and with it, the only compelling justification for abridging society's liberty to compensate for their inequality.

Notes

1. J. R. Pole, *The Pursuit of Equality in American History*, rev. and exp. ed. (Berkeley: University of California Press, 1993), 454.

2. Mary Wollstonecraft, *A Vindication of the Rights of Women*, 2d ed., Carol H. Poston, ed. (New York: W. W. Norton, 1988; 1st ed., 1792).

3. Christine de Pisan, *The Book of the City of Ladies*, Earl Jeffrey Richards, trans., foreword by Marina Warner (New York: Persea Books, 1982). See also Elizabeth Fox-Genovese, "Culture and Consciousness in the Intellectual History of European Women," *Signs: Journal of Women in Culture and Society* 12, no. 3 (Spring 1987): 529–547 [reprinted in this volume, pp. 92–111].

4. Wollstonecraft, *Vindication of Rights*, 194.

5. On Wollstonecraft's political radicalism, see Elissa S. Guralnick, "Radical Politics in Mary Wollstonecraft's *A Vindication of the Rights of Woman*," *Studies in Burke and His Time* 18 (1977): 155–166; reprinted in Wollstonecraft, *Vindication of Rights*, 308–317.

6. On the ERA, see Jane J. Mansbridge, *Why We Lost the ERA* (Chicago: University of Chicago Press, 1986), and Donald G. Mathews and Jane Sherron De Hart, *Sex, Gender, and the Politics of ERA* (New York: Oxford University Press, 1990).

7. Raoul Berger, *Government by Judiciary: The Transformation of the Fourteenth Amendment* (Cambridge, MA: Harvard University Press, 1977), 259–262, 280. See also Elizabeth Fox-Genovese, "Women's Rights, Affirmative Action, and the Myth of Individualism," *George Washington Law Review* 54, nos. 2 and 3 (January and March 1986): 338–374.

8. *Roe v. Wade*, 410 US 113 (1973). For the origins of the right to privacy, see *Griswold v. Connecticut*, 381 US 479 (1965).

9. See Elizabeth Fox-Genovese, "Feminism and the Rhetoric of Individual Rights, Part 1," *Common Knowledge* 1, no. 1 (Spring 1992): 43–53, and "Feminism and the Rhetoric of Individual Rights, Part 2," *Common Knowledge* 1, no. 2 (Fall 1992): 63–93 [reprinted in this volume, pp. 120–31 and 132–43, respectively]; Mary Ann Glendon, *Abortion and Divorce in Western Law: American Failures, European Challenges*

(Cambridge, MA: Harvard University Press, 1987), and Glendon's *Rights Talk: The Impoverishment of Political Discourse* (New York: Free Press, 1991).

10. *Equal Employment Opportunity Commission* v. *Sears, Roebuck & Co.*, 628 F. Supp. 1264 (N.D. Ill. 1986). See also the discussion in Elizabeth Fox-Genovese, *Feminism without Illusions: A Critique of Individualism* (Chapel Hill: University of North Carolina Press, 1991), esp. 70–75, 142.

11. Joan Wallach Scott, "Deconstructing Equality-versus-Difference: Or, the Uses of Poststructuralist Theory for Feminism," *Feminist Studies* 14, no. 1 (Spring 1988): 46.

12. Katie Roiphe, *The Morning After: Sex, Fear, and Feminism* (Boston: Little, Brown & Co., 1993); Naomi Wolf, *Fire with Fire: The New Female Power and How It Will Change the 21st Century* (London: Chatto & Windus, 1993).

13. Charles Fried, "The New First Amendment Jurisprudence: A Threat to Liberty," in *The Bill of Rights in the Modern State,* Geoffrey R. Stone, Richard A. Epstein, and Cass R. Sunstein, eds. (Chicago: University of Chicago Press, 1992), 226.

14. Catharine A. MacKinnon, *Feminism Unmodified: Discourses on Life and Law* (Cambridge, MA: Harvard University Press, 1987), 163–165, 168–171.

15. Laurence H. Tribe, *Constitutional Choices* (Cambridge, MA: Harvard University Press, 1985).

16. Stephen L. Carter, *Reflections of an Affirmative Action Baby* (New York: Basic Books, 1992).

17. On the generalization of rape, see Emilie Buchwald, Pamela Fletcher, and Martha Roth, eds., *Transforming a Rape Culture* (Minneapolis, MN: Milkweed Editions, 1993).

18. For a discussion of acquaintance rape, see Linda A. Fairstein, *Sexual Violence: Our War against Rape* (New York: William Morrow & Co., 1993).

19. Fairstein, *Sexual Violence.*

20. Nicky Hart, "Procreation: The Substance of Female Oppression in Modern Society, Part One: The True Proletariat," *Contention* 1, no. 1 (Fall 1991): 89–108; my response, "Part Two: Feminism and the Spirit of Capitalism," *Contention* 1, no. 3 (Spring 1992): 217–225; and Nicky Hart's response to me, *Contention* 1, no. 3 (Spring 1992): 227–236.

21. *Planned Parenthood of Pennsylvania* v. *Casey,* 112 S.Ct. 2791 (1992).

22. Tellingly, although the decision required minors to consult a parent, guardian, or judge, it did not require adult women to consult their husbands.

23. Elizabeth H. Wolgast, *The Grammar of Justice* (Ithaca, NY: Cornell University Press, 1987), chap. 2.

Fifteen

Severing the Ties That Bind

Women, the Family, and Social Institutions

On the whole, at the opening of the twenty-first century, Western women enjoy a power, education, and privilege unprecedented in human history. And much of this unprecedented power and freedom has resulted from women's political activism on behalf of themselves and other women. Just as the social institutions of the West have both impeded and facilitated women's political activism, so has women's political activism caused both progress and decline in those institutions. Much depends upon your perspective and upon the historical moment you are considering.

Let us begin with the political context: there can be no doubt that the political institutions of Western Europe and the United States have played a role in the emergence of modern feminism and of women's growing role in the social, economic, and political life of Western nations. The ideals of individual freedom and political democracy are distinctly Western and without them it is hard to imagine that women would have moved as readily into political life as they have. The political vocabulary of freedom, equality, and democracy has provided women with the principal justification for their campaign to enjoy the full status of citizenship, especially since there were never principled political justifications for their exclusion from it.

Many women remain dissatisfied with the results of women's access to political life, usually on the grounds that formal equality with men has not netted women an equal share of wealth, power, and prestige. But these days, most activists are likely to focus their attention upon social rather than political institutions and to view political activism as a weapon to effect lasting social change. The impact of women's political activism upon social institutions has been momentous, but its ultimate consequences still remain unclear.

In this essay, I shall briefly consider the current state of the balance sheet and then focus more closely on the specific institution of the family. On the positive side of the ledger, women's political activism of the past few decades has decisively improved the independence and dignity of women as individuals. Women today enjoy opportunities to fulfill their talents, attain an education, pursue a career, run for and win political office that most of our mothers and grandmothers could not have dreamed of. On the negative side, social institutions, especially in the United States, have been decisively weakened, most of all the family.

A word of caution is, however, in order: One of the major consequences of feminist political efforts during the past three or four decades has been decisively to blur the boundary between public and private and, by extension, between political and social institutions. You may recall the early slogan of Second Stage Feminism, "the personal is political." That slogan called for the systematic politicization of personal relations, and many of its goals have been attained. Historically, social institutions have usually been viewed as, in some measure, distinct from political life. During the early nineteenth century, Alexis de Tocqueville visited the new United States and wrote a famous account of what he observed. In *Democracy in America,* Tocqueville commented that many American social institutions were voluntary, which is to say they lacked the legal identity of many European social institutions. He further commented that the egalitarian ideology of Americans and the fluidity of their democratic political institutions made social institutions all the more necessary to the health of the country.

The general situation that Tocqueville described persisted for decades, although specific social institutions changed along the way. Most, however, retained a measure of autonomy from political life. Throughout the nineteenth century and much of the twentieth, the family ranked as the main social institution, and, as an institution, it did enjoy a significant measure of autonomy. In effect, the principles of democracy stopped at the threshold of the private home—a man's castle, as it was proverbially known. As a kind of corporate enclave within the surrounding bustle of competitive individualism, capitalism, and democracy, the family remained tied to hierarchical principles that placed the man, husband and father, in authority over all, including his wife, and placed both parents in authority over their children.

From the beginnings of the woman's movement in the mid-nineteenth century, feminists focused on the injustice of women's subordination to men within the family, and they gradually secured a number of reforms, beginning with a married woman's right to own property in her own name. Second wave feminists even more sharply condemned the family as the cradle of women's oppression, and they successfully campaigned for no-fault divorce, recognition of marital rape, and other forms of assistance for the wives of abusive husbands. Many of these changes represented significant progress for women, many of whom had previously lived in dependence and without any resources they could call their own. As recently as the 1960s it was often extremely difficult for a married woman to get credit in her own name.

Few today would, I think, dispute the positive value of these and related changes, but some are also beginning to worry that they have come at an exorbitantly high price. Their impact has been all the greater because they occurred in conjunction with—and arguably partially because of—a massive movement of married women and mothers of small children into the labor force. Thus, just as the formal bonds of the family were being weakened by legal reforms, women's presence in the family was decreasing because of the time they were spending at work, and women's economic independence from the husband was increasing because of the wages they were earning. And, as more and more people are acknowledging, the most serious casualty of the family's dissolution was children, who are increasingly being turned over to others or left to their own devices.

Feminist political rhetoric has tended to target men as the main obstacles to women's independence and equality, but much feminist political activism has, directly or indirectly, targeted the ties that bind women to children. The campaign to secure and defend abortion on demand is especially revealing in this regard. First, a woman's right to abortion has been defended in political language as an individual right—frequently as a woman's right to sexual freedom. No less significantly, it has been defended on the grounds of privacy. Consider the implications of these two positions. In the first instance, a woman has a right to be liberated from children—the possible consequence of her sexuality. This strategy effectively divorces children from any social institution by labeling them the concern of the woman rather than of a woman and a man. The second argument points in the same direction by reducing privacy to the privacy of the individual rather than the privacy of the couple or the family. As Mary Ann Glendon has argued, this interpretation of the right of privacy is a radical innovation in American law, and it represents a significant departure from the legal norms of Western European nations. Symbolically, the reduction of privacy to the privacy of the solitary individual effectively sounds the death knell of social institutions, especially the family, as organic units with claims upon their members.

Other features of the abortion campaign similarly chip away at the family as a social institution. Feminists have, for example, strongly resisted the idea that a minor should have the consent of a parent or guardian before having an abortion. They argue that since the father or guardian may be the one who has caused the pregnancy in the first place, the requirement that the girl obtain consent simply exposes her to punishment or further abuse. Western European countries handle this danger by allowing a minor to obtain the consent of a judge, but feminist activists have opposed that solution as well, arguing that even a young woman's sexuality is a purely individual matter. Such a radical concept of individualism further weakens the notion that children constitute a social responsibility and not simply an individual possession to be disposed of at will. In a bitter irony, the largest business interests tend to concur with feminist activists in this regard, and in *Planned Parenthood of Pennsylvania v. Casey*, a majority of the Supreme Court argued that women had become accustomed to the free disposition of their sexuality and labor and that unplanned pregnancies should not be allowed to interfere with their ability to support themselves. The opinion amounted to recognition that social institutions, notably the family, have so far decayed that no woman or child can automatically count on their support.

Women's political activism in the United States has disproportionately focused upon securing and defending women's liberation from the binding ties of family and from traditional—or stereotyped—expectations about women's roles. As a result, many feminists have rejected the idea of maternity leave on the grounds that child rearing is as much the man's responsibility as the woman's. Maternity leave, they reason, would officially sanction a woman's special responsibility for children and accordingly reinforce the persisting inequalities between women and men. As a result, the United States stands as one of the few countries in the world that does not offer new mothers some form of maternity leave. All of the Western European countries do so, some quite generously. They also make more generous provisions for state-subsidized day care than we do in the United States.

In contrast, the European pattern has been to be generous to women by being generous to children and the reverse. European countries, with the Scandinavian countries in the lead, are also witnessing some weakening of traditional social institutions, especially the family, but none match the United States in divorce and illegitimacy rates—or in the number of abortions performed. Nor do any match our reluctance to subsidize the care of children. Of eight industrialized nations—Sweden, the Federal Republic of Germany, France, Canada, Australia, Israel, and the United Kingdom—the United States stands alone in neither providing maternity leave nor any universal child allowances. To compound the problems, we do less to support child care and are much less flexible and innovative in the kinds of child care we license than other Western, and many developing, nations. Some of these countries, notably Sweden, also provide housing allowances and health care benefits. And it is worth noting that none of these countries has as high a proportion of children either born to or living with single mothers, or as high a rate of infant mortally. For the richest nation in the world, our record is nothing to boast about.

Sad and intuitively improbable as it may seem, women's political activism has much to answer for with respect to the current state of our social institutions. On this point I am emphatically *not* implying that blame should be laid entirely at the feet of one or another group of women. What I am arguing is that the political agenda of various women's groups has contributed to our current situation if only by failing to campaign vigorously for alternative solutions. Feminist opposition to maternity leave, as I have already suggested, has eased the pressure on business to face up to its responsibilities in this regard. The feminist leadership has also strongly favored policies that encourage women to work full-time throughout their children's early years. This preference has led feminists to campaign for federally-funded day care, but not for child allowances or even for an increase in the tax deductions for children that would make it easier for some women to work part-time or stay home for a few years while their children are young. Nor have feminists mounted a vigorous campaign against the penalty that our tax code imposes upon marriage, presumably because they wish single motherhood to enjoy the same status as marriage. No-fault divorce has benefited some women, but it has harmed many others, and its very existence has tended to weaken both women's and men's willingness to make marriage and family a priority that justifies compromise or even sacrifice in other areas of life.

Conservative women, in contrast, often campaign vigorously for "family values," but more often than not they show no inclination to pay for services that might help less affluent Americans to hold families together. For better or worse, we have moved well beyond the point at which it is realistic simply to exhort people to do the right thing. For numerous and complex reasons, at least half of American marriages may be expected to end in divorce; barely half of adult Americans lives in heterosexual marriages (54.4%); barely a quarter of all households includes a married couple and children; almost a quarter of all American children are born to a single mother (the figure jumps to almost 70% among African-Americans); and a quarter of American children lives in a family headed by a single mother. All of these figures represent substantial changes within the last thirty-five years. During that period, women's fertility dropped dramatically, while out-of-wedlock births increased by 26% and families headed by single mothers by 13%. Nothing suggests that these patterns will automatically reverse themselves in the immediate future, and we may reasonably assume that without substantial support and incentives neither marriages nor two-parent families will regain their standing as foundational social institutions.

There is a disturbing message in all of this: American social institutions today are weaker than those of other Western countries, but elite American women enjoy more advantages and opportunities than women in any other Western nation. (Throughout Western Europe, the rapid rise in immigration and ensuing ethnic diversity is exerting great pressure upon the strength and cohesiveness of social institutions, but has not yet eroded them.) And this hard truth confronts us with a painful question: Must women's gains as individuals come at the expense of social institutions?

Social institutions, by definition, exist to link people into groups. Typically, they possess less authority than the state but more than the isolated individual. Their main purpose and justification lie in their ability to effect goals and facilitate social relations, and in their appropriate sphere they do both better than either the individual or the state. It is further worth noting that, in their absence, the state frequency takes over their functions—often with a marked loss in both social vitality and individual freedom.

Historically, social institutions have often legitimated or reinforced men's advantage over women—an advantage, sad to say, that too many men have abused. No less sad, feminist political struggles have too often sought to correct that imbalance by liberating women from social institutions which, we are learning, tend to crumble without women's commitment. Conservative women's campaigns simply to restore social institutions to some mythical state of normality have singularly failed, primarily because the vitality of social institutions always depends upon their ability to adapt to changing circumstances.

Somewhere between destruction and sterile perpetuation lies the opportunity to modify and revitalize our social institutions to meet the crying needs they were always intended to meet. Of this much, however, we may be sure: No society retains its health and vigor without robust social institutions to draw people into common commitments and to mediate between individuals and the state.

Sixteen

The Feminist Critic and the Woman Writer, or, May the Proper Heroine Still Marry?

Exploring the ways in which women write about their lives, Carolyn Heilbrun impatiently dismisses marriage as "the most persistent of myths imprisoning women, and misleading those who write of women's lives."[1] In writing thus, Heilbrun faithfully echoes the sensibility of the many feminist critics who harbor serious reservations about marriage, which they tend to view as men's preferred method of containing women and thwarting their independent development. In their view, marriage, and especially, seductive narratives of marriage, must be recognized as fetters upon women's ambitions and imaginations. Heilbrun's emphasis upon the role of narrative merits attention, for she clearly ascribes great power to narratives of women's lives, claiming that narratives which link women with marriage constitute myths—implicitly archetypal or hegemonic codifications of women's destiny —and that the imprisoning power of these narratives misleads even the presumably accomplished and independent women who write compellingly of women's lives.

We may readily understand Heilbrun's emphasis upon the importance of narratives—familiar and frequently retold stories—for they do shape our sense of ourselves. We may also agree that marriage has frequently figured as the telos of women's stories or as the inevitable destiny toward which women's lives lead. From the eighteenth-century origins of the modern novel as a genre until well into the twentieth century, if not until our own day, marriage has offered the most usual conclusion to the story of a woman's life, and even since women's stories have begun to include divorce, they have still been likely to conclude with another—better—marriage. Thus, Heilbrun's complaint may be understood as dual: Stories of marriage continue to influence women's sense of their own possibilities, and the long-standing hegemony of the story of marriage leads women writers to recapitulate it, thereby neglecting the opportunity to forge new narrative patterns.[2]

In this spirit, Rachel Blau DuPlessis notes that "[o]nce upon a time, the end, the rightful end, of women in novels was social—successful courtship, marriage—or judgmental of her sexual and social failure—death."[3] The authors of these novels, she insists, wrote to demonstrate the incompatibility of a woman's *bildung,* or personal development, and romance. Yet even they never successfully suppressed their protagonists' "quest" for selfhood, and the quest aspect of their plots "propounds something that the marriage plot with difficulty revokes: that the female characters are human subjects at loose in the world, ready for decision, growth, self-definition, community, insight."[4] The heroism of nineteenth-century female protagonists, who enjoyed no opportunities in work or vocation, lay in "freely choosing the romance that nonetheless, in one form or another, is her fate." And her choice becomes her final act as an "individual agent." Twentieth-century women novelists who have resisted the marriage plot have focused on women's consciousness, for, in DuPlessis's words, "it is logical that narrative, as a site of ideology, should focus on mind, as a site of ideology."[5] Thus, however crudely, their narratives help "to break the reproduction of the status quo."[6]

In a similar vein, Susan Sniader Lanser explores the ways in which even in novels by women the marriage plot "succeeds at the expense of the voice that tells it," and, thereby, "exposes as a fiction the liberty of the female voice in the conventional 'heroine's text': whatever it proclaims, this voice is confined from the beginning in a predetermined (hetero)sexual plot that takes on the powerfully conservative mission of limiting the consequences of voice, rendering 'free' speech a kind of silence already made impotent by the novel's teleology."[7] In a broader perspective, Catherine Gallagher explores the ways in which British realist narratives of the nineteenth century attempted to connect public and private realms, even as the most sophisticated like *Hard Times* and *North and South* "expose contradictions in the ideologies they use as well as the tensions in their narrative methods."[8]

It is striking that these critics, whose theoretical project explicitly focuses upon narrative, apparently remain tied to lingering mimetic assumptions which that theoretical project explicitly opposes. Turning from theory to the literary representation of women in specific texts, they instinctively write as if literature, in some way, represents life—as if a transformation of literary narratives would betoken, or cause, a transformation of the life they represent. Thus, DuPlessis, in acknowledging that the most self-consciously liberatory women writers frequently adopt a didactic and hortatory tone, suggests, however unintentionally, that compelling narratives cannot stray too far from the experience and expectations of readers. So, even while she explicitly reproaches fictions for constraining women's quests for independent selfhood, she implicitly opens the possibility that women have, however inexplicably, valued the fictions she deplores. Women's allegiance to those fictions in turn suggests that, in fiction as in life, the gap between a feminist political agenda and the lives of ordinary women has proved resistant to feminist exhortation, and the more intractable its resistance, the more feminist theorists have turned to language to redress ordinary women's disappointing tendency to cling to traditional stories of women's lives. Postmodern feminist theorists especially emphasize the significance of consciousness—language and narrative—in shaping women's perceptions of their lives.

At the extreme, the postmodernist feminist Judith Butler has argued for the possibility that "this construct called 'sex' is as culturally constructed as gender; indeed, perhaps it was always already gender, with the consequence that the distinction between sex and gender turns out to be no distinction at all."[9] Butler makes no secret of her determination to destabilize received notions of normal or normative sexuality and to represent the destabilization as an attack on illegitimate authority. In her view, "[b]oth masculine and feminine positions are thus instituted through prohibitive laws that produce culturally intelligible genders, but only through the production of an unconscious sexuality that reemerges in the domain of the imaginary."[10] She thus argues that purported sexual differences between women and men are not natural but an artifact of language: Gender, understood as language or culture, creates sex rather than articulating it. Her strategy reinforces and advances the more modest claims of feminist literary critics about the importance of narratives in the shaping of women's consciousness. It also provides a theoretical justification for feminists who argue for the equality of women and men. If sex can be shown to be only a by-product of language or culture, then the foundation for natural differences between women and men crumbles: Sex is what the powerful (however defined) see, not what women and men are. But even if we agree with Butler's claims, which I do not, we still must explain the abiding importance of sexual difference to most women's sense of self.

Butler's intervention, even more than those of Heilbrun, DuPlessis, and Lanser, testifies to the uncertainties and ambiguities of the postmodern situation. The extraordinary sexual and economic revolution of the last thirty years, which has spawned both unprecedented opportunities for women and the modern feminist movement and which has decisively undercut the social centrality of marriage, has called into question the stability of sexual roles and relations. The ensuing preoccupation with gender explicitly challenges the authority of any—including cultural and literary—evocations of women's "traditional" roles and expectations. This climate of skepticism and uncertainty provides the context for current attitudes toward marriage, including Heilbrun's sense that it imprisons women. For the first time, it has become possible for at least some women to live comfortably, and even to bear and raise children, independent of marriage. Under these new conditions, the traditional story of marriage may indeed appear not merely punitive but dysfunctional. Yet even today, marriage, both as a personal relationship and an institution, retains its hold upon many, if not most, women's imaginations, which permits us to consider the possibility that their attachment to the story embodies something more than a misunderstanding of their own interests.[11] Today, as in the past, many women do see marriage as the joining of their public and private identities—an important, if no longer the only, link between their private self and the society to which they belong. In this respect, marriage continues to provide a bridge between the sexes and between generations, a sense of human continuity and roots.

Like other feminist critics, Heilbrun tends to conflate narratives of marriage with marriage as an institution and sometimes appears to suggest that a transformation of narratives might lead women to resist subservience to the institution. Thus, whatever the limitations of her view of marriage as an imprisoning myth, she implicitly acknowledges that, as a narrative, marriage is simultaneously subjective (from the perspective of individual women for whom it signifies their relations with a partner and, by extension, offspring) and objective (from the perspective of society for which it figures as a central and enduring feature of the network of relations that bind individuals and generations to one another). The importance of the objective character of marriage as the fundamental social unit accounts for its status as at once a pledge of mutual faith between individuals, a social contract, and, for the Church, a sacrament. And even after the massive changes of the twentieth century, marriage remains the only personal bond among individuals that enjoys this public status. This official sanction, and the obligations it is taken to entail, underscores the importance of marriage as the fulcrum for the most binding social claims, obligations, loyalties, and sentiments.[12]

Both the persisting narratives of marriage and the anthropological view of marriage as an institution evoke the timeless—transcendent or recurring—dimension of marriage as a common feature of all human societies. In this respect, it is worth noting that the absence of legally binding marriage has commonly figured as one of the salient aspects of slavery, and that absence has contributed to Orlando Patterson's description of slavery as "social death."[13] And, indeed, in the United States and elsewhere, slave women and men strove valiantly to sustain a version of marriage as a binding commitment between individuals and a bulwark for children even when they knew better than any the cost imposed upon the sanctity of those marriages by the absence of legal standing.[14]

Just as societies have relied upon marriage to anchor social relations and the bonds between generations, so have they elaborated narratives of marriage, and, as the forms of marriage have varied, so have the narratives. Most dominant narratives of marriage, nonetheless, share certain features, notably an overarching justification of the institution and some incentive to encourage young women and men's willingness to enter into it. In this respect, these dominant narratives do bind the objective and subjective elements of marriage together in an apparently seamless web. The novel aspect of narratives of marriage in the modern period has been their growing insistence upon love as both the justification for the objective institution and the subjective reason to undertake its possible burdens. Narratives of love and romance have flourished since the dawn of time, but, until the modern period, they have not necessarily been linked to marriage and, in many instances, notably in the case of Courtly Love, have even been seen as inevitably external to it. The tension between true love—the passion that as readily leads to death as to fulfillment—and marriage helps to account for the vital persistence of the notion of love and sexual passion as inherently dangerous, although our contemporary culture is likely to see the danger as externally imposed (perhaps by a crazed stalker) rather than inherent to the passion itself.[15]

Women have never deluded themselves about the dangers that stalk sex and love. If sex is a joining of bodies and love a joining of souls, both are a joining of differences in which women and men seek to lose as well as gain themselves. This game is inherently a dangerous one in which women (and men) may easily get hurt. But throughout time, women, as readily as men, have risked the hurt in their quest for the joy and satisfaction promised by the transcendence or merging of difference. And throughout time, women have spun their own tales of love and sex and transmitted them across generations. The women's fictions that contemporary feminist critics deplore represent a specific chapter in a much older story that sinks its roots in the folk cultures and lore that women themselves have created. And it should not surprise us that, throughout history, women, especially mothers, have encouraged younger women to appreciate marriage as an institutional protection for women's special vulnerability to the dangers that love and sex may entail. Thus have women sought to direct the unruly forces of love and sex toward the willing acquiescence in what are today viewed as the traditional—and perhaps outmoded—roles of wife and mother.

The sexual and economic revolution of the last thirty years has cut women loose from those traditional roles and expectations. Today, women, including the mothers of small children, lead lives that, in many respects, resemble those of men, notably by their unprecedented participation in the labor force. The changes unleashed by the sexual and economic revolution have also resulted in an unprecedented divorce between women's sexual conduct and the morality that, throughout history, has traditionally hedged it in. Even very young girls now freely engage in sexual relations without much, if any, guidance from parents, teachers, or other adults. But women's new freedom has diminished neither the danger nor the appeal of sex and love. If anything, by discrediting the conventions that offered women a modicum of protection, sexual freedom has made them more dangerous than ever. For in the absence of conventions that encourage men to respect women's distinct sexual vulnerability, women enjoy the dubious "freedom" to confront men as equals—the freedom to take pleasure where they find it and to be hurt and abandoned if something goes wrong, which, as feminists are the first to protest, it frequently does.

The literature and lore of all cultures abound with tales of women who have been used and abused, deserted, or simply taken advantage of. Women have always understood the sexual vulnerability that accompanies women's ability to bear children and their special responsibility to care for them. That they have also understood that countless women have found passion, meaning, and fulfillment in their relations with men and their love for children only enriches and complicates their stories. For most women have understood both the dangers and the promise of sex and love as the stuff of everyday life—as an integral part of what it means to be a woman. Thus have they persisted in cherishing a dream of love even as they have recognized that the everyday relations between women and men fall short of the "happily-ever-after" stories of romance. Feminists, who focus upon the gap between the "reality" of women's lives and the fantasy of love stories, tend to disapprove of the love stories. For, they argue, most cultures, especially our own, have deceitfully invoked stories of love and devotion to persuade women to comply with men's designs by the willing assumption of roles that reinforce men's advantage and perpetuate women's subordination. And many tend to object yet more forcefully to stories that emphasize the differences between women and men as if the recognition of difference itself relegated women to a position of dependence or inferiority.

Even feminists, however, have found it difficult to shake the sense that sexual difference is in some way real. Feminist indictments of male brutality invariably, if disingenuously, portray men as naturally brutal. But if we view male brutality as natural or innate and view women as that brutality's ubiquitous victims, how does it not follow that we are assuming men and women to be naturally different? Feminists normally reject that obvious conclusion, lest any recognition of sexual differences be taken to justify policies that exclude women from desirable opportunities. Yet most, even as they cling to the ideal of a sexually neutral equality, perpetuate their indictments of the male brutality that forcefully bars women from the opportunities and rewards to which they are naturally entitled. Meanwhile, other feminists continue to write of women's different sense of morality or women's different "ways of knowing."[16] The contradictions remain puzzling. For it is difficult to view men as sexual brutes and women as victims of male brutality, or to view men as natural predators and women as natural embodiments of mercy and compassion, and still deny that they differ.

Notwithstanding the intractable complexities of the theoretical problem, women persist in living their lives according to their own lights. Most take for granted that, at least with respect to the experience of sexuality and sense of personal relations, women and men do differ. But their easy acceptance of some differences, however elusive, does not undermine their confidence in women's individual talents and accomplishments, nor does it lead them to repudiate the goal of equality in arenas such as women's right to equal pay for equal work.[17] Most women, in other words, seem perfectly comfortable with the idea that a woman may combine quest and romance—that she may perform brilliantly as a pilot or a lawyer or a law enforcement officer or a telephone lineman and still be happy to think of herself as a woman. And, indeed, most of us, including most feminists, do persist in speaking of women as a group, or, better, as members of a sex. But our tendency to do so forces us to confront the meaning we do ascribe to woman or women.

If we ignore the many attributes that women share with men—income, education, ethnicity, race—what remains to distinguish women from the men of their immediate community? Precious little, feminists and many others would answer. What remains may be only a woman's being the daughter of a woman and the physical possibility that her body may bear a daughter (or son) of her own. But however trivial we may deem it, that precious little cannot be discounted, and, protestations to the contrary notwithstanding, it remains the basic difference between women and men. That difference constitutes the core not only of women's greatest vulnerability, but of that sense of self which resolutely resists politicization—the same sense of self that constitutes the wellspring of fantasy, abiding stories, and compelling literature.

Literature, by its nature, feeds off the undisciplined and the unpredictable, which it hammers into the recognizable. The triumph of the most compelling literature lies in its ability to surprise and delight by transforming the idiosyncratic details of a specific experience into a pattern of human response that is unexpectedly familiar to those for whom the details are foreign. Women's writing, especially, has always bridged the gap between women's conversations about their lives and their secret fantasies—between the everyday and the imaginary. Compelling fictions remain as elusive and ungovernable as Zenia in Margaret Atwood's novel *The Robber Bride,* who cannot even be trusted to remain dead and buried.[18]

There can be no doubt that powerful ties bind women's fantasies and, by extension, the most durable myths of woman's nature to women's sexual vulnerability. The very power and resilience of those ties are the true target of Heilbrun and her colleagues' impatience. Women, they seem to be saying, should know better than to continue reading and, all the more, writing narratives that conform to those myths. But as the failure of socialist realism long since demonstrated, literature does not readily follow the dictates of political rectitude. In *The Golden Notebook,* one of the first postmodern novels by a woman, Doris Lessing caustically exposes art's recalcitrant resistance to programmatic imperatives. Her protagonist, the writer and one-time member of the Communist Party, Anna Wulff, notes that as people began leaving the party in the 1950s, there was not an important former activist who did not have a draft of a novel tucked away.[19] Indeed, Anna, who had joined the party out of a burning desire to work with people who saw the problems of the world clearly, sees its inability to accommodate art as emblematic of all its failures.

Nothing could be further from Lessing's—or Anna's—intent than to replicate the forms of previous literature. To the contrary, *The Golden Notebook* may be read as an extended exploration of possible ways to write the postmodern novel and, especially, a possible new ending for the female *bildungsroman.* At the novel's close, Anna's friend and companion, Molly, who, like Anna, is a "free" woman, is planning to marry again, but Anna herself is not. Yet Anna remains no less attached to the dream of love than Molly. And the last of Anna's notebooks, "The Golden Notebook," chronicles her physical, emotional, and psychological merging with her lover, Saul

Green. Anna and Saul part, notwithstanding—or because of—the intimacy that permits them to write a first sentence for one another's next novel. Anna does not renounce the possibilities of sex and love with other men, but she increasingly recognizes that the men to whom she is drawn are fighting their own demons that make the prospects for lasting relations dim. None more implacably expose the bankruptcies and dead-ends of the relations between women and men in the postmodern world than Lessing. Yet even at her most realistic and unsentimental, she suggests that the proliferation of mis-understandings, cross-purposes, and conflicting needs between women and men represent a variation upon an archetypal pattern that binds the two sexes and their offspring.

Lessing's women, even when they are most impatient with the men in their lives, emphatically do not see victimization or unrelenting struggles against male brutality as the main story of those lives. And, if they enjoy greater independence and freedom than the heroines of earlier generations (which is not necessarily the case), it is in their greater freedom from the dic-tates of sexual propriety, their greater ability to support themselves, and their greater willingness to risk some knocks, pick themselves up, and start over. They know, as most women throughout history have known, that they have fashioned their lives from a mixture of pleasure and danger—of good and bad—that has little to do with theoretical abstractions. And more adventur-ous women have always found some pleasure in the danger, at least within limits. Indeed, the main point of *The Golden Notebook* may well lie in its un-relenting insistence that the abstractions will not hold, and irrelevance effec-tively makes the willingness to risk danger a condition of women's lives. In this absence of reliable rule, women rely upon common sense and direct experience. That is what used to be called folk wisdom, and notwithstanding the rapid changes of today, more women live by it than public discussions even hint at.

Today, as in the past, women transmit folk wisdom through stories, through the endless flow of conversation that eases and makes sense of our lives, and binds us to those with whom we share it. Our talk about men, even when harshly critical, often merges with talk of love and romance. It blends with the dreams embodied in the romances we read and the films and soap operas we watch. Romances, films, and soaps obviously spin fantasies that have little to do with everyday life.[20] But for most of us, the lines blur, and it is an easy step from losing oneself in a romance or reading a maga-zine for advice to trading stories with other women. The shared experi-ences of these conversations acknowledge and domesticate the dangers of sexual encounters with men, weaving a web of lore that binds women to one another.

Women rely heavily on stories to make sense of our lives, and as we hear and read stories about other girls and women, we assimilate bits of them into our own experience, anchoring them in our own lives. Susan Douglas argues that genuine women members of the baby-boomer generation invariably know by heart every word of the Shirelles' hit song, "Will You Love Me Tomorrow?"[21] Like the traditional Scottish ballads that women once sang at work, the Shirelles' music evokes women's experiences of love and loss, of the dangers and uncertainties, as well as the delights, of courtship. Such women's songs, like women's stories, help women take possession of their own experience, even when it is painful or ends badly. According to Douglas, the Shirelles, as a girl group that sang girls' music for girls, represented something new in the world of mass media, which had been dominated by men's perspective, but, in telling women's stories for other women, the Shirelles were perpetuating a long tradition. And their listeners were not new in relishing women's stories of women's experience.

Women never outgrow the need for stories about women's lives, even if, as we get older, the stories change. Feminist critics like Heilbrun acknowledge the abiding importance of those stories when they criticize their content and ending. For, if the stories did not matter, who would care about their content and ending? Heilbrun and her colleagues deplore the stories because, notwithstanding the new patterns and expectations of recent generations, many of the stories that women cherish and find touching have much in common with stories that women throughout time have relied upon to make sense of their lives. As Janice Radway has noted with respect to the romances that remain so popular, the stories always contain a measure of fantasy. In some case, especially when real life gets especially painful, fantasy may get the upper hand, although even then, it may provide a safety-valve or an escape that makes the pain more bearable. For some readers of romance, the fantasy of romances simply provides some color or hope in a drab life. And it is worth noting that even the heroines of romances are changing in response to women's broadening expectations for their own lives.[22] But changes and variations notwithstanding, some basic stories continue to shape very different kinds of dreams for the lives of very different kinds of women. Among them, love, marriage, and motherhood have always enjoyed a privileged place.

Across differences of generation, class, ethnicity, and race, marriage and motherhood retain a powerful hold on very different kinds of women's imaginations. Here and there, in response to changing times, we have modified the story, but nothing has replaced it. "Nice" girls may now, without penalty, have sex before marriage, live with men to whom they are not married, or have children on their own, but most continue to hope that sooner or later they will marry. In recent decades, the number of single mothers has dramatically increased, but, more often than not, the women continue to hope for marriage with the father of their child or another. The proliferation of divorce has barely affected the story of marriage at all, as, in the case of Lessing's Molly, failed marriages are followed by others. Even women's intense interest in pursuing their own careers has not, in most cases, led them to abandon the dream that they will also be wives and mothers.

The persistent commitment of many women to marriage and children draws upon wellsprings of feeling and imagination that perversely resist social and political nostrums. Thus, the numbers of women who read gothics and romances suggest that many women do, at some level, continue to entertain fantasies of the strong, daring man who can literally sweep a heroine off her feet. But these same women normally know that the physical strength which can protect is the strength that can bully, batter, and abuse. Some women, even those who know more than they want to about the dangers, cling, against evidence and reason, to the dream of the man who can make everything right and keep them safe. Others, who simply recognize men's fallible humanity, cling to the warmth of connection and belonging.

The image of male strength, like the image of female nurture, springs from children's longing for the security and unquestioning love they expect of fathers and mothers. As little girls grow up and learn more about the realities of the world, vestiges of the myth persist. Even today, when they are learning to be tough and self-reliant, whether in school, at sports, or on the streets, the story of love and marriage lurks in the back of their minds, frequently encouraged by mothers, who, sometimes in spite of themselves, want to see their daughters happily settled. The story seems almost to live a life of its own, coexisting with women's pride in their ability to cope with the challenges life offers them, including difficult men. The same mothers and grandmothers who have perpetuated the story of marriage have always encouraged young women to say and mean, "I will take so much and no more." For most women, the unflinching recognition of men's capacity for brutality, infidelity, and ordinary thoughtlessness coexists with an appreciation of their virtues. Just think of Tony's time-honored combination of love and condescending tolerance toward West in *The Robber Bride*.[23]

Married women do not need to be told that the men they love are more than occasionally impossible. But across differences of class, ethnicity, and race, they recognize men's failings as a consequence of their being men—a product of the difference between women and men. And normally they have little difficulty in distinguishing between the peccadillos a woman learns to live with and the sins she cannot tolerate. In *You Just Don't Understand*, Deborah Tannen explores the way in which differences between women and men surface in their conversational styles, arguing that women speak a different dialect—or "genderlect"—than men.[24] Women, she suggests, tend to favor a language of "connection and intimacy," whereas men tend to favor one of "status and independence." Tannen finds that these differences hold true for all classes, races, and ethnic groups, and her findings seem to have struck a chord, for her book was a bestseller. But then, the sexual differences she observes in conversational style resemble those that others have found in women's and men's taste, sense of morality, patterns of behavior, and ways of thinking about the world. Feminists who resist any acknowledgement of differences between women and men have not been happy with Tannen's conclusions, which they fear might reinforce men's power over women. On the other side, common sense and experience support the view that women do share a lore and culture of everyday life that differ from those of most men. And most women apparently experience sex differently than men.

Women's fiction feeds upon women's lore and culture, which constitutes the bedrock of its intertextuality. Those who view women as perpetual victims apparently slight the massive evidence of women's resilience and even humor in the face of adversity. In recent years, the representations of women's resistance to trivialization or even brutalization have become sharper, and writers like Margaret Atwood capture it with cutting, if subtle, glee that women readers should delight in claiming as their own. But even during the early years of the women's movement, Alix Kates Shulman had the female protagonist of her novel, *Burning Questions,* enter in the index she is compiling for her inconsiderate and bullying husband, "birds, for the. . . ."[25] And previous generations of women writers had their own ways of invoking and celebrating the culture that they assumed women shared. Not for nothing have women invariably proven women writers' most numerous, loyal, and appreciative readers, and it defies credulity that, for generations, they should have devoured women's narratives out of self-hatred or some putative false consciousness.

In *Bearing the Word,* Margaret Homans has thoughtfully explored the experience of women writers who have attempted to write themselves into a language and culture that "depend on the death or absence of the mother" and upon the quest to substitute for her power another power that "men's minds can more readily control."[26] In her view, this androcentric configuration of language and culture condemns women writers to a pervasive tension between their ties, as women, to the literal and their quest, as artists, for the symbolic. For the literal meaning that is natural to them simultaneously "makes possible and endangers the figurative structures of literature."[27] The problem, simply put, is that literal meaning obviates the value of the symbolic elusion to it by collapsing the sign and the referent into one.

This possibility is always, but never more than that, a threat, since literal meaning cannot be present in a text: it is always elsewhere. This positioning of the literal poses special problems for women readers and writers because literal language, together with nature and matter to which it is epistemologically linked, is traditionally classified as feminine, and the feminine is, from the point of view of a predominantly androcentric culture, always elsewhere too.[28]

Homans's concerns remind us of the proclivity of contemporary feminist critics to cling to the literal, which they enjoin women writers to transform. Homans further reminds us, albeit indirectly, that the preeminent quest of the woman writer must ultimately concern her own vocation as artist rather than the destiny to which she consigns her female characters. Since time immemorial, male writers have reached for the symbolic through the representation of female (and male) characters for whom love and connection, including their institutionalization in marriage, figure as dream and as telos. So long as women and men continue to flutter like moths around the dangerous and alluring flame of sexual passion, so long as they hope, against whatever odds, to find abiding meaning in the connections that simultaneously bind and transcend their difference, we may assume that marriage, in its permutations and even its failures, will persist as one of the main weapons in the artist's arsenal of plots. For, if the symbolic rises like the phoenix from the ashes of the literal, it also feeds upon the entwining stories that constitute both culture and individual consciousness. In demanding new plots in order to birth a new world, feminist critics are, however inadvertently, betraying the very women in whose interest they claim to write and, worse, shortchanging those women's capacity to find sustenance in the cultures that have constituted women's past and inform their present.

Those cultures have been grounded in the assumption that women and men differ, and at some level that assumption persists today. Recognition of differences between women and men does not contradict evidence that women may do the same things and hold the same jobs as men with as great success, but it should encourage us to recognize the truth that the ways in which women and men share the world is richly and infuriatingly complex. This truth challenges our imaginations and, above all, the ways in which we think about personal and public solutions to the problems that women confront. The challenge to public policy is daunting, but public policy has never been the main concern of literature or literary theory, both of which primarily focus precisely upon that rich and infuriating realm of imagination and the symbolic—a realm that notoriously eludes institutionalization. The proper concern of writers and critics presumably lies less with support for or

opposition to specific policies than with women's personalities and imaginations, which still have much in common with those of their foremothers.
Women of today, like women of the past, tend to form personalities and
imaginations out of private interactions with those who are closest to them.
In this realm, especially in sexual relations, the differences between women
and men assume their true significance in both life and art.

Today, the myth of marriage till death do us part has lost much of its lus-
ter, in part because so many of the conventions and institutions that sought
to contain men's potential brutality against women by limiting women's freedom have collapsed, in part because women enjoy unprecedented opportunities to independent accomplishment, including economic self-sufficiency.[29]
Yet neither the collapse of those conventions and institutions nor the expansion of women's opportunities has resulted in a utopian sexual equality between women and men, and, on some days, one is tempted to believe it has
fueled an escalating war between the sexes.[30] Ironically, many of the preferred feminist solutions to the perceived problems of sexual violence against
women resemble nothing so much as a restoration of the paternal authority
against which feminists claim to be in revolt—although this time in the guise
of the state. If men are naturally brutal, then their brutality must be forcibly
reined in. Katie Roiphe has made the point clearly.[31] The demand that the
"authorities" protect women from men carries the depressing suggestion that
independent, "liberated" women are not capable of taking care of themselves
or even of avoiding the most dangerous situations.

If feminist theorists and critics tend to view love and marriage as hall-
marks of men's conspiracy to keep women docile, dependent, and in their
place, women, with eyes wide open, have clung to them as central, if risky,
aspects of a woman's life. No more than ordinary women do women writers expect life to be free of risk, but then, most compelling women writers
never did. And if marriage and motherhood continue to figure prominently
in their narratives of women's lives, the reasons for their prominence might
merit reflection. Recent women's fiction has assuredly shed any complacent
tendency to represent marriage as a happily-ever-after resolution of women's
destinies. It abounds with divorces, betrayals, deferrals, and outright abuse.
These days, the story of love and marriage must be revised to take account
of women's working lives or some women's choice not to marry at all. And
yet, neither the changes that have engulfed our world nor the cynicism they
often engender seem to have made a significant dent in the abiding promise
of that story.

Feminists, who frequently argue that marriage and the family constitute
the principal source of women's subordination, have been tempted to see the
commitment to both as a form of escapism, which, in some instances, it is.

But if so, it is an escapism that permeates women's lives as well as their narratives. For generations, romance enshrouded and disguised the economic dependence that forced most women to marry, but romance has survived the collapse of that economic necessity. Neither Sethe in Toni Morrison's *Beloved* nor Tony, Roz, and Charis of *The Robber Bride* depend upon a man for support, nor do Gail Godwin's recent protagonists, Margaret of *Father Melancholy's Daughter* or Alice of *The Good Husband*.[32] Indeed, Godwin, in *The Good Husband*, attributes the traditional role of wife to a man, Francis Lake, who nurses his successful professional wife, Magda Danvers. Yet none of these women characters repudiates the promise of love and connection, nor does any experience a conflict between romance and quest. To the contrary, their commitment to the connection of romance lies at the center of their quest for independent selfhood. All of them struggle to free themselves from the crippling aspects of their past, but their struggles primarily concern their quest to connect on new terms—out of choice rather than compulsion. For today, as in the past, liberation from all connection leads not to fulfillment but to death. Perhaps recognition of the poverty of disconnection accounts for Carolyn Heilbrun's having endowed her own fabulously smart and accomplished fictional heroine, Kate Fansler, with a husband.[33]

The compelling challenge for women writers does not so much concern the obligation to destroy the myths or even to change the plot, which may be a worthy ambition, as to find compelling new modes of representation—new patterns and forms for the writer's voice. And in this challenge, any number are proving wonderfully successful. Toni Morrison's innovative craft is beginning to receive the attention it so richly deserves. But consider also the craft, delicacy, and sheer intelligence of Godwin's *The Good Husband* or Margaret Atwood's *The Robber Bride*. Godwin, like Atwood, has moved well beyond older models in which the main female character was intended to invite the female reader's direct identification. In *The Good Husband*, even the less likable and admirable characters end by engaging the reader's empathy and imagination. In both novels, a running thread about the writing of novels weaves through the formal plot so that how one tells a story emerges as an explicit part of the story itself. Both novelists have the gift of taking the reader into her confidence without ever stooping to simple confession, and the writer's willingness to trust the reader draws the reader into the novelist's imagination and, especially, craft—into the business of writing a novel—without pretension or didactic posturing. Suddenly, one understands the relation between plotting a novel and plotting a life.

Tellingly, both *The Good Husband* and *The Robber Bride* evoke elements of the traditional narratives of marriage in their titles, and it is clear that both authors have set themselves to telling that familiar narrative in a new way. The point is not to smash the core of the narrative, but to twist, turn, and refashion it for today's readers. In *The Good Husband,* Magda Danvers's death—her preoccupation with her "final examination"—contributes to this sense of the relation between the narratives of fiction and the narratives of life. In *The Robber Bride,* Tony's dedication to ancient military history—hardly your stereotypic female preoccupation—does the same. In both novels, each of the primary characters comes marvelously, almost miraculously, alive without the author's ever having issued simplistic invitations to identification. In this sense, *The Good Husband* and *The Robber Bride* stretch and enrich the reader by encouraging us to care about people who may, in essential ways, be unlike ourselves—to see pieces of ourselves in those who are not us and thus to appreciate essential elements of our common humanity. At once powerful and delicate, emotionally inviting and intellectually challenging, these novels, like many other women's novels, should remind us that women writers entrance their readers by fashioning new ways of telling the stories that today, like yesterday, resonate to women's experience and wisdom as well as dreams.

Notes

1. Carolyn Heilbrun, *Writing a Woman's Life* (New York: Ballantine, 1988) 77.

2. For a thoughtful, extended discussion of the change and continuity in Southern women writers' views of marriage, see Sheila M. F. O'Connor, "Wages of Grace: Marriage in the Novels of Augusta Jane Evans, Ellen Glasgow, Eudora Welty, and Gail Godwin," Ph. D. diss. in progress, Emory University.

3. Rachel Blau DuPlessis, *Writing Beyond the Ending: Narrative Strategies of Twentieth-Century Women Writers* (Bloomington, IN: Indiana UP, 1985) 1.

4. DuPlessis 14.

5. DuPlessis 197.

6. DuPlessis 197.

7. Susan Sniader Lanser, *Fictions of Authority: Women Writers and Narrative Voice* (Ithaca, NY: Cornell UP, 1992) 32.

8. Catherine Gallagher, *The Industrial Reformation of English Fiction: Social Discourse and Narrative Form, 1832–1867* (Chicago: U of Chicago P, 1985) 184.

9. Judith Butler, *Gender Trouble: Feminism and the Subversion of Identity* (New York: Routledge, 1990) 7.

10. Butler 28.

11. On women's response to the sexual and economic revolution of the past few decades, see Elizabeth Fox-Genovese, *"Feminism Is Not the Story of My Life": How Today's Feminist Elite Has Lost Touch with the Real Concerns of Women* (New York: Doubleday, 1996).

12. This structural perspective on marriage emerges forcefully from the work of anthropologists. For a discussion of the implications of their work, see Elizabeth Fox-Genovese, *Within the Plantation Household: Black and White Women of the Old South* (Chapel Hill: University of North Carolina Press, 1988) esp. 296–99.

13. Orlando Patterson, *Slavery and Social Death: A Comparative Study* (Cambridge, MA: Harvard UP, 1982).

14. The literature on slavery in the United States abounds with references to slave marriages and the slaves' attitudes toward marriage, but see especially Fox-Genovese, *Within the Plantation Household,* Eugene D. Genovese, *Roll, Jordan, Roll: The World the Slaves Made* (New York: Pantheon Books, 1974), and Herbert G. Gutman, *The Black Family in Slavery and Freedom, 1750–1925* (New York: Pantheon Books, 1976).

15. For the latter view, one must turn to Romeo and Juliet, Tristan and Isolde, or, perhaps, Thomas Mann's "Tristan."

16. Thus Carol Gilligan, whose best-selling book, *In a Different Voice: Psychological Theory and Women's Development* (Cambridge, MA: Harvard UP, 1982), claimed that women have a distinct sense of morality, signed an affidavit in support of Shannon Faulkner's suit against The Citadel. Her work, she insisted, should not be used to justify single-sex education—even as one option among others.

17. This argument is developed in Fox-Genovese, *"Feminism Is Not the Story of My Life."*

18. Margaret Atwood, *The Robber Bride* (New York: Doubleday, 1993).

19. Doris Lessing, *The Golden Notebook,* with a new introduction by the author (1962; New York: HarperPerennial, 1994).

20. Janice Radway, *Reading the Romance: Women, Patriarchy, and Popular Literature* (Chapel Hill: U of North Carolina P, 1984).

21. Susan J. Douglas, *Where the Girls Are: Growing Up Female with the Mass Media* (New York: Times Books, 1994).

22. Radway, *Reading the Romance.*

23. Atwood, *The Robber Bride.*

24. Deborah Tannen, *You Just Don't Understand: Women and Men in Conversation* (New York: Ballantine, 1990) 42.

25. Alix Kates Shulman, *Burning Questions* (New York: Knopf, 1978).

26. Margaret Homans, *Bearing the Word: Language and Female Experience in Nineteenth-Century Women's Writing* (Chicago: U of Chicago P, 1986) 4.

27. Homans 4.

28. Homans 4.

29. Emilie Buchwald, Pamela Fletcher, and Martha Roth, eds., *Transforming a Rape Culture* (Minneapolis, MN: Milkweed Editions, 1993).

30. In 1994, according to a Justice Department study, sixty-two percent of whites killed in spousal abuse were female, thirty-eight percent male. Thus, among whites, for every two women (or slightly less) who are killed by a violent spouse, is one man. This may not be equality, but it is also not the unilateral victimization of women. And black women are even closer to parity than white. Among black couples, women account for only slightly more than half the spousal murder victims (53%) and men slightly less (47%). For an account of the figures on domestic violence, see Katherine Dunn, "Truth Abuse," *The New Republic* 211.5 (1 August 1994): 16–17. On the general problem of feminists' abuse of statistics, see Christina Hoff Sommers, *Who Stole Feminism?: How Women Have Betrayed Women* (New York: Simon and Schuster, 1994).

31. Katie Roiphe, *The Morning After: Sex, Fear, and Feminism on Campus* (Boston: Little, Brown, 1993).

32. Toni Morrison, *Beloved* (New York: Knopf, 1987), Atwood, *The Robber Bride,* Gail Godwin, *Father Melancholy's Daughter* (New York: Morrow, 1991) and her *The Good Husband* (New York: Ballantine, 1994).

33. Kate Fansler's career may be followed in Heilbrun's detective fiction published under the pseudonym Amanda Cross.

Seventeen

Thoughts on the History of the Family

Since the 1950s, but especially since the 1970s, contemporary concerns about the family have generated intense interest in the variety of family forms in different times and places. Recent decades have especially witnessed a veritable explosion of family history, ranging from oral histories of specific families to massive scholarly monographs on the family in specific periods to general interpretations and overviews. This work, at its best, has yielded fascinating results that have decisively expanded our sensitivity to the myriad forms which the purported transhistorical monolith of "the family" may take. Much of it, however, may fairly be viewed as suspect, if only because it was written to serve a specific political or ideological agenda. Above all, for what should be obvious reasons, many of the historical studies of the family originated in a desire to disclose the distinctive, if not unique, features of the family during the period under consideration and thereby to emphasize the difference rather than the similarity among families in different societies and centuries.

Not for nothing has the family captured the attention of historians: How better to expose an institution as the product of human choice rather than natural or divine order than to call attention to its historical variation? Indeed, during the years following World War II, and especially since the 1960s, historians have explored the multiplicity of family forms as well as the changing patterns of family formation and dynamics. Following the pioneering path

"Thoughts on the History of the Family." In *The Family, Civil Society, and the State,* edited by Christopher Wolfe, 3–15. Lanham, Md.: Rowman & Littlefield, 1998. Copyright 1998, Rowman & Littlefield. All rights reserved. Used by permission of the publisher.

254 Thoughts on the History of the Family

traced by the work of the French historian Philippe Ariès, they have, for example, rejected the idea of childhood as a distinct and universal stage of development, insisting that the idea only took shape in Europe during the early modern period. In earlier times, Ariès insisted, children had been viewed as miniature adults.[1] Others, following the lead of Lawrence Stone, have focused upon the changing character of marriage and its relation to the socialization of the young, beginning with childrearing practices.[2] Most historians of the family, notwithstanding differences among them, have tended to follow the lead of Ariès and Stone in insisting upon the close association among the appearance of the idea of childhood and the emergence of the nuclear family, companionate marriage, and, especially, the modern idea of motherhood.[3]

Drawing freely upon psychology, sociology, and anthropology, historians of the family have, on the whole, emphasized the functional or economic character of marital and family relations. The broad functional perspective might be summarized as, "Each society gets the forms of marriage and family it deserves or which best serve its purposes." The economic perspective, which shares many assumptions with the functional, shifts the emphasis to the limits that economic possibilities place upon marriage and family, concluding that the nature of both are shaped by economic forces. Both the functional and economic perspectives converge in their emphasis upon the differences among families according to century, location, or social class. Both have, in this respect, paved the way for the contemporary or postmodern emphasis upon the malleability of family composition and the endless variety of family forms.[4]

The emergence of the contemporary infatuation with the infinite plasticity of "the family" helps to explain the fascination with family history. Having, in our own time, called the very notion of the two-parent heterosexual family into question, we seem compelled to prove that it has never been either naturally or divinely sanctioned and, if anything more important, that most people throughout history have been unwilling or unable to observe its norms.[5] Thus the dominant tendency in family history seems to suggest that there have been as many kinds of families as there have been societies or even individuals. The logical conclusion to be drawn from this work is accordingly that the family, like marriage in which it is anchored, constitutes a relation into which people enter and that they frequently leave according to shifting individual preferences and interests.

In fairness, it is entirely possible that the attitudes toward the family and marriage that many scholars project upon the past may have triumphed in our own time. But, if we are to make any sense of the current debates about marriage and the family, we must understand that the situation of marriage and the family in our time is not merely new but unprecedented. For, until the very recent past, marriage and the family have been universally viewed as the necessary foundation of specific societies and of civilization in general—as the source and manifestation of human and divine order. This understanding of marriage and the family as the most important and abiding system of human relations, as simultaneously necessary to individuals and to society as a whole, has persisted throughout human history. Beneath the surface of changing patterns of marriage and family, the ubiquitous insistence upon the intrinsic value of marriage and family as fundamental goods for the individual and society has endowed the various manifestations and practices with a common character and meaning.[6]

Marriage and the family do change in response to the broad social, economic, and cultural changes as well as in response to political and legal change. To take an easy example, where antimiscegenation laws prevail, a man and woman of different race do not marry, even if they cohabit, and consequently their children enjoy no legal identity as members of their family. Similarly, slaves in the antebellum South could not legally marry although they frequently entered into binding relations with a person of the opposite sex, sometimes with the blessing of a minister. And because these marriages had no legal standing, the children they produced were not legally the children of their biological procreators.[7]

The case of slave marriage throws into relief some of the central features of marriage and the family as legally or religiously constituted institutions. Today, many primarily consider marriage and the family from the subjective perspective of the individual: Do they or do they not further the individual's happiness and fulfillment? Yet if, from the perspective of the individual, marriage and family constitute a subjective story, from the perspective of society they primarily constitute an objective story. Thus, the anthropologist Robin Fox reminds us that marriage figures as a central and enduring feature of "the network of relationships that bind individuals to each other in the web of kinship." And he argues that this network, like marriage itself, has functioned as "the pivot on which most interaction, most claims and obligations, most loyalties and sentiments [have] turned."[8] In other words, notwithstanding variations in form, marriage and the family have served as the primary link between the individual and society or the polity—the essential and irreducible social unit. In this role, marriage and the family typically secured the mutual rights and responsibilities of women and men, recognized the right and responsibility of parents to shape the future of their offspring, and secured the ownership and transfer of property. Until very recently, they preceded and outranked the individual, who was socially and politically defined by them rather than by personal attributes or status. Indeed, in the most important respects, marriage and the family, throughout most of history, have grounded and defined the identity of the individual, who is placed at high risk without their legitimization.[9]

At an accelerating rate during the late nineteenth and twentieth centuries, marital and family ties have increasingly come to be viewed as secular contractual relations, which primarily concern the state, if indeed they concern anyone other than the immediate participants. Throughout history, however, marriage and the family have been of primary concern to the Church or religious authorities, who have viewed them as inherently sacramental. Until the French Revolution, for example, the records of marriages, births, and deaths were not kept by the state, but by the clergy, who inscribed them in the parish registers from which historians have drawn such valuable information. Throughout history, religious authorities have displayed a special interest in marriage, presumably because they, like political authorities, have viewed marriage and the family as fundamental agents and sites of the ordering of human life. And most societies have ascribed a primary role to the family in the religious and moral education of the next generation.[10]

Today, many dismiss the interest of religious and political authorities in the regularization of marriage and the family as further evidence of the curtailment of individual desire by illegitimate authorities. Others, seemingly in growing numbers, demand that religious and political authorities acknowledge, sanctify, or legitimize whatever unions between individuals or groupings of individuals as valid forms of marriage or family.[11] The mistrust of marriage and the family has especially bedeviled feminists, who are wont to charge both with primary responsibility for the subordination and exploitation of women. And there can be no doubt that the feminist movement has decisively contributed to the dismantling of marriage and the family during recent decades.[12] Yet religious and political interest in marriage and the family testifies less to the determination to oppress women and children than to a deep understanding that marriage and the family have everywhere constituted the fundamental social unit—the fulcrum of civilization, the threshold between nature and culture. The core of the religious and political authorities' interest in marriage and the family may, then, be presumed to have derived from their understanding that these are the relations through which people recognize themselves as human beings, through which people define themselves. The question was less one of their imposing marriage and the family upon naturally recalcitrant individuals than of their gaining legitimacy by associating political and religious authority with the fundamental social units into which people grouped themselves.

With respect to the bonds between marriage and family on the one hand and religious and political authority on the other, it is worth noting that both religious and political authority themselves long borrowed heavily from the language of family relations, presumably because that language was taken to be the one that seemed most natural and legitimate to most people. The familial imagery that pervades Christianity begins with God the Father and includes not merely His Son, but the Blessed Mother, and the Holy Family. This same imagery pervaded and structured the early forms of European political authority, which, for centuries, depicted the monarch or the tsar as the father of his people. This form of political authority came appropriately to be known as patriarchalism. In its classic formulation by the British political theorist Sir Robert Filmer, it justified the authority of the monarch as a direct inheritance from Adam, the father of the human race.[13]

In theory, patriarchalism proclaimed a perfect symmetry between the governance of families and the governance of states—both understood to honor and obey the divinely sanctioned authority of the father. But variants of patriarchalism prevailed in societies that restricted its authority to the private realm and did not take it to justify the governance of public affairs. The leading example may well be ancient Rome, which endowed the father of the family with the power of life and death over family members and slaves. The power of the father in the Roman Republic thus exceeded even that of the power of the father in ancien régime France, who still had the authority to demand that the king imprison a son who dared to defy his wishes.[14] Even after the English had forcefully repudiated public patriarchalism and beheaded Charles I, the king who embodied it, they retained traces of its legacy in the assumption that a father would govern the family for which he was responsible, including his adult wife. Thus, in the eighteenth century, when Sir William Blackstone produced his great treatise on English common law, he insisted that in marriage the husband and wife must be one, and that one must be the husband. Blackstone was articulating the law of coverture, according to which the wife lived under the covering wing of her husband, who was held to protect her, govern her, and represent her in the public realm.[15]

The assumption that men naturally govern families, including their wives, has prevailed throughout most of history, although most premodern societies have granted more power to the family as a whole than to the specific husband and father, whom they have tended to view as the delegate of the family—that is, as the steward of an authority that provides for the proper ordering of the family as a whole, which transcends him as an individual. In such a world, it was frequently possible for a woman to step into that role and speak in the name of the family as a whole. Had that not been the case, Elizabeth I would never have succeeded to the throne of her father, and, although questions about the effect her marriage might have upon her role as sovereign persisted throughout her reign and may well have accounted for her never having married, as ruler she proved no more tolerant of challenges to her authority than he.[16]

Not all societies proved as faithful to the principles of delegation as the British, and to avoid complications, the French precociously established or rediscovered the Salic Law according to which a woman could never succeed to the throne. But elsewhere, notably Russia and Austria, women did govern in the name of their families, the interests of which they were believed to represent. Only during the modern and increasingly bureaucratic period did one country after another deem it prudent to institute explicit laws against women's political participation. And they invariably did so following the triumph of liberal, democratic, or individualistic principles that drew a hard line between public and private realms but also opened the way to women's claims to an individual identity independent of the family. Thus, during the second half of the nineteenth century, the United States and many, if not all, Western European countries explicitly barred—or tacitly excluded—women from activities and occupations. In this respect, a kind of sexual segregation emerged in tandem with the racial segregation that succeeded the Northern victory in the American Civil War and the abolition of slavery.[17]

Feminists have frequently been tempted to condemn most, if not all, marital and family relations throughout history as patriarchal. Many even argue that an independent system of patriarchy, grounded in men's presumed universal dominance within the family, has prevailed in all times and places.[18] This charge woefully misjudges the true nature of patriarchy, which has been far from universal. More importantly, it fails to capture the complexity and, above all, the interdependence that have normally characterized the relations between women and men within marriages and families. To grasp the normal state of affairs, we need only remember that the vast majority of human beings have traditionally lived in peasant or farm families in which the contributions, including the labor, of the woman have normally been as important as those of the man.[19] We should also recall that historically most married women have lived under conditions in which the reproduction of the population was the first business of society, in which many pregnancies did not come to term and many babies did not survive infancy, and in which artificial contraception was not—or not generally—available. These were conditions under which the biological difference between the sexes had important consequences and were generally taken to justify significantly different roles for women and men, even when the women also played an important role in provision of the family's resources.[20]

To identify the principal common denominator among the various historical forms of marriage and the family, we could do worse than settle on the widespread belief that marriage and the family articulate the natural sexual division of labor upon which social order and civilization rest. So widespread has agreement been on this matter that, until recently, one would have been hard-pressed to point to a single system of belief, including the great formal religions, a single theory of government, or a single social system that did not regard that "biological" fact as foundational—as an expression of the natural law that underlies and sets limits upon the positive laws of specific states.[21] Only in the very recent past have we witnessed significant opposition to the view of men and women as different and complementary and naturally suited to cooperation within marital and familial bonds upon which the future of the succeeding generation is taken to depend. Indeed, had that purportedly natural relation between the sexes not encountered opposition, we, like other societies, would presumably still regard the family as the natural unit of all human society, notwithstanding differing assumptions about its precise composition and size.

Thus far, I have tried to underscore a few enduring, common elements of marriage and family at the expense of the various forms they may take. But historically, the family, precisely because of its pivotal and indispensable role in linking the individual to society, has demonstrated impressive adaptability: According to circumstances, families may be extended or nuclear, multigenerational or two-generational, matrilineal or patrilineal, matrilocal or patrilocal. They may assuredly be patriarchal, although they have probably never, as Friedrich Engels and others speculated, been genuinely matriarchal.[22] Marriages themselves have varied not merely by monogamy and polygyny, but by whether arranged or freely chosen, whether established on the basis of a bride price or a dowry, and more. Scholars have emphasized the variations, in large measure, to disabuse the complacent assumption that to be legitimate family and marriage must always have observed the model we take for granted. All societies may attempt to ensure their own orderly reproduction through the ways in which they welcome and rear the next generation, but they have not all done so in the same way. Yet the very richness and interest of our new panoramic sense of the diversity of family forms risks obscuring the most important consideration of all. For it may reasonably be argued that none of these seemingly infinite variations matches in significance the sea change that has marked the modern and, especially, the postmodern worlds.[23]

If the modern ideals of companionate marriage and the nuclear family may not claim universal authority, they have nonetheless decisively shaped the ideas of contemporary Americans as well as Western Europeans, and, since World War II, they seem to have exercised some influence within a variety of "modernizing" societies throughout the world. The view of the family as appropriately nuclear and marriage as appropriately the product of the mutual love and choice of the individuals concerned emerged, as Lawrence Stone and others have argued, in Western Europe, notably England, at the dawn of the modern era. Scholars continue to debate the precise origins and causes of the modern ideal of marriage and the family, and most concur that it did not triumph in one fell swoop, much less gain an equal hold upon all social classes or even all regions of a single country. But they increasingly agree that, during the years following 1750, a new ideal of family and marriage was establishing a secure and apparently irreversible foothold among the English upper and upper-middle classes and that inhabitants of Western Europe and the North American colonies were following their lead.

Debates persist about the causes of the change in family size and dynamics toward the end of the early modern period. Some scholars attribute the decisive role to economics and others to ideology, but most concur about the manifestations. The new attitude toward marriage emphasized the importance of individual choice and love rather than the preference for arranged marriage designed to serve the political and economic interest of the larger family. In conformity with this preference for companionship and love between the partners, there emerged a new attitude toward children and motherhood. Elite mothers, who had previously turned their children over to wet-nurses, nannies, and governesses, were now expected to nurse their children themselves and to play a major role in the development of their minds and character. These expectations typically arose more or less in tandem with the first stirrings of political individualism, and they derived from the new interest in children as themselves emergent individuals. Indeed, both political individualism and the new psychology of childhood had a common source in the work of John Locke, in which childhood was viewed[24] as a distinct— and formative—stage of life during which children's impressionable minds and hearts were molded by the loving attention and firm discipline of parents, especially the mother. Whether as effect or cause, these new convictions about marriage, childhood, and family life generally accompanied an older age at first marriage for women and a gradual decline in the number of children per family. And the whole was ensconced in a view of the family as a private sphere, safely removed from the hurly-burly of public life, and informed by the glow of intimacy and love.[25]

Most of us recognize this constellation of attitudes, if only because it prevailed among Europeans and Americans until at least the upheavals of the 1960s and still prevails among many today. What we not so readily recognize is that this view, which so many of us cherish, contained within itself the seeds of its own ultimate destruction. Companionate marriage and the loving, child-centered, private family assured tremendous benefits to many people and to society at large, but they also created an array of problems, including men's abuse of women and children, the personal unhappiness of husbands and wives, and the psychic misery of children. We need not exaggerate the abuses, which have occurred in all families in all times and which may actually have diminished during the nineteenth and early twentieth centuries, but do need to acknowledge them. In recent years, it has become commonplace—in some circles, obligatory—to denounce the repressive and abusive character of the "patriarchal" bourgeois family. But whatever that family was, it was not patriarchal, and it arguably served its members better than any known alternative.

Ironically, the very emphasis upon love and mutuality between husband and wife and among parents and children that fostered the best features of this family also opened the way to its erosion. For example, once one assumes that a marriage must be grounded in love, how does one prohibit divorce when love dies? By the 1920s, divorce had, indeed, become much easier to obtain and was beginning to lose its social stigma. Thereafter, especially in the United States, the divorce rate skyrocketed—all in the name of true love and the fulfillment of individuals. The bonds of the nuclear family were steadily loosening, but the decisive blow came with the extraordinary sexual and economic revolution of the last thirty years.[26] That dual revolution has spawned both unprecedented opportunities for women and the modern feminist movement, and has decisively undercut the social centrality of marriage. These explosive changes have given us no-fault divorce, abortion on demand, rampant unwed motherhood, and "children's rights," and now threaten us with same-sex marriage as well.

The numbers that chronicle the proliferation of divorce, the children born to unwed mothers, the children who live all or a large part of their childhood without a resident biological father, and the other casualties of our current attitudes and practices are staggering. But there is a real danger that single-minded attention to the quantitative magnitude of family disruption will obscure the dramatic significance of the qualitative change. For, seen in historical perspective, our contemporary situation is indeed something new under the sun. To be sure, there are many who deny that qualitative change has occurred, arguing, for example, that the proliferation of divorce more often than not results in the formation of new marriages.[27] And in truth, many, if not most children in the seventeenth-century Chesapeake lost one or both of their parents before they reached their teens. Workers in nineteenth-century Paris frequently lacked the resources to marry and lived in common law marriages, which meant their children lacked legal standing. Until the twentieth century, most people died much younger than they die today, which meant that marriages did not last as long as those of today, and the surviving partner often remarried, which meant that many children grew up without either a biological mother or a biological father in residence. As for the contemporary reliance upon day care and nannies, was such not the experience of countless children throughout history, especially among the well-to-do? All of which and more is true, but the use to which these facts are being put entirely misses the point.

For before the last thirty years or so, no known society has rejected some form of marriage and family as the ideal—and as a norm to which most people were expected to aspire. Exceptions to and violations of the norm were recognized as exceptions and violations. Today, if we credit our senses, we are witnessing a concerted attempt by a portion of the elite to deny the value of the norm. In its place, we are offered marriage as the personal fulfillment of the individual, who must be free to switch partners at will. And we are offered family as "families"—whatever combination of people choose to live together on whatever terms for whatever period of time. It is possible that adults may survive this madness, although one may be permitted to doubt. It is doubtful that any significant number of children will survive it, as the mounting evidence of their distress amply warns. History suggests that, since the dawn of time, one of the principal tasks of civilization has been to bind men to families—to hold them accountable for the children they father and for the children's mother. The modern period slowly eroded elements of that accomplishment, while it introduced some salutary reforms. But it left the ideal intact. Since the 1960s, the postmodern elite has, as if with the snap of the fingers, exploded it. What may emerge from the wreckage is anyone's guess, although the initial signs do not inspire confidence.

Permit me then to conclude with this thought: At first glance the history of marriage and the family may appear to offer a wondrous array of diversity, but that first glance, like others, is more deceptive than trustworthy. For, on closer inspection, history teaches that civilization has always been accompanied by—indeed grounded in—an ideal of marriage and the family that attempts to join the biological difference of men and women in the common project of responsibility for the next generation.

Notes

1. Philippe Ariès, *Centuries of Childhood: A Social History of Family Life,* trans. Robert Baldick (New York: Alfred Knopf, 1962).

2. Lawrence Stone, *The Family, Sex, and Marriage in England, 1500–1800* (New York: Harper & Row, 1977).

3. See, for example, Randolph Trumbach, *The Rise of the Egalitarian Family: Aristocratic Kinship and Domestic Relations in Eighteenth-Century England* (New York: Academic Press, 1978); Elisabeth Badinter, *Émilie, Émilie: L'Ambition féminine au XVIIIème siècle* (Paris: Flammarion, 1983); Jacques Donzelot, *The Policing of Families,* trans. Robert Hurley (New York: Pantheon, 1979); Cissie Fairchild, "Women and Family," in *French Women in the Age of Enlightenment,* ed. Samia I. Spencer (Bloomington: Indiana University Press, 1984), 97–110. See also Elizabeth Fox-Genovese and Eugene D. Genovese, *Fruits of Merchant Capital: Slavery and Bourgeois Property in the Rise and Expansion of Capitalism* (New York: Oxford University Press, 1983), ch. 11 "The Ideological Bases of Domestic Economy: The Representation of Women and the Family in the Age of Expansion."

4. Initially Talcott Parsons and his students pioneered in applying Weberian theory to family history. See, for example, Neil Smelser, *Social Change in the Industrial Revolution: An Application of Theory to the British Cotton Industry* (London: University of Chicago Press, 1959). Many subsequent histories of family life, including some excellent ones, have adapted a functional perspective to their own purposes. See, for example, David Levine, *Family Formation in an Age of Nascent Capitalism* (New York: Academic Press, 1977); David Levine, ed., *Proletarianization and Family History* (Orlando, FL: Academic Press, 1984); Hans Medick, "The Proto-Industrial Family Economy: The Structural Function of Household and Family during the Transition from Peasant Society to Industrial Capitalism," *Social History* 1, no. 3 (Oct. 1976): 291–315; Michael Anderson, "Family, Household, and Industrial Revolution," in *The American Family in Social-Historical Perspective,* ed. Michael Gordon, 1st ed. (New York: St. Martin's, 1973); Michael Anderson, *Family Structure in Nineteenth-Century Lancashire* (Cambridge: Cambridge University Press, 1971); Michael Anderson, Frank Bechhofer, and Jonathan Gershuny, eds., *The Social and Political Economy of the Household* (Oxford: Oxford University Press, 1994); Peter Laslett, *Family and Household in Past Time* (Cambridge: Cambridge University Press, 1972). For a general sampling, see *The American Family in Social-Historical Perspective,* ed. Michael Gordon, 2nd. ed. (New York: St. Martin's, 1978) and 3rd. ed. (New York: St. Martin's, 1983). For a more explicit anthropological perspective, see, for example, Jack Goody, *Production and Reproduction* (Cambridge: Cambridge University Press, 1976); Nancie I. Gonzalez, *Black Carib Household Structure: A Study of Migration and Modernization* (Seattle, WA: University of Washington Press, 1969). And, for a critique of functionalism, Christopher Lasch, *Haven in a Heartless World* (New York: Basic Books, 1977).

5. Good examples of this attitude may be found in Louise A. Tilly and Joan W. Scott, *Women, Work, and Family* (New York: Holt, Rinehart & Winston, 1978) and Darret B. Rutman and Anita H. Rutman, *A Place in Time: Middlesex County, Virginia, 1650–1750,* 2 vols. (New York: Norton, 1984).

6. The intrinsic value of marriage and family embodied in the changing forms of both emerges from a wide variety of studies. See, for example, Charles Rosenberg, ed. *The Family in History* (Philadelphia: University of Pennsylvania Press, 1975); Jack Goody, Joan Thirsk, and E. P. Thompson, eds., *Family and Inheritance: Rural Society in Western Europe, 1200–1800* (Cambridge: Cambridge University Press, 1976); Georges Duby, *Le Chevalier, la femme et le prêtre: le mariage dans la France féodale* (Paris: Hachette, 1981); Frances and Joseph Gies, *Marriage and the Family in the Middle Ages* (New York: Harper & Row, 1987); Barbara A. Hanawalt, *The Ties That Bound: Peasant Families in Medieval England* (New York: Oxford University Press, 1986); David Herlihy, *Medieval Households*

(Cambridge, MA: Harvard University Press, 1985); Ernest Bertin, *Les Marriages dans l'ancienne société française* (Genève: Slatkin, 1975; orig. ed., 1879); Christiane Klapisch-Zuber, *Women, Family, and Ritual in Renaissance Italy,* trans. Lydia G. Cochrane (Chicago: University of Chicago Press, 1985); Suzanne Fonay Wemple, *Women in Frankish Society: Marriage and the Cloister, 500–900* (Philadelphia: University of Pennsylvania Press, 1981); Herbert G. Gutman, *The Black Family in Slavery and Freedom, 1750–1925* (New York: Pantheon, 1976); J. Hajnal, "European Marriage Patterns in Perspective," in *Population in History: Essays in Historical Demography,* ed. D. V. Glass and D. E. C. Eversley (London: E. Arnold, 1965); Paul Ourliac and J. de Malafosse, *Le Droit familial,* vol. 3 of *Histoire de droit privé* (Paris: Presses universitaires, 1968); Martine Segalen, *Mari et femme dans la société paysanne* (Paris: Flammarion, 1980); Jean-Louis Flandrin, *Families in Former Times,* trans. Richard Southern (Cambridge: Cambridge University Press, 1979).

7. I offer a more extended discussion in *Within the Plantation Household: Black and White Women of the Old South* (Chapel Hill: University of North Carolina Press, 1988). See also Eugene D. Genovese, *Roll, Jordan, Roll: The World the Slaves Made* (New York: Pantheon, 1975); Gutman, *Black Family;* James Hugo Johnston, *Race Relations in Virginia and Miscegenation in the South, 1766–1860* (Amherst, MA: University of Massachusetts Press, 1970).

8. Robin Fox, *Kinship and Marriage: An Anthropological Perspective* (Harmondsworth: Penguin, 1974).

9. For a fuller discussion of the issues, especially the relation of individualism to family cohesion, see Elizabeth Fox-Genovese, *Feminism without Illusions: A Critique of Individualism* (Chapel Hill: University of North Carolina Press, 1991).

10. For a fuller discussion, see James Gustafson, *Ethics from a Theocentric Perspective,* 2 vols. (Chicago: University of Chicago Press, 1984), 2: 153–84. See also Duby, *Le Chevalier, la femme et le prêtre;* Steven Ozemont, *When Fathers Ruled: Family Life in Reformation Europe* (Cambridge, MA: Harvard University Press, 1983).

11. William N. Eskridge, Jr, *The Case for Same-Sex Marriage: From Sexual Liberty to Civilized Commitment* (New York: Free Press, 1996); Sanford M. Dornbusch and Myra H. Strober, *Feminism, Children, and the New Families* (New York: Guilford Press, 1988); Sharon Elizabeth Rush, "Breaking With Tradition: Surrogacy and Gay Fathers," in *Kindred Matters: Rethinking the Philosophy of the Family,* ed. Diana Tietjens Meyers, Kenneth Kipnis, and Cornelius F. Murphy, Jr. (Ithaca, NY: Cornell University Press, 1993), 102–142. For the opposing position, see, for example, Maggie Gallagher, *The Abolition of Marriage: How We Lost the Right to a Lasting Love* (New York: Regnery Publishing, 1996) and David Popenoe, *Life without Father: Compelling New Evidence That Fatherhood and Marriage Are Indispensable for the Good of Children and Society* (New York: Free Press, 1996).

12. See, for example, Carole Pateman, *The Sexual Contract* (Stanford, CA: Stanford University Press, 1988); Rosalind Coward, *Patriarchal Precedents: Sexuality and Social Relations* (London: Routledge & Kegan Paul, 1983); Ellen Willis, *No More Nice Girls: Countercultural Essays* (Hanover, NH: Wesleyan University Press, 1992); Adrienne Rich, "Compulsory Heterosexuality and the Lesbian Experience," *Signs: Journal of Women in Culture and Society* 4 (1980)[: 631–660].

13. Sir Robert Filmer, *Patriarchia and Other Writings,* ed. Peter Laslett (Oxford: Basil Blackwell, 1949). See also Fox-Genovese, *Feminism without Illusions* and my "Property and Patriarchy in Classical Bourgeois Political Culture," *Radical History Review* 4, nos. 2 & 3 (Spring/Summer 1977): 36–59 [reprinted in this volume, pp. 1–20]. See also

Gordon Schochet, *Patriarchalism in Political Thought: The Authoritarian Family and Political Speculation and Attitudes Especially in Seventeenth-Century England* (New York: Basic Books, 1975).

14. Suzanne Dixon, *The Roman Family* (Baltimore: Johns Hopkins University Press, 1992); Judith P. Hallett, *Fathers and Daughters in Roman Society: Women and the Elite Family* (Princeton: Princeton University Press, 1984); Louis de Loménie, *Les Mirabeau: Nouvelles études sur la société française au XVIIIè siècle*, 5 vols. (Paris, 1879–1891).

15. William Blackstone, *Commentaries on the Laws of England*, 4 vols. (Chicago: University of Chicago Press, 1979; orig. ed., 1765–1769). See also, Margaret J. M. Ezell, *The Patriarch's Wife: Literary Evidence and the History of the Family* (Chapel Hill: University of North Carolina Press, 1987).

16. J. E. Neale, *Queen Elizabeth I* (New York: Doubleday-Anchor Books, 1957).

17. See, for example, Carroll Smith Rosenberg, *Disorderly Conduct: Visions of Gender in Victorian America* (New York: Alfred Knopf, 1985); Ellen Carol DuBois, *Feminism and Suffrage: The Emergence of an Independent Women's Movement in America, 1848–1869* (Ithaca, NY: Cornell University Press, 1978); Mary Roth Walsh, *Doctors Wanted: No Women Need Apply: Sexual Barriers in the Medical Profession, 1835–1975* (New Haven: Yale University Press, 1977); Joan D. Hedrick, *Harriet Beecher Stowe* (New York: Oxford University Press, 1994); Brian Harrison, *Separate Spheres: The Opposition to Women's Suffrage in Britain* (New York: Holmes & Meier, 1978); Martha Vicinus, *Independent Women: Work and Community for Single Women, 1850–1920* (Chicago: University of Chicago Press, 1985); Mary Lyndon Shanley, *Feminism, Marriage, and the Law in Victorian England, 1850–1895* (Princeton: Princeton University Press, 1989); Steven C. Hause with Anne R. Kenney, *Women's Suffrage and Social Politics in the French Third Republic* (Princeton: Princeton University Press, 1984).

18. Gerda Lerner, *The Creation of Patriarchy* (New York: Oxford University Press, 1986) and my review of it in *Journal of the American Academy of Religion* 55, no. 3 (Fall 1987): 608–12.

19. Olwen Hufton, *The Prospect Before Her: A History of Women in Western Europe*, vol. 1, 1500–1800 (New York: Alfred A. Knopf, 1996), esp., 137–76, "On Being a Wife." See also, for example, M. Mitterauer and R. Sieder, *The European Family: From Patriarchy to Partnership from the Middle Ages to the Present* (Oxford: Oxford University Press, 1982); J. Goody, *The Development of the Family and Marriage in Europe* (Cambridge: Cambridge University Press, 1983); Elizabeth Fox-Genovese, "Women and Work," in *French Women and the Age of Enlightenment*, ed. Samia I. Spencer (Bloomington: Indiana University Press, 1984), 111–127 [reprinted in this volume, pp. 75–91]; François Lebrun, *La vie conjugale sous l'ancien régime* (Paris: Armand Colin, 1975); Yves Castan, *Honnêteté et relations sociales en Languedoc (1750–1780)* (Paris: Plon, 1974); Segalen, *Mari et femme*; Flandrin, *Families in Former Times*.

20. Hufton, *Prospect Before Her*; Olwen Hufton, *The Poor in Eighteenth-Century France* (Oxford: Oxford University Press, 1974); E. A. Wrigley and R. S. Schofield, *The Population History of England 1541–1871* (London: Edward Arnold, 1981); William Goode, *World Revolution and Family Patterns* (New York: Free Press of Glencoe, 1963).

21. Robert P. George and Gerard V. Bradley, "Marriage and the Liberal Imagination," *The Georgetown Law Journal* 84, no. 2 (Dec. 1995): 301–320. See also Robert P. George, "Natural Law and Positive Law," in *The Autonomy of Law*, ed. Robert P. George (Oxford: Clarendon Press, 1996), 321–34, and John Finnis, *Natural Law and Natural Rights* (Oxford: Clarendon Press, 1980).

22. Frederick Engels, *The Origin of the Family, Private Property and the State* (New York: International Publishers, 1972); Karen Sacks, *Mothers and Wives: The Past and Future of Sexual Equality* (Westport, CT: Greenwood Press, 1979).

23. For a fuller discussion of the significance, see Fox-Genovese, *"Feminism Is Not the Story of My Life": How the Elite Women's Movement Has Lost Touch with Women's Real Concerns* (New York: Doubleday, 1996) and on some of the implications of the recent sea change, see Richard A. Posner, *Sex and Reason* (Cambridge, MA: Harvard University Press, 1992), and reviews of Posner by Robert P. George, "Can Sex Be Reasonable," *Columbia Law Review* 93, no. 3 (April 1993): 783–794, and Elizabeth Fox-Genovese, "Beyond Transgression: Toward a Free Market in Morals," *Yale Journal of Law and the Humanities* 5, no. 1 (Winter 1993): 243–64.

24. John Locke, *Two Treatises of Government,* ed. Peter Laslett (Cambridge: Cambridge University Press, 1967, and John Locke, *An Essay Concerning Human Understanding,* 2 vols., ed. Alexander Campbell Fraser (New York: Dover, 1959). See also Elizabeth Fox-Genovese, "Property and Patriarchy in Classical Bourgeois Political Culture," *Radical History Review* 4, nos. 2 and 3 (Spring/Summer 1977): 36–59 [reprinted in this volume, pp. 1–20].

25. Notwithstanding some persisting disagreements about timing and effect on the lives of the mass of the population, this view has attained general acceptance, and versions of it pervade most of the vast literature on family and women's history, some of which is cited above.

26. For an elaboration, see Fox-Genovese, *"Feminism Is Not the Story of My Life."*

27. Mary Jo Bane, *Here to Stay: American Families in the Twentieth Century* (New York: Basic Books, 1976).

Eighteen

Equality, Difference, and the Practical Problems of a New Feminism

That we are in sore need of a new feminism can hardly be doubted, and the answer to why we need one could hardly be more disconcertingly simple: the old one has failed. But a wide gap separates recognition of the need from the prospects for meeting it. In recent years recognition of the need has only grown, especially among women of faith. Pope John Paul II has insisted upon its urgency in a series of reflections: his "Letter to Women," written to delegates at the opening of the Beijing conference; his collected Angelus reflections of 1995, *The Genius of Woman;* and his *Mulieres dignitatem.* Sadly acknowledging that "unfortunately even today there are situations in which women live, *de facto* if not legally, in a condition of inferiority," John Paul insists that the prevalence of injustice makes it all the more "urgently necessary to cultivate everywhere a culture of equality, which will be lasting and constructive to the extent that it reflects God's plan."[1] Catholic and other Christian women have been taking up the challenge, although most have focused more upon the theory—philosophy and theology—of the problem than practical programs. What I shall, with no disrespect intended, call the retreat to theory testifies to the daunting complexity of the cultural, political, and practical problems.

The mere suggestion that feminism has failed, much less that it has failed women, would outrage mainstream feminists, although they frequently complain that the gains of the movement are in imminent danger of being reversed. A significant percentage of North American and western European women doubtless concur that, since the 1960s, feminism has decisively contributed to a dramatic improvement in the position of women as individuals, as it undisputably has, although some would legitimately argue that gains on the one hand have carried losses on the other. The gains have been so rapidly and thoroughly integrated into the social fabric of First World nations that there is no reason to reiterate the ways in which feminism has contributed to increasing the dignity and independence of women. Not counting myself among those who seek to return women to the bedroom and the kitchen—were such a return even possible—I have no wish to minimize the intrinsic value of those gains, which, in many respects, are setting a standard for the rest of the world. In much of the world, women face problems that are virtually unimaginable for many of us, and although many of those problems are specific to their devalued situation as women, many are common to the men and children of their communities. Feminists regularly remind us that more needs to be done if women are to attain genuine equality with men, and so it does, especially in the developing world, but it remains debatable whether much of what feminists view as necessary—notably, free access to abortion—will truly serve the interests of women.[2]

Any new feminism must necessarily build upon the "old," even as it struggles to redress its wrongs. Few would contest that feminism has done much to improve aspects of the lives of many women, but as those who seek to formulate a new feminism know, the "improvements" have often come at a daunting cost that feminists are loath to acknowledge. In the first instance, the old feminism has not equally improved the lives of all women—or even all aspects of the lives of the privileged women it has most directly benefited —and it has had demonstrably negative consequences for many aspects of the lives of many women. Yet more important, the strategies of the old feminism have seriously undermined essential features of our culture and moral life, notably our ability to value and nurture human life in all its diversity, our respect for a uniform standard of justice, our willingness to honor any form of natural or divine authority (although other forms of authority are flourishing), our willingness to nurture children and protect childhood, and our ability always to see other persons as ends in themselves—never means to another end.[3]

At the center of this web, theory and practice meet in a union as inseparable as that of soul and body, and here they confront the abiding feminist conundrum—the challenge of reconciling women's difference from men with their equality to them. Increasingly, both secular and Christian theorists claim to have moved beyond this alleged impasse, which they impatiently dismiss as no impasse at all. Some Catholics have even followed the aggressively secular Joan Scott in arguing that we err in viewing difference and equality as opposites when the true opposite of difference is similarity and that of equality is inequality. Others, notably Pia de Solenni, are drawing upon classical Catholic theology to argue that the souls of women and men have always been equal in the eyes of God even as they have also been different and, consequently, called to different roles. The theorists who pursue these discussions from the ground of orthodox Catholicism (including respect for the magisterium and the pope) frequently invoke the analogy of Christ's relation to the church, his bride, or that of the virgin Mary, mother of the church and preeminent exemplar of faith.[4]

Both analogies command respect—nay, admiration—and both capture essential spiritual qualities that a new feminism must include, but spiritual significance notwithstanding, they offer neither an adequate answer to the claims of the old feminism nor an adequate foundation upon which to build a new feminism in the world. Yet more dangerous, they implicitly retreat from the real terrain of struggle, namely, the equality of women and men in the world. However much secular feminists have protested the opposition of equality and difference in theory, they have never freed themselves from it in practice. And for evidence of their abiding attachment to equality as sameness, we need look no further than their unyielding defense of abortion on demand at all stages of a pregnancy, including after birth. Their desperate attachment to this demand reflects nothing more nor less than a commitment to guarantee women the same—"no fault"—sexual freedom they believe men have always enjoyed, which amounts to a covert demand to equalize the physiological difference between women and men. The danger for the prospects of a new feminism lies in the possibility that Christian feminists are effectively restricting their "reconciliation" of equality and difference to the realm of theory, and a viable new feminism must directly confront the realm of practice. For most women understand their lives within the context of the realm of practice or as mediated by its problems.

Equal but different has assuredly not satisfied dissident Catholic feminist theologians like Rosemary Radford Ruether and Elisabeth Schüssler Fiorenza, who are becoming ever more radical with the passage of time. Their demands begin with the sexual liberation of women, grounded in the right to abortion, and extend to women's ordination to the priesthood. They impatiently dismiss the pope's appeal to women "to promote a new feminism which rejects the temptation of imitating models of 'male domination,'" and they deplore his claim that "the experience of motherhood makes you acutely aware of the other person, and at the same time, confers on you a particular task."[5] Their vision of an egalitarian feminist future would leave as little of orthodox Catholicism standing as secular feminists have left of mainstream Protestant churches, respect for marital fidelity, and the two-parent heterosexual family.[6] But restiveness with difference between women and men, especially when it might call for differentiation of roles, much less women's deference to men, has permeated virtually all Christian churches and is leaving a clear mark on the thought of women who consider themselves faithful rather than dissident Christians.

The main Protestant churches, with the Methodists and Episcopalians in the lead, have spawned strong radical feminist movements within their ranks, as the series of "Re-imagining" conferences attests. The Presbyterians join the Methodists and Episcopalians in ordaining women, and many Protestant churches are revising their texts and liturgy in the direction of gender-neutral language and practice. Thus groups such as Christians for Biblical Equality, who apparently see themselves as devout and faithful Christians, express growing dissatisfaction with failures to promote full equality between women and men, whether within marriage or in the leadership of the church as pastors, deacons, and elders. Firm proponents of requiring biblical translations to use gender-inclusive language, they also oppose traditional notions of male headship in marriage.[7]

Many members of Christians for Biblical Equality, like many Catholic women who engage these questions, apparently reject a representation of themselves as radicals, much less as rebels against the teachings of their faith. Many claim to respect the value and significance of sexual difference. Problems only arise with attempts to discuss how that difference should play out in practice: What, if any, social, political, economic—or even familial—roles should be allotted according to sex? Or, to borrow loosely from *Annie Get Your Gun,* what is there that men can do that women cannot do as well or better? What is there that women do that men should not also be obliged to do? The mere posing of such questions underscores the prevailing assumption that men have had the better part—the powers, the thrones, the glory —from which they have unjustly excluded women. This quest for "biblical equality" constitutes a thinly veiled attempt to redress that imbalance, but to do so with Christian charity rather than anger.

Proponents of these and similar positions apparently see themselves as the pioneers of a new Christian feminism, but close examination of their ideas suggests that either they suffer from a breathtaking lack of realism or they are privileging the claims of feminism over those of Christianity by attempting to force Christianity to conform to feminist demands. More important, their attempts to reconcile difference and equality within a Christian context sadly misestimate the magnitude of the task, as much at the level of theory as at the level of practice.[8]

At the level of theory, the discussion must begin with the recognition that feminism originated as the handmaid of individualism and, from the start, has been tied to and informed by the ideals of individual liberty and the equality of individual rights. As an ideology, feminism, which did not receive its official name until late in the nineteenth century, has consistently focused upon securing women's legal equality with men, notably their right to hold property in their own name, to vote, to obtain a divorce and retain custody of children should it be granted, to attend institutions of higher learning, to enter any profession of their choosing, and more. Also from the start, many—although emphatically not all—women's rights activists have been hostile to organized and revealed religion, primarily because they have deplored traditional religious teachings about the appropriate roles of women and men and, especially, their inclination to favor men's domination of women.

Deep resentment of traditional religions' propensity to proclaim women's ordained subordination to men has often blinded women's rights advocates to Christianity's consistent teaching on the equality of all souls in the eyes of God, captured in the familiar words of Saint Paul: "There is neither Jew nor Greek, there is neither slave nor free, there is neither male nor female; for you are all one in Christ Jesus" (Gal. 3:28). By the same token, those who understand the ideal of equality tend to treat all lapses from the ideal as abuses or transgressions. Both perspectives thus slight the rich complexity of Christian—and especially Catholic—thought. The first perspective focuses upon embodied life in this world, while the second focuses upon the innate worth of disembodied souls. But Catholicism views body and soul as indissolubly linked, hence the insistence upon the resurrection of the body. This aspect of Catholic theology opens the door to an understanding of equal but different, but it does not begin to solve the difficulties and contradictions of women's position in the modern—or postmodern—world.

Historically, a comprehensive understanding of equal but different has only flourished in premodern or prebourgeois hierarchical societies, for they, unlike modern individualistic societies, cultivated a notion of difference as organic interdependence. Consequently, while the absolute worth of individuals might be understood as equal—at least to God—their functions in the world were understood as highly differentiated and only under the most exceptional circumstances as interchangeable. Since the great bourgeois revolutions of the seventeenth and eighteenth centuries and the massive cognitive and epistemological revolution that simultaneously provoked, accompanied, and resulted from them, the understanding of equality and difference has undergone a sea change. The premises of individualism, with their emphasis upon autonomy, independence, and self-determination, have made it virtually impossible to imagine an equality grounded in difference, with the result that feminists who seek equality for women have almost invariably been led to deny or abstract from sexual difference.[9]

Here we need not linger over the intellectual convolutions, beginning with the substitution of gender (understood as a social construction rather than an innate attribute) for sex, by which secular feminists have sought to deny the relevance of female bodies to women's social roles and needs. Suffice it to say, they have produced an array of bizarre conclusions, ranging from the rejection of all claims of difference as invidious "stereotyping" to demands for aggressive affirmative action programs to "level" the playing field. Perhaps this contradiction affords their main lesson and offers a salutary caution to Christian women who seek to formulate a new feminism. Difference cannot be wished away, and attempts to legislate away its consequences invariably end in an ominous strengthening of the state that enforces the programs to eliminate it. Unfortunately, the problems that plague the efforts of secular feminists, to reconcile equality and difference, plague those of Christian feminists as well.[10]

Notwithstanding a discourse of mutual love and respect between women and men, Christians for Biblical Equality cannot easily disguise its discomfort with traditional female roles. In recent years discussions of "servant leadership" have proliferated, apparently with a view to binding men to the roles of service traditionally performed by women. The challenge to present the role of servant as admirable and desirable has nonetheless proved daunting, especially since the very attempt to do so betrays the extent to which the secular disdain for service has penetrated Christian thought. It is difficult to ignore the powerful bonds between individualism and secular feminism on the one hand and a rejection of authority, whether natural or divine, on the other. And if we recognize the force of those bonds, we are led, however unwillingly, to recognize that the rejection of authority—and binding covenants—lies at the core of feminism and of the individualism from which it derives. In this perspective we may grasp the emphasis upon self-realization, liberation, and all the rest as neither more nor less than the refusal to be bound by any obligation to God or man. Not for nothing did Elizabeth Cady Stanton devote the last years of her life to a bitter critique of the Bible, which she published as a revised version of the original, entitled *The Woman's Bible*, and entitle her last important piece "The Solitude of the Self."[11]

Catholic feminists have tended to embrace the goals and claims of secular feminists, and their attempts to introduce feminism into the church have constituted a protracted and increasingly insolent challenge to the magisterium on all fronts. Catholics who are seeking a new feminism in keeping with the wishes of Pope John Paul II have scrupulously attempted to avoid those challenges, but for the most understandable of reasons, their contributions to the discussions have tended to remain highly abstract. Doubtless they understand all too well that their invocations of the virgin Mary and the church as the bride of Christ will never satisfy those who view feminism as the defense of women's right to self-determination and self-realization. So, again for the most understandable of reasons, they dodge the tough practical questions: male headship in marriage, marriage as a sacrament, contraception, abortion, homosexuality, extra- and premarital sex, the responsibilities of mothers, and more.

However much Catholic theologians and philosophers, including Saint Teresa Benedicta of the Cross (Edith Stein), Hans Urs von Balthasar, and Pope John Paul II, have emphasized the equal dignity and worth of women and men, they have also consistently insisted upon the difference between them, invariably emphasizing women's special vocation as the bearers and custodians of life. Just as men embody a distinct—and often unmeasured—ambition for power and domination, so do women manifest a special vocation for the care of life, which requires a measure of self-denial and self-abnegation. Nothing in feminism suggests that a woman's true vocation lies in sacrificing her own interests and desires to those of others, and even devout Catholic women have not found it easy to ground a new feminism in women's willing renunciation of self. In this respect the early efforts to formulate a new feminism have been slow to challenge the old feminism's individualist premises. My point is not to minimize the difficulty of the task: individualism has so thoroughly permeated our culture that no sphere, including religion, remains immune to its influence.[12]

Catholic thought, notably but not exclusively on the nature of the human person and the culture of life, nonetheless offers opportunities, which have yet to be pursued, to break through the prison house of individualism. Pope John Paul II in particular has written extensively on the fallacies in understanding the human person as an autonomous or isolate entity. The human person, he insists, exists only in relation to others, just as the three persons of the Trinity exist in relation to one another. Throughout his philosophical writing and, since his ascension to the papacy, in his encyclicals and letters, he has explored the idea and substance of the person as the combination of subjective perception and objective position, and he has countered the abstract concept of the individual with attention to the role of action and choice in the development of the person. Drawing upon a theologically informed existentialism, he has consistently argued, "an existential metaphysics of actual being (*esse actu*) is required to situate the moral agent in the actual context in which one acts."[13] The focus upon action and its context underscores the embodiment of the person and his or her moral and social connection to others. Thus the person cannot be understood as idea or intent—or by extension, desire—in the abstract, but only as idea or intent (or desire) in action. In this perspective no person can be autonomous— "an island," to borrow from John Donne—for each of us remains bound by interdependency and mutual responsibility to all others, and those bonds impose distinct limitations upon the individual freedom of any person. If this identification of the person with action imposes constraints upon individual freedom, it also offers a rich new understanding of freedom, namely, the inherent respect for human dignity that dictates that each person be viewed as an end and never as a means.[14]

If the essence of the human person lies in the union of action and intent —makes subjective consciousness palpable in embodied action—the reality of the person depends upon and cannot be understood or lived without the limitations upon individual freedom imposed by the coexistence of others. Thus does a proper understanding of the human person's relation to freedom return us to the realm of moral authority or, in the words of John Finnis, "moral absolutes."[15] This logic inescapably leads to the conclusion that moral imperatives are linked to the essence of the human person, whose very existence depends upon the independent reality of others. The defense of individual autonomy, liberation, and self-determination that lie at the core of secular feminism reduces to little more than autism—the isolation and anomie of the disconnected.

Catholic theology offers innumerable examples of connection as the core of a living—and lived—faith. In various ways, countless saints have pointed to connection with God as the fulcrum of their being, implicitly echoing the words of Saint Augustine, "Our hearts are restless, O Lord, until they rest in you." This spirit of connection echoes the lessons of humility embodied in the life of the virgin Mary. For as Balthasar has written, "Faith is the surrender of the entire person: because Mary from the start surrendered everything, her memory was the unsullied tablet on which the Father, through the Spirit, could write his entire Word."[16] It is difficult to imagine a starker contrast with the secular feminist imperative that each woman should be free to construct herself—to choose the life she wants even at the cost of other lives. Bluntly put, the contrast opposes the woman who chooses to sacrifice herself for the good of others and the woman who chooses to sacrifice others for her own good. And until we plumb the depths of the contradiction, we shall have poor prospects for constructing a truly new feminism.

Among the many connections that figure so prominently in Catholic theology and faith, the connection between mother and child, as represented in Mary's motherhood of Jesus—Mary the Theotokos—and her motherhood of the church, enjoys a special place and provides a bridge to the lives of ordinary women. Secular feminists have generally deplored women's "imprisonment" in the responsibilities of motherhood and perhaps even more the identification of women with motherhood. In their canon, self-realization requires liberation from domestic servitude to others and the right to play an independent role in the world. The defense of women's right to liberation from children fuels their passionate and uncompromising defense of women's right to abortion on demand, which amounts to a demand for women's liberation from connection.[17]

Secular feminists would vehemently protest the claim that they seek freedom from connection and no less vehemently deny that their ideal of liberation constitutes the cutting edge of the "culture of death." But any new feminism must begin with the recognition that both charges are true. As the bearers of life, women, including those who never bear a child, possess a special affinity for connection and, consequently, potentially embody a special gift for connection. Nowhere is it written that each woman will realize that potential, which must find its realization in specific actions within specific contexts. And we all know that women are capable of chilling cruelty as well as heroic and sacrificial love. In situations, like our own, that discourage any binding connection, the probability that many women will fail in the realization increases exponentially, and massive failures of connection are precisely what is signified by Pope John Paul II's evocation of the culture of death. That women's most fervent aspirations for themselves have taken the form of a revolt against binding connection represents a tragedy of staggering proportions. For if women reject connection, who will embrace it?

My point is embarrassingly simple: there may be innumerable "other" feminisms, but there will be no new feminism until there is a feminism of life. Countless women, including many secular feminists, will doubtless concur, insisting that they "support" the culture of life. Feminists for Life is forging the path and doing admirable work for which we should all be grateful. But for the best of reasons, members of this group emphasize their kinship with the ideals of Susan B. Anthony and Elizabeth Cady Stanton, both of whom opposed abortion but otherwise embraced the essentials of individualism. Even they seem reluctant to tell women that their support for life will frequently require the surrender of their autonomy—their right to choose in many areas. And herein lies our greatest challenge: those who view women's binding connection to the children they conceive as a form of enforced service are not wrong. Nor are those who point to the staggering difficulties of reconciling care for children with worldly success. Nor yet are those who protest that women's primary responsibility to children reinforces their subordination to men, or at least precludes their complete equality with them. As Jesus instructed his disciples, "No one can serve two masters; for either he will hate the one and love the other, or he will be devoted to the one and despise the other. You cannot serve God and mammon" (Matt. 6:24).

Recognition of a binding obligation to others—especially children, but also husband and frequently other members of an extended family—usually forces a woman to adopt a new perspective on her job or career in the world and even, if only for a finite period, relegate it to second place, if not put it on hold for an extended period. This necessity inescapably undermines a woman's ability to compete equally with men in the public world, at least for the short term. A woman's choices for life and fulfilling obligations to others do not, however, necessarily bar her from one or another form of worldly accomplishment. Most women today may expect a significantly longer life span than their foremothers, and countless numbers are finding ways to move in and out of jobs and careers in conformity with the other priorities in their lives. The great secret of such intermittent and unorthodox careers is that those who pursue them frequently prove more successful than their sisters who pursue more conventional tracks.

We should never forget that a woman's experience in domestic life, especially if it includes a serious measure of reflection, self-examination, and meditation, may do more to prepare her for subsequent success in a job or career than innumerable years in a mind-numbing "rat race." There are no guarantees that all women will draw such benefits from running a house and caring for children, but there is a high probability that those who enter into those tasks from the foundation of a strong marriage and in a spirit of willing service and joy in the fostering of human life will. Much depends upon the maturity and faith that permit a woman to choose to assume those obligations for her own reasons rather than responding like the adolescent who is being coerced by her parents. In addition, it has become widely accepted among people of differing economic status that fathers as well as mothers may participate actively in the care and education of children. The difference lies in the inability of fathers to nurse infants and the special bond that pregnancy creates between mother and child. These considerations point to a primary responsibility for women during the first two or three years of a child's life, by which time patterns have been established, which easily lead to an extension of that sexual division of labor within families—especially if more children have been born or are desired or if the parents have decided upon homeschooling.

For feminists, any presumption that women will have primary responsibility for children, much less that they will compromise their careers (and they rarely attend much to the wishes of less affluent women who only hold mere "jobs"), represents a betrayal of women's needs and rights. Their positions on these matters reflect an underlying conviction that justice will free women effectively to become men. Typically those who have most actively opposed feminist positions on women's rights and needs have fallen into the trap of seeing women as fit only for motherhood and service to others. Tragically this unilateral opposition to everything feminism represents has resulted in a general failure to attend to the variety of options from which women may choose. In particular, it has led many of those who most sincerely attend to the needs of children and the fostering of a culture of life to slight the gift of women's vocations to a single life.[18]

The world has a crying need for the talents and dedication of women, who are more than capable of fulfilling innumerable public roles with distinction—and in a spirit of charity and fidelity as well. Single women may choose to live and work as members of religious communities, as independent laypersons in the secular world or in an intermediate status, as for example do the numeraries of Opus Dei and the consecrated members of Commune et Liberazione. In the latter cases they work in the secular world, sometimes living in a community and sometimes on their own, but take vows of fidelity. In any of these capacities, and others, single women bring unique and sorely needed gifts to a vast array of occupations, none of which should be closed to those who have the qualifications for them. The point is not to "condemn" all women to marriage and motherhood, which many women still regard as their highest vocation, but to imagine feminism as a mansion with many rooms and to understand that some choices preclude others—at least in the short run. A new feminism must encompass and honor vocations for single women, just as it must support the distinct vocations of women who are wives and mothers. Both vocations offer ways in which women can contribute to rebuilding a culture of life.

True dedication to the culture of life requires respect for authority, if only the authority of God's commandment not to kill. In practice, that dedication normally also requires respect for the authority of children's nonnegotiable needs and perhaps the authority of a husband—or at least of the sacrament of marriage. There can be no genuine dedication to the culture of life without the surrender of some of our "rights" and a large chunk of our "autonomy." The essence of the culture of life lies in our ability to see others as like ourselves and to see Jesus in each and every one of them. Secular feminism has uncritically embraced the dominant male version of success and insisted that women have an equal right to reap its fruits. This single-minded focus upon worldly success has blinded secular feminists to the understanding that the success they covet also embodies many, if not all, of the attributes and policies they otherwise deplore: brutal competition, the quest for domination, exploitation of the planet and its resources as well as of people, and more.

Edith Stein, a favorite student and assistant of Edmund Husserl, never doubted women's intellectual capabilities or the world's need for their dedicated participation in its work. Yet Stein, recently canonized as Saint Teresa Benedicta of the Cross, also believed the nature of women's contributions differed from those of men. Thus, she cautioned, a man's "one-sided endeavor to achieve perfection easily becomes a decadent aspiration in itself; our desire for knowledge does not respect limits placed on it but rather seeks by force to go beyond these limits; human understanding may even fail to grasp that which is not essentially hidden from it because it refuses to submit itself to the law of things; rather, it seeks to master them in arbitrary fashion or permits the clarity of its spiritual vision to be clouded by desires and lusts."[19]

In emphasizing women's greater propensity to nurture human persons and the earth, Stein never restricted their roles to family responsibilities. To the contrary, she insisted upon women's independent right to vocations in the world and, especially, to the intrinsic value of those vocations. But her enthusiasm about women's vocations did not change her belief that woman's nature differs from that of man in important ways. Many contemporary feminists see any admission that women may differ from men in nature or needs as a shameful capitulation and betrayal of women's rights. On a purely empirical level, most women do not agree, and a new feminism must respect many women's desire to marry, bear and rear children, and anchor a web of binding and loving connections. Beyond the desires of individuals, however, the fate of our world now hangs in the balance.

Many will see a betrayal of justice—and assuredly of feminism—in any suggestion that women may bear a special responsibility to nurture the culture of life, which alone can protect our future. But those who do are, however inadvertently, acknowledging their own imprisonment in outmoded, and increasingly dangerous, ideas. No doubt the ideals of service and sacrifice run directly against the grain of our culture, but if we deny their claims we place ourselves at high risk. Until now, feminism in general—and we all know there are marginal exceptions—has waged a fierce battle to permit women to behave like men and, in the areas in which they cannot, to guarantee them the same results as if they had. A new feminism requires that we muster the courage and the faith to reverse this paradigm. Women throughout the world are in desperate need of policies that respect and protect them as women—not policies that ensure their access to abortion so that they can become as "free" as men. A feminism grounded in the defense of a woman's right to "choose" to have an abortion is inescapably a feminism that promotes the culture of death.

It is never easy to go against the grain, especially when doing so exposes one to social and economic risks. But without the will to defy prevailing ideas, we will condemn ourselves to more of the same. Jesus, in time and place, was profoundly countercultural. A new feminism must follow his lead and direct women's efforts to formulating a new model of the way to be human. Who knows? If we succeed in defending a culture of life in which personhood is understood as mutual recognition rather than autonomy and no person is ever objectified as the means to an end, men—within the constraints of their differences from us—may follow.

Notes

1. *Pope John Paul II on the Genius of Women* (Washington, D.C.: United States Catholic Conference, 1997), p. 22, passage from the Angelus reflections, June 25, 1995. See also Pope John Paul II's "Letter to Women," dated June 29, 1995, and released at the Vatican July 10, 1995; and his *On the Dignity and Vocation of Women: Mulieres Dignitatem*, released in 1987.

2. The heated debates over CEDAW (Convention on the Elimination of All Forms of Discrimination against Women) in 2002 focus precisely upon the different views of the programs that will benefit women and communities even as they reveal the intensity of opposition between the different sides. On October 15, 2002, Cybercast News Service reported that feminist groups, including the Religious Coalition for Reproductive Choice, the National Organization for Women, the National Abortion and Reproductive Rights Action League, hysterically protested President Bush's nomination of Dr. David Hager to the Food and Drug Administration Advisory Panel on the grounds that Hager might be in a position to roll back approval of RU486. On October 17, 2002, the Associated Press reported that following a speech at the Cooley Law School in Lansing, Michigan, Sara Weddington told the *Lansing State Journal* that if Republicans won the fall elections, there would be an imminent danger that *Roe v. Wade* would be overturned.

3. See my development of this argument in Elizabeth Fox-Genovese, *Women and the Future of the Family*, with responses by Stanley I. Grenz, Mardi Keyes, Mary Stewart Van Leeuwen, ed. James W. Skillen and Michelle N. Voll (Grand Rapids: Baker, 2000).

4. Joan Wallach Scott, "Deconstructing Equality-Versus-Difference: Or, the Uses of Poststructuralist Theory for Feminism," *Feminist Studies* 14, no. 1 (1988): 33–50; Pia de Solenni, "The New Feminism: Contributing to a Philosophical and Theological Renaissance" (paper delivered at the Pontifical College of the Holy Cross, November 9, 2001), and her "*Fides et Ratio:* A Context for Developing the New Feminism" (paper delivered at the Twenty-Fifth Annual Convention of the Fellowship of Catholic Scholars, September 28, 2002). See also R. Mary Hayden Lemmons, "Equality, Gender, and John Paul II," *Logos: A Journal of Catholic Thought and Culture* 5, no. 3 (Summer 2002): 111–30.

5. John Paul II, *Evangelium vitae*, #99.

6. "The Campaign for a Conservative Platform," *Conscience* 16, no. 3 (Autumn 1995): 11, 14, quoting *Evangelium vitae. Conscience* is the pro-choice Catholic journal edited by Rosemary Radford Ruether. See also Elisabeth Schüssler Fiorenza, "Feminist

Theology as a Critical Theology of Liberation," in *Churches in Struggle: Liberation Theologies and Social Change in North America,* ed. William K. Tabb (New York: Monthly Review Press, 1986), pp. 46–66; Rosemary Radford Ruether, *Disputed Questions: On Being a Christian* (Nashville: Abingdon, 1982); Elisabeth Schüssler Fiorenza, *Discipleship of Equals: A Critical Feminist Ekklesia-logy of Liberation* (New York: Crossroad, 1993); and for a general discussion of feminist theologians' attitudes toward Mary and women's relation to the church, Maurice Hamington, *Hail, Mary? The Struggle for Ultimate Womanhood in Catholicism* (New York and London: Routledge, 1995).

7. For a brief account of the 2002 meeting of Christians for Biblical Equality, see Judith Person, "Christian Meeting to Study Sex Roles," *Washington Times,* September 24, 2002, available online at http://www.washtimes.com/culture/20020924–21282920. htm. For examples of the Protestant arguments, see Mary Stewart Van Leeuwen, "Re-Inventing the Ties That Bind: Feminism and the Family at the Close of the Twentieth Century," and other contributions in *Religion, Feminism, and the Family,* ed. Anne Carr and Mary Stewart Van Leeuwen (Louisville: Westminster John Knox, 1996). See also Mary Stewart Van Leeuwen et al., *After Eden: Facing the Challenge of Gender Reconciliation* (Grand Rapids: Eerdmans, 1993). For similar arguments from a Catholic, see Regina A. Coll, *Christianity and Feminism in Conversation* (Mystic, Conn.: Twenty-Third Publications,1994), and Corinne Patton, "Catholic and Feminist: We Are Called to Be Both—Response to Elizabeth Fox-Genovese," *Logos: A Journal of Catholic Thought and Culture* 2, no. 4 (Fall 1999): 27–38.

8. For preliminary criticisms of these attempts, see Elizabeth Fox-Genovese, "Catholic and Feminist: Can One Be Both?" *Logos: A Journal of Catholic Thought and Culture* 2, no. 4 (Fall 1999): 11–26, and my "Response to Corinne Patton," pp. 39–48 in the same issue; Donna Steichen, *Ungodly Rage: The Hidden Face of Catholic Feminism* (San Francisco: Ignatius, 1991); and Francis Martin, *The Feminist Question: Feminist Theology in the Light of the Christian Tradition* (Grand Rapids: Eerdmans, 1994).

9. For a discussion of the distinct character of individualism and feminism's relation to it, see Elizabeth Fox-Genovese, *Feminism without Illusions: A Critique of Individualism* (Chapel Hill: University of North Carolina Press, 1991).

10. The leading proponent of these arguments is probably Judith Butler, *Gender Trouble* (New York: Routledge, 1990) and her *Bodies That Matter: On the Discursive Limits of Sex* (New York: Routledge, 1993).

11. Elizabeth Cady Stanton and the Revising Committee, *The Woman's Bible,* pts. I and II (Seattle: Coalition Task Force on Women and Religion, 1974; original ed., 1898). For a preliminary discussion of the radicalism of her religious views, see Elizabeth Fox-Genovese, "Contested Meanings: Women and the Problem of Freedom in the Mid-Nineteenth-Century United States," in *Historical Change and Human Rights: The Oxford Amnesty Lectures, 1994,* ed. Olwen Hufton (New York: Basic Books, 1995), pp. 179–215 [reprinted in this volume, pp. 167–96].

12. See James Davison Hunter, *Before the Shooting Begins: Searching for Democracy as the Culture Wars Rage* (New York: Free Press, 1994). See also Elizabeth Fox-Genovese, "How Abortion Has Failed Women," *Crisis* 18, no. 3 (March 2000): 32–37.

13. Kenneth L. Schmitz, *At the Center of the Human Drama: The Philosophical Anthropology of Karol Wojtyla / John Paul II* (Washington, D.C.: Catholic University of America Press, 1993), p. 126. For a thoughtful introduction to Karol Wojtyla / John Paul II's thought, see this work by Schmitz. See also Rocco Buttiglione, *Karol Wojtyla: The Thought of the Man Who Became Pope,* trans. Paolo Guietti and Francesca Murphy (Grand Rapids:

Eerdmans, 1997), and George Weigel, *Witness to Hope: The Biography of John Paul II* (New York: Cliff St. Books, 1999).

14. For the development of Karol Wojtyla's thought on these questions during his years as a professor at the University of Dublin, see his *Person and Community: Selected Essays,* trans. Theresa Sandok, O.S.M. (New York: Peter Lang, 1993).

15. John Finnis, *Moral Absolutes: Tradition, Revision, and Truth* (Washington, D.C.: Catholic University of America Press, 1991).

16. Augustine, *Confessions* 1.1; Hans Urs von Balthasar, *Mary for Today,* trans. Robert Nowell (San Francisco: Ignatius, 1996; original ed., 1987), p. 45.

17. See Jaroslav Pelikan, *Mary through the Centuries: Her Place in the History of Culture* (New Haven: Yale University Press, 1995), and my review of it, "The Evolution of Mary: From the Gospels to Mariology to Feminist Critiques," *Books and Culture* 3 (May–June 1997): 34–36. For an extreme—but starkly honest—version of the argument that women should not be burdened by responsibility for children and should treat an unwanted pregnancy as an invasion by a hostile intruder, see Cynthia Daniels, *At Women's Expense: State Power and the Politics of Fetal Rights* (Cambridge: Harvard University Press, 1993).

18. For the ways elite feminists have ignored the concerns and interests of the majority of women, see Elizabeth Fox-Genovese, *"Feminism Is Not the Story of My Life": How the Feminist Elite Has Lost Touch with the Real Concerns of Women* (New York: Doubleday / Nan Talese, 1996). On the value of a distinct role for men as fathers, see W. Bradford Wilcox, "Religion, Convention, and Paternal Involvement," *Journal of Marriage and Family* 64 (August 2002): 780–92.

19. Edith Stein, *Woman,* trans. Freda Mary Oben (Washington, D.C.: ICS Publications, 1987), p. 70.

Nineteen

Feminism and the Unraveling
of the Social Bond

It has not been easy to acknowledge that feminism has promoted the unraveling of the most binding and important social bonds. Not easy, but unavoidable. Like countless other women who cherish improvement in the situation of women in the United States and throughout the world, I was initially quick to embrace feminism as the best way to secure our "rights" and our dignity as persons. Like countless others, I was seriously misled.

As a child, I dreamed of becoming the first woman president of the United States and of having twenty-three children. I have accomplished neither, but the spirit that informed those dreams has continued to inform my aspirations for a just and humane society. Beginning in the 1960s, the feminist movement seemed to offer an appropriate strategy for promoting full social participation for women. Coming in the wake of the Civil Rights movement, the women's movement seemed an overdue response to the social, legal, and economic liabilities that curtailed women's access to countless opportunities. Many of us rather uncritically responded to the call to work for the improvement in women's situation, even when we had nagging doubts about the leaders or particular strategies of the movement.

My own doubts were rooted in my erstwhile dream of twenty-three children and the attendant assumption that I would be blessed with a loving and enduring marriage. Naïve as my expectations may seem today, they had never included the possibility that feminism would require the sacrifice of marriage and children—a binding connection to other persons.

Although not at the time a practicing Christian, I had been imbued with traditional Christian values and teachings, laced with a strong dose of Calvinist morality. That Calvinist legacy, especially as conveyed by the grandmother I adored, prepared me to respect the claims of duty and loyalty, especially to the family members to whom our obligations are greatest. Never was I promised a rose garden, but I was taught to find unexpected rewards in hard work and self-denial. Coming from this background, I found no appeal in the rhetoric and goals of "liberation," and sexual liberation in particular did not rank high on my list of women's just demands. But for the movement as a whole, sexual liberation rapidly moved to the top of the charts.

In 1973, most of us knew much less about abortion than we know today. Thus I, among many, did not immediately grasp its ominous implications. I never much liked the idea of abortion, but mainly because I mistrusted the language of "rights" in which it was couched. How, I asked myself, could we justify giving one person the "right" to take the life of another? The only solution I could see was to defend a social consensus about the beginning of life and to argue that viable life only begins at what the Church once called "quickening," namely after three months.[1] But even before my reception in the Church, my opposition had gradually stiffened. Euthanasia, or what is euphemistically known as "assisted suicide," played a growing role in my thought, for, in the case of euthanasia abuse was so easy—and so often self-serving and convenient. Ronald Dworkin's *Life's Dominion* forcefully brought home the complacency with which we privileged intellectuals decide for others which "quality of life" is worth living.[2] And those thoughts brought me back to abortion. How can we ever be sure that an "unplanned pregnancy" will not be a blessing?

Feminism has officially declared that no woman should ever suffer the burdens of an undesired pregnancy, a position that feminists prefer to translate into the platitude that each child must be "wanted." But children are not convinced by platitudes. A mother's right to bear only the children she chooses puts the children on a very short leash: wanted one moment, they can never be sure of still being wanted the next.

But then feminism has, from the start, cast the care for children as work fit only for servants, or at least as work that no woman should ever be compelled to shoulder. That attitude, as the King of Siam said to Anna, "is a puzzlement." He was referring to the modern practices that were pressing for an increase in equality of status between a monarch and his subjects and between a man (king that he might be) and a woman. But the early glimmers of modernity that troubled His Majesty were the direct precursors of the feminism that today is sundering relations between women and men and parents and children.

As rules go, the words of the Preacher have held up as well as any: "The thing that hath been, it is that which shall be; and that which is done is that which shall be done: and there is no new thing under the sun. Is there any thing whereof it may be said, See, this is new? It hath been already of old time, which was before us." (Ecclesiastes 1:9–10) The book of Ecclesiastes abounds with assurances about continuities, and it warns against the vanity of pretenses, whether to wisdom or to accomplishment or to abiding fame. And well into the twentieth century, its vision seemed to prevail. Its verses afforded Ernest Hemingway the title for *The Sun Also Rises,* which he borrowed from "The sun also ariseth, and the sun goeth down, and hasteth to the place where he arose," (Ecclesiastes 1:5) just as it afforded Pete Seeger "To every thing there is a season, and a time to every purpose under heaven." (Ecclesiastes 3:1)

Throughout history, societies and cultures have revered and relied upon tradition. Even Western civilization, with its predilection for revolutions, has viewed human nature as essentially unchanging. And although patterns of relations between the sexes have varied widely, the understanding of human nature has everywhere been grounded in sexual difference. Chinese and Andean peasants have assuredly differed about the specifics, as both differed from the citizens of ancient Athens and from the nobles of medieval or early modern Europe. Yet each group, in its own way, took the difference between the sexes as an article of faith and took the sexuality of nubile young women as a matter of great consequence. The seeming universality of these patterns lends a patina of plausibility to feminist arguments that human history is nothing but the saga of men's domination of women. Feminists insist that patriarchy has constituted the oldest, most intractable, and most enduring social system and that the oppression of women trumps all competitors, notably oppression by class and race.

Competition over who suffers the greatest oppression persists, but its outcome does not affect the claim that sexual difference has constituted the cornerstone of the practical and symbolic life of all cultures and civilizations. Men and women's specific social, political, and economic roles have varied widely from one society to another, but notwithstanding the surprising variety in the allocation of male and female roles, most—if not all—societies have insisted on the significance of sexual difference itself. Yes, moralists, pundits, official story-tellers, and other custodians of community mores have typically insisted that nature has ordained women for one or another specific role, frequently—although not always—in obedience and subservience to male kin. But cross-culturally, the point is not so much the specific roles as the difference between the roles of women and those of men.

This distinction is central to an understanding of our contemporary situation and especially to the broadside attack on women's "natural" roles within families. The attitudes and customs that have restricted women to specific roles have proven easy targets for feminists. Recent decades have witnessed the collapse of the obstacles to women's participation in countless occupations. It has become increasingly difficult to argue that women cannot enter virtually any occupation or profession they choose, including some for which nature, arguably, has not endowed them. We now have women who serve as police chiefs or sheriffs, serve in the armed forces, serve as fire fighters, and who have made it impossible for any to doubt women's ability to excel as athletes. The growing popular recognition of women's abilities paved the way for radicals to conflate this new (and often guilty) acknowledgment that women had been excluded from many opportunities, with the claim that there is no natural difference between the sexes. The sleight of hand is worthy of an accomplished magician, and, like the best feats of magic, it has successfully displaced public attention from what is really happening.

What is really happening may well be what the Preacher of Ecclesiastes thought we would never see: something new under the sun. For throughout the twentieth century, and at an accelerating rate toward its close, the peoples of the globe experienced a magnitude and rate of change without precedent in human experience. Between the opening of the century and its close, the world's population increased threefold. As recently as 1900, most of the world's people lived on the land and worked in subsistence agriculture, usually with hand tools that had changed little for centuries. Even the economically dynamic United States did not become fifty percent urban until 1920. Until then, Britain was alone in having more than half its population in cities, torn from the familiar social and moral context of rural life. The twentieth century revolutionized the life of agricultural people throughout the globe. As 2000 dawned, more that half of the world's population lived in cities. During the same period, life expectancy rose from forty-five to seventy-five years, and, in the 1990s, the risk of dying in childbirth was at least forty times less than a mere fifty years before, although some forms of abortion may be causing a new—and largely hidden—increase in those risks.

In the short run, these changes produced an increase of population, but the increase resulted from medical advances that defer death rather than from an increase in births. Recent demographic studies confirm that hysteria about overpopulation is sorely misguided. Some parts of the world have experienced an increase in births, but even this increase does not portend more of the same in the future. Since the first decade of the twenty-first century, the dramatic decline in birth rates in the most highly developed countries had been followed by an unexpectedly sharp decline in the less developed countries. That decline resulted in part from the continuous appearance of new viruses and epidemics that resist existing drugs, but also from an increase in abortion and perhaps a growing use of contraception.[3]

In the most highly developed countries, notably the United States and Western Europe, but also Japan, declining birthrates have resulted from choices that apparently reflect a desire to maximize material affluence. But the decline in births has also increased the dependence on immigration to fill necessary jobs and support the health and retirement expenses of the indigenous population. Decline in birth rates is more ominous in southern Africa, where half or more of the population risks being wiped out by the devastating spread of AIDS. As much as eighty percent of all children there are likely to be orphans within a few years, many of them infected with HIV. Meanwhile, the enforced limitation of births in China is resulting in a surplus of boys that bodes ill for China's internal and external peace. Together with the breathtaking technological advances that have literally transformed the world, these changes have had a powerful impact on the attitudes and culture of those who have lived through them.

In one century, we have effectively doubled the material progress of all previous history, and, in so doing, cut ourselves adrift from most of the accumulated wisdom and practices of previous centuries. Across the globe, peoples are being wrenched from traditional communities, some moving to the cities of their own countries, others swelling the waves of migration that are transforming the developed world. Some are profiting from new opportunities, but many more are suffering a sharp decline in their quality of life, and something between ten and thirty percent of the world's population has fallen into an underclass that has "lost touch with the labor market, with the political community, and with social participation more generally."[4]

The global economy is drawing peoples into a tightening web. It gravitates to the cheapest labor, continually strives to reduce the number of workers, and, by its very material success, promotes a growing social, political, and moral disfranchisement among those it touches—whether rich or poor.

The same tendencies that are consigning the poorest among us to the scrap heap of crime, drugs, disease, and early death are seducing the wealthiest into the moral bankruptcy that inexorably derives from the repudiation of responsibility for others.

Throughout the most highly developed nations, secularism has launched a full-scale attack against tradition, especially against belief in any form of divine or natural authority. The privileged of the earth deny that any authority may legitimately limit the freedom of the individual, who obeys only the dictates of personal will or desire. Meanwhile, within the developed nations and especially beyond their borders, religious fundamentalists are vehemently rejecting what they view as the social and cultural corruption of modernity.

In different ways and at different rates, both secularism and fundamentalism have contributed to what Pope John Paul II has designated the culture of death—a culture that holds human life cheaper and cheaper until it drains it of all intrinsic value, a culture that transforms people into objects or even obstacles. This self-portrait has little appeal for the affluent of the developed world, who have no patience with the idea of the culture of death, and even less with the picture of themselves as its purveyors. Caught up in a world overflowing with commodities and armed with a science that promises to extend and even create human life, they find it easy to take their unprecedented material prosperity as the standard for human fulfillment.[5]

This unprecedented material prosperity has flourished against the backdrop of the bloodiest and perhaps the most eventful century in history. Its unending succession of local and global wars has perpetrated an unprecedented slaughter of combatants and non-combatants alike. The wars have triggered a massive displacement of peoples and a seemingly continuous drawing and redrawing of national boundaries. In their accelerating indifference to the distinction between military and civilian targets, they have encouraged the proliferation of brutality and terror. Those caught in the grip of the wars have demonstrated the ability to survive "theoretically intolerable conditions," but their very endurance has deadened the rest of us to our "accelerating return to what our nineteenth-century ancestors would have called the standards of barbarism."[6] Arguably, the twentieth century witnessed the horrors that Moses promised to the children of Israel should they turn away from their God.

Together with the revolutionary developments of the century, the proliferating atrocities inexorably hardened lines both within and among nations and between the affluent and the dispossessed, imposing unprecedented hardship on some while showering unprecedented material prosperity on others. According to Eric Hobsbawm, the century was "the age of extremes," and the most striking characteristic of its close may well have been the tension between the "accelerating process of globalization and the inability of both public institutions and the collective behavior of human beings to come to terms with it."[7] These words, written by a great Marxist historian, might well have come from a Christian. Privately, individuals may cope well, but mediating institutions—notably families and churches—are in disarray.

Critics of both Left and Right have bemoaned the centrifugal pull of modernity on social institutions, and notwithstanding vehement disagreements, both groups have especially focused on the dehumanizing tendencies of the economy and urban life. At the same time, feminists have sharply attacked the social, religious, and political institutions of the West for their oppression of women, whom they excluded from the benefits of individualism. In this instance, feminist hostility seems sorely misplaced since the very institutions they are attacking fostered the emergence of modern feminism. The ideals of individual freedom and political democracy are distinctly Western—and Christian—and their political vocabulary of freedom, equality, and democracy has provided women with the principal justification for their campaign to enjoy the full status of citizenship.[8]

Many women remain dissatisfied with the results of women's independent access to public life, usually on the grounds that formal equality with men has not netted women an equal share of wealth, power, and prestige. But it is hard to deny that the change—improvement—in women's situation has been revolutionary. Indeed, if there is a negative side to these developments it lies in the dramatic erosion of social institutions, most of all the family. One of the major consequences of feminist political efforts during the past three or four decades has been decisively to blur the boundary between public and private and, by extension, between political and social institutions. In this respect, the chickens of the early slogan of Second Stage Feminism, "the personal is political," have come home to roost in the growing politicization of personal relations.

Since the middle of the nineteenth century, but at a rapidly accelerating rate since the 1960s, feminism has been waging a relentless attack on all institutions, notably the family and the Church, that have curtailed women's autonomy, and, in this respect, it has become the cutting edge of the most destructive aspects of modernity. Feminism has primary responsibility for a redefinition of the right to privacy that substitutes the individual for the couple or the family and that, as Mary Ann Glendon has cogently argued, represents a radical departure from American and Western European legal norms. Symbolically, the reduction of privacy to the privacy of the solitary individual sounds the death knell of social institutions, especially the family, as organic units with claims upon their members.

My point is neither to deny nor minimize the abuses to which women have been subjected. Had not the abuses so often been so egregious, the revolt against them might not have been so destructive. But they were, and we are left with the wreckage—and the question of whether the improvement in women's position in the family and in the world was worth the price, which, today, seems daunting. More troubling yet is the question of whether the struggle to improve women's situation was waged on the right grounds or for the right reasons. At issue is not the legitimacy of women's complaints, but the inherent justice of feminists' proposed solutions, which have pushed individualism to its most destructive limits in the claim that a woman's freedom from oppression depends on her right to have an abortion at any stage in a pregnancy.

From a social perspective, the succession of Supreme Court decisions on abortion since *Roe v. Wade* in 1973 has furthered the tendency to dissolve the family as an organic unit into the random collection of its current members. *Planned Parenthood of Central Missouri v. Danforth* (1976) denied the husband's right to participate in his wife's decision to continue or terminate a pregnancy.[9] By this logic, the husband has no more stake in his wife's pregnancy than any other individual—and, consequently, as Tiffany R. Jones and Larry Peterman argue, "there is nothing of one's own in the most serious sense left for husbands in the family."

Planned Parenthood of Southeastern Pennsylvania v. Casey (1992) drove the consequences home, holding that a husband "has no enforceable right to require a wife to advise him before she exercises her personal choices." She has no obligation to obtain her husband's consent for an abortion and no obligation to notify him she is having one. The very idea that a husband has an interest in his wife's pregnancy reflects "a different understanding of the family" from that which these court rulings advance.

Casey made explicit the social and economic assumptions that underlie the case for abortion on demand: since women had become accustomed to the free disposition of their sexuality and labor, an unplanned pregnancy should not be allowed to interfere with their ability to support themselves—or force a man or the government to do so for them. If the woman can afford a child, she has the right to carry her pregnancy to term, and if she cannot, she must have the "right" to abort it. For feminists the right to abortion is necessary to the defense of women's sexual liberation. For elite men and women, it is too often the defense of their freedom from economic responsibility for those less fortunate than they. The consequence of both attitudes is to reduce an unborn baby to the status of a material object—a possession to be disposed of at will. It should make us thoughtful that, on this point, the largest and most powerful business interests and the feminist activists agree.

In defending abortion as the cornerstone of women's liberation, feminists, whether intentionally or naively, expose the contradictions at the heart of the movement—and its moral bankruptcy. In truth, those who claim that there are "many" feminisms have a point—albeit a very limited one. In my judgment, there are not many feminisms, but one, if only because there is only one official political movement, and it has the Democratic Party in a vise. But there are many different feminist positions on a variety of questions, and they are often in contradiction. Some feminists attach great importance to differences among women by race, ethnicity, and class. Others do not. Some see women as innately nurturing and loving, others reject the idea of any innate attributes. Feminists may see themselves as women of faith or as resolutely secular, as fundamentally the same as men or as radically different from them, and so on *ad infinitum*. But, in the end, the vaunted diversity of feminisms is little more than a question of fashion or style.

Feminism rests upon the conviction that no one has the right to tell a woman what to do—to abridge her right to self-determination—or to compromise her absolute equality with men. All the variants on feminism are thus united by a fierce commitment to individualism and equality, and all fundamentally reject the notion of legitimate authority. The right to woman's "liberation" from the thralldom of womanhood to which her foremothers were bound ultimately depends upon her liberation from binding ties to others and especially to tradition or historical precedent. The "difference between the sexes" is but another of those lies that were perpetrated on women to keep them barefoot and pregnant—or fashionable and pregnant as the case might be. The real kicker was the pregnant, for pregnancy and the children to which it led did more even than men to exclude women from the full range of opportunities and occupations. Thus feminism, which had originated in the commitment to defend women as a sex, came to repudiate sex in favor of "gender," and feminists rapidly convinced the culture at large that to use any other term was *ipso facto* an act of discrimination.[10]

This line of reasoning led directly to the defense of abortion on demand as the only sure guarantee of women's individual rights and their equality with men. For feminists, the issue was not the taking of a human life but "choice"—the protection of a woman's right to choose her own destiny. Most resented the suggestion that a woman who had an abortion was killing her child, although a few candid souls, notably Cynthia Daniels, did—and justified the killing on the grounds that the child was a predator, draining her very substance.[11] Daniels was rare in her willingness to defend abortion as a woman's right to fight for her own survival, but those who lacked her candor shared her conviction that at issue was the right of survival. Increasingly, abortion emerged as the litmus test of what it means to be a feminist. "Feminists for Life" is making a brave attempt to contest this terrain, but have yet to make much political headway.

The radical individualism of the pro-abortion feminists runs directly counter to Catholic teaching on matters of faith and morals and Catholic theology of the human person. In the simplest possible terms, to grant one person the "right" to kill another is to succumb to the ultimate objectification. Recently, there has been a concerted attempt to dismiss the position as political partisanship, but it is deeply misguided. The Church, Denver

Archbishop Charles Chaput recently wrote, "is never partisan, but that doesn't change the fact that abortion is the central social issue of this moment in our national history—not the only issue, but the foundational issue; the pivotal issue. For Catholics to ignore it or downplay it or 'contextualize' it would be an act of cowardice."

Catholics for a Free Choice openly opposes Church teaching on abortion and, in defending a woman's right to have an abortion, effectively embraces a Protestant, or even secular, notion of individualism. Many other Catholics nurture a more covert opposition to Church teaching and, especially, to the authority of the Magisterium. A favorite cause among these dissenters is women's access to the priesthood. Many find the cause a matter of simple justice—how can we deny women the same opportunities as men? How can we stifle a woman's conviction of the "vocation" to the priesthood? Time and space preclude my offering a full answer here, but the simple answer is that the case for women priests depends entirely upon secular arguments and, whatever the intentions of those who advance them, effectively encourages the subjection of the Church to Caesar's laws. Doubtless there are women who could become excellent, dedicated priests, but the Church—especially these days—offers other opportunities for the exercise of their gifts. And they have yet to answer the arguments about the direct descent from the apostles or, as far as I can tell, to grasp its true implications, notably the importance in Catholicism of embodiment. We believe in the Real Presence and the resurrection of the body. Admitting women to the priesthood would be to undercut the material grounding of both and thus to sacrifice the essence of Catholic theology and faith to the personal ambitions of individuals. Surely, we can do better.

The radicals and secularists have so thoroughly co-opted the debate over feminism—over women's nature, vocation, and destiny—that it has become virtually impossible to recognize how much is really at stake. For under the guise of, "How could any charitable person deny this promising young woman the opportunity to develop her talents to the full and in precisely the way she sees fit?" we are being asked to concede the very notion of the human person as necessarily connected to others. Sadly but inescapably, the sexual liberation of women—appropriately known as the sexual revolution—has led to the disintegration of the family, the objectification of the person, and the repudiation of all binding ties among individuals. Pray recall that the same Saint Paul who gave us the beloved words, "In Christ there is neither" also gave us, "For you were called to freedom, brethren; only do not use your freedom as an opportunity for the flesh, but through love be servants of one another." (Galatians 5:13) And he left the Galatians, to whom these remarks were addressed, with the cautionary, "Do not be deceived; God is not mocked, for whatever a man sows, that he will also reap. For he who sows to his own flesh will from the flesh reap corruption." (Gal 6:7–8)

In practice, the sexual liberation of women has realized men's most predatory sexual fantasies. As women shook themselves free from the norms and conventions of sexual conduct, men did the same.[12] There can be no doubt that women's situation has demanded improvement—and continues to do so throughout much of the world. But the emphasis upon individual rights at the expense of mutual responsibility and service is not the way to secure it. Worse, it is destroying the fabric of our society as a whole because it is severing the most fundamental social bonds. Binding ties constrain women, but they constrain men as well. As Danielle Crittenden has noted, the family "has never been about the promotion of rights but the surrender of them—by *both* the man and the woman."[13]

The point is emphatically not to blame women, who often suffer from these developments. By destroying the stigma that condemned women for sexual activity outside of marriage, the ethos of sexual liberation, combined with the feminist campaign against marriage and motherhood, has directly contributed to our declining birth rate, the proliferation of single parents, and the number of children born outside of marriage. The new economic forces and systems that have come to dominate global life systematically erode institutionalized family life.[14] The new multi-national economic giants have no need for stable families, which may actually interfere with their ability to manage workers and sell goods.

Under these conditions, we cannot expect the world of production to foster the restoration of a responsible and ordered social and moral life. In the United States—and much of the Western world—women have always borne a disproportionate responsibility to embody moral precepts, and women have been noticeably more likely than men to practice the virtues of faith in everyday life. Today, feminism has taught us to view the practice of these virtues as work fit only for servants. In this scenario, a child, rather than a joy, a blessing, a promise for the future, becomes only a burden. The idea that sexual freedom is an individual right, which must be liberated from any reproductive consequences, has decisively contributed to the terrifying cheapening of life that has dominated the twentieth century and is opening the twenty-first. What most of its defenders fail to recognize is how well it supports the most sinister aspects of a global economy that is pulling people out of family and community settings and, in so doing, seriously eroding our ability to imagine and defend an idea of the human person as one who must never be objectified—must never be treated as a means rather than an end.

Notes

1. "Women's Rights, Affirmative Action, and the Myth of Individualism," *George Washington Law Review* [54] (Fall 1986)[: 338–74].

2. Ronald Dworkin, *Life's Dominion: An Argument about Abortion, Euthanasia, and Individual Freedom* (New York [: Knopf], 1993), and my review in *The Washington Post* (1993).

3. Phillip Longman, *The Empty Cradle: How Falling Birthrates Threaten World Prosperity and What to Do About It* (New York [: Basic Books], 2004), and Marina Melenic, "Decline and Fall," *The American Spectator,* online edition (June 14, 2004). See also, LifeSiteNews.com, Wellington, June 15, 2004, reports on newly released statistics on New Zealand that reveal "a steady increase in the abortion rate in New Zealand," which "had 1130 more abortions in 2003 than 2002." Of these abortions, one in three were on women who had already had an abortion, and "and the jump was even higher for women between the ages of 15 and 20, from 20 to 21 per 1000. One in ten had already had two or more abortions."

4. *The Oxford History of the Twentieth Century,* ed. Michael Howard and Wm. Roger Lewis (New York: Oxford University Press, 1999), 337.

5. For a thoughtful discussion of the assault on tradition, see Eric Miller, "Alone in the Academy," *First Things,* no. 110 (February 2004): 30–34.

6. [Eric J.] Hobsbawm, [*The Age of Extremes: A History of the World, 1914–1991* (New York: Pantheon Books, 1994),] 13.

7. [Hobsbawm, *The Age of Extremes,* 15.]

8. Kwame Anthony Appiah, *In My Father's House: Africa in the Philosophy of Culture* (New York: Oxford University Press, 1993); Orlando Patterson, *Freedom, Vol. 1: Freedom in the Making of Western Culture* (repr. ed., New York: Basic Books, 1992).

9. 428 U.S. 52 (1976), at 70, cited by [Tiffany Jones and Larry Peterman, "Whither the Family and Family Privacy?" 4 *Texas Review of Law and Politics* (Fall 1999)].

10. For an introduction to the theories on sex and gender, see Judith Butler.

11. Cynthia Daniels, *At Women's Expense: State Power and the Politics of Fetal Rights* Cambridge, MA: [Harvard University Press,] 1993.

12. George A. Akerlof, Janet L. Yellen, and Michael L. Katz, "An Analysis of Out-of-Wedlock Childbearing in the United States," *Quarterly Journal of Economics* CXI (1996): 277–317. It should be noted that Akerlof, Yellen, and Katz write from the liberal rather than the conservative end of the political spectrum. Indeed former President Clinton appointed Janet L. Yellen to the Council of Economic Advisors.

13. Danielle Crittenden, *What Our Mothers Didn't Tell Us: Why Happiness Eludes the Modern Woman* (New York: Simon & Schuster, 1999), 110.

14. For the sexual and economic revolution, see Elizabeth Fox-Genovese, "*Feminism Is Not the Story of My Life*" (Doubleday 1996). See also Francis Fukuyama, *The Great Disruption: Human Nature and the Reconstitution of Social Order* ([New York:] Free Press, 1999), and the discussions by Alan Wolfe, "The Shock of the Old," *The New Republic,* No. 4411 (August 2, 1999): 42–46, and also David Brooks, "Disruption and Redemption," *Policy Review,* No. 95 (June & July, 1999): 72–77.

Selected Bibliography of Works by Elizabeth Fox-Genovese

Compiled by Ehren K. Foley

This bibliography provides a listing of those works written by Elizabeth Fox-Genovese that deal substantially with the themes of this volume. It is divided into books, coauthored books, edited and coedited works, and articles, including contributed chapters and review essays. Items in each section are listed chronologically by date of original publication. Included are items in this volume, related items in other volumes of this series, and those items that were excluded from this volume by constraints on space or by editorial decision. While the bibliography does strive for comprehensive coverage, it doubtless falls short of that goal. Several conscious omissions are worth noting. The bibliography does not include the many short book reviews and articles that Fox-Genovese authored during her career. It also omits those items that deal with themes addressed in the other volumes of this series, though there is some overlap between volumes. A full sense of the breadth of Fox-Genovese's work therefore requires perusal of each of the first four volumes of the selected edition of Elizabeth Fox-Genovese's writings and its accompanying bibliography.

Books
1991
Feminism without Illusions: A Critique of Individualism. Chapel Hill: University of North Carolina Press, 1991.

1996
"Feminism Is Not the Story of My Life": How Today's Feminist Elite Has Lost Touch with the Real Concerns of Women. New York: Nan A. Talese, 1996.

2008
Marriage: The Dream That Refuses to Die, edited by Sheila O'Connor-Ambrose. Wilmington, Del.: Intercollegiate Studies Institute, 2008.

Coauthored Books
2000
With Stanley J. Grenz, Mardi Keyes, and Mary Stewart Van Leeuwen; edited by James W. Skillen and Michelle N. Voll. *Women and the Future of the Family.* Grand Rapids, Mich.: Baker, 2000.

Edited and Coedited Works

1983

With Susan Mosher Stuard. *Restoring Women to History: Materials for Western Civiliza-tion I.* Bloomington, Ind.: Organization of American Historians, 1983.

1984

With Israels Perry. *Restoring Women to History: Materials for Western Civilization II.* Bloomington, Ind.: Organization of American Historians, 1984.

With Susan Mosher Stuard, and the assistance of Rufus Fears and Marc Mayer. *Restoring Women to History: Materials for United States I.* Bloomington, Ind.: Organization of American Historians, 1984.

1995

With Virginia Bernhard. *The Birth of American Feminism: The Seneca Falls Woman's Con-vention of 1848.* St. James, N.Y.: Brandywine, 1995.

Journal Articles and Sections of Books

1977

"Property and Patriarchy in Classical Bourgeois Political Theory." *Radical History Review* 4, nos. 2–3 (1977): 36–59.

1978

"Yves Saint Laurent's Peasant Revolution." *Marxist Perspectives* 1 (Summer 1978): 58–92.

1979

"The Personal Is Not Political Enough." *Marxist Perspectives* 2 (Winter 1979): 94–113.

1980

"The New Female Literary Culture." *Antioch Review* 38 (Spring 1980): 193–217.

1982

"Gender, Class, and Power: Some Theoretical Considerations." *History Teacher* 15 (Feb-ruary 1982): 255–76.

"Placing Women's History in History." *New Left Review* 133 (May/June 1982): 5–29.

1984

"Women and Work." In *French Women and the Age of Enlightenment,* edited by Samia I. Spencer, 111–27. Bloomington: University of Indiana Press, 1984.

"Women's Studies in the 1980s: Now More Than Ever." *Women's Studies Quarterly* 12 (Fall 1984): 25–28.

1985

"Two Steps Forward, One Step Back: New Questions and Old Models in the Religious History of American Women." *Journal of the American Academy of Religion* 53 (Sep-tember 1985): 465–71.

1986

"The Claims of a Common Culture: Gender, Race, Class, and the Canon." *Salmagundi* 72 (Fall 1986): 131–43.

"Women's Rights, Affirmative Action, and the Myth of Individualism." *George Washington Law Review* 54 (January/March 1986): 338–74.

1987

"Culture and Consciousness in the Intellectual History of European Women." *Signs* 12 (Spring 1987): 529–47.

"The Empress's New Clothes: The Politics of Fashion." *Socialist Review* 17 (January/February 1987): 7–30.

"Women and the Enlightenment." In *Becoming Visible: Women in European History*, 2nd ed., edited by Renate Bridenthal, Claudia Koonz, and Susan Stuard, 251–77. Boston: Houghton Mifflin, 1987.

1989

"The Feminist Challenge to the Canon." *National Forum* 69, no. 3 (Summer 1989): 34–36.

1990

"Between Individualism and Fragmentation: American Culture and the New Literary Studies of Race and Gender." *American Quarterly* 42 (March 1990): 7–34.

"Socialist-Feminist American Women's History." *Journal of Women's History* 1 (Winter 1990): 180–210.

"Whose Women's Studies?" *Chronicles: A Magazine of American Culture* 14 (September 1990): 50–52.

"Women in Agriculture during the Nineteenth Century." In *Agriculture and National Development: Views on the Nineteenth Century*, edited by Lou Ferleger, 267–301. Ames: Iowa State University Press, 1990.

1991

"Conservative Feminism and Economic Reality: A Response to Katherine Kersten." *Policy Review*, no. 57 (Summer 1991): 83.

1992

"Feminism and the Rhetoric of Individual Rights, Part One." *Common Knowledge* 1, no. 1 (1992): 43–53.

"Feminism and the Rhetoric of Individual Rights, Part Two." *Common Knowledge* 1, no. 2 (1992): 63–73.

"Feminist Rights, Individualist Wrongs." *Tikkun* 7 (May/June 1992): 29–34.

"The Legal Status of Families as Institutions." *Cornell Law Review* 77 (1992): 992–96.

"Procreation and Women's Rights: A Response to Nicky Hart." *Contention: Debates in Society, Culture, and Science* 1 (Spring 1992): 217–25.

1993

"From Separate Spheres to Dangerous Streets: Postmodernist Feminism and the Problem of Social Order." *Social Research* 60 (Summer 1993): 235–54.

"Mixed Messages: Women and the Impact of World War II." *Southern Humanities* 27 (Summer 1993): 235–46.

1994

"Difference, Diversity, and Divisions in an Agenda for the Women's Movement." In *Color, Class and Country: Experiences of Gender,* edited by Gay Young and Bette J. Dickerson, 232–47. London: Zed, 1994.

"Religion and Women in America." In *World Religions in America: An Introduction,* edited by Jacob Neusner, 259–74. Louisville, Ky.: Westminster / John Knox Press, 1994.

1995

"At Cross-Purposes: Feminism and the Christian Faith." *Regeneration Quarterly* 1 (Fall 1995): 6–11.

"Beyond Autonomy: Sex, Repression, and Violence against Women." *Common Knowledge* 4, no. 3 (1995): 64–71.

"Contested Meanings: Women and the Problem of Freedom in the Mid-Nineteenth-Century United States." In *Historical Change and Human Rights: The Oxford Amnesty Lectures 1994,* edited by Olwen Hufton, 179–215. New York: Basic, 1995.

"The Female Experience in American Religion." *Religion and American Culture: A Journal of Interpretation* 5 (Winter 1995): 16–21.

"Feminism, Children, and the Family." *Harvard Journal of Law and Public Policy* 18 (Spring 1995): 503–8.

"A New World for Women and Blacks?" Special issue, *World and I* (June 1995): 44–53.

"Rethinking Abortion in Terms of Human Interconnectedness." *Studies in Pro-Life Feminism* 1 (Spring 1995): 91–105.

1996

"Beyond Individualism: The New Puritanism, Feminism, and Women." In *The New Salmagundi Reader,* edited by Robert Boyers and Peggy Boyers, 578–93. Syracuse, N.Y.: Syracuse University Press, 1996.

"Strict Scrutiny, VMI, and Women's Lives." *Seton Hall Constitutional Law Journal* 6 (Summer 1996): 987–90.

1997

"Abortion and Morality Revisited." *Human Life Review* 23 (Summer 1997): 50–59.

"Rethinking Sexual Harassment." *Partisan Review* 64 (1997): 366–74.

"The Wages of Women's Lib." *World and I* 12 (November 1997): 32–37.

"Women and Equality: Promise or Deception?" In *Reason and Republicanism: Thomas Jefferson's Legacy to Liberty,* edited by Gary L. McDowell and Sharon L. Noble, 251–70. Lanham, Md.: Rowman & Littlefield, 1997.

1998

"The Feminist Critic and the Woman Writer, or, May the Proper Heroine Still Marry?" In *(Trans)Formations of Cultural Identity in the English-Speaking World,* edited by Jochen Achilles and Carmen Birkle, 175–94. Heidelberg: Winter, 1998.

"Severing the Ties That Bind: Women, the Family, and Social Institutions." *Intercollegiate Review* 34 (Fall 1998): 26–30.

"Thoughts on the History of the Family." In *The Family, Civil Society, and the State,* edited by Christopher Wolfe, 3–15. Lanham, Md.: Rowman & Littlefield, 1998.

"Women in a Changing World: The Consequences and the Implications." In *Toward the Renewal of Civilization: Political Order and Culture,* edited by T. William Boxx and Gary M. Quinlivan, 1–11. Grand Rapids, Mich.: Eerdmans, 1998.

1999

"Catholic and Feminist: Can One Be Both?" *Logos: A Journal of Catholic Thought and Culture* 2 (Fall 1999): 11–26.

2000

"How Abortion Has Failed Women." *Crisis: Politics, Culture, and the Church* 18 (March 2000): 33–37.

2003

"Deadly Choice: Abortion as a War against Women." *Touchstone* 16 (September 2003): 36–41.

"Wrong-Turn: How the Campaign to Liberate Women Has Betrayed the Culture of Life." In *Life and Learning XII: Proceedings of the Twelfth University Faculty for Life Conference at Ave Maria Law School, 2002,* edited by Joseph W. Koterski, 11–22. Washington, D.C.: University Faculty for Life, 2003.

2004

"Equality, Difference, and the Practical Problems of a New Feminism." In *Women in Christ: Toward a New Feminism,* edited by Michele M. Schumacher, 297–311. Grand Rapids, Mich.: Eerdmans, 2004.

"Feminism and the Unraveling of the Social Bond." *Voices: Women for Faith and Family* 19 (Michaelmas 2004): 9–14.

2005

"Which 'Roe Effect'?" *Society* 42 (July/August 2005): 27–29.

"Why Must Religious Tradition Be Reconciled with Feminism—Restorative, Radical, or Otherwise?" *Common Knowledge* 11, no. 1 (2005): 105–11.

Index

This index includes only names, titles, and places, as they appear in the text.